Learning for a Complex World

Learning for a Complex World

A Lifewide Concept of Learning, Education and Personal Development

Edited by

Norman J Jackson

AuthorHouse™
1663 Liberty Drive
Bloomington, IN 47403
www.authorhouse.com
Phone: 1-800-839-8640

© 2011 by Norman J Jackson. All rights reserved.

No part of this book may be reproduced, stored in a retrieval system, or transmitted by any means without the written permission of the author.

First published by AuthorHouse   08/16/2011

ISBN: 978-1-4567-9370-8 (sc)
ISBN: 978-1-4567-9371-5 (hc)
ISBN: 978-1-4567-9372-2 (ebk)

Printed in the United States of America

Any people depicted in stock imagery provided by Thinkstock are models, and such images are being used for illustrative purposes only.
Certain stock imagery © Thinkstock.

This book is printed on acid-free paper.

Because of the dynamic nature of the Internet, any web addresses or links contained in this book may have changed since publication and may no longer be valid. The views expressed in this work are solely those of the author and do not necessarily reflect the views of the publisher, and the publisher hereby disclaims any responsibility for them.

Dedication

For all the people whose ideas I have drawn upon
and the students, colleagues, friends and family
who have helped turn my ideas into reality.

Educational Vision

A fresh hope is astir. From many quarters comes the call for a new kind of education with its initial assumption affirming that *education is life* - not merely preparation for an unknown kind of future living......The whole of life is learning, therefore education can have no endings.
Eduard Lindman 1926:6

Contents

Acknowledgements — vii

Contributors — ix

Editor's introduction — xii
Norman Jackson

Foreword — xiv
The living testimony of a lifelong-lifewide learner
John Cowan

1 The lifelong and lifewide dimensions of living and learning — 1
Norman Jackson

2 Lifewide education: a transformative concept for higher education? — 22
Ron Barnett

3 A holistic model for learning and personal development — 39
Colin Beard and Norman Jackson

4 Developing capability through lifewide education — 61
Norman Jackson

5 Authoring your life : a lifewide learning perspective — 76
Marcia Baxter Magolda

6 An imaginative lifewide curriculum — 100
Norman Jackson

7 Freedom to learn: a radically revised pedagogy to facilitate Lifewide Learning in the academic curriculum — 122
John Cowan

8 Connecting lifewide learning to life-based Learning — 137
Maret Staron

9 Lifewide learning habits of students 160
Jenny Willis and Norman Jackson

10 Immersive experience – a rich but challenging environment 194
for transformative learning
Sarah Campbell and Norman Jackson

11 Surrey Lifewide Learning Award: a learning partnership 222
to support lifewide learning
Norman Jackson, Charlie Betts and Jenny Willis

12 Learning through work 261
Norman Jackson, Jenny Willis, Sarah Campbell
and Michael Eraut

13 Adapting to another culture: an immersive experience 286
Novie Johan and Norman Jackson

14 Lifewide education: an emergent phenomenon in 308
UK higher education
Charlie Betts and Norman Jackson

References 322

Index 341

Lifewide Education Community Interest Company 347

Acknowledgements

The story that is our life unfolds in unpredictable ways but the detail reveals itself in the many situations we encounter or create in the different spaces and places we inhabit every day. This book focuses attention on the value of seeing education as a personal lifewide project. How I have come to hold this belief is the result of what I have learnt from many people - my parents and family, teachers, friends and colleagues, and people who I never met but who shared their thoughts through their writing or other creative expressions. I am who I am because of you and without you this book would not have been written.

Mentors are very special people who share their wisdom, provide encouragement and support, and when necessary act as a critical friend. Throughout this project, and long before, I have benefitted enormously from Professor John Cowan's presence and guiding hand and his rich and insightful stories which illustrate in a practical way the principles and practices of lifelong and lifewide learning.

All but one of the contributors to this volume have been involved in the work of the Surrey Centre for Excellence in Professional Training and Education (SCEPTrE), at the University of Surrey. Each of them recognised the potential in the idea of lifewide learning and education and each has added value to our initial ideas and evolving practices.

I would like to pay a special tribute to the SCEPTrE Team. Charlie Betts, the Surrey Lifewide Learning Award Coordinator, was instrumental in developing the learning partnerships, through which students' lifewide learning could be recognised and valued. Dr Jenny Willis made a significant contribution to our programme of research and evaluation, and Clare Dowding and Susan Wood provided excellent administrative support for the project as a whole. Our talented and committed student partners - Sarah Campbell, Jake Payne, Jessica Lo, Clare Fellows, Chris Stanage, Jon Kennedy, George Prassinos and Ieva Bachtiarova, contributed to our research, participated in our educational designs, helped create, pilot and evaluate tools and technology, and document our work through filming.

Trying to bring about educational change in a university can be a daunting and sometimes demoralising affair when most people want to keep doing the same thing and anything that is not perceived to be academic is not considered worthy of attention. I am forever grateful to colleagues who did not take this view and who provided much encouragement and support to the SCEPTrE Team. They include: Professors David Airey, Michael Kipps, Neil Ward and Shirley Price and Dr Janko Calik, Dr Simon Usherwood, Jane Leng, Osama Khan, Sally Eadie, Dr Russ Clark and Nigel Biggs. As an employer responsible for the development of new graduate recruits, John Watkins provided invaluable advice, encouragement and support.

Throughout our project the students who participated in the Lifewide Learning Award and our other educational enterprises, were our main source of inspiration. Your voices permeate this book and your involvement and feedback convinced us that what we were trying to do was right.

Books are written and re-written and in the re-writing process, Professor John Cowan provided many useful suggestions for improving draft chapters and Dr Jenny Willis and Charlie Wilson (Perfect Write) provided excellent editorial support.

This educational project would not have been possible without the financial support of the Higher Education Funding Council England (HEFCE). We hope that we have honoured the expectation for Centres of Excellence in Teaching and Learning to pioneer innovative approaches to teaching and learning and to share what has been learnt with the wider community.

Contributors

RONALD BARNETT is Emeritus Professor of Higher Education at the Institute of Education, University of London. He is a recognized world authority on the conceptual and theoretical understanding of the university and higher education. Three of his many books, *Realizing the University in an age of supercomplexity*, *Engaging the Curriculum in Higher Education* (with Kelly Coate, 2005) and *A will to Learn: being a student in an age of uncertainty* (2007) influenced SCEPTrE's work. Ron contributed to SCEPTrE's research programme and helped develop the concept of lifewide education.

MARCIA BAXTER MAGOLDA is Distinguished Professor of Educational Leadership at Miami University of Ohio (USA). She teaches student development theory in the Student Affairs in Higher Education masters and doctoral programs. Her scholarship addresses the evolution of learning and development in college and young adult life and pedagogy to promote self-authorship and she has authored and edited over seven books on this subject.

COLIN BEARD is Professor of Experiential Learning and a Faculty Teaching Fellow in the Sheffield Business School at Sheffield Hallam University. He is an expert practitioner in designing and facilitating experiential learning, completing a doctorate and co-authoring a key text in the field. His expertise is recognised in a National Teaching Fellowship Awarded by the Higher Education Academy. Colin developed the holistic model of learning that underpins our concept of lifewide education.

CHARLOTTE BETTS known as 'Charlie' by our students, was the Coordinator for the Surrey Lifewide Learning Award. She was responsible for the day to day operation of the scheme and facilitating the learning partnerships that underpinned the scheme. She is also a practising professional artist and an educational consultant.

SARAH CAMBELL is an excellent example of someone who appreciates the opportunities that life provides to develop herself as a whole person. After working in the music industry for several years, she studied psychology at the University of Surrey graduating with a first class honours degree in June 2010. She has now embarked on an MSc and PhD in the Psychology Department at the University of Surrey and her personal story shows how her lifewide experiences have shaped her interests and determined the career pathway she has chosen.

JOHN COWAN is an extraordinary teacher whose career spans over 45 years during which he has championed and practised student-centred learning. During that time he has placed an ever increasing emphasis on preparing students to exercise stewardship over their lifewide development while at University, and in lifelong learning thereafter. John worked closely with SCEPTrE to develop and apply the concept of lifewide learning and education and took on the role of 'external auditor' which helped the delivery team check the effectiveness of its support and judgments.

MICHAEL ERAUT is Emeritus Professor at the Sussex Institute of the University of Sussex and a world expert and leading researcher into how professionals learn in work place settings. His books include the highly acclaimed *Developing Professional Knowledge and Competence*. In 2007 he completed an ESRC-funded five-year study of how professionals learn in the early part of their careers. His work with SCEPTrE helped to transfer and adapt some of this research knowledge to the work placement and part-time work contexts of lifewide learning and personal development.

NORMAN JACKSON was responsible for leading the research and development work on which this book is based in his capacity as Professor of Higher Education and Director of the University of Surrey Centre for Excellence in Professional Training and Education (SCEPTrE). Prior to this he worked in senior positions with a number of national bodies including HMI, HEQC, QAA, LTSN and HEA and it is through this work that he formed his view of how UK higher education needs to change. An important focus of his work has been concerned with the role of higher education in developing students' creativity. He is currently Managing Director of Chalk Mountain Education and Media Services Ltd. and Director of the Lifewide Education Community Interest Company.

NOVIE JOHAN is Lecturer in Hospitality Management at the University of Surrey and currently completing her Doctoral dissertation on the educational value of the GAP Year. She was co-facilitator and researcher in SCEPTrE's 2010-11 Cultural Academy.

MARET STARON is principal of a Sydney based consultancy 'Mindful Creations'. Her passion continues to be learning and development. She wonders about how we retain (or don't retain) our passion for learning, growth and change, and how we can acknowledge and value the interrelationship of head, heart and hope in organisations. Maret has examined these issues in her thesis for her Master of Science (Hons), from the University of Western Sydney, as well as through the many projects she has led in the Australian VET sector.

JENNY WILLIS Following a Fellowship study awarded by SCEPTrE in 2008/09, Jenny joined SCEPTrE's team as lead researcher on projects relating to 'learning to be professional' and 'lifewide learning'. She is an active contributor to national and international conferences and has publications in the field of work-integrated learning and Co-op education, and professional development.

Editor's introduction

Ten years ago I helped to establish the imaginative curriculum network for people who cared about students' creative development in higher education. The thought of an imaginative curriculum has energised me ever since and when I was appointed to lead the Surrey Centre for Excellence in Professional Training and Education (SCEPTrE) at the University of Surrey, I knew that I had been given a fantastic opportunity to turn the idea of an imaginative curriculum into a reality. Our ideas for an imaginative curriculum slowly formed around a lifewide concept of learning and education. This concept, in my view, holds the promise for a more complete education, connecting in a profound and dynamic way the opportunities and support provided by universities and colleges, with what learners do to develop themselves in the many spaces and places they inhabit while they are engaged in study.

The ideas and practices described in this book have been developed in response to the wicked problem of how higher education might better prepare students for the challenges that lie ahead of them as they grapple with a world that is becoming ever more complex, more challenging, more uncertain and more disruptive. In doing this the contributors believe that lifewide education is the future direction for a higher education system that needs to transform itself to better serve its moral purpose - to make a positive difference to students' future lives.

According to some commentators our society is confronting a growing social aspiration gap in which we simply cannot create the society most of us want to live in by replicating what we are currently doing. If we accept this perspective then there is an urgent need for us to rethink the way we educate people and encourage and support them in their endeavours to develop themselves to become the people they need to be in order to create the society they want to live in. The approach described in this book offers one possible way forward.

Douglas Thomas and John Seeley Brown have coined the term 'a new culture of learning'[1] to describe the phenomenon that is emerging as we shift from the traditional stable structures for learning of the 20th century to more fluid and transient, technology-enabled structures of the 21st century. Learning is all around us and our concepts of lifewide learning and education are very much a part of this cultural phenomenon.

The SCEPTrE Centre, was one of 74 publicly-funded Centres for Excellence in Teaching and Learning (CETLs) established between 2005 - 2011. Although SCEPTrE no longer exists the ideas it brought into existence live on and the Lifewide Education Community Interest Company has been formed to continue to develop and promote lifewide learning and lifewide education. Any revenues from this book will be used to support the not for profit work of this organisation.

Professor Norman Jackson
Director SCEPTrE December 2005 to March 2011
Director Lifewide Education CIC www.lifewideeducation.co.uk

August 2011

1 Thomas, D. and Seely Brown, J. (2011) *A New Culture of Learning: Cultivating the Imagination for a World of Constant Change.* Available through Amazon

Foreword

Confessions of a lifelong-lifewide learner

John Cowan

Preamble
I have taken great pleasure in being part of SCEPTrE's lifewide learning project during 2009–2010. Consequently, I am delighted to have been invited to contribute here a personal perspective on my own lifelong-lifewide journey of learning and personal development. In this foreword I will draw upon two papers I wrote for SCEPTrE in 2010, revisiting them now with a new emphasis on the interaction of the two words in that hyphenated adjective 'lifelong-lifewide'. For when I reread these papers, I noticed that they focussed beyond incidents and influences relating to my *lifewide* learning and development, in the immediate demands of my situation at the time. The generalisable lessons that I learnt were to serve me well and be consolidated and extended in subsequent life, where they featured as significant strands in my ongoing *lifelong* development as a person.

I shall attempt in what follows to abstract some examples of lifewide learning as these occurred, summarise the transferable learning which subsequently ensued for me and show how this influenced my lifewide learning and development in later life. In so doing, I will add some side comments as footnotes to provide a richer and more conversational perspective – by amplifying, and by questioning myself.

Lifewide learning in my schooldays
I had to wear spectacles even before I went to school. My eyesight was weakening rapidly, and at that time the (inaccurate) professional wisdom was that the less I read, the less deterioration would ensue. So my reading outwith school was restricted to thirty minutes per day. I relied upon my mother to read to me, to enable me to do my homework. She also faithfully read for my diversion, at a time when we had radio but no television. In her company I met many wonderful characters in literature that I have ever since regarded fondly

as personal acquaintances of mine, rather than as characters in books[1]. Not unreasonably, my mother did all she could to manage me in more than my use of my eyes. But I yearned to be my own person, and steadfastly resolved to make as many of my own decisions as possible. So, despite my mother's caring involvement and natural wish to manage me, I was determined to study, revise, prepare and manage my time and leisure in my own way. I went on making my own decisions when they mattered to me, even when some of them subsequently turned out to have been unwise[2]. I learnt from my mistakes![3]

My father, who was a lecturer in a then technical college, encouraged and supported me in all sorts of ways. He was a gentle gentleman, who was ever on the lookout for people in need of assistance, which could include his son. He gave help willingly and with pleasure. He demonstrated in his life, and shared with me, his concept of a 'pool of goodwill' to which we should all contribute without expectation of direct return from the person whom we have been able to assist, and from which we can all draw at some time or another[4].

Having been evacuated after the Clydebank blitz, I was to be taught during and after the Second World War in six different Scottish schools. In all of them, the learning was teacher-directed[5]. I was taught by several authoritarian and brutal teachers for whom the punishment of 'the belt' was a routine classroom activity. One took exception to my use of green ink, and threatened to belt me every time I used it in his classwork. Deviously and pig-headedly[6], I determined to be my own person. I ejected the green ink from my pen before his French classes, and refilled it with the watery school ink from the desk inkwell. This yielded horrible results, as the rubber reservoir in my fountain pen had become stained each evening with the green which now melded unattractively with the blue. 'You said I wasn't to use green ink, Sir, and I haven't. Can you belt me for doing what you told me to do?' I knew it was pointless to argue with him about my right to use green ink. I just outmanoeuvred him tactically (if not tactfully), until

---

[1] Why is this not mentioned in the account of lifewide learning which follows here? (see ending.)
[2] My commitment to encouraging my own children (and my students) to make their own decisions was probably a reaction to my own childhood experiences and my determination then to be my own person.
[3] Lifewide learning can come from negative as well as positive experiences.
[4] My rewarding commitment, many years later, to unpaid educational development work in developing countries was influenced by values and practices I had admired in my father. This emerged slowly.
[5] Which is not necessarily bad, pedagogically. I found it effective to be instructed how to titrate using a burette, or how to integrate by parts.
[6] When and with what effect does determination become pig-headedness?

he gave up in desperation. And I avoided being belted, having even in these days seen the strength of intimating grounds for appeal to a higher authority[7].

Fortunately, I was also taught by a few splendid characters. One, especially, revealed to me the delights of the integral calculus, which I'm sure I would never have discovered if left to my own devices[8]. Another introduced me to a range of wonderful English literature to which I often return. Generally, however, I soon learnt to concentrate on working out what was being asked of me in the examination system, and to concentrate on doing it well. I did not know then that I was sussing out, and following, the hidden curriculum[9]. My lifewide learning in this, however, was more general than that; it was about finding out what people expected of me in various situations, and as far as possible responding accordingly[10].

At secondary school, I became secretary of the Rowing Club, selecting and organising crews and travel arrangements – my first experience of management, on a small scale[11]. I sensed from conversations between officials in the boathouse that it was likely that there would soon be a requirement for schoolboy oarsmen to be competent swimmers. Such a requirement, once made official, would have had to be respected. I grasped the bull by the horns, and went to consult our rector. I pointed out to him that our regatta-winning first crew contained three non-swimmers, whose exclusion would be a serious blow to our prospects. We negotiated a short-term agreement, ahead of the anticipated ruling that all oarsmen must be able to swim. It was agreed that our non-swimming oarsmen might continue to train and represent the school in this their final school year, provided they took swimming lessons[12]. Anticipating the problem had made it possible for me to avoid it[13].

An extra-mural activity which I enjoyed, and which also contributed to my lifewide learning, was the Drama Club. The master in charge was a Physics

---

[7] I must have been quite an unattractive schoolboy. Being successful is not always the key to being likable – something I've found in lifelong development.
[8] The seeds of a love for mathematics led me to become an admirer of elegance in proofs a decade later.
[9] Lifewide learning is not assessed. What's the equivalent of the hidden curriculum, as a driving force, then?
[10] a) Notice how often lifewide learning broadens out into generalities. b) Not necessarily agreeing or conforming, but consciously taking account of that they expected of me.
[11] Seizing an opportunity as it arose – a characteristic of lifewide learning. I was soon to learn that schoolboys can be harsh critics of what they deem as incompetence. This was basic and important lifewide learning.
[12] Success (on a small scale). How critical is this in the early stages of lifewide learning?
[13] I was learning the secrets of how to be successful in a proactive way. Don't sit back and wait for things to happen; work on a solution to a problem that has yet to fully emerge.

teacher, who had been in the Scottish National Players for several years. He would take us to local theatres and music halls (including the infamous comedians' graveyard of the Glasgow Empire). We would sit at the back of the gallery and watch the stagecraft with him. One of our many lessons was to watch and see that a comedian, however successful in raising laughs, would not win attention without beginning effectively, and would not be applauded warmly unless the closing two or three minutes had also gone down well with the audience[14]. Beyond this point, the general lifewide learning for me was the value of observation as a way into reflective[15] learning and development.

In my schooldays, then, my lifewide learning featured[16] the development of:
1. autonomy: making my own decisions about what mattered to me
2. goodwill: casting my bread on the waters of the pool of goodwill, without expecting immediate return
3. tactics: avoiding direct argument and preferring to manoeuvre tactically
4. expectations: finding out what was expected of me, and delivering it with minimum effort
5. observing: carefully and thoughtfully observing, before engaging in new challenges
6. anticipation: anticipating and dealing with problems before they arose[17].

I have implied so far that this lifewide learning was valuable[18] to me. But soft words butter no parsnips. It behoves me here to test out this claim. Are there facts from the next stages in my life which bear out that belief or assertion?

Subsequent use of my lifewide learning from my schooldays
1. Autonomy: In 1987, I was interviewed for the post of Scottish Regional Director of the Open University (OU). The interview, by five OU personalities, went badly. When it passed to the Vice-Chancellor to conclude the questioning, he commented: 'You don't seem to appreciate, Professor Cowan, that we're looking for a manager who will live above the shop three hundred and fifty days in the year.' I responded that this was not how I had read the job description. 'Indeed,' asked the VC, 'and how did you read the job description?' I replied, 'I thought you were looking for someone whose first priority would be the quality

---

[14] My enduring lifelong learning was the usefulness of objectively observing a new situation, and reflecting on how to engage with it – *before* so doing.
[15] Reflection has been important to me all my life. Maybe it is taken for granted in what follows here. Why?
[16] I notice that my chosen headings all relate to general abilities or beliefs and values, though they arise in the first instance from particular uses of abilities. None feature coverage of content.
[17] Perhaps this was the beginning of my appreciation of living in a constantly changing world.
[18] Valuable – or satisfying?

of the learning experience of OU students in Scotland. But that's obviously not what you want, so clearly I'm not your man.' I went home, happy that I had held out, even in failure, for the values[19] to which I wished to subscribe as a senior university teacher[20]. The next morning I was phoned and offered the job. I sought confirmation that my interpretation of the job description had been accepted before I agreed to take up the post. I was so reassured[21]. There ensued ten fruitful and fulfilling years. In that period, alone amongst regional directors who were primarily administrators, I was the OU's academic maverick[22] regional director, concentrating on what I believed to be important.

2. Goodwill: As a young lecturer, I was saddened to learn of the problems facing a young Iranian researcher in our department. He had been schooled in Scotland, and gone on to obtain his degree there. Now he was having problems in confirming permanent residence. I did my best for him, dealing with several MPs in so doing. The campaign was successful[23]. He thanked me warmly. I was glad to have been able to help him towards a good solution. Some fifteen years after these events the OU in Scotland was having great problems obtaining suitable accommodation in central Edinburgh. I approached my former student, now a multi-millionaire property developer. He bent over backwards to obtain and refurbish wonderful accommodation for the OU in Scotland, at a viable rental. The bread cast on the waters years before was returned in great measure.

3. Tactics: As a young professional engineer, I specialised in jobs which had to be completed within tight time schedules[24]. In these settings, my lifelong learning developed my already established ability to manoeuvre tactically. On one occasion we were to tackle a difficult job, in a restricted site where it was impossible to increase the already large amount of expensive plant on site, or the number of men working there (having already planned for twenty-four-hours-a-day working). An obstructive foreman, determined to cover himself should we not finish in time, disputed the relationship between the resource to be provided and time available for completion in my carefully considered plan. I did not argue. Instead I manoeuvred tactically. I arranged to meet with the foreman and his non-union gang, and tabled my estimate of time required

---

[19] Where had these come from?
[20] At the time, I was contemplating a final appointment which would take me on to retirement.
[21] Was this my self-discovery of a male version of what was being taught to women in assertiveness courses? It was driven by my passion for what mattered to me.
[22] Is this a role I have relished during my lifewide learning? If so, is that significant?
[23] Was I attracted to this as another difficult battle to fight – or as a cause to pursue?
[24] Serendipitously, my first such challenge had led to an effective response, judged impressive by the client and my line manager.

(which occupied the full period for which I had scheduled), and the costs, including overtime and plant hire, which was a major item. The men followed their foreman in expressing grave doubts about the practicality of my scheme. I then offered to share with the squad *half* the saving in the considerable plant hire costs if we finished within the scheduled period. In addition, however long the job took within the scheduled period, I was offering to pay each man for the full period including overtime. My offer was taken up – and the weekend job was completed by four o'clock on the Sunday afternoon, ahead of my plan. The job cost less than my estimate, as we saved a lot on our sharing of saved plant hire; and the men went home earlier than they had planned, with full wages and a bonus. Tactics paid off[25].

4. Expectations: As a consulting engineer, I extended my practice of finding out what was expected of me – in this case by clients – and providing it to the best of my ability. I was often asked to advise on remedial measures for old or damaged structures. One early client waved my thorough report at me, and told me: 'I pay you to use your expertise and act for us as our engineers. I don't want long reports. Get it all on one side of foolscap, telling me what needs to be done, why, how much it will cost and how long it will take.' Another client asked for supplementation to a fairly detailed report. 'There's a lot of money to be spent on this work. I need a full report in which you explain to me your analysis of the problem and the situation, detail what you propose and why (with some consideration of possible options), and provide a detailed estimate of costs and a schedule for completion of the work.' In subsequent jobs, clients were given what they expected of me, with the same professionalism behind each report[26].

5. Observing: When I was in mid-career, my Head of Department persuaded me to represent our region on four central committees of our professional body. For almost eighteen months, I went to London to sit in meetings where most members were prominent and influential professional personalities. For a while I did not contribute to the discussions; but I observed carefully. In due course, I went on to use effectively what I had learnt from my observations, and from elsewhere[27].

---

[25] But was it ethical?

[26] My lifewide learning continued, lifelong. Never again would someone have to tell me what kind of report they had wished; from then on, I asked before writing. And I hope I also went on to find out what my students expected of me.

[27] a) How well? There's not much being said here about where I obtained my criteria for my self-judgements? b) On the first occasion when I prepared my students for group work, I used that splendid Henry Fonda film *Twelve Angry Men*. We set ourselves to watch Fonda reverse the voting of his eleven fellow jurymen. During this, we noted what made characters effective, and ineffective, in these group discussions. I learnt as much as my students did!

I had seen, for example, that if I expected to disagree with a strong personality and effective debater, I should arrive early and sit near him on his side of the table. He would find it difficult to confront someone alongside him.

I had seen that succinct statements, worded clearly in short sentences, were more likely to engage the members' attention; so I prepared accordingly in hastily scribbled drafting and redrafting of possible wording on the margin of my agenda paper, before contributing.

I had seen the devastating power of the pertinent question to puncture a bubble of pomposity or lack of accuracy; and I used questions accordingly.

For a while I kept a score in my reflective diary of tactics that had paid off for me. It was quite effective[28]. Observation had extended my lifewide learning into yet another area.

6. Anticipation: As a university teacher committed to being innovative, I built upon my ability to anticipate problems and avoid them before they arose. I foresaw trouble when I launched the then utterly radical provision of a major course offering full self-assessment within an undergraduate degree. For this required approval by the Board of Moderators of my professional bodies, and I could foresee that the elderly and conservative visiting panel members would be horrified to discover that I was already allowing my students to choose what they would learn, how they learnt and to what standard – with their self-assessment providing final marks which contributed to their degree ratings. Early in the visit, it was apparent that moderators were highly unlikely to be persuaded to approve self-assessment and self-direction. Tentatively, I suggested that they would not be able to give approval until a suitably qualified panel had rigorously investigated my students' learning outcomes and their coverage of essential professional objectives. Sternly, they agreed. I told them that 'it just so happened' that I already had such an evaluative report, from an evaluation team whose members had impeccable professional qualifications and were currently serving the professional bodies in that capacity. Would the visitors like to see it? They expressed keen interest. So I passed over the report in which the professional experts whom I had invited had endorsed the outcomes of this self-assessed and self-directed course. Hoist with their own

---

[28] I suppose this reflects my ongoing search for the secrets of how to be effective.

petard, the moderators were obliged to approve – because I had anticipated and coped with the problem before it arose[29].

I admit that there is evidence in my schooldays and beyond of extra-curricular lifewide learning which was to prove of lifelong and deepening significance to me. But what of development which began during my undergraduate studies and apprenticeship?

Lifewide learning in my undergraduate studies and apprenticeship
When I was seventeen I went, as an immature entrant, to university, where again the teaching was authoritarian and the lecturers far from approachable. I had wanted to become a lawyer. But that called for four years of study, and the opticians advised that my eyes would not last for more than three years of intensive reading. So I opted instead to study civil engineering, motivated by the prospect of designing and building useful things. Ironically, after six months, as I became physically mature, my eyes began to stabilise[30]!

In my first three-month summer vacation, I entered indentured employment with a firm of consultants, having sought and found an apprenticeship which offered me training continuing into the two years after graduation. The firm, with which I was to work in various capacities for fourteen years, employed many apprentices and few engineers or journeymen. Consequently, the apprentices were often expected to undertake tasks well beyond their professional status[31]. In this setting my relevant lifewide experience was of taking full responsibility for my own learning and development. This featured when I had only been there a few weeks. I was asked whether I could design reinforced concrete beams. I saw an opportunity to do something more interesting than simply colouring in prints of drawings, and dishonestly declared confidence. Quickly, I went off and found a couple of readable books in the office library, and went home that evening to teach myself how to design reinforced concrete beams. It was exciting and motivating to go on site when my calculations and drawings were becoming reinforced concrete foundations for an electricity sub-station. There was also scope for further learning when I had to solve the practical problems which my naive detailing had sometimes created[32].

---

[29] But I did not always succeed. I foresaw the most effective relationship for the OU in Scotland with the new Scottish Parliament long before events developed. I did not persuade my VC; I failed. It was only ten years after I retired that I saw the OU change policy, under a new VC, to follow the line I had advocated.
[30] Perhaps this confirmed the wisdom of making my own decisions, rather than relying on advice?
[31] I wonder how different my lifewide learning might have been without this serendipitous circumstance?
[32] And so an activity arising from lifewide learning led to further engagement in lifewide learning

Everything I did that summer was either self-taught, or taught to me by other apprentices[33] – like how to set up and use surveying instruments. Senior apprentices also taught me effectively and supportively, and modelled for me the practices I wished to follow and abilities I set out to acquire. That same pattern was to apply in my second summer. However, little of what I studied at university was of any direct use to me. Even the university course in surveying techniques, when at last that subject featured in our timetables, was primitive in coverage compared to what was expected of me in practice, and in which I had already acquired considerable expertise. Worse still, it did not equip me to survey existing steel buildings sufficiently accurately to allow new steelwork extensions to be designed, detailed and fabricated – to fit. So quickly I went off again to discover for myself how to do these things.

In my first summer after leaving school, I became an officer in a Christian boys' club, which had recruited me to its Sunday meetings while I was at senior school. I managed to have a week at their summer camp, based in a forestry hut on the remote shores of Loch Fyne. My first appointment was as boating and bathing officer. They reckoned that my boating experience was without question, and that as the one non-swimmer in the camp, I would not mind manning the safety boat at swimming parades[34]. Here it also was that I put into practice my Drama Club teacher's advice about public speaking. Each officer took an evening epilogue, when apart from conveying an evangelical message, our task was to catch and retain interest. I concentrated hard on beginnings and endings.

In my second year, I was camp quartermaster. For a camp which lacked motorised transport, this entailed ordering all that we would need for the advance guard and the seven-day camp of sixty-five boys. I had the assistance of my predecessor's record, but I had to adjust this for changes in menus and numbers. Woe betide me if I under-ordered, or missed something out[35]. Equally, I should not over-order, lest camp budgeting suffered. When I returned home, my last task was to write up my records in 'the Portavadie book', with my advice to whoever would do the job next year. This was my first experience of reflective record keeping, something I was to continue in one setting or another, from family holidays to innovative teaching.

---

[33] Peers are often the most effective teachers. Watch children teaching children to play Monopoly, and see how much more effective they are than adults. This, of course, is socio-constructivism.
[34] Health and safety requirements?
[35] More learning by anticipating and avoiding mistakes.

I made one innovation that year at camp. I dabbled in entrepreneurship[36]. I learnt at a late date that we were to have a visitor, who would be coming down by car. I contacted him, and asked him to bring us a refrigerated container of ice-cream. This luxury I had to sell cost-effectively. So I negotiated to share the cost amongst my customers. Thus the first wafer cost (1951 values) twelve pounds. Once I had a second customer, the wafer cost went down to six pounds – and so on. My satisfied, but hard-up, customers became my keen salesmen.

In due course I graduated, having again found out what the examiners expected of me, and having supplied it in good quality[37]. But in my heart of hearts, I was far from convinced of the professional or other value of my education. Admittedly, I had relished the wonderful abstractions of the various courses in mathematics, when an inspired teacher helped me to acquire a lifelong joy in the concept of elegance in mathematical proofs and in computer programming. And an imaginative lecturer in geology had inspired me to see and read the countryside as if for the first time I had shed dark sunglasses[38]. But I still felt dissatisfied[39]. I kept wanting to equip myself beyond my professional requirements[40].

And so it was that I began a habit which was to persist for the rest of my life. In the August of that summer, I undertook something akin to self-appraisal[41]. In that first scrutiny, I came to the conclusion that my first class honours degree said little about me, except that I was an intellectual savage with a sound background in engineering theory. I knew little or nothing of art, literature, music, ballet or drama. I decided that I wanted to make good that deficiency and become a rounded person[42]. I consulted friends and acquaintances who seemed better equipped in these areas than me. I asked them to suggest what I should do, read, study, experience, to open up my education as a whole person. Some suggestions led me into richnesses which have occupied me for

---

[36] Why?

[37] And without much respect for a system in which the hidden curriculum dominated – and someone like me could identify that. But why was I never tempted to lead a revolt against a system for which I had little respect? Maybe because I saw no chance of success?

[38] Perhaps this is appreciating how different lenses allowed me to see and appreciate the world from an entirely different perspective? (Apologies for the pun.)

[39] Interesting that so much of my self-taught lifewide learning is driven by my own sense of need and insufficiency, which compares unfavourably with my formal education, which was mainly driven by someone else's idea about what I should be good at.

[40] In the beginning, this aspiration for breadth was disciplinary. But not for long.

[41] How did this begin? I cannot remember.

[42] Notice my growing awareness of my need for life balance. But why is there no mention of that in the rest of this account?

all of my life, and have in turn opened door after door into other wonderful areas and experiences[43].

In my self-appraisals, I naturally also reviewed my professional competences. Visits to construction sites had shown me that my knowledge of the trades in the construction industry was slight, superficial and (in my judgement at that time) inadequate. I decided to sign up for evening classes leading me to a Higher National Certificate in Building. I didn't want to be able to construct timber roofs, install central heating or lay bricks. But I wanted to know enough to tell whether I was working with a competent joiner, plumber or bricklayer; and also to know the questions I should be asking, in order to tap into their advice and experience[44].

For some time after graduating, my spare time was mainly devoted to competitive rowing. I was a member of several Scottish Championship crews. I was powerfully influenced by an older man who was our stroke, and who held strong views about self-imposed discipline – for the crew and generally in life. Jack was in a way an avuncular or older brother hero figure for me, someone to whom I looked up, not least for the way he trained his thirty-two-year-old body to be competitive. From him, I learnt to never admit defeat[45]. We raced once at Aberdeen, and he caught a bad crab at the start of the final race. It was obviously hopeless to continue. Even before we had properly begun, we were lengths behind against a top crew. Yet he furiously drove us pointlessly on – to catch up, and then to lead and to win. I lost more than eight pounds on that unforgettable afternoon – but we had won, by a canvas. And I had learnt that day *never* to be put off because a challenge seems impossible[46].

In the twelve years which followed graduation, I learnt a great deal on my own and from professional colleagues, and made relatively little use of my formal education. I swiftly gained professional status, and specialised in a variety of fields in civil engineering. I was a section leader at twenty-three years old, leading a section mainly consisting of apprentices of my own style and age or, in the case of our draughtsman, of more than my age. My section specialised in doing jobs against the clock which others had declared impossible or had

---

[43] Note that self-directed learning which is totally focused on one aim can miss many other worthwhile possibilities.
[44] I've often envied in later years the wonderful professionalism of top-rate advocates and architects. This is seen in their ability to ask perceptive questions of a professional like me, as if they were well versed in my discipline. I wanted to be such a professional, asking good questions, learning from the answers, and so contributing genuinely to interdisciplinary decisions and problem-solving.
[45] How important has learning from my 'hero figures' been to my lifewide learning?
[46] Maybe I *still* had to learn the distinction between being determined and being pig-headed.

proved by their failures to be so. But I never accepted that[47], and always managed to deliver. My most noteworthy (and final) 'impossible' contract involved the re-roofing of an important paper mill building, set in the midst of other buildings. The re-roofing had to be completed in the sixteen-day holiday period, or we would never have contracts from that firm again. The most competitive tender insisted on a three-month contract period. I worked out a way to meet the sixteen-day window of time, by constructing the roof first above the old building, then beginning demolition of the old structure while hanging the columns below my new roof, and finally concreting the new foundations. It seemed crazy to all but me. I had to take full responsibility for men, management and plant in a direct-labour arrangement. I had little sleep in the first five days on site. But we completed the task almost a day ahead of schedule. For me, the lifewide experience of doing something that many fellow professionals had judged impossible had a surprise effect. Tackling tasks which were structurally impossible had lost its challenge and thrill. It was probably time to move on[48].

Leading the motley crew of likeable individuals in my section had been a big challenge initially for someone with no training in leadership other than as a young officer in a boys' club. I soon found, as I had in the camp kitchen, that groups who enjoy each other's company will usually work well together, and do a fair amount of laughing together. In the drawing office, I arranged professionally relevant diversions. For instance, I insisted[49] on a challenge to anyone (including myself) who was going out of the office to visit a site or conduct a survey. When any of us came back from such a site visit, we had to tell the others about something relevant to engineering which we had learnt, and which no one else in the section knew already. If they failed, or if they came back with something that someone in the section already knew, they had to stand us all a beer. The pecuniary hardship of an apprenticeship community meant that we all learnt to question and understand, and shared a lot in this way.

What, then, featured in my lifewide learning in this phase of my life? There were many strands interwoven[50]. Amongst the elements of my rambling tale, I hope

---

[47] Surely an over-simplification. There must have been some requests which were, indeed, impossible. How did I distinguish?
[48] Of this, more later. Maybe an important feature for lifewide learning is learning when to move on.
[49] Why? And where did this idea originate?
[50] How important were my reflective conversations with such as Jack, and my fellow apprentices? Very influential, I judge – even if I didn't know it was socio-constructivism!

you can discern as I do that I was learning and developing, again in terms of generalisable abilities and value.
1. self-direction: to take responsibility for my own learning and development – planning, monitoring and evaluating it
2. self-protection: to refrain from going public on what I was thinking and proposing, until I knew I could show that I could crack the problem
3. self-enhancement: to equip myself beyond my current professional requirements
4. persistence: not to give up in the face of apparent defeat
5. co-operation: to learn from and with my juniors and peers
6. flexibility: to be open to changing my mind, or starting again
7. capability: to learn, and learn quickly, and often informally, in order to achieve what mattered to me.

Consequent lifelong learning in later life

Was all of this lifelong, as well as lifewide? Did it prove generalisable and transferable forward in time? Once again, I believe that examples from my subsequent life and career may illustrate, although not prove, that this was so.

1. Self-direction: Under this first heading, I have a profusion of examples; but then it is an important principle.

When I became a father, I felt committed to respect the autonomy of my children in their decision-making. This began seriously when they moved up to secondary school. I told them that *I* was paid by the month, so *they* should be paid by the month too. I would cover school fees and club subscriptions and family holidays. They should manage the rest. 'To begin with, estimate how much you will require from me each month,' I asked. They estimated for a week, and multiplied by four. I pointed out that eleven months in the year had virtually four and a half weeks. So I multiplied their weekly estimate by four and a half, and then increased the total liberally to cover items which I felt they had neglected. This largesse strained their ability to self-manage. My first son had spent his allowance before the first month was up – so he had to walk to and from school for the last days. I told him that *I* had nothing more coming in before the end of the month, so neither had *he*[51].

---

[51] I found it supportive that my children, after a family discussion many years later, reported that this delegation of financial responsibility had been the most formative experience in their childhood. All followed it when they raised their own families.

Initially, my firstborn son was a brilliant pupil in primary school, so it was easy for me to say that he should make his own decisions, since they were obviously working out well. However, when he moved to secondary school, and was more interested in extra-mural activity with the audio-visual sound crew than in preparing for his important examinations, I found it was more difficult to remain disengaged[52].

When my second son failed some examinations in engineering at his university, I foolishly departed from my principles and offered tutorial assistance with a subject which I was competent to teach. Fortunately, he adhered to *my* principles, so to speak, and politely declined. I then had the sense to let drop the suggestion I should never have raised.

When my daughter, with a good record at school, did not know what professional area she should pursue in her forthcoming university studies, I *almost* managed to refrain from giving advice. However, I advised just once, but only in general terms, that she should study what attracted her, and trust that she would discover in what followed what she would want to do. She opted to study Music, though she did not want to teach. After a year, around the time of the Children in Need campaign, a visiting speaker came to talk about music therapy[53]. My daughter quickly discovered what she wanted to do with her music, as a therapist to the severely disadvantaged.

My commitment to autonomy in everyone's learning and development extended from my family to my students. To first-year students who so wished, I delegated responsibility to decide what they would study, and how they would study, around the Properties and Use of Engineering Materials. In a presentation while I was in Colombia, they earned us an Education for Capability Award for 'A Course without a Syllabus'. Then some years later (as I have already mentioned), I pioneered a self-directed and self-assessed course in Design at third-year level, which was accepted by our professional bodies[54].

2. *Self-protection:* All of the latter activity was not free from criticism and disapproval[55]. When I was appointed Scottish Director for the Open University,

---

[52] The big question when things go wrong is: 'Should I think again – or persist?'
[53] Yet another example from my experience of serendipity triggering off extensive and valuable lifewide learning – in this case, for my daughter.
[54] In this respect I was encouraged many years later, after I had written a book about being an innovative university teacher. The great authority, John Biggs, was kind enough to describe it in his own book of that time as 'The clearest example of practice-what-you-preach that I have seen'.
[55] Was this a consequence of being innovative, or of being successful – or just of my interpersonal style? I've often wondered.

my supportive and scholarly Deputy Director, Judith George, presented a slim paperback to me one day. She described it, tongue in cheek, as a five-hundred-year-old handbook for educational developers like me. The immediate quotation from Machiavelli towards which she directed me was his advice that:

Nothing is more difficult to undertake, more perilous to conduct or more uncertain in its outcome, than to take the lead in introducing a new order of things. For the innovator has for enemies all those who have done well under the old, and lukewarm defenders amongst those who may do well under the new.

And then I noted for myself that 'No enterprise is more likely to succeed than one concealed from the enemy until it is ripe for execution'.

The more I have thought about these words, the more accurately they sum up my experiences in trying to bring about radical changes in a Civil Engineering programme, and in dealing with the challenges I was about to face in enhancing support for isolated Open University students in Scotland. Plagued by petty objections and criticisms from academically conservative colleagues, I had already learned the hard way the wisdom of the old Scots saying that 'Fools and bairns (children) should never see a job half done'. Eventually, hard experience had shown me that it was time enough to present what I had been doing when I had assembled firm evidence to table, and had ingathered objective external judgements in support of my innovations[56]. Then I could confidently and effectively take the stance, in the words of our national poet, that 'My skill may weel be doubted; / but facts are chiels that winna ding, / an downa be disputed [My skill may well be doubted (pronounced 'dooted'); but facts are like children who will not change their story, and should not be disputed[57]].

On reflection, then, a great deal of my lifewide learning in the field of autonomous learning in my later years as an innovative teacher was about how to stall scrutiny, badly informed criticism and obstruction[58]. I stalled until I had strong evidence of the effectiveness of what I was doing, so that the merits of student-centred learning could not validly be doubted.

---

[56] Echoes here of anticipating problems and coping with them before they happen. Lifewide learning is interwoven.
[57] Some quotations mean a lot to me. I have also found them useful. If a junior felt unable to do something, I might quote KoKo's protest that a man cannot cut his own head off, to which Pooh-Bah responded sternly, 'A man can try!'
[58] But my tactical commitment to ingathering objective data to inform my self-judgements was growing. Is this a desirable feature of lifewide learning?

3. Self-enhancement: In my time with the OU, I studied for a degree in Social Sciences, to broaden my learning to cover another disciplinary area – and to give me experience of being an open and distance learner. One course I especially valued was Professional Judgement and Decision Making[59].

Before I retired from the OU, I found myself assisting the Social Sciences course team in the University of the Highlands and Islands Project, where we designed some innovative modules. I taught on some of these for three to four years after retirement, until they had no further need of me. Thus my lifewide learning, driven by personal needs and interests, became the foundation for later professional practice. So it seemed natural (in my last year with the OU) to study a module in Arts about Homer's poetry, again widening my disciplinary base[60] and connecting me back to my love of literature developed at my mother's knee.

4. Persistence: I suppose the origin for me of explicit learner-centredness in my teaching occurred in my very first lecture to a final-year Design class. I had a catastrophic failure, and had to steel myself to find the resolve to try again.

I had prepared this important[61] lecture assiduously, and was determined to offer interesting examples and valuable content. Within five minutes of my opening, it was apparent that the students were bored to tears. I went home almost in tears myself, convinced that I had made a dreadful error in leaving the employment I had so much enjoyed in the design office. That evening, I prepared for my second lecture, determined to be more interesting and to have richer content than in the first one. If anything, the second was worse than the first. I left the lecture room in absolute despair. As I walked down the corridor, a student – to whom I shall be forever grateful and with whom I am still in contact after forty-five years – walked alongside me and asked politely whether I knew what was wrong. I responded that I did indeed know what was wrong: I had been boring. And I just didn't know how to rectify that. 'No,' he advised me, 'you weren't boring. It was just that you lost us all in the first five minutes. We aren't up to that speed and depth.' I thanked him, and went home with a spring in my step to prepare something more straightforward, and to explain in clearer detail at a pace which allowed assimilation[62]. From that day to this, finding out from my

---

[59] Maybe rather late in my development. Self-directed lifewide learning may sometimes omit or delay experiences?
[60] Lifewide learning can eventually become an established feature of my practice. Then I need a new challenge or opportunity or variety.
[61] Well, it was important to me!
[62] What would have happened if he hadn't spoken to me? Serendipity again.

students about the learning experiences which I create for them has been a fundamental feature of my approach as a teacher. And that, in turn, has led to umpteen worthwhile learning and development experiences for me over the years. The student's insight made a powerful impact on me, bringing me important lifewide learning about the value of dialogue with students. And that leads me on to my next feature and example.

5. *Collaboration (and co-operation):* Throughout my teaching career I have sought feedback and advice from my students. I have then joined with them in becoming action researchers of our joint purposes, discovering how we could together make our learning and teaching relationship more effective. Eventually, I initiated similar activity on the part of some OU tutors in Scotland. One result of that has been the publication of papers jointly written with students. Other results have included restructuring of handouts, clarification of standards from past examples and my facilitation of online discussions in Taiwan.

6. *Flexibility:* My lifewide learning has often arisen from family incidents[63]. Some years ago my late son had taken up an attractive offer of appropriate employment while he still had a little work to do to complete his PhD. In his new job, he went to Paris with a van full of valuable equipment, his thesis, his laptop and disks. The van and contents he parked in a top-security car park. He returned after booking into his hotel to find that the van had been stolen. He phoned home to break the news, and my wife came through broken-hearted to tell me about our son's disaster. When he spoke to me later and asked what I thought, I just looked forward and said quite sincerely that I was sure his second thesis would be better than his first one[64].

A few months later, I had a message from Lewis Elton about a conference paper which I had carefully written to the declared limit of 4,500 words, and had had accepted. At a late date he had decided papers should only take up 3,000 words. I was tempted to withdraw, but getting this thinking published was important to me. So I hastily began again, to produce 3,000 words – in poor grace. Long after the conference, I allowed myself to bitterly compare the two versions, to see what damage the curtailment and rewriting had done. To my astonishment, I found that I believed that the 3,000-word version was the better paper. I had learnt that starting again from scratch is no bad thing.

---

[63] Our families and other close personal relationships are one of our most valuable resources and sources of insight. They have a habit of teaching us things we thought we already knew. I'll spare my wife's embarrassment by not relating the many ways in which she has contributed to my lifewide learning – and especially to learning from my mistakes.
[64] And it was.

Often a complete change of direction can be transformative. A major development for me as a teacher happened when I was five years into the job of lecturing. I wanted to teach better than those who had taught me. I had a vague vision of establishing a teaching unit in the department where I was employed. However, I felt I could make better progress as a teacher than I had so far managed to do. So I signed up for a summer school at University of Manchester Institute for Science and Technology, run by a wonderful man called Bill Morton. It was a condition of attendance that we agreed to be in residence full time, and to undertake no social engagements outwith the school programme. We lived together, and Bill lived with us.

The programme was a wonderful combination of workshops, guest presenters and interesting speakers at our evening dinners – and time with Bill[65]. He epitomised what Carl Rogers[66] has described as congruence, establishing a relationship with each of us in which, from the outset, he was genuine and real. In our conversations, especially in the residence in the evenings, he talked with us a lot about our aspirations and where they came from. He was genuinely interested in each of us. And in his conversations with us, as they developed, he shared with us his own aspirations, which centred on supporting student learning. He explained to us, without preaching to us, or trying to sell us his views and values.

I went back home as a convert, as did many others whose development as teachers had been lifewide during that fortnight. No longer did I want to establish a teaching unit. I wanted to establish a *learning* unit. My fortnight-long experience of lifewide learning had shown me what learner-centred activity could deliver, for me and my students. And my friendship with Bill Morton had shown me the kind of teacher I wished to become.

I would summarise all of this by saying that I was constantly trying to develop the capabilities I needed to achieve success and so I was trying to find ways that enabled me to do so. For example, I was increasingly putting my neck on the line to take risks in the belief they would lead to success. I put my trust in others to lead us to success; and I tried to create conditions and provide leadership that enabled others in my team to achieve their own successes[67].

---

[65] A powerful influence on me.
[66] Another powerful influence. I am still rereading Rogers, and finding ideas I have missed.
[67] But, in all honesty, none of this was done consciously at the time – at best, it was intuitive. However, in the fullness of time, I began to see the merits of such an approach.

Lifewide learning within my university career
Professional life was becoming less challenging, and more humdrum. For gradually, each new and even more demanding challenge felt less and less demanding, and more to be 'just another impossible job'. It was probably time to find new challenges.

Accounts of my lifewide learning as a university teacher have already featured in the examples I have given of transfer forward in time. So it will suffice to amplify that by reiterating how I was inspired early on by the writings of Carl Rogers and especially by the course directed by Professor Bill Morton. I came home from that, tore up all my carefully prepared lecture notes from the previous five years and decided to start anew. I moved as quickly as my conservative colleagues could tolerate[68] towards what was then called independence (or more accurately autonomy) in learning. I progressively offered my students meaningful choices in the rate and approach which they took to their learning, the outcomes which they pursued and their assessment of the consequent learning and development, which was objectively evaluated as a distinct improvement. As a result, I became less and less concerned with the content which my students would cover, and more with the capabilities[69] which I wanted to help them to develop and with what *they* wanted to learn. For I hoped that – as soon as possible – they would responsibly and ably take full charge of their own learning and development.

I went on to research (consecutively) in four different fields, to publish in all of them and to gain higher degrees in two of them – and all of this activity was almost entirely self-directed and self-managed[70]. Mindful of my father's example, I took advantage of British Council funding to undertake staff and curriculum development work in Third World countries, without a fee, for at least three weeks in every year – and gained great strength (and confidence[71]) from these demanding experiences. Eventually (as you now know), I was to take a further undergraduate degree (in social sciences). As a result I have taught in my career in four quite distinct discipline areas. Additionally, a feature of my teaching, which is partly a consequence of my advancing years and partly a

---

[68] Their toleration was low! Fortunately, the one exception was my highly supportive Head of Department.
[69] I have long mourned the demise of the influence of the Education for Capability Manifesto. That is why I am so heartened by the adoption of the capability-based approach to lifewide learning advocated in this book (see Chapter 3).
[70] This is an interesting contrast with present-day postgraduate supervision, where fear of adverse dropout rates seems to have led to authoritative direction by many supervisors.
[71] It's easier to take risks outwith your own academic territory. If you fail, which I never actually did, you don't have to live on with the consequences of failure!

consequence of the rapidity with which the world is changing, has been that almost everything I have taught has been outwith the curricula of the courses I took as a student[72]. And that has called for more self-direction on my part – and on the part of my students. It has also reinforced my belief in the transferability of generic abilities underpinned by values and beliefs developed through the experiences I have had applying such generic abilities in different contexts.

My lifewide learning still owes a lot to my juniors, in age if not in wisdom. Please bear with me as I close my anecdotes with a long composite tale eventually involving my seven-year-old granddaughter. It begins back in my days with the British Council. For some years I worked on educational development activities abroad, partnering an expert in that field, Alan Harding. On one occasion in Egypt, a rotund Turkish academic called Baha asked if he might observe one of our planning sessions. Readily we agreed, provided he only spoke with us after we had finished. He honoured that agreement zealously. So at the close, Alan asked Baha what he had observed. Baha thought for a few moments, and then observed slowly that John did ninety-five per cent of the talking, and Alan did ninety-five per cent of the thinking. We laughed – and I hope I learned[73]. Since then, more and more I have disciplined myself to try to summarise, at least silently in my mind, what others are saying to me, before deciding what I should say to them. I don't always succeed in that resolve, but I judge this lifewide learning has made a difference in me.

One of Alan's favourite ways into development activities which stress learning rather than teaching was to make use of Kipling's famous rhyme[74]:

> I keep six honest serving men
> They taught me all I knew
> Their names are What and Why and When
> And How and Where and Who

For years I used this theme in introductions to some of my own workshops. But then it dawned on me, as someone committed to self- and peer-assessment, that there was a seventh question which was also very important to me, as a query that all learners should pose of themselves. This was and is: 'How well?' 'How well did I do that?' or 'How well do I want to do this?' Feeling self-satisfied

---

[72] Is this not true for most of us? The half-life of an electronics degree is said to be less than four years. And new methods of learning emerge rapidly. E-learning is now being overtaken by ubiquitous-learning.
[73] Because, at the time, this truth hurt?
[74] The Elephant's Child Rudyard Kipling (1902)

by this awareness, I extended my list (but not the poem) to cover *seven* important questions which serve learning.

Then, one Friday afternoon, this being the 'in-service training' time for local primary school teachers, my granddaughter was with us as usual. She was working her way through her busy list of things she wanted us to do. Having cleared the list, she was wont to ask, 'What n'else, Granpa?' I once found myself thinking about her question. It dawned on me that she was posing another important question for anyone promoting learning. Learners, like curious children, should constantly be asking themselves: 'What *else* should I be considering, what *other* options need to be explored, is there *another* possibility?'

I notice that all of my examples so far have involved the active involvement of a third party in my lifewide learning[75]. I now close by pointing out that this agent can be of any age. For it was thanks to seven-year old Rebecca that my lifewide learning took my list of questions to facilitate learning from seven to eight.

The 'Helen Wood' question
In a workshop for part-time staff of the Open University in Scotland who sought Staff and Educational Development Association accreditation as university teachers, I challenged participants to identify the ability which lay at the core of their disciplines. Dr Helen Wood, after pondering, said that as a chemist, what was most important to her was to look at data and spectra, and notice what was not there. I rate that a central challenge in most disciplines[76].

So what have I omitted in this long tale of lifelong-lifewide learning? A lot. I haven't thought sufficiently analytically about the role of serendipity in my lifewide development, and how I might or might not have developed in its absence. I have only hinted at the importance to my development of relationships of two kinds. There is the 'hero figure', such as Bill Morton; there is also the 'buddy', which Alan Harding was to become once he refused to occupy the pedestal on which I still (privately) place him. I've profited from having many splendid buddies. And I haven't expanded on the influence of passion for my aims which Richard St John mentions amongst other qualities for success, which seem to me more qualities which are missing in the unsuccessful. I

---

[75] I have reached this point late in this piece but it should be clear to you that my lifewide learning has essentially been a social affair kindled and emerging from some of the most important relationships in my life.
[76] As in the classic incident of the dog which did not bark in the night.

haven't distinguished 'watchful anticipation', which is knowing that in an unpredictable and emergent world not everything can be controlled, and so the unexpected emerges and we have to be prepared in order to recognise it. Given that I am arguing that lifewide learning is emergent, I should have drawn attention to this phenomenon. Space precludes dealing with these and other omissions in an already overlong foreword.

However, I feel a need to squeeze in just one last example, guilty that it only occurred to me when I was adding the questioning marginal comments. I asked myself why I had said nothing about the role of familiar readings and literary characters in my lifelong experience. Suddenly, I remembered that the two most used volumes on my bookshelves, even beyond Rogers, are the glorious eleventh chapter of the Epistle to the Hebrews[77], which surely inspired that great Luther King speech in which he repeatedly told that 'I have a dream...'. The second is a book given to me as a boy by my scatty godmother, a book which I cannot recall my mother ever reading to me, which contained the adventures of 'Stalky & Co'. Stalky was a maverick schoolboy, derived from Kipling's own schooldays. He rebelled against authority. He mostly succeeded. He often took a stance for something which mattered to him on principle. I wonder how much that book shaped the young John Cowan.

Some provisional sense making
My views about learning to be professional through lifelong lifewide learning have originated from the life history on which I have touched here. From Machiavelli: 'The more sand has escaped from the hourglass of our life, the clearer we should see through it.' I am now almost seventy-nine years old. I still regularly teach undergraduates and postgraduates – though not full time and mostly online. Each summer I still carry out a self-appraisal[78], pinpointing what should feature on my forthcoming agenda for development. I identify the understanding I wish or need to acquire, and the abilities I should hone or develop. My aim is always to feel reasonably satisfied with my updating and uprating[79] of my personal and professional competences.

In this I am greatly in debt to Norman Jackson. At an age when most old men like me would be left in peace to sit by the fireside in their slippers, I found myself encouraged by him to write two reflective pieces in which I looked back over my life experience. In so doing, just as Moliere's M. Jourdain had

---

[77] A catalogue of heroes who fought against the odds!
[78] With assistance, as ever, from peers and colleagues who help me to identify unperceived needs.
[79] I draw a distinction here. I am currently updating myself on new thinking about e-moderation. I am needing to up-rate my creative skills with PowerPoint.

discovered late in life that he had been speaking prose for over forty years, I discovered, with Norman's prompting and to my delight, that I had been profiting throughout my life from what he explained to me was lifewide learning[80]. This learning and development had gone far beyond, and was much more important to me than, what I had learnt in the various courses I have taken in my formal education[81] and the academic awards I have gained.

I now look forward with great anticipation to learning what the contributors to this volume have to share with us about this vital aspect of all our learning, and to the unanticipated things that will surely emerge through the relationships of those engaged in creating this book.

---

[80] Incidentally, Norman has confided in me that I am also an important part of *his* lifewide learning enterprise.

[81] Perhaps I was fortunate in being unfortunate. I was unfortunate to be taught by men who stirred up my will to do better for myself than they were doing; and I was unfortunate to be taught my engineering by lecturers of whom only one had practised as a senior engineer. I was fortunate that I therefore felt free to manage my own learning and development.

Chapter 1

The lifelong and lifewide dimensions of living, learning and developing

Norman Jackson

Synopsis
This Chapter introduces the idea of 'lifewideness' and explains why it is worthy of examination and why it is an important concept for student development. It tries to show how the idea complements and adds value to the well-known concept of lifelong learning and argues that a lifewide education could enhance a university's ability to recognise and value learning and personal development that is essential for survival, success and personal fulfilment in a complex modern world.

Introduction
Dellas and Gaier (1970) define personal creativity as the desire and ability to use imagination, insight and intellect, feeling and emotion, to move an idea from one state to an alternative, previously unexplored state. This book tries to move the idea of *lifewideness*, an idea that has so far received little conceptual or practical attention in education, to a more examined, meaningful and useful state. Our primary concern is to add value to the educational experiences and personal development of higher education students. Our aim is to influence the prevailing concepts of learning and personal development in higher education, by recognising and valuing what students do to make their own education more complete.

Why should the idea of lifewideness be examined? As we develop deeper understandings about the sorts of learning and development that are required for living a successful and fulfilled life in a complex modern world, it becomes more and more apparent that our educational institutions need to pay more attention to developing learners as whole people. Focusing so much attention on the cognitive development of individuals misses the point of what well rounded education should be about. By examining the idea of lifewideness we are opening up the possibility for a more complete education: one that recognises that formal education is just one part of an individual's whole life: a life that is full of opportunity for learning and education.

To be successful and fulfilled in life we have to develop ourselves so that we are able 'to negotiate and act on our own purposes, values, feelings, and meanings rather than those we have uncritically assimilated from others' (Mezirow 2000:8). Hodge *et al.* (2010) suggest that this requires 'a shift from uncritical acceptance of external authority to critical analysis of authority in order to establish one's own internal authority. This internal authority is what developmental theorists call self-authorship, or the capacity to define one's beliefs, identity, and social relations (Baxter Magolda 2001, 2004, 2009; Kegan 1994).' This book develops the argument that by adopting a lifewide concept for learning and education, our education institutions can facilitate learner progression towards such complex learning achievements as are embodied in the principles and practice of self-authorship.

How does lifewideness relate to lifelong learning? Most people are familiar with the idea of lifelong learning to represent an individual's learning and development throughout the whole of their life-span. But the complementary concept of lifewideness, the learning and development that occurs more or less contemporaneously in multiple and varied places and situations throughout an individual's life course, is less familiar. Yet for students who are studying in higher education (only one part of their lifelong learning journey), it is the lifewide dimension that they actually notice and participate in every day.

Lifewideness is a simple idea. It recognises that most people, no matter what their age or circumstances, simultaneously inhabit a number of different spaces – like work or education, running a home, being a member of a family, being involved in a club or society, travelling and taking holidays and looking after their own wellbeing mentally, physically and spiritually. We live out our lives in these different spaces and we have the freedom to choose which spaces we want to occupy. In these spaces we make decisions about what to be involved in, we meet and interact with different people, have different sorts of relationships, adopt different roles and identities, and think, behave and communicate in different ways. In these different spaces we encounter different sorts of challenges and problems, seize or miss opportunities, and aspire to live a useful and productive life and achieve our ambitions. It is in these spaces that we create, with others, the meaning that is our life.

> an experience we have in place A resonates at a deep level with something I am encountering in place B. The resonance makes me examine my experience in Place A more closely in search of profound answers to the deep quest of who I am and who I want to become.
> (Paul Thomas; 10/12/10)

The potential for who we might become resides in the possibilities afforded by the spaces and opportunities in our lives, but we have to recognise these opportunities and act upon them. More than this, our lives are often shaped by others, and we have to create opportunities from the situations they create for us. Turning other people's projects into projects from which we draw meaning and benefit is an important talent for sustaining a self-fulfilled life.

Why is this important to higher education? By reframing our perception of what counts as learning and development, and developing the means of recognising and valuing the learning and development gained in a learner's lifewide experiences – learning that is not usually assessed within an academic programme – higher education could enable learners to develop a deeper appreciation of how, what, when and why they are learning in the different parts of their lives. Heightened self-awareness is likely to help learners become more effective at learning through their own experiences and this should be an essential outcome of a higher education experience that prepares people for the challenges of a complex, ever-changing world.

The book tries to show that the idea of lifewideness provides us with a powerful concept within which other ideas and accumulated wisdom can be integrated. In his book *The 8th Habit: From Effectiveness to Greatness*, Stephen Covey examines and gives meaning to the idea of 'voice' – 'the unique personal significance we all possess – the voice of hope, intelligence, resilience and the limitless human potential to effect positive change'. According to Covey (2004:5) voice lies at the nexus of talent (your natural gifts and strengths); passion (those things that naturally energise, excite, motivate you); need (including what the world needs enough to pay you for [and the needs you identify and feel a need to fulfil[1]]); and conscience (that still, small voice within that assures you of what is right and that prompts you to actually do it).

This set of ideas and meanings connects in a profound way an individual's identity and spirit with their capabilities, attitudes, needs, motivations and purposes so necessary for achieving, within an ethical framework that guides personal decisions and actions. This representation of voice seems to me to embody the essence of what underlies and gives expression to our unique personal significance. And the idea of lifewideness provides the context through which our unique voice is applied in everyday situations.

Furthermore, at a time of increasing instability and rapid change, lifewide learning and the practice of lifewide education hold the promise of engaging individuals more systematically and more deeply in the development of the capability and agency necessary for them to create and sustain a good quality of life (Alkire 2008). These ideas hold the promise of enabling individuals to both achieve a sense of personal fulfilment and social well-being and gain recognition for the learning and development that has been gained through leading the life we choose to lead.

Maslow (1943) developed a framework for analysing the motivational forces (needs and purposes) behind human behaviour (both reactive and proactive) and growth (personal development). His model contains five levels of need:

1. biological and physiological basic needs – air, food, drink, shelter, warmth, sex, sleep, etc.
2. safety needs – protection from elements, security, order, law, limits, stability, etc.
3. belongingness and love needs – work group, family, affection, relationships, etc.
4. esteem needs – self-esteem, achievement, mastery, independence, status, dominance, prestige, managerial responsibility, etc.
5. self-actualisation needs – realising personal potential, self-fulfilment, seeking personal growth and peak experiences.

Because the lifewide concept of learning and development embraces the whole of a person's life, lifewideness must engage with the full spectrum of a person's needs and the opportunities available to them to satisfy their needs and realise their potential. It provides a more holistic vehicle for encouraging and supporting self-actualisation than a traditional higher education approach that focuses primarily on disciplinary learning. Baxter Magolda (2004) highlights the significance of this process through the concept of self-authorship.

> The complexities young adults face in trans-disciplinary contexts after college, as well as the complexities inherent in disciplinary learning during college, require something beyond skills acquisition and application. They require transformation from authority dependence to self-authorship, or the capacity to internally define one's beliefs, identity and social relations.
> (Baxter Magolda 2004:145)

Hodge et al. (2010) are critical of traditional approaches to teaching and learning in higher education which do not prepare people for the demands and challenges of living and working in a trans-disciplinary world.

> To discover new ideas, learners must possess an internal set of beliefs that guide decision making about knowledge claims, an internal identity that enables them to express themselves in socially constructing knowledge with others, and the capacity to engage in mutually interdependent relationships to assess others' expertise. These capacities cannot be cultivated solely by engaging actively with the raw materials and tools of the academy or by participating in a student-centred classroom, although these are essential. Instead, they emerge gradually when educators foster students' holistic growth through continuous self-reflection, seamless and authentic curricular and co-curricular experiences that steadily increase in challenge, and appropriate levels of support.
> (Hodge et al. 2010:2)

A lifewide concept of education allows educators, and empowers learners, to address these concerns. Because it embraces the whole of a person's life, lifewideness includes all of a person's experiences in their cognitive, personal and social development. Lifewideness is fundamentally concerned with the way we create, engage with, sense, and make sense of our own experiences. Learning and developing through our experiences has been described by Beard and Wilson (2005:2) as 'a sense making process that actively engages the reflective inner world of the learner as a whole person (social, physical, intellectual, emotional, spiritual, etc) with the rich "outer world" of their learning environment (space & place, artefacts, people, cultural etc)'. Learning is both a sense-making and a meaning-making process. A lifewide concept of education values an individual's search for meanings and purposes and from in their life.

Inspiring student voices
This inspiring story, told by a final year undergraduate student, illustrates very well the wonderful interplay of life as a journey and life as a rich set of parallel

and interfering relationships and situations through which people are changed and come to understand themselves better. It captures her search for deeper meanings and purposes in her life and reveals her journey of self-realisation and self-authorship.

The volunteer trip I organised was to a small town in Uganda. This was something I had thought about for years and finally had the means to do. I approached the Students' Union and asked whether there was a programme already set up. I was referred to a local non-government organisation called Experience Culture and I was inspired by a visit to their website which informed me of the work they were doing in Uganda. I got in touch with them and they invited me to join them in their work. I emailed the entire university asking who wanted to come with me and soon realised just how much I had bitten off! The response was overwhelming and I tried to be as fair as possible while only being able to choose five other students. Once the group was assembled I started to organise the next steps and fundraising. I soon found that while students are generous to causes, it is difficult to stir up enthusiasm towards raising money without pitching the idea in an incendiary manner. It took a lot of planning and long hours often through the night to try to make our fundraisers enticing and fun, while maintaining the focus on the cause itself. Over the next 6 months, we came up with ideas such as the sale of sweets at student events, a decorated bake sale, a pub quiz, a giant dodgeball tournament and a music concert at the university. Any money raised was to be a donation towards the children's home and medical centre we would be working at....Being the organiser and perceived leader of a group was new to me and extremely daunting; this proved to be one of the most marked times of my life, during which I grew immensely as a person, and developed my confidence through a comforting sense of achievement.

We started work immediately upon our arrival in Uganda... Working so closely with the students, teachers, hospital workers and volunteers was a wonderful experience, and we soon came to view the world through their eyes, with emotional and profound results. At the children's home we taught lessons in and out of the classroom, sports and games, and sex education. This was probably where I was most at peace while in Uganda, as the love and simple kindnesses the children bestowed upon us were almost magical. Their excitement towards learning was contagious and I looked forward to spending time with them every day. It was a sharp realisation to see the stark differences between the culture and attitudes in Uganda and back home where complacency and over-indulgence are rife.

At the medical centre we helped out at AIDS clinics, helped with filing and went on 'field trips' out into rural communities to teach about HIV/ AIDS, sex education and health and nutrition. Our donations were spent on a library for the children's home, which we painted ourselves, shoes for the children and mosquito nets for those in the communities. I could not help but be moved by the experience of seeing families living in conditions of extreme poverty and illness. One particularly draining day of work involved us going out into a community far away to try to obtain support for Sarah, an eleven-year-old girl who was HIV-positive, and had walked forty-one kilometres barefoot to the medical centre to ask for help. We negotiated with her family for four hours to try to get them to provide shelter and food for her in order for her to receive drug treatment from the medical centre. It was entirely surreal to be sitting under a tree in the African sun, fighting for someone's chance of survival, with the desperation and urgency of the conversation all too apparent. This difficult, drawn out negotiation was absolutely worth it when they finally agreed, ultimately saving her life. The knowledge that we have helped at least one person in this way is something I cling to when it feels that we are just one drop in an ever-present ocean of suffering that often threatens to overwhelm us.

These experiences we had in Uganda changed me and spurred me on to try to make a bigger difference and try to sustain what we had started and in my second year we [me and my sister] set up a 'volunteering society' [to continue the work we had begun]. Pioneering this society was daunting to say the least, with every step unpaved, and layers of bureaucracy to manoeuvre past.

I cannot fully explain the feeling of wholeness that accompanies helping someone in a significant way. Every new experience adds to my person, and expands or alters my perspectives. I feel that it has helped me to grow in so many ways, especially in terms of confidence and my capabilities for dealing with unfamiliar situations and to create new opportunities for myself and others. I feel spurred on to continue what we started and more, and truly believe that I am now much better equipped to achieve these goals. Through the various activities I have undertaken while at university I have improved my understanding and insight into myself, and others. I have also realised that while an idea may start as just an idea, or may seem like just a drop in a vast ocean, it can manifest itself as a wonderful compilation of events; a tidal wave whose ripple effects extend continuously outwards.

This very personal story shows how an individual has created and connected her lifewide experiences to form her lifelong journey, and how these experiences create the foundation for future (lifelong) intentions and actions that unfold in a different time and place. This story also reveals an individual's resolve to act or change because she has witnessed or been part of something through which she has changed: new insights and beliefs have been gained and her will to do more has been stimulated. The power of this learning manifests itself in this person's preparedness to engage with complex uncertainty, making informed, insightful and sometimes emotionally engaged choices about what to do or try to do next. Her willingness to put herself into new and unfamiliar, even risky, situations where neither the contexts nor the challenges are known seems to have forged a stronger identity so that she becomes more complete in the way she aspires to be. The story also illuminates how an individual's will to persevere and her own agency can overcome the obstacles that are encountered when she wants to achieve something in a world that is organised with priorities that are different to her own. Above all, the story illustrates the powerful synergy between an individual's lifelong and lifewide journey and her development as the person she wants to be and become. This story of self-actualisation is the underlying story of lifewide learning and personal development.

The lifelong-lifewide paradigm

This story, told by a student in her third year at university, illustrates well the lifelong dimension of learning (over two years) and the lifewide dimension – some of the opportunities she took to develop herself in different parts of her life during this period. Lifelong learning is a well-established concept in the world of educational policy. It represents all the learning and development we gain through living.

> Lifelong learning is the continuous building of skills and knowledge throughout the life of an individual. It occurs through experiences encountered in the course of a lifetime. These experiences could be formal (training, counselling, tutoring, mentorship, apprenticeship, higher education, etc.) or informal (experiences, situations, etc.) Lifelong learning is the 'lifelong, voluntary, and self-motivated' pursuit of knowledge for either personal or professional reasons. As such, it not only enhances social inclusion, active citizenship and personal development, but also competitiveness and employability.
> (Wikipedia 06/05/10)

Lifewide learning is a concept within the lifelong learning paradigm. It emerged in a report (NAES 2000) by the Swedish National Agency for Education.

> The lifelong dimension represents what the individual learns throughout the whole life-span. Knowledge rapidly becomes obsolete and it is necessary for the individual to update knowledge and competence in a continuous process of learning. Education cannot be limited to the time spent in school, the individual must have a real opportunity to learn throughout life. The lifelong dimension is non-problematic, what is essential is that the individual learns throughout life. The lifewide dimension refers to the fact that learning takes place in a variety of different environments and situations, and is not only confined to the formal educational system. Lifewide learning covers formal, non-formal and informal learning.
>
> (NAES 2000:18)

The idea quickly spread through the policy community and became incorporated into the thinking of economists concerned with measuring value in lifelong learning. A presentation entitled 'Measuring the Impact of the New Economy in Education Sector Outputs' dated 2002 on the UK Government Statistics Office website makes reference to 'measuring lifewide learning'. Richard Desjardins (2004), building on the work of Tuijnman (2003, cited by Desjardins 2004), utilised the idea of lifewide learning in his conceptual framework for the economic evaluation of lifelong learning and these ways of thinking were incorporated into a number of reports by the Organisation for Economic Co-operation and Development for example (OECD 2007:10)

> Learning does not occur just in school – it is both 'lifewide' (i.e. it occurs in multiple contexts, such as work, at home and in our social lives) and 'lifelong' (from cradle to grave). These different types of learning affect each other in a wide variety of ways. Their impact in terms of the outcomes of learning is equally complex – whether it is in the economic and social spheres, the individual and collective, the monetary and the non-monetary. Further complicating the picture are substantial gaps in our knowledge base on a number of issues, including the following:
>
> - The cumulative and interactive impacts of lifewide and lifelong learning
> - The potential impacts of informal learning, later interventions in adulthood or even different types of formal education
> - And the impacts of different curricula (general, academic, vocational) and impacts of different learning at different stages.

The OECD 'Report on the Social Outcomes of Learning' (OECD 2007) provides a useful conceptual framework with which to frame the issues relating to the social outcomes of learning. In this framework learning from formal education and from the diverse contexts that make up people's lives combines to create human and social capital.[2] 'The knowledge, skills, competencies and attributes embodied in individuals facilitate the creation of personal, social and economic wellbeing (OECD 2001:18), where competencies are defined in terms of the capability to perform in particular situations; or 'The ability to successfully meet complex demands in a particular context through the mobilisation of psychological pre-requisites including cognitive and non-cognitive aspects' (Rychen and Salganik 2003, OECD 2007:43).

The Hong Kong primary and secondary school system is the only education system to have adopted a lifewide concept of learning and education.

> Life-wide Learning (LWL) refers to student learning in real contexts and authentic settings. Such experiential learning enables students to achieve certain learning goals that are more difficult to attain through classroom learning alone. It helps students to achieve the aims of whole-person development and enables them to develop the life-long learning capabilities that are needed in our ever-changing society.
> (Government of Hong Kong Education Bureau website)

When viewed from these perspectives, our project to explore the potential role of lifewide learning in the UK higher education setting has the potential to encourage students to become more conscious of the importance of their lifewide learning enterprise while they are studying at university. In raising the awareness of learners of the importance of informal learning in their lifewide experiences, we advance the proposition that they are more likely to be prepared for their lifelong journey of learning and change, and be more conscious of the way in which they learn and develop themselves through the many opportunities and challenges that their life affords. In raising such awareness in individuals, a second proposition might be advanced namely, that lifewide education affords the opportunity to enhance economic, social and personal well-being outcomes from our educational system. This is the ultimate added educational value of the lifewide learning project.

The 'wicked problem' we share

How teachers prepare their students for a lifetime of uncertainty and change, and enable them to work with the ever-increasing complexity of the modern world, is a challenge shared by higher education institutions and educationalists all over the world. How we prepare ourselves for our own unknown futures is a problem we all share.

The now famous 'Shift happens'[3] YouTube video clip portrays, in a deliberately provocative way, the sort of globally connected, fast-changing and uncertain world in which our students' futures lie. While we might question some of the statistics in the film, the central message is clear. We live in a world where change is exponential and we are currently helping to prepare students for jobs that don't yet exist, using technologies that have not yet been invented in order to solve problems that we don't know are problems yet.

If we uphold the educational values of trying to make a positive difference to students' lives then we have a moral and professional responsibility to prepare them for the lifetime of uncertainty, change, challenge and emergent or self-created opportunity that lies ahead of them. It may sound dramatic but the reality is that the majority of our students will have not one but several careers; they will have to change organisations, roles and identities many times and be part of new organisations that they help to create or existing organisations that they help to transform. Many will have to invent their own businesses in order to earn an income or create and juggle a portfolio of jobs requiring them to maintain several identities simultaneously. Preparing our students for a lifetime of working, learning and living in uncertain and unpredictable worlds that have yet to be revealed is perhaps one of the greatest responsibilities and challenges confronting universities all over the world.

Preparing students for an increasingly complex and uncertain world is a 'wicked problem' (Rittel and Webber 1973; Conklin 2006). What emerges from all the technical, informational, social, political and cultural complexity that we are immersed in are problems which cannot be solved through rational, linear problem working processes because the problem definition and our understanding of it evolve as new possible solutions are invented and implemented.

Douglas Thomas and John Seely Brown (2009) crystallise the educational challenge to living in a world of constant and rapid change.

> The educational needs of the 21st century pose a number of serious problems for current educational practices. First and foremost, we see the 21st century as a time that is characterised by constant change. Educational

practices that focus on the transfer of static knowledge simply cannot keep up with the rapid rate of change. Practices that focus on adaptation or reaction to change fare better, but are still finding themselves outpaced by an environment that requires content to be updated almost as fast as it can be taught. What is required to succeed in education is a theory that is responsive to the context of constant flux, while at the same time is grounded in a theory of learning. Accordingly, understanding the processes of learning which underwrite the practices emerging from participation in digital networks may enable us to design learning environments that harness the power of digital participation for education in the 21st century.
(Thomas and Seely Brown 2009:1)

Barnett (2000), meanwhile, summarises the challenge of preparing students for a supercomplex world.

Higher education is faced with not just preparing students for a complex world, it is faced with preparing students for a supercomplex world. It is a world where nothing can be taken for granted, where no frame of understanding or of action can be entertained with any security. It is a world in which we are conceptually challenged and continually so. ...

This supercomplexity shows itself discursively in the world of work through terms such as 'flexibility', 'adaptability' and 'self-reliance'...... In such terminology, we find a sense of individuals having to take responsibility for continually reconstituting themselves through their life span.
(Barnett 2000:257-258)

That traditional forms of discipline-based higher education do prepare students for a complex changing world is undeniable, in so far as so many people are able to take on and be successful in roles that are far removed from their initial disciplinary training. That we recognise we can do better is also undeniable, as institutions and educational professionals continually strive to enhance the effectiveness of the curriculum in preparing students for their world after they have graduated. This point in time is merely the point at which we take stock of the situation and think again about the most appropriate direction to travel.

The most powerful argument for a lifewide curriculum is that it contains more potential for learning than any other curriculum! Adopting the concept of a lifewide curriculum shifts us into a more experience-based view of learning (Andreason *et al.* 1995) when learners use their experiences as the resource for learning by reflecting on, evaluating and reconstructing their experiences in order to draw deeper meaning and grow self-theories (Dweck 1999) from them in the light of prior or parallel experiences.

An experience-rich curriculum that engages with the full breadth of a learner's life provides an environment within which a more holistic conception of learning and individuals' sense of being in the world can be nurtured. We can appreciate much more fully the rich dimensions of learning through belonging, doing, sensing, feeling, thinking and being (Beard 2010; Beard and Wilson 2005; and Chapter 3).

Experience of working and learning in different environments is essential to developing a repertoire of 'ways of knowing' and 'being able to come to know'. Experiential knowing is part of action and it lies at the heart of the epistemology of practice. It complements but is different to explicit and tacit knowledge and can only be gained through acts of doing and being (Cook and Brown 1999).

At the heart of the lifewide learning idea is the deep moral purpose of fostering learners' will or the spirit to be and become (Barnett 2005). An individual's lifewide enterprise contains far more opportunity for her to exercise her will than that part of her life that is only associated with an academic programme. But will alone is not enough; alongside this intentionality learners must have the agency (the thinking capacity, skill, behaviours, qualities and self-awareness) to engage in ways that will enable them to act and adapt, to influence events, achieve their goals and learn through their experiences. They must be, or learn to be, agentic learners (Bandura 2001). The student narrative contributions to this book demonstrate unequivocally that learners' lifewide learning enterprises contain far more opportunity and potential for the development of human agency than a formal education programme alone.

Looking beyond higher education to the professional worlds to which most of our students aspire, we can see the sorts of qualities, skills, dispositions, agencies and ways of knowing and being that are required through the study of professionals doing what they do in their work (e.g. Eraut 2007, 2008 and 2009; Billett 2008, 2009a and b). While higher education has always sought to prepare learners for these professional worlds, the challenge is embedded in the question: 'Can we create even better educational designs that will enable learners to be better prepared for the sort of world we imagine in the future?'

The informational world has added its own complexity. Indeed one of the main reasons the world has become so complex is the volume, immediacy, availability, diversity and speed of producing and using this information. To participate fully in this world we need information handling and processing skills, and digital literacies that were just not necessary even a few years ago. Although formal education plays an important role, many of the skills required and ways of being in the web-enabled information world are gained from experiences of using technology in the social-networked world outside the classroom (Thomas and Seeley Brown 2011).

The utilisation of new media in a strong social context has given rise to what Jenkins *et al.* (2006) describe as a *participatory culture* with relatively low barriers to artistic expression and civic engagement, strong support for creating and sharing one's creations, and some type of informal mentorship whereby what is known by the most experienced is passed along to novices. A growing body of scholarship suggests potential benefits to personal development of these forms of participatory culture. Access to this participatory culture functions as a new form of the hidden curriculum, shaping which youth will succeed and which will be left behind as they enter school and the workplace (Jenkins *et al.* 2006). By embracing a lifewide concept of learning these forms of capability can be recognised and valued within a learner's self-determined development.

Tackling the wicked problem

Directly or indirectly, the problem of how we prepare people for a complex and unpredictable world is the main force driving change in tertiary education and it will always be so. But what we do in response to this challenge is only one part of the educational equation. Learners are busy preparing themselves through the many things they do and involve themselves in outside formal education every day of their lives. It is the recognition that personal education is both a partnership between learners and the providers of formal opportunities, and a self-motivated and self-determined project that makes the idea of lifewide education so appealing and valuable.

This book has been formed around the attempts of one university-based educational development centre to engage with this wicked problem. We defined our problem in terms of 'learning for a complex world' as this seemed to capture the essence of the challenge and the opportunity that we thought we were tackling. With the help of a talented facilitator (Julian Burton), we turned our initial thinking into a symbolic picture (Figure 1.1) that tells a story about people being in a world where day to day the things we need to think about and involve ourselves in emerge through the situations in which we choose to engage or find ourselves.

Figure 1.1 SCEPTrE's metaphorical wall picture which helps to visualise the idea of learning in and for a complex world

At the heart of our concept is the notion of 'will' (Barnett 2005) – the willingness to learn through the whole of life's experiences, the willingness to see self-development as a necessary, holistic and integrated process which evolves through participation in the opportunities that life affords. It is the will to be and become a certain sort of person that drives people to create their enterprises for learning and self-development.

But will alone is insufficient to engage in the opportunities that life affords. It also requires agency: 'Between stimulus and response there is a space. In the space lies our freedom and power to choose our response. In those choices lie our growth and our happiness' (Covey 2004: 4). In the space where we have the freedom to choose what we do, we make decisions that are based on our beliefs, values and what we know and don't know, and can or can't do, and how we feel. For example, we can choose to be positive or negative, to create or try something new or replicate what we have done before, to behave ethically or do something we know is wrong, or to persevere with something difficult or abandon it.

In drawing on Stephen Covey's ideas we have identified a key building block in the lifewide idea: namely, that our lives are made up of multiple streams of situations that require us to make decisions and to act on these decisions, or not if we choose this course of action. A significant part of the complexity in our lives, and the way we ultimately learn to deal with complexity, comes from our experience of engaging with the multiplicity of situations we encounter within our daily lives. And in our family and wider social world, the way we help others deal with their situations is also part of our complexity.

A lifewide curriculum

Formal education, although very important, is only one part of the experiences that make up our lives: experiences that are generally not recognised as being relevant to a student's higher education learning enterprise which has been traditionally formed around either learning about one or more subjects which may or may not be directly related to a career pathway. Yet observation of what students actually do to develop themselves while they are at university shows that their development as a person involves far more than studying a subject (Chapters 9- 13). It involves them immersing themselves in a whole-of-life experience, the results of which shape their identity and destiny (for example story of one student's volunteering in Uganda described above).

As a generalisation, when designing an academic curriculum, designers typically begin with their purposes and imagined outcomes. They think about the content (knowledge), create a design around the content, encourage learning and the use of content through prescribed teaching and learning activities, provide some supporting resources (usually text based) and assess learning against criteria that reflect the answers they hope to get for the problems and challenges they set. There is a predictability and linearity in this form of formal learning that is quite different to the learning that emerges from doing things in the world outside formal education. There is little or no room for outcomes that are not desired or anticipated by the teacher or outcomes that learners individually recognise as being valuable to themselves if they are not also deemed valuable by the teacher.

But what if we were to begin with the learner and their life, and see the learner as the designer of an integrated meaningful life experience? An experience that incorporates formal education as one component of a much richer set of experiences that embrace all the forms of learning and achievement that are necessary to sustain a meaningful life. These ways of thinking are both disturbing, because higher education seems to be neglecting important things, and exciting because of the potential to improve the current situation.

Turning ideas into new realities

But it is one thing to have ideas and another to create meaningful and useful educational practices that give concrete expression to the ideas. Anyone who has tried to innovate within a university knows that this is a 'messy business'. For any change agent, university organisations are a challenging mix of collegial, individualistic, managerial and bureaucratic entities that often combine to dismiss or stifle any emergent practice that challenges the status quo. Furthermore, nothing is static: the challenge is to bring about change in an environment that is already full of change - much of it that no one wants to make! Ewell is particularly helpful in explaining why universities are difficult organisations in which to accomplish innovation (Ewell 2005) and many of his insights and conclusions are directly applicable to our own experiences of trying to bring about change. Our project to persuade our university to adopt a lifewide concept of higher education was not successful. But neither did it fail, trying to innovate but not succeeding, especially in a climate of cost-cutting is the normal and acceptable risk of engaging in educational innovation. The seeds for fundamental change have been sown and have taken root in the hearts and minds of individuals who have been influenced by our work. These people are adapting their practices and innovating in ways that honour the idea of lifewide education. Beyond our university, this book attempts to spread our ideas and practices more widely and only time will tell whether we have been successful in influencing others.

I have always believed that significant change - like the changes accompanying the systematic introduction of Personal Development Planning (QAA 2000) in UK higher education, should be viewed at the scale of at least a decade or even a generation. Our attempts to bring about fundamental change in one institution should be judged on this time scale. More importantly, when considering educational change of the type we are advocating, it is the global not the local level that is important. Our research has shown that there are many institutions in the UK that have already embraced some of the ideas and practices advocated in this book. These institutions are the true pioneers for a new and more complete higher education.

About the book

This book is primarily for teachers and other educational practitioners who are interested and involved in helping students maximise the learning and development they gain from their higher education experience. The authors contributing to this book hope that their attempt to examine and give practical meaning to the idea of lifewideness makes sense to you and helps you to support and facilitate the development of students and / or staff in your professional context. We also hope that it might have meaning for you in your own life.

In recent years, universities in the UK have been encouraged to evaluate what they do through the lens of the student experience. This has resulted in an increasing institutional interest and awareness in the way in which students integrate higher education with their life across and beyond the campus. (NASPA and ACPA 2004). This book is also written for people who work in the Student Care Services who support students as they engage in and are shaped by their whole life experience while they are at university.

For the decision makers who are trying to bring about the cultural change necessary in adopting a lifewide approach to education, we hope the contributions in this book will reinforce your conviction that this is the right thing to do and provide useful conceptual and practical information that will help you achieve your educational ambitions.

The book is organised into four parts. The introduction to lifewide learning begins in John Cowan's Foreword. A self-proclaimed lifelong/lifewide learning enthusiast, John provides his personal interpretation of how the learning and personal development he gained in the lifewide dimension of his life have shaped him as a person.

Part 1 (Chapters 1-8) to introduce the key concepts of lifewideness: lifewide learning and personal development, lifewide education and lifewide curriculum. In Chapter 2 Ron Barnett proposes that lifewide education has the potential to transform our thinking about the purpose of higher education and proclaims that lifewide learning is already a reality. Any holistic model of education also requires a holistic view of learning and personal development and in Chapter 3 Colin Beard and Norman Jackson develop such a model. Lifewide education lends itself to a capability-based approach and the reasons for this and the nature of capability required for living a successful and fulfilled life are considered in Chapter 4. Lifewide learning is powerfully linked to the concept of self-authorship developed by Marcia Baxter Magolda, and in Chapter 5 she draws attention to the importance of personal experiences in the world outside higher education that enable learners to encounter and develop the epistemological, intrapersonal and interpersonal complexity necessary for surviving and prospering in a complex and disruptive world. She also elaborates her ideas for Learning Partnerships that would support and enable learners' to develop the capabilities and dispositions necessary for self-authorship. The consequence of adopting a lifewide concept for education is that we also need a lifewide concept of curriculum and this theme is developed in Chapter 6. A lifewide curriculum embraces three curricular domains - the academic, co-curriculum and extra-curriculum and a more complete education involves exploiting the opportunities for learning and development in all three domains. But what role do teachers play in promoting and facilitating lifewide education? In Chapter 7 John Cowan sets out to answer this question, advocating that a new pedagogy is required to support and sustain lifewide learning and connect and integrate students' learning outside and inside formal education. Part 1 concludes with a contribution from Marat Staron (Chapter 8) relating the concept of lifewide learning and education to the 'life-based learning' concept developed for work-based learning situations in the vocational education and training (VET) sector in Australia.

Part 2 focuses on the lifewide learning experiences of students and is based on research undertaken at the University of Surrey using questionnaires, reflective essays and interview techniques. Through several on-line questionnaire surveys Jenny Willis and Norman Jackson (Chapter 9) show the wide range of experiences students have outside the formal curriculum and the significance of these experiences to their personal development. The stories told by students through a series of essay competitions and interviews reveal the deeper meanings and values in such experiences. The analysis of student narratives also forms the basis for Chapter 10 in which Sarah Campbell and Norman Jackson consider the educational importance of immersive experiences, concluding that such experiences provide important vehicles for self-actualisation and self-authorship.

Part 3 provides a practical example of a Lifewide Education Learning Partnership to encourage and support learning and personal development using the example of the Lifewide Learning Award Framework developed at the University of Surrey. In Chapter 11 Norman Jackson, Charlie Betts and Jenny Willis outline the Award Framework and describe the ways in which learning and personal development were achieved and represented by students and validated by assessors. This is followed by examples of learning in two different contexts. The first case study (Chapter 12) focuses on the work environment. Norman Jackson, Jenny Willis, Sarah Campbell and Michael Eraut describe research into how people learn and develop through the process of work and relate this to student development in work placement and part-time work. The chapter describes a Learning Partnership that was developed to support learning through part-time work and it shows the type of learning achieved and represented by students in a pilot. The second case study focuses on the cultural environment and in Chapter 13 Novie Johan and Norman Jackson describe a Learning Partnership aimed at revealing the personal changes and development that occur when students make the difficult transition from living in one culture to another.

In *part four* (Chapter 14), Charlie Betts and Norman Jackson take a helicopter view of the UK higher education system to reveal what can only be described as an 'emergent movement' to embrace learning and personal development gained through co- and extra-curricular experiences. They offer a way in which institutions might compare, evaluate and quality assure their emergent practices through 'benchmarking' and offer an ecological perspective on an educational system that would promote, support and value lifewide learning,

This movement must be viewed in the context of a higher education system that has been in a state of flux and transformational change for over thirty years. In 2011 we are about to enter a new stage in this process as UK higher education becomes an essentially privately-funded affair. The consequences of such a profound change cannot be fully appreciated until it happens but one thing is certain, students and their parents are going to expect the maximum benefit from the significant financial investment that will be made.

One of the ways in which this might be achieved is by giving serious attention to the ideas outlined in this book and embracing the ideals and practices of a more complete lifewide education. Our hope is that the ideas in this book might usefully contribute to the enormous change and challenge that lies ahead. This is why we have chosen to frame our book with Eduard Lindeman's optimistic vision. This is also our vision for a more complete lifewide education.

'A fresh hope is astir. From many quarters comes the call to a new kind of education with its initial assumption affirming that *education is life* - not merely preparation for an unknown kind of future living......The whole of life is learning, therefore education can have no endings' (Lindman 1926:6).

Endnotes
1 My addition.
2 It should also be noted that The National Institute of Adult Continuing Education (NIACE) adopted the same constructs in 2007 when it launched a 'Lifelong, life-wide learning: Commission of Inquiry' into an adult learning strategy for economic success, social justice and fulfilment: www.niace.org.uk/lifelonglearninginquiry/default.htm. See also Schuller and Watson (2009).
3 At the time of writing the original YouTube clip posted three years ago (www.youtube.com/watch?v=ljbI-363A2Q) has had over five million hits and subsequent versions have had another five million hits.

Chapter 2

Lifewide education: a new and transformative concept for higher education

Ronald Barnett

Synopsis
This chapter introduces the idea of lifewide education and considers the challenge and opportunities it affords. In an age of liquid learning, many students are more in the world than they are in universities; and many of their extra-curricula experiences are yielding experiences of significant learning and value to their personal development. Facilitating such extra-curricula learning and personal development, recognising it by some form of accreditation and opening spaces for systematic reflection on such lifewide learning are the makings of a new pedagogical function for the university. Lifewide education thus offers the possibility of a transformative concept for higher education.

Introduction
If lifelong learning is learning that occupies different spaces through the lifespan – 'from cradle to grave' – lifewide learning is *learning in different spaces simultaneously*. Such an idea throws into high relief issues precisely of spaciousness – of authorship, power and boundedness; for characteristically pursued in different places under contrasting learning conditions, the various learning experiences will be seen to exhibit differences in authorship, power and boundedness, as well as in other ways. In turn, such a conception of lifewide learning suggests a concept of liquid learning, a multiplicity of forms of learning and thence of *being* experienced by the learner contemporaneously. This concept of lifewide learning poses in turn profound questions as to the learning responsibilities of universities: do they not have *some* responsibility towards the *totality* of the students' learning experiences? Does not the idea of lifewide *education* open here, as a transformative concept for higher education?

In sum, the idea of lifewide education promises – or threatens – to amount to a revolution in the way in which the relationship between universities, learners and learning is conceived.

If a liquid age has arrived, perhaps liquid learning has also arrived.[1] The tense is important – 'has' arrived; not 'is arriving' or 'will soon arrive'. The future is already here. There is an understandable tendency to cash out such a thought in terms of e-learning, especially the new generations of interactive learning, of 'virtual life' learning and multimedia learning, with the learner learning through various media simultaneously. Here is liquid learning in full measure, it may seem, with its pedagogical frames weakening, and manifold experiences running together beyond the boundaries of disciplines, conventional standards of communication and sure understandings.

Certainly, a narrative of liquid learning in terms of digital learning could be developed and such work is already implicitly in hand (for example, Luke, 2002; Bayne, 2008; Savin-Baden, 2008). Here, though, another narrative is proposed; a narrative of liquid learning in terms of multiple and simultaneous spaces. The two qualifiers are crucial: multiple *and* simultaneous. This form of liquid learning is the phenomenon of an individual inhabiting several learning spaces simultaneously and, in those spaces, experiencing not just contrasting learning experiences but even *contending* learning experiences. The phenomenon is not new: for one hundred and fifty years or more, individuals while at work might avail themselves of informal and formal learning experiences locally available (through, for instance, university extension programmes) and those extra-mural opportunities (outside the walls of the workplace) might even lead to revolutionary thoughts and activities. Today, in a liquid age, however, individuals inhabit simultaneously as part of their lives multiple learning spaces: work, non-work, family, leisure, social networks, occupational networks, social engagement and manifold channels of news, information and communication, not to mention physical and global mobility (actual and virtual), burst open the possibilities for learning.

In their medieval inception, right up to the middle of the twentieth century, universities saw themselves as total learning institutions. Their buildings – colleges – were turned inwards to quadrangles. They were locked at night. Entry was severely restricted. They offered learning spaces secluded from the world. This situation was not dissolved but accentuated with the formation of the disciplines. 'The ivory tower' was a powerful and not unfair image, in its depiction of research as a socially secluded activity. But the last half-century has witnessed fundamental changes to universities: now they are in the world and the world is in universities. There is mutual 'transgressivity' across their boundaries (cf Nowotny, Scott and Gibbons, 2001:21). Universities have become liquid institutions, a shift accentuated by the marketisation of higher education.

In these shifts, students are no longer entirely enfolded within universities but become customers engaging in market relationships with their universities. They have an independence from their institution: their market independence is mirrored by a new contractual relationship (they have legal rights which can and are increasingly enforced in the courts) and by a social and economic independence. Students have their own networks outside the university, virtual and physical. And they have an economic independence. Their very indebtedness aids this economic independence in a way. From being in debt (to banks, to the state, to the taxpayer, to private sector organisations and even to family members), they are now released from dependence on the university. In this regime, students become not just economic and social nomads but they also become *learning nomads*, increasingly inhabiting all kinds of social and economic situations that afford different kinds of learning. In this milieu opens the phenomenon of *lifewide learning*.

Lifewide learning and lifelong learning

Life*wide* learning, it is surely already apparent, is fundamentally different from life*long* learning. Life*long* learning is learning across time, and ideally, as the term implies, more or less throughout a lifetime. It reminds us that learning can go on almost 'from cradle-to-grave'. In this context, university education is simply an experience at a moment in time in an unfolding learning journey through life. It is possible that an individual may experience university education more than once in his lifetime; but then we simply see university education as a series of stages – and perhaps intermittent stages – in that lifelong learning journey. In essence, lifelong learning is a series of learning experiences in successive time zones of a life.

Lifewide learning, in contrast, is learning in different places simultaneously. It is literally learning across an individual's life at any moment in time (Jackson, Chapter 1). These places of learning may be profoundly different. These learning experiences will be marked by differences of power, ownership, visibility, sharedness, cost and recognition.[2] The idea of lifewide education, in other words, reminds us that learning occurs in – as we may term it – learning *spaces*.[3] In this context, university education may be itself seen as occurring in different learning spaces and may well have its place *alongside other learning spaces that the student inhabits* while taking his formal programme of studies. So, for 'lifelong education', we may read learning in different intervals of time; and for 'lifewide education', we may read learning in different space(s) during the same interval of time.

Certainly, an individual's learning journey through life can be seen as involving both lifelong learning *and* lifewide learning. His learning will be moving forward through his lifespan (lifelong learning) *and* will involve many learning spaces (lifewide learning); and often, at any one time, the individual will be experiencing several forms of learning all at once. So the *timeframes* of lifelong learning and the *spaces* of lifewide learning will characteristically intermingle.

Through time and across space, the relationships between lifelong learning and lifewide learning are even more complex. For the learning experiences that an individual undergoes simultaneously in lifewide learning will themselves be associated not only with different timeframes but with forms and spaces of learning that have different rhythms. Within a short period of time, as well as being committed to his course of study – itself a complex of learning experiences with different pacings – a student may participate in a university sports team and its events, a weekly church service, some sessions in paid employment and a two-month charitable commitment in a developing country. Each of these activities has its own rhythm; fast and slow time jostle in the student holding onto his learning spaces. In addition, from time to time these commitments may overlap or clash; and so the student has to 'manage his time' and determine priorities as the various responsibilities are heeded.

Oakeshott (1989:101) spoke of university life for the undergraduate as 'the gift of an interval'. It was time out, a *spacious* space into which the student stepped, outside of the mainstream of society's structures. Now, much of that idea is passé. Higher education represents not an interval between stages of the press of the responsibilities of youth, but is rather a set of learning and developmental spaces *in addition* to those of the wider world in which the student is immersed and continues to be immersed. Now, the student is a person in society – whose age may range characteristically from eighteen to fifty (and sometimes beyond that range, even among undergraduates) – and his university education offers a set of learning experiences alongside many others enjoyed by the student already or that may be taken up while the student is enrolled at the university. Accordingly, if it is still to do work for us, Oakeshott's idea of higher education as 'an interval' needs reinterpretation: in an age of lifewide learning, just what kind of interval might higher education offer?

Places for a student's lifewide learning

We may distinguish different forms of, and spaces for, a student's *lifewide* learning. While being a student, he may be involved in learning activities and learning processes (the examples offered are 'real examples', revealed in recent interviews at the University of Surrey):

- *within a course*, some of a more *cognitive* kind (writing an essay, tackling computational problems) and some of a more *operational* kind (in a laboratory, in the creative design studio)
- within a course, *off-campus* and assessed (in the clinical setting, conducting a mini-survey)
- within a course, off-campus but *not accredited* (a field trip, even sometimes the work experience component of a 'sandwich' course)
- *on campus*, and *unaccredited* and *not linked* to the student's course (writing for a student newspaper, working on a student e-journal, running a sports or social society, running a student bar, working in a student shop)
- *voluntary* and unaccredited *but linked* to the student's course (joining with a few other students and composing musical scores for each other's assessment, but outside the students' courses)
- *on campus*, *not linked* to the student's course and *accredited* by a university (taking a language course recognised in some way by the university and separately from the student's degree)
- not linked to the course, *off campus* and *accredited* by an agency *other than* the university (taking a St John's ambulance course, taking a language course offered by an agency in the private sector)
- not linked to the course, off campus and *unaccredited* (singing in a choir, starting up entrepreneurial activities and trying to make some money in the process, engaging in voluntary work, perhaps in a developing country).

This classification of a student's lifewide learning spaces and activities through which new learning and development occurs allows us to make five general points:
- The student's learning often takes place in *a number of sites.*
- The student's formal course of study may constitute a *minority* of the learning experiences undergone by a student while he is registered for that course of study. (In some courses in the humanities and social sciences, after all, 'contact time' may amount to less than ten hours per week.)

- Much of the learning that a student achieves while at university is currently *unaccredited*, and involves unaccredited learning that is both *within* the course of study and unaccredited learning that is *outside* the course of study (either on or off campus).
- Much of the student's learning is *personally stretching*, whether it is on or off campus, and whether it is part of a formal course of study or not; it may involve situations quite different from anything hitherto experienced (across social class, ethnicity, language, nation and other forms of social, cultural and economic differentiation).
- Much of the student's experience outside the course of study is highly demanding, and may involve high degrees of responsibility (perhaps for others) and accountability such that it leads to major forms of personal development on the part of the student.

Forms of lifewide learning

One might be tempted to try to categorise the forms of learning achieved by students – whether on their course or outside of it – in terms of skills and knowledge. A student who becomes a member of the university's horse-riding team will gain much *knowledge* about horses and will learn also the *skills* of horse-riding. One might want to stretch the notion of skills here to include, for example, 'team skills' or even – if captaincy of the team is involved – 'leadership skills'. And the interviewees used the term 'skills' in reflecting on their learning. But the language of knowledge and skills is insufficient to capture the complexity of the learning processes that many are undergoing. Here are the voices of some of my interviewees at the University of Surrey:

1. '[I was working] with UNICEF ... for a month, and I was volunteering and I was working with internally displaced people, people affected by war. [And I was] educating them about the journey (back to their home countries) and also what they're going to find when they go back, like what to expect in terms of how the water is, how the schools were, how the land ... if there were any mines, or any other diseases ...'
2. A recent graduate: '... it was quite an adjustment when I came out of an environment, first of all where I was given feedback and support all the time; where I had grades that I could measure myself against ... it was never a question of skills ...'
3. 'I think I've probably grown up a lot as a person ... I've had a lot more responsibility and I've tried to push myself into doing things that I wouldn't have done before I came. [For example], last year, I created a new society

for the university. That involved quite a lot of responsibility and taking control and I've never been in that, sort of, leadership position before.'
4. A captain of a university sports team: 'I used to be quite shy ... but coming here and having to work in groups of people. I like having something separate from ... my academic work. It definitely ... boosts my enthusiasm. Getting out there every week and doing something you enjoy.'
5. A student with several interests and activities, including a part-time job: 'You have to be different in different contexts because obviously it's not appropriate to be sort of completely yourself all the time. ... You have to sort of keep going ... amidst pressure. To me, it'd seem like you're sort of letting other people down ...'

'... when I'm at work, [that] sort of gives you confidence with mostly with working with others ...'
6. A student involved in several societies involving different ethnic and religious groups: 'so if you look at a person ... every star has a right to twinkle ...'

In these quotations, these interviewees are reflecting on themselves and their learning and their development in ways that are not easily caught by talk of knowledge or skills. 'Enthusiasm'; keeping going 'amidst pressure'; growing in 'confidence'; believing that every person in the world 'has a right to twinkle'; overcoming one's 'shyness'; growing up 'as a person'; empathising with others so as to be able to help them; becoming self-reliant; and bearing the pressure of personal responsibility: terms, ideas and dimensions such as these might be caught in part by talk of knowledge (coming to know, say, more about oneself) or skills (learning, say, the skills of self-management) but those domains – of knowledge and skills – are ultimately inadequate to capture the profound forms of human development that are taking place through the students' varied forms and places of learning. Indeed, one interviewee (2) is quite clear: 'it was never a question of skills'. What is in question here in all of these quotations, surely, is the way in which each student is becoming more fully human.

In comprehending students' lifewide learning, therefore, we need to supplement the domains of knowledge and skills with a sense of a student's *being* and, indeed, his continuing *becoming*. Here, a language of dispositions and qualities may be helpful. In the quotations above, for example, we can see the *dispositions* of:
- a willingness to learn about oneself (student 3)
- a preparedness to put oneself into new situations (1)
- a preparedness to be creative in interpersonal situations (1; 3; 5)
- a preparedness to move oneself on, into another place (2; 3; 4)

- a will to help others (1)
- a willingness to adjust one's approach and self-presentation, according to context (5)
- a will to keep going, even in arduous settings (5).

We also see the *qualities* of:
- enthusiasm (4)
- confidence (5)
- empathy (5; 6)
- care (for others) (1)
- energy (3)
- self-reliance (2; 3).

These two lists of dispositions and qualities are by no means exhaustive and could easily be developed further by drawing on the full extent of the interview data.

All of the students *were* developing their knowledge and their skill sets. For example, the students I interviewed were developing *skills* for managing the many demands on their lives, for juggling the complexities of their lives and in analysing situations to determine how best to be effective; and some of the interviewees were quite explicit about how they were developing such skills. They were also developing their *knowledge* in different ways (such as gaining knowledge of first aid, of commercial practices, of national and even international organisations). So the domains of skill and knowledge remain important in understanding the learning achievements of students in their lifewide learning.

However, in addition to developing their *knowledge* and their *skills*, all of my interviewees were developing their *dispositions* and *qualities* as well. And in developing their dispositions and qualities, they were developing as persons. In developing their *dispositions*, they were developing a greater preparedness to go on, to engage with life and to throw themselves into and engage with strange situations. In developing their *qualities*, they were developing their own personas, and a way of imparting their own stamp on the activities into which they threw themselves. The totality of the student's learning experiences, we can see, is altering their *being-in-the-world*. This being is not fixed but is now in a process of perpetually becoming as the students engage with a continuing interplay with their environment, moving this way and that, and so unfolding in often unpredictable ways.

This set of considerations implies, perhaps, in developing any kind of self-profiling among students – for example a 'Record of Achievement' or University Certificate alongside their course of studies – that students should be encouraged to reflect on how they have developed as *persons*. Whether the language of 'dispositions' and 'qualities' could be operationalised in any such initiatives on the part of the university would have to be subject to a kind of action research. Perhaps at least the idea of 'qualities' might be found to be helpful in students' self-monitoring processes (even if the idea of 'dispositions' turns out to be somewhat too abstract a notion for practical purposes).

Some intermediate questions
These reflections raise some challenging questions and reflections for any university.

1. *What is or should be special about the student's course of study, if anything?* One student interviewed was a member of a small group of students who met regularly and produced for each other's scrutiny artistic creations that were intimately linked to the purposes of their degree course but which were entirely independent of the course in that they were unprompted and were invisible to the tutors on the course. Students may be *more* active intellectually and imaginatively in the learning spaces outside their formal course of study. What, then, should be the aims of the student's course of study?
2. *What implications arise for the university, if any, from the students being in receipt of income from some of their learning activities?* Both on campus and off-campus, students are often in receipt of income. This income takes many forms: salaried (from an employer for regular work); wages for occasional work; self-earnt, from entrepreneurial activities. Might students feel *more* involved in and committed to such activities (generating immediate income) than to their university studies? They may also be accorded considerable degrees of dignity, autonomy and responsibility in some of their experiences outside their course.
3. *What is the value, if any, of a student's lifewide learning for their academic studies?* Is there a relationship here, or are their wider learning achievements held separate from their experiences on their academic programmes? (I return to this matter further on in the chapter.)
4. *To what degree should the university take an interest in the student's informal and extra-mural learning?* It may be that, for some students at least, its value lies precisely in its *not* being formalised and in the student retaining learning and developmental spaces that are their own, independent of the

university. For many students, however, some positive stance on the part of the university towards students' achievements, learning and development outside their course would be valued. (I return also to this matter.)

In short, taking all of these questions together, what is the learning value of a student's informal, non-accredited and extra-mural learning and what stance should the university take towards it?

The university and lifewide education

Both lifelong and lifewide learning put challenges in the way of university education but they are different challenges. If a student's university education is going to be succeeded, as it will be, by yet further forms of learning later in life, then that is one set of considerations. The university has then a responsibility to consider how it can help in enabling students to be effective learners through the rest of their lives. To that extent, a university would then be deliberately contributing to a student's *lifelong* education. The student's university experience would be designed to enable him to make further progress in his later learning experiences (both formal and informal).

However, if a student's university education is, *at the same time*, being accompanied by all manner of other learning and developmental experiences, then that is another set of considerations. Here, the university would recognise that the student is engaged in a process of life*wide* learning *during the period of his registration as a university student*. Then the question arises: what is to be the stance and approach of the university towards the student's wider learning experiences? Does the university ignore them or does it take them into account in some way? Does the university see its offerings as part of the student's lifewide learning? Does it thereby take on the role not merely of higher education, or even of lifelong education, but now of life*wide education*? That is to say, in some way, the university comes to understand that it has a responsibility of *contributing to the enhancement of the student's lifewide learning that he is experiencing while studying at the university*. In this way, the university may come to play a deliberate part in contributing not only to the student's intellectual and professional development but to the development of the student's *lifeworld*. As Pollard puts it: '... higher education courses have to become more meaningful in terms of students' lives-as-lived and in relation to development through the lifecourse' (Pollard, 2003:178).

There are a number of forms of possible university response in recognising students' lifewide learning and so developing the university's role in lifewide education (and they are *not* incompatible):
- encouraging and facilitating students in gaining worthwhile experiences beyond their programme of studies
- accrediting students' wider lifewide learning experiences
- offering opportunities for systematic reflection on those learning experiences such that the learning and personal value of those experiences are enhanced; here, the university would be attending to and enlivening the 'biographicity of [the student's] social experience' (Alheit and Dausien, 2002:17)
- shaping the university's own courses so that they offer the student the best chance of maximising the learning potential of their lifewide experiences (and, in so doing, bring about a greater positive relationship between the students' learning experiences both on and beyond their courses and enhancing the students' total lifeworld).

These forms of possible response on the part of the university are, in a sense, *levels* of response, for they denote increasing levels of engagement with the student's extra-curricula learning and development; and they are not mutually exclusive forms of possible response by the university.

The academic value of lifewide learning

Here, I want to pursue question 3 from the earlier section 'Some intermediate questions': *What is the value, if any, of a student's lifewide learning for their academic studies?* To what extent is there a relationship between the experiences and the personal development achieved by students in their lifewide learning and their academic studies? Here are some student voices on the matter:

Q: So, do you think that that side of your life is separate from your degree or does it help you, would you say?
A: I think it helped me in a way ... because when I'm there I'm relaxed. ... It's separate in a way and it's associated in a way because there you see people from class as well. They'll help you as well with your course.

Q: Do you think [that these different kinds of experience] help each other?
A: ... well, especially the society stuff definitely helped my degree – if for no other reason than just feeling more accessible to the lecturers and the tutors ... [in] being more confident in talking to them.

Q: You're being exposed to quite different kinds of setting. There are some links here, do you think?
A: I suppose that when I was at work I'd have to talk quite professionally to sort of senior people to me and then that would ... apply [to my interacting] with staff within the university.

In these quotations, and the earlier quotations, we see that students' learning and personal experiences are extending beyond their courses and:
- offered a space in which they can meet informally but in collaborative experiences and so develop more collaborative relationships *within* their courses
- helped them to gain more confidence in themselves that *carried over into the courses*, not least in their relationships with their tutors and lecturers
- developed a kind of generalised enthusiasm for learning which enhanced the degree to which they engaged with their formal programme of studies.

In other words, the idea – already suggested – is reinforced that, *in the university's own interests*, it makes sense for a university to acknowledge and to respond to, in some ways, their students' extra-curricula learning. Here, the idea is reinforced via the voice of the students themselves.

Towards a classification of learning spaces

If higher education is to respond to students' lifewide learning, then a classification of learning spaces becomes more than a theoretical exercise, it has potential educational value. Learning spaces may distinguished – it is already evident – by means of a number of dimensions:
- *Authorship*: What degree of ownership does the learner have in the activity in question? To what degree can the learner author his own activities? Where does the power lie in the framing of a learning space?
- *Accountability*: To whom is the learner accountable? What form does that accountability take?
- *Responsibility*: For what range of activities is the learner responsible? Is the learner responsible for other people?
- *Framing*: How bounded are the activities of the learning space? To what degree are they regulated by formal and tacit rules and conventions?
- *Sociability*: To what degree is the activity of the learning space personal and to what degree is it a matter of interaction and even possibly collaboration?
- *Visibility*: How public is the activity?
- *Complexity*: What is the level of the intellectual, emotional and practical demand? How complex is the activity?

- *Money:* How is the activity financed? What are its costs? Is there an income stream attached? Is the learner responsible for managing the income?

It follows that, in theory, a profile could be developed for any learning space: and each learning space could be interrogated as to how it stands in relation to each of these eight dimensions. Alongside such a profile, each profile could also be assessed as to the degree it helped to develop the kinds of dispositions and qualities identified earlier. The temptation might arise here to employ the term 'matrix' – that each learning space be analysed both against the dimensions of learning space and the dispositions and qualities that it might engender. Such a temptation should be resisted, for the idea of learning space now developing here is too messy and too inchoate to be caught adequately by such a regimented term as 'matrix'.

The straight and the smooth

In their book, *A Thousand Plateaus*, Deleuze and Guattari (2007) distinguish smooth and striated spaces. Striated spaces are characterised by walls, enclosures and roads between enclosures; smooth space is 'a field without conduits or channels' (ibid. 409); it is nomadic, 'marked only by "traits"'. 'Smooth, or nomadic, space lies between two striated spaces ...' Are these not helpful metaphors for us here? Lifewide learners, we may say, are precisely nomadic learners, comfortable in moving from one learning space to another, even if those learning spaces are themselves bounded and subject to laws and procedure. Lifewide learners inhabit both striated spaces (the spaces of their different learning experiences, each with its own rules of procedure, however informal) and smooth spaces, the spaces of transition from one space to another, the spaces in which they can take a view of their learning and gather it into themselves. It is smooth space that is crucial for it is in smooth space that the learner moves; is not held in a particular learning space but always has the potential to move to another learning space. 'Smooth space is a field without conduits or channels' (ibid. 409). In smooth space, the learner decides on his own map and makes up his own territories. Smooth space is iconoclastic.

Of course, there is no sharp break between such smooth and striated spaces (as Savin-Baden (2008) observes[4]). Striated spaces have their own space for movement, for the learner's spontaneity, daring and adventurousness. Smooth spaces are always in danger of being taken over and subjected to rules and procedures and become striated spaces.

Are there here student-types; those who love the freedom of smooth spaces, who will not be confined by any space, and those who prefer to reside in striated space, not necessarily content with the offerings of their course, but rather lacking the courage to voyage onto the slipperiness of smooth, unbounded space? On the one hand, the nomad who hangs onto open space, even at the risk of overload of experience and missing appointments; on the other hand, the hermit who clings to his course as the only source of learning nourishment. The nomad is always wandering in and across learning spaces; and always preparing for new learning voyages.

There is a problem here. Does not the formal recognition of lifewide learning experiences and even achievements on the part of the university represent the sequestration of smooth space by striated space? Deleuze and Guattari observed that: 'One of the fundamental tasks of the State is to striate the space over which it reigns, or to utilize smooth spaces as a means of communication in the service of striated space' (Deleuze and Guattari 2007:425). After all:

> Each time there is an operation against the State – insubordination, rioting, guerrilla warfare, or revolution as act – it can be said that ... a new nomadic potential has appeared, accompanied by the reconstitution of a smooth space or a manner of being in space as though it were smooth. .. It is in this sense that the response of the State against all that threatens to move beyond it is to striate space.
> (Deleuze and Guattari 2007:426)

Is the university not acting in the same way when it seeks to recognise lifewide learning? Is this not a process of corralling the unconfined into the confined? To bring it under control? Not necessarily. The educational value of the university's response to lifewide learning depends on the character of the learning space that the university opens up. As noted, there is no firm division between smooth and striated spaces. The challenge to universities, therefore, in responding to students' lifewide learning is to optimise smooth learning spaces. That is to say, to open spaces to the student that are both in themselves open and that encourage the students concerned to roam across their manifold learning spaces and so enhance the smooth properties of those learning spaces. The smooth and the striated both need each other. Here opens the need for and the value of systematic reflection.

A student observed that:

> ... I've sort of looked and sort of maybe reflected more on things that I have done that I wouldn't really [have considered] an experience until now. Sort of swimming and part-time work – I would just not really [have] related them at all until [I started on the SCEPTrE Learning through Experience Certificate].

Here, we glimpse the possibility that the benefits of students' lifewide learning can be *enhanced through structured reflection*. Enabling students to come into a space in which they can draw out of themselves the learning that lies within them as a sediment of their wider experiences, and of which they are unaware, itself is a valuable experience. The multiple learning spaces of lifewide learning become landing points from which other learning spaces can be viewed. This is not merely a process of reflecting on the student's lifeworld but is a process that helps to make sense of and so bring into focus the student's lifeworld. No wonder that so many interviewees say, when invited to reflect on the value of their manifold learning experiences, that they grew in confidence. How are we to comprehend this non-specific idea unless we bring in a sense of a person gaining a sense of themselves as a distinct human being engaging in a lifetime's work of continuous becoming, having multiple learning experiences and growing through those experiences?

This is not to say that all those learning experiences are seen in a positive light. To the contrary: some experiences, subjected to the gaze of critical self-evaluation, will be seen as unsatisfactory. But that is often ultimately a positive experience, for the student can then turn in another more satisfactory direction:

> I came to uni wanting to be a clinical psychologist ... but working ... with children with autism (and) by going to work at Broadmoor, it's kind of led me to realise that I don't want to be a clinical psychologist. ... At the moment, I'm thinking that I want to go into animal behaviour ... rehabilitating captive animals back into the wild and breeding and things like that. So quite a strong focus.

Experience, assimilation, reflection, accommodation: these are complex processes of personal transition and the universities can assist this process by opening spaces for systematic reflection.

Such a movement on the part of the university begins an inversion of the university's educational function, for here, the university would be orienting itself towards the student's lifeworld. To adapt another term from Deleuze and

Guattari, the university would here be helping students *perpetually* to be 'becoming-learners'.

Conclusions

For two hundred years, the university has built its educational mission around knowledges that it has sequestered unto itself. The student was held in the university. Gradually, the student has been released back into the world (with sandwich years, clinical experience and real-world projects, and acceptance that students will take employment during vacations and increasingly often work while learning). Now, in an age of liquid learning, students are as much as if not more in the world than they are in universities; and many of their extra-curricula experiences are yielding experiences of significant learning and personal development.

The university is, therefore, faced with the challenge of its stance in the face of such extra-curricula learning. Facilitating such extra-curricula learning, recognising it by some form of accreditation and opening spaces for systematic reflection on such lifewide learning are the makings of a new pedagogical function for the university. Now the university turns itself outwards and shifts its pedagogical purposes from a concern with the intellectual growth of the student to a concern with his lifewide development; his total lifeworld indeed. This is a university that frames a mission for itself in part around lifewide education. Here, there is a journey not only for the individual student but also for the university, the ultimate endpoint of which is a yet further transition in which the university begins to consider the implications of lifewide learning for the character of its own programmes of study and the student's pedagogical experience therein. This would be the ultimate revolution.

Endnotes
1 The idea of the 'liquid' is taken from Zygmunt Bauman. To my knowledge, Bauman has not actually employed the term 'liquid learning' but he has observed the implications for learning that arise from a 'liquid life' (Bauman, 2006:118–19, 123).
2 This chapter was originally written as a paper for a keynote presentation at the 'Enabling a More Complete Education Conference' held at the University of Surrey in April 2010.
3 There is the makings of a literature on the idea of 'lifewide learning', for example, Skolverket (2000), Pollard (2003), Slowey and Watson (2003), Alheit and Dausien (2003), Clark (2005) and Jarvis (2007). Two variants of 'lifewide learning' seem to be present: on the one hand, a sense that learning should connect with and is dependent upon a learner's wider life, and on the other hand, a sense that lifewide learning includes

the informal and experiential. The concept being suggested in this chapter – that of lifewide learning as *simultaneous* learning across *multiple* learning sites – overlaps *both* of those variants but is somewhat distinct from them.

4 The paper has been written alongside a reading of Maggi Savin-Baden's (2008) book, *Creating Opportunities for Knowledge Creation in Academic Life*. Although the conception of learning spaces there seems somewhat different from that adopted here (a sense of learning space as offering spaciousness as against, here, a view of learning space as a space in which learning may be spacious *or* congested), that book ranges across many of the issues raised in this paper – and many other issues besides – and offers a brilliant résumé of the matters it raises. It also adeptly draws on the categorisation of striated and smooth cultural spaces advanced by Deleuze and Guattari (to which this chapter also refers). The book should be seen, I believe, as essential reading on the matter of learning space and the responsibilities upon educational institutions raised by modern scholarship thereupon.

Chapter 3

A holistic model for learning and personal development

Colin Beard and Norman Jackson

Synopsis
Learning is a rich and complex phenomenon but higher education often tends to view and value learning as essentially cognitive. The value of a lifewide concept of higher education lies in its capacity to embrace and celebrate a richer and more holistic view of learning and personal development and in its ability to enable learners to see that their own development is accomplished through what they do in the many spaces and places that make up their lives. A lifewide concept of education values and recognises learners' attempts to develop and use all their senses and embraces all their physical, intellectual, spiritual and emotional experience. Lifewide education encourages learners to experience themselves as developers and users of knowledge in all its varied forms to become more aware of who they are and the person they want to become. In other words, it enables and empowers them 'to formulate a personal strategy to address the most important quest human beings face - the need for their lives to have enduring meaning'[1]. This chapter examines and commends a holistic model of learning and development to take advantage of the opportunities that lifewide education affords.

Learning and developing as a person
Learning, and the effects of learning on our personal development, is a complex phenomenon. It emerges through our physical, intellectual, emotional and spiritual engagement with experiences involving the human, natural and material worlds. As Kegan points out, learning is fundamentally a meaning-making process.

> The activity of being a person is the activity of meaning-making. There is no feeling, no experience, no thought, no perception, independent of a

meaning-making context in which it *becomes* a feeling, an experience, a thought, a perception, because we are the meaning-making context.
(Kegan 1982:11)

Rogers (1983) captures the essence of this meaning-making process very well.

> I want to talk...........about LEARNING – the insatiable curiosity that drives the adolescent boy to absorb everything he can see or hear or read about gasoline engines in order to improve the efficiency and speed of his 'cruiser'. I am talking about the student who says, 'I am discovering, drawing in from the outside, and making that which is drawn in a real part of me.' I am talking about any learning in which the experience of the learner progresses along this line: 'No, no, that's not what I want'; 'Wait! This is closer to what I am interested in, what I need'; 'Ah, here it is! Now I'm grasping and comprehending what I need and what I want to know!'
> (Rogers 1983:18–19)

Any comprehensive view of learning as a meaning-making process must involve consideration of all the things that influence the way we create meaning, namely the social (other people/society), psychological (inner psyche/self), emotional (feelings), sensorial/bodily (kinaesthetic/senses) and cognitive (thinking) dimensions of being.

Learning involves personal change – it involves acquiring new or modifying existing personal knowledge, behaviours, skills, values, beliefs, attitudes and qualities that are the inner and outer manifestations of who we are. While thinking and doing are important dimensions of learning, sense awareness and feeling awareness should also be considered to be fundamental to the development of the self, and our sense of who we are, our *being*. If the sensorial-bodily world is central to human communication and self-awareness, we might usefully ask difficult yet fundamental questions about the experience of learning:

- Where and when does the learning take place and what is the significance of the contextual environment?
- What kind of learning activities do learners engage with?
- In what form is the learning experience initially received and perceived in its immediate sensorial form?
- How are the emotional dimensions of learning experienced and what effect do they have?
- How are so-called intelligence and knowledge developed and applied?

- In what way does transformation and personal change occur, and how is it understood and applied?

Figure 3.1 Six dimensions of learning (Beard 2010:10)

Connecting the Inner and Outer Worlds of the Learner					
1 OUTER WORLD OF LEARNER		2 Sensory Interface	3 INNER WORLD OF LEARNER		
SIX PRACTICAL QUESTIONS					
1 Learning Environment	2 Learning Activity	3 Senses	4 Affect – Emotions	5 Reason – Mind	6 Learning and change
WHERE	WHAT	HOW	HEARTS?	MINDS?	CHANGE?
where ... with whom, and in what contextual circumstances, does learning take place?	what will the learners actually do?	how will learners receive this experience?	what is the nature of the emotional engagement?	what is the nature of the cognitive engagement?	how can learners be encouraged to change?
SIX DIMENSIONS OF LEARNING					
BELONGING	DOING	SENSING	FEELING	THINKING & KNIOWING	BEING & BECOMING
Potential to engage the less tangible – Formless	Focus on tangible things FORM				Potential to engage the less tangible . Formless

In Chapter 2 Barnett provides persuasive evidence, drawn from a small interview-based study, that students view their own development not just in terms of their academic experiences, but of their whole being and becoming in the world. It therefore makes sense to consider learning and development in the holistic way that being and becoming require. The holistic model for learning proposed by Beard (2010) and reproduced in Figure 3.1, provides a useful framework to help us understand how our whole being is involved in learning. In this representation of learning there are three components to a learner's world –

his inner world, his outer world and the sensory interface between these worlds. Learning is represented in six dimensions: sensing, belonging, doing, feeling, thinking and being/becoming, and each of these dimensions is now considered in turn.

Sensing
In order for learning to emerge through experience, it is said that 'the learner must be actively present and be self-aware of his or her interaction with the social and/or material environment' (Illeris 2002:157). What is it, then, to be present and self-aware? Gergen (1999) provides an example of his own early self-awareness, articulating the pleasure of his writing and learning.

> I grew up with fountain pens. As a child they were as 'natural' to me as my family. My father's pen seemed to produce an endless stream of mathematical scribbles that somehow transformed themselves into papers in journals. Meanwhile my mother's musings gave way to bursts of inspirational writing – short stories, travelogues, and the best letters a boy away from home could ever receive. The pen was destined to become my life. And so it did, as I slowly worked my way toward a professorship in psychology. I loved to ponder and to write; the sound of the pen on paper, the flowing of the ink, the mounting columns of 'my thoughts' – all produced a special thrill.
> (Gergen 1999:1)

The rich sensory awareness described by Gergen is part of a wider sensory intelligence (SI), and like other intelligences (Gardner, 1983; Goleman,1995, 2006) it can be developed through mindful effort and through engagement with diverse situations and experiences. Self-awareness requires a high state of self-knowledge of our internal state and our connectivity to the external world.

> All of our experiences of our life-world begin with bodily sensations which occur at the intersection of the person and the lifeworld. These sensations initially have no meaning for us as this is the beginning of the learning process. Experience begins with disjuncture (the gap between our biography and our perception of our experience) or a sense of not-knowing, but in the first instance experience is a matter of the body receiving sensations, e.g. sound, sight, smell and so on, which appear to have no meaning. Thereafter we transform these sensations into the language of our brains and minds and learn to make them meaningful to ourselves – this is the first stage in human learning.
> (Jarvis 2009:25)

Sensory awareness involves an integrative (re)connection of the perceptual–conceptual relationship. Sheets-Johnstone (2009) refers to the problem of languaging experience and learning. Language, she suggests, is clumsy and inadequate in describing, for example, affective states and bodily movement. Abram (1997) highlights how the sensorial world has been affected by speech and written text, both linear communication forms. He points to the lineage of the alphabet and shows how the direct sensorial connectedness to the outer world was initially through pictographic and rebus-like meanings within written form, still clearly present in Chinese writing. Abram argues that the human senses, intercepted by the written word, are no longer gripped and fascinated by the expressive shapes and sounds of particular places, and calls for a return to our senses in order to be more present and aware. Similarly, Lakoff and Johnson (1999) challenge the dominant Western views of philosophy, and argue that thought is mostly unconscious and that reason is not dispassionate, but emotionally engaged. Reason, they argue, is not purely literal, but largely metaphorical and imaginative. We use terms like 'higher' education, 'grasping' the subject, 'step-by-step' reasoning, and 'supporting' evidence: everyday speech contains a milieu of kinaesthetic-spatial metaphors that highlight a corporeal lineage. These writers further encourage an embracing of the whole of a learner's life, as a lifewide education optimises the opportunity for learners to engage in experiences that utilise all their senses and connect these to their meaning-making processes.

Belonging
The 'where' is the environment, place or space, the location, the social and more than human context providing the external stimuli and ambience for the learning experience to wholly or partly occur. In the lifewide learning paradigm these are the everyday spaces and places where we encounter or create situations and have our experiences. There are, of course, social, political, and cultural dynamics operating in these spaces. The 'where' of learning relates to the wider sense of being-in-the-world, and to our sense of 'belonging' and so we refer to this dimension as the 'belonging' dimension.

Belonging in the world has considerable theoretical complexity (Cannatella 2007) and it is increasingly recognised as a key element in student transition and transformation. Learning to belong is an experience that is common to all students as they begin their university or college career. Belonging forms the basis of much wider philosophical debate. Palmer and Owens (2009), for example, refer to 'not belonging' as a prevalent theme within accounts of higher education first-year student learning experiences at university. Their work suggests that the transition between one place (homeland) and another (university and beyond as studentland) can result in an 'in-between-ness' – a betwixt space. This phenomenon is particular pronounced when a student comes from another country to study in the UK and enters a culture that is very different to their own (see Chapter 13). Turning point experiences for students in the process of belonging have revealed a cast of people and evolving relationships, symbolic objects and contrasting motivations that both liberate and constrain the students' transition into university life. The significance of lifewide education is that learners' journeys of learning to belong can be recognised and validated. Such journeys happen over and over again during students' time at university. By honouring the different places and spaces that make up learners' lives we can help them recognise the important learning that emerges from the process of learning to belong. Chapter 6 gives further consideration to the where of learning through the examination of the life spaces/places that learners inhabit.

Doing
The 'what', in Beard's model, is concerned with what people are doing or going to do through which learning will or might occur. Learning involves an active dimension: expressing and receiving information (e.g. symbolic/language) that is used to represent and communicate our world by various means such as reading, writing, drawing, building, playing, performing, enquiring, solving, listening and talking. Learning by doing is a central tenet of experiential learning, as signified in the Western interpretation of the popular Confucian aphorism *I hear and I forget, I see and I remember, I do and I understand.* In the real world outside formal education, we often say that learning by doing is the best form of learning, because by this act we can witness directly whether someone is capable of doing and achieving something. In the higher education learning context of 'doing', teachers seek to actively involve students in purposeful learning activities that might involve lectures, seminars and real or simulated experiences within or outside the university, involving practical work or concept building. Learning might involve a wider mathematical challenge or the solving of a significant problem, yet all such activities will nevertheless be part of a wider and longer multidimensional journey of learning within an educational design called a course or programme. This dimension of learning and development is thus referred to as the 'doing' dimension, and in higher education it involves a pedagogy that facilitates individual examination of the sequence, shape and form of the learning experiences to embrace complex conceptual areas such as constructing and deconstructing something, solving

abstract or concrete problems or engaging in purposeful enquiry and developing knowledge that is relevant to the task.

The significance of lifewide education is that the entirety of a person's life spaces and places for learning contains far more potential for 'doing' than only the formal educational spaces they inhabit. And the sort of doing that students do in some of their life spaces outside formal education is highly relevant to becoming who they want to be – for example, a particular sort of professional practising in a particular field. The significance of lifewide education is that it can embrace all of a learner's spaces and places for doing things, and encourage her to be more aware of what she is doing and of what she is learning in the process. By embracing lifewide education the promise is that learners can be encouraged to be more mindful of the freedoms and opportunities available to develop themselves in ways that they believe will enable them to become who they want to become.

Feeling
The fourth dimension of learning concerns the emotions through which we perceive, interpret and emotionally respond to the stimuli from the external environment; we internalise the external learning experience. This is the 'feeling' dimension, concerning 'affect', a general term often used to include emotions, feelings and moods. The way we feel about an experience will have a strong impact on what we learn from it. Our feelings about a situation often emerge again as we recall the situation. Emotions are part of our social and cognitive self. They are pervasive, interwoven into facets of our inner and outer world. They are also linked to the roots of our identity. While emotional experiences and emotional intelligence underpin learning, many educators have only recently given more attention to emotional literacy, emotional intelligence and emotional competency (Goleman 1995; Mortiboys 2002). Our lives are always experienced as waves of differing emotions as the 'ups' and 'downs' of life. Different emotions, in size and frequency, create the essential rollercoaster form of the emotional self in student life (Beard et al. 2007). The role of positive emotions in learning seems to be a neglected area: we tend to focus on stress and fear and anxiety and deficit models of learning. Rarely is space provided to discuss and celebrate the pleasures associated with learning. While negative states can be destructive, they can also be positively harnessed. They can also be changed, and simply changing an emotional state from negative to positive can be the outcome of learning. Chapters 10 and 13 highlight the importance of this process in the context of students' immersive experiences.

Emotional blocks to learning can include fear and risk aversion, as well as the need for perfection and control. 'Reframing' emotions can alter the inner emotional scripts in our minds, helping us to access the positive potential in negative scenarios. Students who show anxiety before giving presentations can reframe their fear. Students who hold their hands up on white-knuckle rollercoaster rides do this to increase their feelings of fear: fear is fun! If a presentation in front of peers is seen as scary then it too can be reframed, in a similar vein. It can be seen as okay or even fun to 'feel the fear', the dry lips and shaky knees. Negative experiences have potential to be transformed, in the mind. Helping people to be conscious of their emotional experience can allow them to better manage and self-support their own learning. Helping learners to sense, surface and express both positive and negative feelings rather than deny or censor them requires skill and care. It enables the colour and richness of the feelings of learners to surface and be expressed and (re)considered. The significance of lifewide education is that because it embraces all of learners' life spaces, including those spaces where they have their white-knuckle rides, fall in and out of love and experience feelings of success and failure, it embraces the whole of their emotional experience as well. How they learn to cope with, manage and make the most of their emotional self can be acknowledged, recognised and valued.

Knowledge and knowing
The fifth dimension of the model focuses on the scope and form of cognition (mind) and forms of knowing and knowledge. The significance of lifewide education lies in its potential to embrace all of learners' life spaces: their spaces for thinking, knowing, developing and using different forms of knowledge.

> By talking of 'knowledge', rather than of 'knowledges' or 'knowings', we take, albeit implicitly, a stance on the basic metaphysical question, 'What is?'. By extension, our stance favours some epistemologies over others. The metaphysics are not trivial: if knowledge is plural, then intentions, curricula and pedagogies need to afford the development of knowledges; if we prefer to speak of 'knowings', we may be trying to suggest provisionality and situatedness, each of which implies rather different intentions, curricula and pedagogies than does 'knowledge'.
> (Knight 2006:1)

How learners understand what knowledge is and the way they develop the knowledge and knowings necessary for being in the world is of fundamental importance as we plan our strategies to enable them to prepare for their future.

Questions of learner epistemology – such as *what is knowledge? how is it acquired? what do we know? how do we come to know what we know? how do we use our knowledges and ways of knowing to develop more knowledge?* – are of higher order significance than questions about pedagogy (the method and practice of teaching and support for learning), which should follow. But all too often, higher education takes a narrow view of what thinking, knowledge and knowing are. Disciplinary education tends to value codified and theoretical knowledge and its utilisation by learners in abstract problem solving. This is not to say that handling complex information in this way is not useful – far from it: it is an essential process for enabling learners to develop the cognitive maturity required to function effectively in a modern world. Cognitive maturity (Baxter Magolda 2004a:6-10) is characterised by the ability to reason and think critically and creatively, analyse situations and consider the range of perspectives necessary to make good decisions on how to act, and metacognitive and reflective capacity to create deeper meanings and enduring understandings. Cognitive maturity requires knowledge to be viewed as contextual recognising that multiple perspectives exist.

> Contextual knowers construct knowledge claims internally, critically analysing external perspectives rather than adopting them uncritically. Increasing maturity in knowledge construction yields an internal belief system that guides thinking and behaviour yet is open to re-construction given relevant evidence. Cognitive outcomes such as intellectual power, reflective judgement, mature decision making and problem solving depend on these epistemological capacities.
> (Baxter Magolda 2004a:9)

By adopting a lifewide concept of higher education learners can engage with the rich complexity and messiness of the knowledges and knowings that they encounter in their everyday 'doings'. In other words in all the contexts that form their lives. They do this anyway and the central educational proposition of this book is that by encouraging and supporting them in this enterprise they will gain more benefit from and recognition for their own learning and development.

Boisot (1998) provides a useful conceptual aid for viewing these different sorts of knowledge (Figure 3.2). Using the two-by-two matrix of codified/abstract and uncodified/concrete knowledges he shows schematically the relationship between the knowledge that is embodied in everyday thinking and practices – our personalised working knowledge that we use to deal with situations – and more abstract/symbolic and codified knowledge such as that which we find in books, reports and working papers.

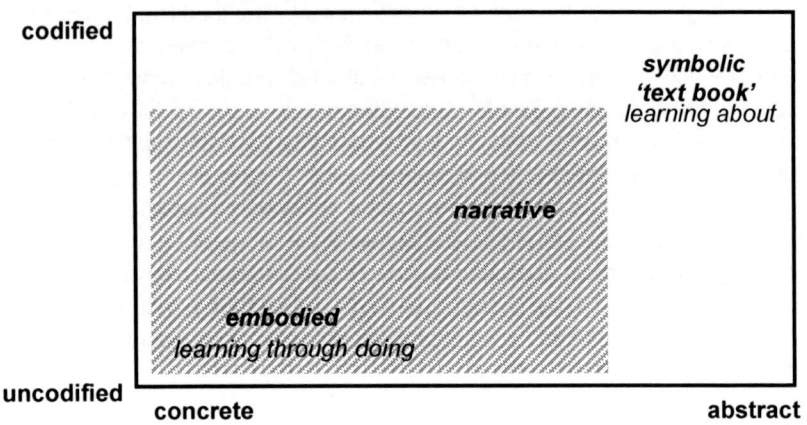

Figure 3.2 Conceptual framework for viewing knowledge. Adapted from Boisot (1998)

codified

symbolic
'text book'
learning about

narrative

embodied
learning through doing

uncodified

concrete   abstract

Our personal embodied knowledge mainly populates the shaded area. It has been created or co-created with others through our participation in the things we do and the extraction of meaning through our reflections on the situations we have encountered. It includes knowledge that we have gained from codified sources and from every other source (including what we have sensed and felt). Thomas and Seeley Brown (2009 2011) help us understand the nature of this embodiment.

> *Homo Faber* no longer divorces knowledge from knowing, or explicit from tacit understanding. Instead, *Homo Faber* invites us to think about the ways in which the two are inherently connected and supplemental to one another. Through creating we come to understand and comprehend the world, not merely as a set of objects, artefacts, or creations, but as coherent entities which we come to dwell in and which we make sense of the "jointness" and interconnection of the parts that constitute the whole, both at the explicit level of the object itself and at the tacit level in terms of its social context and relations. It is this level of tacit knowledge, that which is known, embodied and most importantly *felt* that begins to constitute a basis for a new understanding of learning.
>
> (Thomas and Seeley Brown 2009:8)

Narrative or storytelling provides a communication medium, often rich in metaphor, that links these two domains the embodied and codified knowledge domains. Bauman (1986) argues that oral narrative is constitutive of social life itself.

> When one looks at the social practices by which social life is accomplished one finds – with surprising frequency – people telling stories to each other, as a means of giving cognitive and emotional coherence to experience; constructing and negotiating social identity; investing the experiential landscape with moral significance in a way that can be brought to bear on human behaviour; generating, interpreting and transforming the work experience; and a host of other reasons. Narrative here is not merely the reflection of human culture, or the external charter of social institutions, or the cognitive arena for sorting out the logic of cultural codes, but is constitutive of social life in the act of story telling.
> (Bauman 1986:113–14)

It is to be expected that a lifewide concept of education will be rich in individuals' embodied knowledge and that the way such embodiments will be communicated is through the stories they tell about their experiences and the illustrations they give of their embodied practices. Michael Eraut has developed a rich conception of personal knowledge based on his observations of the knowledge people develop and use in work situations (2009, 2010a, 2011 and Chapter 12). This type of representation is also relevant for lifewide education.

> I argue that personal knowledge incorporates all of the following:
> - *Codified knowledge* in the form(s) in which the person uses it
> - *Know-how* in the form of *skills and practices*
> - Personal *understandings of people and situations*
> - Accumulated *memories of cases* and *episodic events* (Eraut 2000, 2004)
> - Other aspects of personal *expertise, practical wisdom* and *tacit knowledge*
> - *Self-knowledge, attitudes, values* and *emotions*.
>
> The evidence of personal knowledge comes mainly from observations of performance, and this implies a *holistic* rather than *fragmented* approach; because, unless one stops to deliberate, the knowledge one uses is already available in an *integrated form* and ready for action.
> (Eraut 2010:2)

For lifewide education to have any meaning our educational practices must:
- value and respect these forms of knowledge and embodied knowing
- enable learners to represent their embodied learning and to communicate it through the telling of stories about their experiences and embodied practices
- and be able to recognise and value such learning within these experiences and embodied practices.

Thomas and Seeley Brown (2009) argue that the traditional model of learning in formal education, which is focused on codified knowledge has been grounded in the concept of *thinking and learning about* i.e. knowledge is something to be studied and accumulated. But the real world outside formal education is more concerned with *learning through doing* and putting the things we learn into action, often within the context of an epistemic community. They describe (Thomas and Seeley Brown 2011) the emergence of a *new culture of learning* and summarise the development and use of knowledge thus:

> *Homo Sapiens:* '(hu)man as knower' is a fundamental statement about what it means to be human. It is also an ontological statement about learning. There are three senses in which learning happens in relation to change. The most basic sense is 'learning about' which corresponds to contexts in which information is stable. We learn about things which are stable and consistent and not likely to change over time. The second sense is 'learning to be,' which requires engagement with an epistemic community and provides a sense of enculturation in practices which allow one to participate and learn how to learn and even shape practices within that community. The third sense, which emerges out of a context of rapid and continual change, is a sense of *becoming*. This sense of learning is itself always in a state of flux, characterised by a sense of acting, participating, and knowing. This sense of knowing requires us to be reflectively aware and reflexively responsive to our learning and to the continuing changes we need to make in order to adapt.
>
> (Thomas and Seeley Brown 2009:5)

> *Homo Faber :* '(hu)man as maker)' no longer divorces knowledge from knowing, or explicit from tacit understanding. Instead, *Homo Faber* invites us to think about the ways in which the two are inherently connected and supplemental to one another. Through creating we come to understand and comprehend the world, not merely as a set of objects, artefacts, or creations, but as coherent entities which we come to dwell in.

[This] is more than simply making; it is making within a social context that values participation. It is akin to what Polanyi (1967, 1974) has described as "indwelling," the process by which we begin to comprehend and understand something by connecting to it and, literally, living and dwelling in it. In that way, making also taps into the richness of becoming......In fact, we may go so far as to say, there can be no sense of becoming, particularly as it relates to learning, without the dimension of....indwelling.

(Thomas and Seeley Brown 2009:7-8)

These are not just abstract ideas; they are the reality of learning, being and becoming in the real world outside formal education. Although people may not be able to articulate their understandings in these ways, they will come to realise these things in their own way, through their own experiences. It is, however, a moral responsibility of any education system that purports to help people prepare themselves for a lifetime of learning to help them develop and appreciate these perspectives in ways that make sense to themselves. The value of a lifewide concept of learning is in the opportunity it provides to encourage learners to see and experience knowledge and knowing in all its forms and to appreciate and value themselves as the developers and integrators of their own knowledge. Because it can embrace the social dimensions of a learner's life, it can also enable learners to appreciate their role in the co-creation and validation of knowledge in the different parts of their lives. And because it embraces a rich conception of knowledge and learning, a lifewide conception of education can support the learning partnerships that enable these forms of learning and complex achievement to be validated.

Being and becoming

The sixth dimension of Beard's holistic integrated model of learning concerns the 'being-becoming' dimension. Here we are dealing with the underlying psychoanalytic theories of identity which attempt to explore the inner self, and the influences that affect our ability and willingness to be and become a different person. Carl Rogers, drawing on his professional experience as a psychotherapist, has much to say about what it means to become a person: meanings that he believes can be applied to the process of becoming beyond the therapeutic context (Rogers, 1961:123).

> the goal the individual most wishes to achieve, the end which he knowingly and unknowingly pursues, is to become himself.

> When a person comes to me, troubled by his unique combination of difficulties, I have found it most worthwhile to try to create a relationship with him in which he is safe and free. It is my purpose to understand the way he feels in his own inner world, to accept him as he is, to create an atmosphere of freedom in which he can move in his thinking and feeling and being, in any direction he desires. It is my experience that he uses it to become more and more himself....
>
> (Rogers, 1961:108-109)

According to Rogers the process of becoming involves the following processes:
- examining the various aspects of his own experience to recognise and face up to the deep contradictions he often discovers (ibid:109)
- the experiencing of feelings - the discovery of unknown elements of self (ibid 111)
- the discovery of self- in experience - to find the patterns, the underlying order, which exists in the ever changing flow of experience (ibid 114)

What Rogers' analysis of becoming reveals is the need to understand our inner self but it is easy to neglect or disown our inner self because it is hard to experience or describe. Gardner (1993), whose work challenged the old monolithic notion of a single intelligence quota (IQ), commented that the 'sense of self' placed most strain on his multiple intelligence theory: the self goes beyond intelligence. Cell (1984:9) remarked that: 'In learning to live with less self-awareness, we also diminish those distinctively human possibilities for freedom, creativity, caring, and ethical insight which are based on that awareness'. Cell devoted a whole chapter to 'Learning and the struggle to be'. He noted (ibid. 9) that: 'Our sense of worth becomes less and less tied to having approval from others and more and more grounded in knowing ourselves to be the creators of meaning and value.' The experience of learning should ideally intensify our sense of freedom and liberate our creative potential in order that we might usefully make a contribution to society.

According to Rogers (1961) what emerges from this process is a different person, one who is:
- more open to his experience - the individual is more openly aware of his own feelings and attitudes and more aware of reality as it exists outside of himself (ibid 115)
- more trusting of himself (ibid 118)

- more confident in his own choices, decisions and evaluative judgements - less and less does he look to others for approval or disapproval; for standards to live by; for decisions and choices (ibid 119)
- more content to be a process (for ongoing self-discovery) rather than a finished product

> It means that a person is a fluid process, not a fixed and static entity; a flowing river of change, not a block of solid material; a continually changing constellation of potentialities, not a fixed quantity of traits.
> (Rogers 1961:122).

Here then is the essence of becoming: an essence that is echoed over and over again in the narratives of students engaged in their lifewide learning experiences.

Holistic model of personal action

Beard's (2010) holistic model of learning helps us appreciate the dimensions of learning but they can only be realised through an individual's decisions and actions. It therefore makes sense to connect this holistic model of learning to a holistic model for personal decision making and action. The essence of this process is described by Stephen Covey.

> Between stimulus and response there is a space. In the space lies our freedom and power to choose our response. In those choices lie our growth and our happiness.
> (Covey 2004: 4)

This process of creating and dealing with situations is fundamentally a process of self-regulation as described by Schunk and Zimmerman (1998) and Zimmerman (2000). Self-regulation can be represented as a continuous process involving forethought (planning and decision making), action/performance and self-reflection on action/performance (Figure 3.3). Concepts of self-regulation developed through empirical studies of students engaged in learning can be directly related to the processes through which professionals develop knowledge and learn through work (see Chapter 12). The dispositions and capability for self-regulation are integral to the concept of being an effective learner and to the concept of lifewide learning and education. In the UK Personal Development Planning (PDP) has been introduced to encourage the systematic development of practice (QAA 2000). The dimensions of PDP can be related to the construct of self-regulation (Jackson, 2010a).

Figure 3.3 Capability modelled as a process of self-regulation. Based on Zimmerman (2000:26)

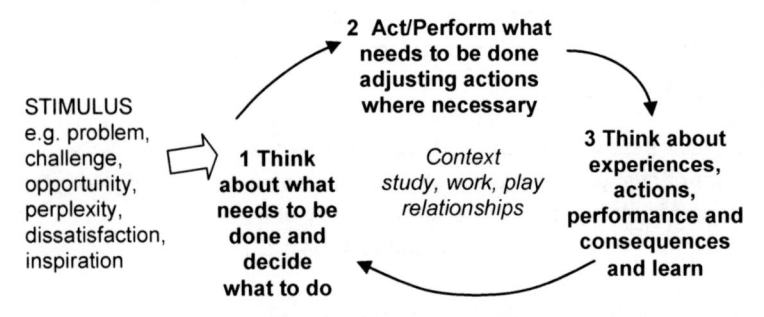

```
                            2  Act/Perform what
                               needs to be done
                               adjusting actions
   STIMULUS                    where necessary
   e.g. problem,
   challenge,                                          3 Think about
   opportunity,       1 Think         Context          experiences,
   perplexity,        about what    study, work, play  actions,
   dissatisfaction,   needs to be    relationships     performance and
   inspiration        done and                         consequences
                      decide                           and learn
                      what to do
```

The model of self-regulated learning provides a scientific explanation of the processes that underlie the actions through which learning and personal development occur. The integrated model of self-regulation (Figure 3.3) has three components.

Forethought
People don't engage in tasks or set goals and plan and work strategically if they are not motivated by strong personal agency. In particular, self-efficacy (personal beliefs about having the means to learn or perform effectively) and outcome expectations (personal beliefs that the outcomes will be worthwhile) are key features of personal agency.

This is where decisions are made to engage with a situation. Where they are assessed, ideas are born and decisions are made about how to approach and work with a particular situation. Ideas on how to tackle a situation may be born from rational or intuitive thought processes. The more analytical/rational brain analyses tasks, sets goals and develops strategies. The intuitive brain may provide an idea or insight to a way of thinking about a problem. What is planned is influenced by contexts, self-efficacy, expectation of immediate and longer-term outcomes, levels of intrinsic interest and goal orientation (e.g. learning for assessment or mastery of a process or skill). For example, for some people the opportunity to be creative is a major stimulus and source of energy and motivation to thinking and subsequent actions. The way they will experience the situation and the potential for learning in the situation will be strongly influenced by this orientation to thinking and doing.

It is important to have knowledge that is relevant to the job in hand. In a new situation we often lack the knowledge we need to solve a problem or meet a challenge so knowing how to acquire knowledge or seek help are important aspects of dealing with a situation. The ability and motivation to be curious, to problematise and to imagine/find and explore perceived problems through questioning are important features of creative thinking at this stage. Asking the right questions and not being afraid to ask questions is essential. So is 'seeing' the potential of situations to provide many possible right answers. The ability to generate ideas (generative thinking) and to critically evaluate ideas to distinguish those that are most useful and motivating is important. This way of thinking draws on memory of past experience and also imagination stimulated by things outside of our own experiences. It is a creative as well as an analytical process.

Action and performance
In the process of acting on our thinking we are integrating our knowledge and applying it within a situation and creating our knowing: knowing that is relevant to the particular situation, and also more generally which might we utilise in future situations. This knowing relates to the holistic model of learning proposed by Beard (2010) and described earlier in this chapter. The doing (acting and performing) part of the self-regulation model distinguishes many sub-processes e.g. notions of self-instruction, help-seeking and using the environment to create resources for learning. These are all crucial to dealing with situations. 'Doing' is the process of engaging with emergent problems in real time, the structuring of the environment to create resources for learning, the adaptation and transfer of ideas to new contexts, the use of a repertoire of communication and inter- and intra-personal skills to achieve a goal, the juggling and prioritising of numerous tasks and the nurturing of relationships are all manifestations of the integrated actions we employ. These things all rely on self-efficacy and personal motivation to sustain them. We must also be aware of the consequences of our actions and adjust them if necessary.

Reflection and meaning making
The third element of the self-regulation model relates to the thinking we do after an event, after we have performed. This process allows us to stand back, to see the bigger picture and make more sense of what happened than when we were implementing our actions. Comparing our own performance and attributing causal significance to results requires evaluation against criteria, standards or previous performance - what is good/poor performance attributed to?

Value of the self-regulatory model of being and becoming
The self-regulatory model provides a comprehensive explanation for our being in the world. By integrating prospective and retrospective thinking processes with our actions and experiences it engages with our becoming. The strength of the model is in its ability to integrate our critical (analytical) and creative (imaginative and intuitive) cognitive process, our emotional, sensorial and physical worlds. Emotions like *anger* (resentment, annoyance, hostility and even outrage), *sadness* (dejection/depression, flatness, energyless, loneliness), *fear* (anxiety, misgiving, apprehension) and *enjoyment* (contentment, satisfaction, pride and even pleasure) are all part and parcel of our engagement in the situations that make up our lives. How we feel about or sense something has a major effect on whether we want to pursue something or abandon it. The interplay of emotions, beliefs, actions and contexts is complex and unpredictable but we need to be conscious of them as they will impact on our decision making processes. The roots of self-efficacy, our senses of personal and professional satisfaction with what we have done and our willingness to adapt and become a different person, lie in these attitudes of mind. The model of self-regulation acknowledges all of these things and helps us see how we engage in situations and learn from and through our experiences of 'doing'.

Self-regulation in an unpredictable changing world
We might usefully add one further dimension to this explanation of how a person is actively engaged in learning and developing themselves through their self-determined life experiences. The model of the autodidactic (self-instructed) learner (Tremblay, 2000) incorporates the self-regulating model of learning but sets it in a context of emergence (Figure 3.4).

An autodidactic process is heuristic, iterative and contextual. Situations may be orchestrated but they might equally be conditions of coincidence. An individual's learning project does not develop in a linear way and the actions necessary for the realisation of a task are not presented in a sequential and predictable manner. Knowledge and knowing emerge through action. The process is a continuous experiment in which action and reflection share the same space. Theory (self-theory) develops from action and the knowing that emerges through action. This is an appropriate conception of the way that people approach learning as a sustained experiment in which action and reflection on action and the shaping of future actions share the same space. Autodidactic learners are dependent on the resources for learning that are available in their immediate environment and learning projects are shaped through taking this into account. Autodidactic learners often do not plan to use particular resources but see and exploit opportunities as they arise; they seize every opportunity that chance offers them to learn.

Figure 3.4 The autodidactic model of learning (Tremblay 2000)

- The process develops without prior condition
- Knowledge emerges through action and the individual is open to recognising and exploiting its value
- The individual works with the process heuristically

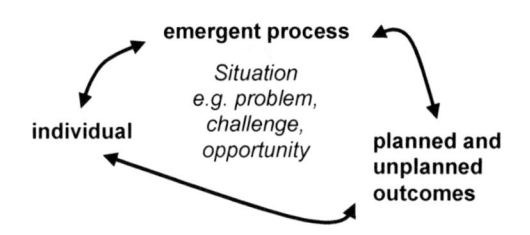

```
                    emergent process
                      Situation
                    e.g. problem,
       individual    challenge,
                     opportunity      planned and
                                      unplanned
                                      outcomes
```

- The individual creates her own rules and vocabulary for learning
- The individual is strongly self-regulating

- The individual and the environment are reciprocal determinants
- The individual gains knowledge through a complex, diversified and expanding web of resources

It might be argued that the ultimate objective of lifewide education is to support learners as they develop and implement the dispositions, qualities and capabilities that enable them to be self-regulating/ autodidactic learners. This conception of people engaging in learning is quite different from conceptions of learners and learning held by most HE teachers yet, if they pause to reflect, it is the world that they themselves inhabit and the concept of behaviour and learning that most closely approximates their own professional life.

Value of a lifewide education

Who we are and who we become is the result of our being (of being and becoming ourselves) in all the spaces and places we choose to inhabit or are chosen for us engaging with all the dimensions of learning that are considered in Beard's holistic model of learning (Figure 3.1). The value of a lifewide concept of education is in its capacity to embrace and celebrate this richer and more holistic view of learning and personal development than has traditionally been the case in higher education. By embracing the holistic model for a self-regulating/autodidactic learner (Figures 3.3 and 3.4) we can appreciate the complexity of our thinking and actions when we engage with situations and see how the holistic model of learning advocated in this chapter is a necessary part of this complexity.

By helping learners to become more aware of their being in the world, we have the potential for them to gain deeper understandings of how the parts of their lives connect and how the development they gain from these different experiences is integrated to enable them to become who they want to become. This second year student shows us that she has learnt this valuable lesson while she was studying for her law degree and holding down a fulltime job! Implicit in what she is saying is that by drawing from her lifewide experiences of learning and development she is becoming the person (the barrister) that she would like to be.

> When I first started, I saw the separate sections of my life – my study, my work, my social life and my personal life – when in fact they are not separate. They are an integrated and connected whole. By taking elements of each of these areas, I can get somewhere near that formula that is going to get me a great pupillage and a tenancy.

Becoming different by being willing and able to adapt and change, is a necessity in a world that is full of both evolutionary and radical, often disruptive, change. There are particular points in our lives where this process dominates our being. These points are the transition points where we move from situations and environments with which are familiar into territories that are unfamiliar for example, leaving school and home and going to university or college, and starting a job. These life-changing experiences engage us physically, intellectually and emotionally and they require us to learn and develop in a holistic way. They are particularly important as people make the transition from youth to adulthood.

> there is so much to be learned..... academically, emotionally, socially, societally and most of all in terms of identity
> (Illeris 2009:404).

The significance of a lifewide concept of education is that we can utilise the educational value in becoming a different person embedded in the life-changing event that involves leaving home, going to university or college and learning to live more independently. Chapter 10 reveals that immersive experiences that students consider to be transformative, occur throughout and across their life course. The promise of a lifewide education is that transformative experiences that shape our lives provide a source of deep personal meaning making.

The work of Carl Rogers (1961) reveals the detail in the significant process of becoming a different person. A lifewide concept of education enables people to examine the various aspects of their own experience to recognise and appreciate the opportunities they have to learn and develop, resolve contradictions, experience feelings, discover unknown elements of themselves and create more meaningful lives.

Closely, allied to the above is the fact that an individual's lifewide experiences require them to learn holistically and integratively as they grapple with the opportunities, uncertainties and risks that emerge through the things they do everyday of their life. This set of conditions provides an ideal and natural context for the development of cognitive maturity - the ability to think with sufficient complexity to deal with complex indeterminate situations - and what Baxter Magolda (2004a&b, 2009) calls becoming authors of our lives. Baxter Magolda (1999, 2001, 2004, 2009) demonstrates the importance of developing students' conceptions of knowledge, and their understanding of their own and others' role in its co-creation and utilisation and how such conceptions shape an individual's identity and sense of being in the world.

> Despite diversity across contexts, environments that promoted self-authorship consistently operated on three key assumptions ... Learners were exposed to epistemological, intrapersonal and interpersonal complexity via three assumptions. First, these environments conveyed *knowledge as complex and socially constructed* ... [this way of thinking] gave rise to the second assumption – that *self is central to knowledge construction.* Encouragement to define themselves and bring this to their way of learning, work and relationships emphasised the intrapersonal growth, the internal sense of self, needed for self-authorship. The third assumption evident in these environments was that *authority and expertise were shared in the mutual construction of knowledge among peers* ... These three assumptions were closely linked in environments that promote self-authorship.
> (Baxter Magolda 2004:41–2)

Adopting a lifewide concept of education enables us to take advantage of the full range of opportunities that students have for developing epistemological, intrapersonal and interpersonal complexity, a theme which Marcia Baxter Magolda addresses in Chapter 5.

Endnotes
1 Willimon and Naylor (1995)

Chapter 4

Developing capability through lifewide education

Norman Jackson

Synopsis
Capability is the power or ability to do something or to perform a certain role. It is an important concept in education and human development. Our capability represents 'the *real opportunity* that we have to accomplish what we value' (Sen 1992). Students value their own development as it improves their chances for a fulfilled and productive life. We talk a lot about student-centred learning that encourages independence, self-motivation and self-management, but if we respected learners as the designers and architects of their own life experiences, which includes by choice a higher education, we would have more chance of realising this goal. This Chapter considers capability from a number of perspectives and argues that a more complete education values, supports and recognises students' efforts to develop their own capability through the freedom and opportunities they have across all the spaces and places in their lives.

Why is capability so important?
Chapter 1 drew attention to a key building block in the lifewide learning idea; namely, that our lives are composed of multiple streams of situations that require us to evaluate options and make decisions about what to do or what not to do. Chapter 3 developed a holistic model for the patterns of thinking and actions that enable us to deal with or create situations - based on the idea of self-regulation (Zimmerman, 2000). Attention was drawn to Stephen Covey's explanation of what happens in the decision making space where we make choices.

> Between stimulus and response there is a space. In the space lies our freedom and power to choose our response. In those choices lie our growth and our happiness.
>
> (Covey 2004:4).

In this space where we have the freedom (or restricted freedom) to choose what to do, we make decisions that are based on what we and others value, what we know and don't know, what we believe is right or wrong, what we think we can or can't do and how we feel about the different options available to us. But in order to turn our thoughts and feelings into effective action we need both the will and capability to act. This chapter focuses on the idea of developing capability through a lifewide concept of education.

Capability is the power or ability to do something or to perform a certain role. It is an important concept in education and human development; it refers to (Sen 1992:40) 'the various combinations of functionings (beings and doings) that [a] person can achieve'. It also reflects a 'person's freedom to lead one type of life or another ... to choose from possible livings' (ibid. 40). Our capability represents 'the *real opportunity* that we have to accomplish what we value' (ibid. 31). Sen draws attention to the inter-relationship between the *functionings and beings* that enable people to accomplish something and the *opportunity* they have (available to them) for utilising these functionings to achieve something that they and/or others value. The difference between a capability and functioning is the same as an opportunity to achieve something and the actual fulfilment of that thing. The notion of capability is 'essentially one of freedom – the range of options a person has in deciding what kind of life to lead' (Dreze and Sen 1995:11). These authors emphasise the importance of choosing a life one has reason to value, where choices have been determined through considered thought and reflected upon.

Walker (2006), inspired by Sen's seminal work, presented a strong case for a capability approach in order to encourage fresh thinking and reflect ethically upon the purposes and values of higher education in relation to student development, agency and learning, public values and democratic life, and the pedagogies that support these things. Walker develops a coherent, value-based philosophy that is consistent with lifewide education, which provides a context within which learners can choose to reveal, in a thoughtful, reflective and appreciative way, the kind of life they choose to lead or would like to lead. The approach to lifewide education we are advocating aims to provide learners with a supportive, empowering and enabling framework to draw deeper meanings and fulfilment from their lives, gaining recognition for capabilities they develop and demonstrate through participation in the experiences they create for themselves.

Lifewide education also holds the possibility of engaging individuals more systematically and more deeply with the way in which they secure and sustain a good quality of life for themselves (Alkire 2008) and for others, and for maintaining a sense of personal well-being in a world of continuous, rapid and sometimes disruptive change[1]. Allied to this it affords opportunities for a strength-based approach, rather than the more usual deficit oriented approach, to capability development. Linley (2008:29) defines a strength as 'a pre-existing capacity for a particular way of behaving, thinking, or feeling that is authentic and energising to the user, and enables optimal functioning, development and performance'. O'Connell summarises the key features of a strength-based approach thus.

> A strength-based approach is a positive psychology perspective that emphasises the capabilities and strengths of the individual. It starts with and accentuates the positive. Strengths-based approaches are developmental and process-oriented. They identify and reveal internal strengths and resources (resiliencies) that exist within an individual, family, or group as they occur in specific problems and contexts (Egeland *et al.*:1993)...The strength-based approach 'honour[s] the innate wisdom of the human spirit, the inherent capacity for transformation of even the most humbled and abuse' (Saleeby 1997). The basic premise of this approach is 'that people possess inherent strengths or assets that hold the key to their ability to cope with stress and trauma. Instead of diagnosing deficits and prescribing treatment to address them, strength-based therapists help clients identify and build on their capacities' (Barton 2005). Every individual, group, family, and community has strengths. To detect them, the social work practitioner must be genuinely interested in and respectful of their client's stories, narratives, and accounts, as well as the interpretive angles they take on their own experiences (Saleeby 1997).
> (O'Connell 2006:2)

O'Connell was writing in the context of social work practice but a strength-based approach can be used in any relational developmental situation (like coaching, mentoring, careers guidance and the learning partnerships advocated in Chapters 11-13). Evidence that a strength-based approach has positive effects on dispositions and beliefs that relate to capability is provided by Govindji and Linley (2007). A study of 214 university students showed that people who used their strengths more reported higher levels of subjective well-being (i.e., happiness) and psychological well-being (i.e., fulfilment). They also found that people who used their strengths more reported higher levels of self-esteem and self-efficacy, which is a scientific conception of confidence – the belief that they were capable of achieving the things they wanted to achieve. Lifewide education recognises that while acknowledging and acting on weaknesses, it is valuable to personal development, the strength-based approach encourages people to discover what they are good at and invest time and energy in developing their talents through the experiences that they believe will nurture these talents. Maret Staron explores the strength-based idea further in Chapter 8.

Perspectives on capability

The concern for capability advocated in this book is not new. In 1979, the Royal Society of Arts published an 'Education for Capability Manifesto'. The campaign it supported ultimately led to a capability approach to higher education being advocated in the 1990s as part of a Government-funded Enterprise in Higher Education programme (EHE). The 'capability movement' was motivated by the desire to better equip learners for the challenges they would face in a modern world. The same values and motivation that underlie our advocacy for lifewide education. Participants in this movement believed that by developing students' capability they would have more functionings, opportunities and freedoms to choose how to lead a productive and fulfilled life and this would ultimately benefit society and the economy.

Stephenson, one of the leaders of the UK capability movement, described capability as:

> an integration of knowledge, skills, personal qualities and understanding used appropriately and effectively – not just in familiar and highly focused specialist contexts but in response to new and changing circumstances. Capability can be observed when we see people with justified confidence in their ability to:
> - Take effective and appropriate action
> - Explain what they are about
> - Live and work effectively with others
> - Continue to learn from their experiences as individuals and in association with others, in a diverse and changing society
>
> (Stephenson 1998:2)

He also emphasised the integrated and action-oriented nature of capability, its relationship to confidence and knowledge, skills, and values, and the making and execution of judgements about what is right and wrong.

> Each of these four 'abilities' is an integration of many component skills and qualities, and each ability relates to the others. For instance, people's ability to take appropriate action is related to specialist expertise which in turn is enhanced by learning derived from experiences of earlier actions. Explaining what one is about involves much more than the possession of superficial oral and written communication skills; it requires self-awareness and confidence in one's specialist knowledge and skills and how they relate to the circumstances in hand. The emphasis on 'confidence' draws attention to the distinction between the possession and the use of skills and qualities. To be 'justified', such confidence needs to be based on real experience of their successful use............capability is not just about skills and knowledge. Taking effective and appropriate action within unfamiliar and changing circumstances involves ethics, judgements, the self-confidence to take risks and a commitment to learn from the experience.
> (Stephenson 1998:3)

More recently, Cairns and Stephenson (2009:16) argue that capability is a holistic concept which encompasses both current competence and future development through the application of potential, bringing their concept of capability closer to Sen's (1992) integrated notion of functionings and opportunity. In their opinion the concept of capability is applicable across individuals and organisations and it includes:

- the capacity to operate in both familiar and unfamiliar situations
- the utilisation of creativity/innovation
- being mindful about change and open to opportunities/uncertainties
- being confident about one's abilities
- being able to engage with social values relevant to actions
- engaging with learning as a self-directed process
- operating to formulate and solve problems.

Cairns and Stephenson (2009:17) identify three elements to capability:

- *ability* – to carry out observable behaviours to a level of acceptable performance and potential skills and attributes that can be realised with effort and opportunity

- *self*-efficacy – defined as the confidence of the individual, acts as a motivational force and with success a confidence builder supporting further risk taking, persistence and capable behaviour
- *values* – the way individuals' actions are guided by a personal set of values and their ability to articulate any values issues associated with that action.

According to Cairns and Stephenson (2009:18) capable implementation of actions requires:
- *Mindfulness – awareness and openness to change.* Mindful people are conscious of their thinking and working out of solutions and progress
- *Self-management.* All learners need to be self-managing and responsible for their own learning and development.
- *Effective problem formulation and problem solving.*

The educational philosophy that underpins this book builds on these understandings. They are the things that enable us to act within the self-regulatory model proposed in Chapter 3. Here I would like to emphasise four aspects of capability. The first is *imagination*. Capable people are able to comprehend a situation, to think with sufficient complexity to deal with it and to imagine what might be. How we nurture rather than stifle imagination, as well as critical thinking, is an important question for higher education and the lifewide education concept provides an opportunity for nurturing and celebrating the imaginations of our students (Chapters 9-13 provide abundant evidence of this).

The second characteristic of capable people is that they have the *will* to succeed. Without the will to try, even if you don't succeed, nothing is possible. You have to be willing to involve yourself in a situation in order to influence it. Belief in ourselves and our own capacity and ability to effect a change or make a difference is an integral part of our willingness to try. How we nurture will in an educational world that forever seeks compliance with the will of teachers is another difficult challenge for higher education and lifewide education offers more scope for students to make use of and demonstrate their wilfulness in a variety of contexts and situations.

Knowing that you are able to do something in order to deal with a situation also feeds into our preparedness to try. The third dimension of capability is *ability*. We have to develop practical skill and knowledge of how and when to use the skill in an appropriate manner to turn ideas into effective action: action that will one way or another have an impact. Skill is not a checklist of things we can do but an *integrated set of functionings* that are adjusted in response to the ongoing monitoring or 'sensing' of our effects as the results of our actions emerge. Here we return to the conundrum of what knowledge and skills do we choose to help students' develop for a rapidly changing world? Perhaps the overarching capability is the ability to develop and utilise new knowledge and skill when it is needed and to combine and adapt existing knowledge and skills in order to improvise in new and unfamiliar situations.

The fourth component of capability is *self-awareness* the ability to recognise and evaluate the effects we are having and adjust what we are doing if necessary. Our ability to sense and observe situations and make sense of what is happening feeds into our self-regulatory action-oriented mechanism to help us refine our actions and intentions. Our preparedness and ability to reflect on a situation enables us to learn from our experience so that we can have more immediate effect and more impact in the future. Reflection is the key sense and meaning making process in our life and it ultimately feeds into what we value and our sense of satisfaction and fulfilment. The challenge for higher education is to develop this habit in ways that are meaningful and relevant to students' lives and lifewide education provides a rich context that is full of opportunity, achievement, uncertainty, mistakes and failures that are so necessary to stimulate this metacognitive process.

The successful application of capability in different situations produces effects or impacts and awareness of these nourishes our *confidence* and sustains our willingness to try to achieve things that we or others value. But in order to turn ideas and feelings into action we need *opportunity* – we have to be provided with opportunity and we have to recognise and make good use of it when we see it, or be able to create our own opportunities. So linked to opportunity is *freedom* – without the freedom to choose and the freedom to create opportunities, our ability to achieve will be limited by the decisions of others. If we have the freedom (autonomy) what is possible is only limited by our imagination, willingness and capability.

Contexts for developing and utilising capability

Stephenson (1998:4) made the distinction between dependent and independent capability, using the idea that the situations we encounter may be categorised according to whether they are within a familiar or unfamiliar context and whether the problem (challenge or opportunity) is familiar or unfamiliar (Figure 4.1).

Much of our life is spent in familiar situations where we don't have to pay much attention to what we are doing and we can reproduce the response and routine practices that we have done many times before (position W, Figure 4.1). Stephenson considered this space to be one in which we practised dependent capability and he related this to traditional teaching approaches adopted in higher education.

Figure 4.1 Relationship between capability, context and the nature of problems, challenges and opportunities (adapted from Stephenson 1998:5). Letters refer to scenarios described below[1]

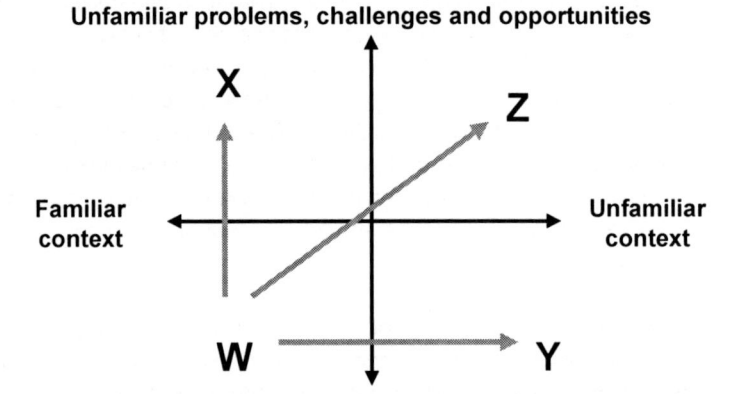

Unfamiliar problems, challenges and opportunities

X   Z

Familiar context   **Unfamiliar context**

W   Y

Familiar problems, challenges and opportunities

Position W can apply to the work-place, the home, community activities or artistic pursuits. Good performance in position W may require technical skills and knowledge of the highest order, or at the simplest level. We give students information about the context; the more complex the context, the more information we give them. We give them information about the kinds of problems they will meet, and details of the solutions which have been found to be effective. We might even give them practice in the implementation of the solutions and evaluation of their effectiveness. We seek to develop student capability in position W by passing on other people's experience, knowledge and solutions ... the resultant capability is essentially a dependent capability.

(Stephenson, 1998:4)

In any aspect of our life we can suddenly be confronted with a problem, challenge or opportunity that we have not encountered before in a context with which we are familiar (position X, Figure 4.1), or we may find ourselves in a new context dealing with problems that we have encountered before (position Y, Figure 4.1). Such situations require us to develop new contextual understandings and invent and try out new practices and ways of behaving. We have to have the will, capability and confidence to learn and adapt to the new situations. Stephenson viewed performance in these environments as involving a degree of independent capability.

Life also has a habit of putting us in situations, or we put ourselves into situations, in which both the contexts and challenges are unfamiliar (position Z, Figure 4.1). In such situations the resources and support we depend on in more familiar settings may not be available to us and we have to rely on our own resources and create new sources of support. We have to develop new contextual understanding and create, adapt and implement ideas, formulate and invent solutions and develop new practices rather than replicate things that we have done before. Stephenson viewed performance in this environment as an expression of independent capability.

> In position Z, we have less familiarity with the context and we have not previously experienced the problems with which we are faced. The slavish application of solutions perfected for familiar problems may have disastrous effects in position Z. To a large extent we are on our own, either individually or collectively [and] we have to take much more responsibility for our own learning. By definition, we must inform ourselves about the unfamiliar context and not simply remind ourselves of what we were taught or trained to do. By definition, we must formulate the problems we have to deal with, not remind ourselves of problems previously learned. We must devise solutions and ways of applying them without the certainty of knowing the outcome, as a way of learning more about both the context and the problem. ... We need confidence in ourselves, and in our judgements, if we are to take actions in uncertainty and to see initial failure as a basis of learning how to do better. When taking action in position Z, intuition, judgement and courage become important; there is no certainty of consequences based on previous experience.
>
> (Stephenson 1998:5)

This conceptual framework provided by Stephenson (ibid.) provides a useful tool for thinking about the situations in which we involve ourselves on our lifelong - lifewide journey. The added value that lifewide education brings to this way of thinking is that at any point in time we may be involved in one, several or all of the environments portrayed in Figure 4.1 in our different life spaces. It must also be apparent that lifewide education provides learners with the opportunity to learn through venturing into spaces and places where both the contexts and the challenges are unfamiliar (position Z in Figure 4.3) and this is crucial to the development of capability that learners need to become the authors of their own lives (Baxter Magolda 2004a) a theme that is developed in Chapter 5.

We can use this framework to encourage students to think about the sorts of situations they are using to develop themselves and invite them to reflect on whether they are restricting themselves to contexts and challenges that are familiar and comfortable, or whether they are involving themselves in unfamiliar problems and contexts that will require them to develop resourcefulness and new forms of independent capability. Chapters 10 and 13 discuss the latter types of situation in more detail.

The challenge of complexity

The human condition is to try to understand situations in order to make good decisions about how to act (or not to act). Some situations are easy to comprehend: they are familiar and we have dealt with them or something like them before and we are confident that we know what to do. Others are more difficult to understand and some are impossible to understand until we have engaged in them. The Cynefin framework (Figure 4.2) developed by Snowden (Snowden 2000; Snowden and Boone 2007) and described by Callaghan (2009) helps us appreciate the nature and level of complexity in different types of situation. The framework was originally developed to aid understanding of situations and how to deal with them in organisations, but the concept can also be used to evaluate personal situations. There are four domains within the framework.

In the *simple* domain things have a simple cause and effect – you do X and you are very likely to get Y. The environment is familiar and understood. You will probably have had many similar experiences that can be directly related to the situation. You know that 'what you do' is likely to have a particular result. And if you do the same thing in a similar situation the same result will happen. At the other extreme is the *chaotic* domain where there is no perceivable relationship between cause and effect. If this situation happens in your life, you feel totally out of control and overwhelmed. In these situations your natural response is to act, sense what happens and then act again until you get yourself into a more understandable and comfortable situation. Between these two extremes there are two other types of situation.

Figure 4.2 The Cynefin tool[3] to facilitate thinking about situations of differing complexity (Snowden 2000, Callaghan 2009)

COMPLEX	COMPLICATED
Cause and effect only make sense in retrospect. Situations are not predictable and are unlikely to be repeatable but principles learnt can be used again.	Cause and effect may be widely separated but with effort a relationship can be made. Situation is analysable and knowable.
CHAOTIC	SIMPLE
No cause and effect relationships. Situation is not perceivable.	Cause leads to a predictable effect. Relationships are repeatable. Situation is known

Complicated situations are not single events but involve a stream of interconnected situations (many of which may be simple) linked to achieving a goal (like solving a difficult problem or bringing about a significant innovation or corporate performance). They can be difficult to understand: there are cause-and-effect relationships but you have to put some effort into working out the relationships by gathering information about the situation and analysing it to see the patterns and look for possible explanations of what is happening. Engaging in these sorts of challenges is the way you become more expert in achieving difficult things and a lot of professional work is like this.

Complex situations are the most difficult to understand. They are not single events but involve multiple streams of variably connected situations linked to achieving a significant change in the pattern of beliefs and behaviours (culture) in a society or organisation. In such situations the cause-and-effect relationships are so intertwined that things only make sense in hindsight and sometimes well after the events have taken place. In the complex space, it's all about the inter-connectivity of people and their evolving behaviours and patterns of participation that are being encouraged or nurtured through the actions of key agents. The results of action will be unique to the particular situation and cannot be directly repeated. In these situations relationships are not straightforward and things are unpredictable in detail. People involved may not know the cause of the change that they have been involved in or ascribe the source of change to something that is quite removed from the trigger for change. The sort of factors being dealt with in the complex space are things like culture, trust and leadership, and the way you make progress in understanding what is happening is to sense the patterns of change and respond accordingly.

In developing capability for dealing effectively with situations we are developing the ability to comprehend and appraise situations, and perform appropriately and effectively in situations of different levels of complexity. We do this intuitively throughout our lives because that is what life is about. Formal education can equip us with knowledge, understanding and ways of thinking that can assist us in particular contexts but it is limited in so far as it cannot offer us the experiences of actually dealing with situations as they arise in the world outside the classroom. That is why programmes that integrate learning in work and institutional environments have so much more potential to develop capability for dealing with situations where knowledge and capability are grown and applied in situations that are not controlled. A lifewide concept of education simply extends this opportunity into other aspects of students' lives.

Capability and self-regulation

Chapter 3 argued that lifewide education needs to be underpinned by a holistic model of learning embedded in the self-regulating[4] practices of individuals. This framework for observing, sensing and evaluating situations, making decisions and plans for action, implementing action and adjusting actions in response to feedback and then reflecting on actions and their effects, defines the fundamental set of capabilities we need to accomplish anything of significance. This process of self-regulation is remarkably similar to what Eraut (2009:6) defines as the basic epistemology of practice in professional work situations, namely:

- *Assessing situations* (sometimes briefly, sometimes involving a long process of *investigation and enquiry*) and continuing to monitor the situation

- *Deciding what, if any, action to take*, both immediately and over a longer period (either on one's own or as a leader or member of a team); [In complex situations this stage also includes *Designing (planning) the action*]
- *Pursuing an agreed course of action*, performing professional actions – evaluating the effects of actions and the environment and adapting as and when necessary
- *Metacognitive monitoring of oneself*, people needing attention and the general progress of the case, problem, project or situation; and sometimes also learning through reflection on the experience.

The capability to do something is defined and judged in terms of the appropriateness of what is being done, how well it is being done and the effects of what has been done. Eraut focused on the capability exhibited by professionals in fulfilling their work role. He defined capability in terms of 'what individual persons bring to situations that enables them to think, interact and perform' (Eraut 1997; 1998), and 'everything that a person (or group or organisation) can think or do' (Eraut 2009:6). In his research into how professionals learn through work, he identified over 50 aspects of professional activity which he called learning trajectories. At any point in time professionals are either developing or regressing within a particular trajectory depending on the experiences they are gaining through their work which enabled them to develop and use their capability. This highlights the important fact that the capability to do anything is a dynamic phenomenon that grows and wanes according to the opportunities available for practice and further development. The added value of a lifewide education is that there are more opportunities for the development and application of capability across all of a students' life spaces than there are within an academic programme.

The final perspective on capability offered in the chapter comes from the work of Richard Greene (2004[4]) who describes '32 capabilities of highly effective people in any field' and distils these down to eight general capabilities.

> Highly effective people have eight general capabilities. The first four such capabilities are ways of using liberty they make for constructing, establishing, and founding enduring changes in lives and the world. They have ways, when encountering difference and otherness, of keeping what is new, difficult, and unknown or challenging from being absorbed and assimilated to their existing models and preferences. They have ways of preserving the otherness of what they encounter.

Second, they have ways of unearthing the most buried, subtle, intimate, and vital forces and things inside themselves and examining them for possible use or improvement. Third, they have ways of bringing order to their own selves and to the selves of those in groups around them. Fourth, they have ways of turning insights, ideas, experiences, and the like into impacts on society, actual changes in how things are arranged and done. The second four general effectiveness capabilities are ways of protecting novelty from erosion by large, traditional, already established powers of the world. Fifth, they have ways of doing things with style and verve rather than doing them perfunctorily. Sixth, they have ways of upping the performance of all dimensions of their selves, work, and lives, not just some or a few. Seventh, they have ways of influencing people, in many channels, modes, and means. Eighth, and last, they have ways of operating with new commonsenses, they borrow or invent, that make their automatic reactions up-to-date and future-looking.

(Greene 2004:5)

Greene's detailed research-based account of the capabilities of high-performing people who are effective in their field, provides a comprehensive, explicit and inspiring vision for human development. But this research focuses on exceptional people, the high achievers in their field, and it might be argued that the capability constructs developed for exceptional people cannot be applied to individuals with more modest achievements. However, Greene's powerful way of framing capability – *'they have ways'* – points to the repertoire of strategies, skills, ways of thinking and behaving that people possess in order to achieve the things that they value in life. I believe that similar capabilities to those described by Greene can be recognised in the lives of some of the students who have been involved in piloting the Lifewide Learning Award (for example the student narrative in Chapter 1).

Our goal is draw attention to the possibility that a lifewide concept of education offers more potential for enabling people to develop, use and demonstrate the sorts of complex capability Greene portrays than more traditional forms of curriculum. It offers the possibility of being able to recognise the emergence of such complex capabilities through the ways and means in which students choose to live their lives.

The will to be capable

Our will and values determine the choices we make about the sort of person we want to be and the sort of life we want to lead. 'Will is the most important concept in education. Without the will nothing is possible' (Barnett 2005: 15). We cannot achieve anything of significance. We cannot strive to be creative or make decisions about a situation we find ourselves in, we cannot act in ways that are ethical and appropriate to the situation and we cannot learn how to deal with the situation without the will to do so. Ultimately, it is our will to develop capability in and for a particular set of situations that determines what we can and can't do.

Greene's (2004) analysis and synthesis of the capabilities of highly effective people reveals the complex nature of what capable people are able to do. They do these things not just because they are able to but because they want to, inspired by the value and meaning that they derive from what they are doing and from the feedback they receive from the results of their efforts.

A fundamental question for higher education curriculum designers is *what forms of experience nurture the spirit and self-belief that will enable learners to become who they want to become and enable them to develop the capability that will enable them to cope and keep on coping with the considerable challenges they will experience in their future personal and professional lives?* The central proposition of this book is that a lifewide concept of education offers more opportunity for achieving this worthwhile goal than an academic, discipline-based programme alone.

Endnotes
1 For example, the global recession of 2010–11.
2 Stephenson's original diagram only described two fields which he labelled X and Y. These have been relabelled W and Z on ,y diagram so that two other fields can be described
3 visit http://en.wikipedia.org/wiki/Cynefin. Shawn Callaghan provides an excellent introduction by in the form of a YouTube podcast.
4 In the UK, the terms 'self-management' or 'managing self' are often used to denote the executive capability required to think about, plan, organise and execute actions strategically. Self-regulation is a well-researched phenomenon that engages more fundamentally with the learner's psychological processes underlying intentional actions and behaviours.

Chapter 5

Authoring your life: a lifewide learning perspective

Marcia B. Baxter Magolda

Synopsis
Navigating the complexities of twenty-first-century life requires self-authorship, or the development of an internal voice to guide one's beliefs, identity and relationships. Competing demands of adulthood introduce the limitations of uncritically following external authority and help adults realise that although they cannot control reality, they can choose how to respond to it. Establishing their internal criteria for what to believe, how to identify themselves and how to relate to others yields an internal voice to co-ordinate external influence. Developing self-authorship is an arduous task and is more likely when higher education contexts are intentionally designed to assist learners in transitioning from external to internal definition. The three-dimensional nature of self-authorship and the notion that this personal growth is a necessary component of complex and holistic learning, supports the central thesis of this book which advocates a lifewide concept of higher education. Learning partnerships in which educators respect learners' voices, discourage simplistic solutions to complex problems, encourage learners to develop their own personal authority and engage in mutual learning, support learners in self-authoring their lives. Examples of learning partnerships in multiple contexts illustrate how educators can intentionally capitalise on learners' experiences to reinforce learners taking responsibility for their own lifewide and lifelong journeys for learning.

Introduction
Regardless of where you live in this world, young adults are faced with the challenging task of managing uncertainty, complexity and constant evolution in twenty-first-century society. Thus higher education's role in preparing them for success in adult life extends beyond information acquisition to transformational learning (Kegan 1994; Mezirow 1990). Jack Mezirow describes transformational learning as '... the process by which we transform our taken-for-granted frames

of reference (meaning perspectives, habits of mind, mind-sets) to make them more inclusive, discriminating, open, emotionally capable of change, and reflective so that they may generate beliefs and opinions that will prove more true or justified to guide action' (Mezirow 2000:7–8).

Transformational learning involves what Kegan (1994) calls the growth of the mind, or the remaking of one's meaning making about knowledge, identity and social relations. Kegan's conception of the mind incorporates conceptions of self and relationships. The evolution of meaning making in three dimensions – epistemological, intrapersonal and interpersonal – undergirds the ability to manage and be comfortable with uncertainty, complexity and change. The concept of lifewideness advanced in this book resonates with this holistic view of human development and the transformational learning it supports. It is also consistent with calls for educational reform that focus on both intellectual and personal maturity.

Professional associations in the US have long focused on holistic student development, advocating a vision of education that includes intellectual, physical, social, emotional and spiritual dimensions (American Council on Education 1949). Historically, US higher education included a student affairs component, or a co-curriculum, that addressed most of these dimensions while the intellectual dimension was the purview of teachers through the academic curriculum. However, collective research on the college experience (e.g. Kuh *et al.* 1990; Kuh *et al.* 2005; Pascarella and Terenzini 2005) confirms that learning cannot be parsed in this way because it occurs in multiple dimensions in both these arenas. This research resonates with Barnett's concept of learning in multiple spaces (Chapter 2, this volume).

Contemporary reports from US educational reform associations call for blending learning in the curriculum and co-curriculum based on the understanding that all dimensions are essential for learning. For example, *Learning Reconsidered: a Campus-wide Focus on the Student Experience* (Keeling 2004:5) advocates learning as 'a complex, holistic, multi-centric activity that occurs throughout and across the college experience'. This report outlines student outcomes that encompass cognitive complexity, interpersonal and intrapersonal competence, and civic engagement. Similarly, *Putting the World into World-class Education* (DfES 2004) lists becoming informed, active, responsible global citizens as the first of eight key concepts. Effective citizenship and learning extend beyond skill acquisition to achieving complexity on the three dimensions of development (Baxter Magolda 2004c; King and Baxter Magolda 2011). Epistemological maturity is required to analyse and judge the validity of multiple perspectives to make wise decisions. Personal maturity is necessary to enable acting autonomously yet collaboratively and acting with integrity. Relational maturity is required for effective collaboration that integrates multiple perspectives in an uncertain and complex world. Kegan (1994) portrayed these three dimensions of development as integrated throughout the lifespan and defined self-authorship as the point at which adults take internal responsibility for their belief systems, their identity and the nature of their social relations. Much of the student development research in the US suggests that college students need more opportunities and support to develop the capacities that would enable them to meet these demands (e.g. Baxter Magolda 2001, Baxter Magolda *et al.* in press; Kegan 1994; Torres 2010; Pizzolato 2004). Longitudinal research with US college students also indicates that movement towards self-authorship is central to young adults' abilities to succeed in complex work, educational and personal environments (Abes and Jones 2004; Baxter Magolda 2009; Torres 2010). In this chapter, I describe the concept of self-authorship, how it develops, learning partnerships to promote its development and linkages between self-authorship and lifewide education.

Self-authorship

The concept of self-authorship emerged from the constructive-developmental research tradition based in the work of Jean Piaget, William Perry and Robert Kegan. Constructivism refers to humans' tendency to construct meaning by interpreting their experiences. Developmentalism suggests that these constructions evolve over time through periods of stability and transition to become more complex. Piaget (1950) described increasingly complex ways of making meaning on the part of children. Perry (1970) extended this notion in his research with college students to outline what he called a scheme of intellectual development. Perry's scheme, while focused on intellectual development, did include the dimension of self, as did the work of Belenky *et al.* (1986) on womens' ways of knowing. Kegan (1982) made explicit the intersection of the epistemological, intrapersonal and interpersonal dimensions. In doing so, he described a series of meaning-making structures that evolved from relying on external others for meaning making to taking responsibility for one's own meaning making. He labelled one of the latter ways of making meaning in that journey 'self-authorship'. My twenty-five-year longitudinal study (Baxter Magolda 1992, 2001, 2009) of one group of US college students expands the possibilities of this journey and describes a similar trajectory from external definition to internal definition. Hamer and van Rossum's (2010) twenty-five-year research programme in Dutch universities paints a similar portrait, as do contemporary

US studies on various student groups (e.g. Abes and Jones 2004; Pizzolato 2003; Torres and Hernandez 2007).

One way to portray this evolution is through the metaphor of rules and exceptions. We typically have 'rules' we use to make sense of our experiences. These rules come from prior experiences, including information from authorities, and assumptions we make resulting from these experiences. When we encounter an experience that does not fit with our rule, we typically view it as an exception. This allows us to maintain our original rule. However, when too many exceptions have occurred, we revise our rule so that it more effectively captures our experiences. Piaget called this process equilibration, suggesting that humans want to be in balance and reconstruct their meaning making to account for dissonance. This process refers to the basic structure behind our meaning making, or *how* we make meaning, rather than to the content of what we think.

The significance of our lifewide experiences is that the more diverse our experiences are the more we are likely to encounter situations that do not conform to the rules we have formed. A good example is participating in travel where we are exposed to a culture very different from our own. Although this might be a transient experience it is likely to expose us to new ways of making meaning that are very different to what we are used to and, consequently, our own ways of thinking may be challenged. Similarly, daily interactions with others in our own community whose race, ethnicity, religious faith, social class or sexual orientation differs from ours provides exposure to multiple perspectives that potentially challenge our meaning making.

One portrait of self-authorship
I began a longitudinal study of *young adult* learning and development in 1986 involving one hundred and one college students at a US university. I interviewed them annually throughout their college experience and have continued to interview them annually since their graduation. Most were eighteen when they began college and are now in their early forties. I share an overview of the journey toward self-authorship here based on their stories (for more detailed stories see Baxter Magolda 1992, 2001, 2009). It is important to emphasise that this journey is nuanced based on personal characteristics (e.g. race, ethnicity, sexual orientation), context (e.g. social class, culture) and the intersections between the two. It also varies depending on whether young adults encounter the appropriate demands for self-authorship and the requisite support for it, a topic addressed later in the chapter.

Following external formulas
Although the journey toward self-authorship varies according to upbringing, personal experiences and schooling, over half of the one hundred and one students I interviewed upon their college entrance had acquired a way of knowing that privileged the voice of external authority. They believed that knowledge was certain, authorities had it and their role was to acquire it uncritically (Baxter Magolda 1992). Jim explicitly articulated this view:

> The information is cut and dried. It is either right or wrong. If you know the information, you can do well. It is easy because you just read or listen to a lecture about the ideas, then present it back to the teacher.
> (Baxter Magolda 1992:xi)

These students also relied on external authorities to help them make decisions. For example, when asked about choosing her major, Carmen shared, 'I did not really decide. My mother suggested majoring in zoology, so I did' (Baxter Magolda 1992:89). Participants looked for external formulas for learning, how to view themselves and how to relate to other people.

Over the course of their college experience, most encountered exceptions to this rule when professors insisted that knowledge was often uncertain and that learners should critically evaluate knowledge claims. Most altered their original rule to believe that knowledge was uncertain in some fields, but still relied on some form of external authority for some process for ascertaining the truth. Thus they followed external formulas for how to decide what to believe and how to view themselves and relations with others. Mark, who developed more complex ways of knowing during college, still turned to external formulas as he attended law school:

> I came here and I tried to figure out what the legal culture figures is success. I knew a Supreme Court clerkship was [success], so one of my goals was to aim towards that. So I got here to law school and I figured out, 'Okay, well, to be a success here you have to get to know some professors who are influential with judges to get a good clerkship, to get in the pipeline, to get in the star system here. Also get on *Law Review*. Write a paper here that you can publish.' I thought, 'Okay, this is kind of the plan then, step by step.' The ultimate plan for success in the legal culture.
> (Baxter Magolda 2001:41)

Although Mark was no longer relying on specific authority figures for what to believe, he focused on ascertaining what others regarded as success so he could follow that plan. After one year of law school, he reported:

> I said, 'Is this map of success given to me by the legal culture really a map at all to success?' And it depends on your definition of success. A great resume or accolades, yeah, that's the chart to a sign of prestige, that's the way to go. But I realized that I couldn't be a person who sacrificed happiness to that goal of prestige ... I never dreamed that I would be unhappy working on the law journal. I didn't think it would be as tedious and boring as I found it. That never figured in. There was no way law school and its classes could be as big a turnoff as they were.
> (Baxter Magolda 2001:46)

Like many of his peers, Mark began to look to himself for deciding what to believe. Most participants did so because they encountered problems with external formulas in their work or personal lives. Either following the formulas did not lead to the intended outcome, or they achieved the outcome and found it unsatisfactory. Resolving this dissonance led to a crossroads marked by tension between external influences and one's internal voice.

Crossroads

Abandoning external formulas left my participants unsure of how to proceed due to tension between their emerging internal voices and external influence. They recognised the importance of listening to their internal voices and trying to bring them into conversation with external voices. Kurt, in his mid-twenties, captured this phase of the journey:

> I'm the kind of person who is motivated by being wanted, I think. I've gone to a couple of workshops and, either fortunately or unfortunately, I'm the kind of person who gets my self-worth on whether or not other people accept me for what I do or other people appreciate what I'm doing. ... I'm coming from a position where I get my worth and my value from other people, which is, I think, wrong for me to do. But that's where I am right now. I feel like whether or not I choose to be happy is dependent upon me and only me. If I say, 'You made me mad,' or the converse, 'You made me happy,' then I'm giving all of the power that I have to you. The power of choice is mine; I have a choice of how I want to perceive each and every situation in my life. ... Obviously I'm not to that point yet because I choose to make myself happy and make myself sad on what other people are thinking. But I think I'd like to

> someday get to a point where I can say, 'Okay, that's your perception. I am not dependent on you for my happiness or my sadness.' And I think that would be a very strong, very spiritual place to be.
>
> (Baxter Magolda 2001:98–9)

Kurt was aware of his internal voice and knew he could and should be using it to guide his life. However, he had not developed his internal voice sufficiently to co-ordinate others' perceptions about him. He struggled at work because he acted in ways to gain his co-workers and supervisors' approval. He also struggled in personal relationships because he sacrificed his needs to those of others.

Lauren, also in her mid-twenties, was experiencing the crossroads but was working on cultivating her voice to sort out her feelings and priorities. Talking about a situation with her boyfriend she shared:

> He came home with me to [my parents' house] and I was totally gung-ho. I'm like, 'This is it; I know it.' And then after they gave me their feedback, they liked him but they were just not sure. And after they said that, all of a sudden I didn't like him as much anymore. It was nothing that he did to me; it was not the way he acted. It was nothing. But it was because of what they said; all of a sudden I started changing my mind. Yes, that's exactly true. But then my sister, on the other hand, is the opposite and is like, 'Just go with how you feel.' And my friends, my close friends here are like, 'Just go with how you feel.' So now it's gotten better. I'm trying to really think of what I want and not what they want. So this relationship is continuing, which they're not upset about at all, but I will tell you they have told me, 'Come on, this really isn't going to work. It's too far.' And that does affect me. But I'm really trying to take the attitude where maybe I need to find out for myself. But I will admit always in the back of my mind what they think still lingers over my decisions.
>
> (Baxter Magolda 2001:99)

A short time later Lauren moved to where her boyfriend lived so that she could work out for herself how she felt. Despite their awareness of the need to use their own voices to co-ordinate external influence, it took many of my participants until their mid to late twenties to navigate through the crossroads to place their voices in the foreground. In many cases, their intrapersonal or interpersonal capacities were not yet sufficiently developed to support their epistemological insight. Developing those capacities, and thus the internal voice to co-ordinate internal influence, yielded self-authorship for most of these learners by their late twenties.

Key components of self-authorship

Following my longitudinal study participants through their thirties prompted me to identify three elements within self-authorship: trusting the internal voice, building an internal foundation and securing internal commitments. The first element involves growing to trust the internal voice by using it successfully in multiple contexts over time. Dawn, diagnosed with MS at age thirty-three, described trusting her internal voice:

> Finding the balance between [going with the flow] and me saying I have control over myself, not letting this condition get the best of me. Knowing how to make things happen and let things happen. When you find the balance between those things, life is spectacular. That is kind of a trust thing – trusting that you know yourself enough to dance that line. Know when to make something happen and when to let it happen. Trusting yourself that you know that space. I don't quite know myself enough to trust that yet. I'm working on it. I'm getting close. That deepest self-knowledge to know you can stay there at that middle point and have that balance. That is a constant process for me. To be able to say this is my life and it's on my terms; I love that.
>
> (Baxter Magolda 2004b:xx–xxi)

Dawn conveys the key characteristic of trusting one's internal voice: realising that reality is beyond one's control but that you can use your internal voice to shape your reaction to reality. Most made this discovery through one of life's many challenges, including health problems, work struggles or relationship difficulties, emphasising again the value of lifewide experiences in promoting development.

Trusting the internal voice led to building a philosophy of life based on internally established beliefs and values. At some point in their thirties my study participants reported that these ideas moved from being in their heads to being in their hearts. They felt these internal commitments became second nature to them. Dawn described this latter element:

> It's starting to feel – more like wisdom than knowledge. To me knowledge is an awareness of when you know things. You know them as facts; they are there in front of you. When you possess the wisdom, you've lived those facts, that information so fully that it takes on a whole different aspect than just knowing. It is like you absorbed that information into your entire being. Not just that you know things. It is something deeper. Knowledge is brain –

wisdom comes from a different place I feel like. Something deeper connecting with your brain so that you have something different to draw from. A point where knowing you are going to do something – the knowledge has a deeper level – internal, intuitive, centered in entire being, the essential part of you that just – makes the basic knowledge pale by comparison.
(Baxter Magolda 2007:71)

Securing internal commitments helped participants feel settled and enabled them to live out their convictions. It also helped them deal effectively with major health challenges, career changes, relationship complexities and their wide range of work and family responsibilities.

Factors that mediate developmental growth
Complex interactions of individual and environmental factors influence development. Although the majority of developmental research suggests that few eighteen- to twenty-four-year-olds in the US reach self-authorship, Pizzolato (2003) reported that those who entered college despite lack of parental and community support exhibited early self-authorship because they had to figure out how to pursue college on their own. She reported that differences in their personal characteristics and coping strategies mediated their ability to maintain their self-authorship in the face of the marginalisation they experienced at college. Torres and Hernandez (2007) observed that some Latino/a students became self-authoring during college, in part due to having to address racism and the complexity of negotiating family relationships. Torres (2009) also described differences among Latino/a students' acceptance or rejection of negative stereotypes due to their perceptions of oppression or privilege, and noted that those with more complex developmental capacities were better able to reject negative stereotypes. Abes and Jones (2004) found similar evidence in studying lesbian students, who with increased developmental complexity were able to reject heterosexist assumptions prevalent in society. These examples imply that marginalisation due to social class, race, ethnicity or sexual orientation provides dissonance that may lead to abandoning external formulas. They also raise the possibility that dissonance in any area of one's life might affect growth in all three dimensions and thus affect learning in other arenas. Research suggests that learners foreground different dimensions (i.e. epistemological, intrapersonal and interpersonal) in ways that further nuance the developmental journey (e.g. Baxter Magolda 2010; King 2010; Pizzolato 2010). This reinforces the notion that lifewide experiences stimulate developmental growth and that lifewide education is crucial to promoting self-authorship because different learners meet these challenges in different places in their lives

and deal with them in different ways. The personalised support provided informally by an individual's own support network or the support offered by a formal learning partnership provides the support necessary to keep the challenges from being overwhelming.

Learners whose lifewide experiences provided dissonance prior to college may come to the college experience aware of their internal voices and committed to further developing them. These learners are likely to recognise and take advantage of the many curricular and co-curricular opportunities to promote their epistemological, intrapersonal and interpersonal growth. Intentional partnerships to assist them in maximising these opportunities could help them refine their internal voices during college, yielding a stronger preparation for navigating life's challenges. Learners whose lifewide experiences have not yet challenged their meaning making may come to college unaware of the need for an internal voice and resistant to educators' efforts to get them to challenge external formulas. These learners require different kinds of partnerships and perhaps more immersive experiences to help them make significant progress toward self-authorship during college. Efforts to make them aware of the shortcomings of following external formulas and the value of their internal voices must precede support to help them cultivate and refine their internal voices. Efforts to spark this awareness include structured opportunities for learners to reflect on their experience, intentional conversations to help learners establish their own learning goals, pedagogy that fosters critical thinking and encourages learners to appreciate the emergent and collaborative nature of real world learning, and an environment that both challenges and encourages them to engage in the learning opportunities they have in all parts of their life. Perhaps explicitly conveying to learners that their lifewide experiences are an integral part of their learning and growth would emphasise the crucial role of personal maturity in adult life. Emphasis in the UK on the Personal Development Planning process (Quality Assurance Agency for Higher Education 2009) and in the US on engaged learning reflects the perspective that lifewide experiences should be linked to formal learning experiences to promote personal maturity. The concept of self-authorship is one way to capture the personal maturity required to succeed in contemporary life.

Promoting self-authorship through 'learning partnerships'

Throughout the longitudinal interviews learners shared their best learning experiences and the characteristics of learning environments that helped them develop more complex ways of making meaning. These included classroom and co-curricular learning environments, as well as personal, work and relational environments they encountered during and after college. I synthesised their ideas into the Learning Partnerships Model (LPM), a model of practice to intentionally promote self-authorship in higher education (Baxter Magolda 2004a, 2009). The LPM is a combination of three means of supporting learners and three means of challenging them. Educators support learners in moving toward self-authorship by validating them as knowers, situating learning in their experience and defining learning as mutually constructing meaning. Educators do so by:

- respecting their thoughts and feelings, thus affirming the value of their voices
- helping them view their experiences as opportunities for learning and growth
- collaborating with them to analyse their own problems, engaging in mutual learning with them

(Baxter Magolda 2009:251).

Educators challenge learners to develop self-authorship by portraying knowledge as complex and socially constructed, emphasising self as central to knowing, and sharing authority and expertise. Specifically, they do so by:

- drawing participants' attention to the complexity of their work and life decisions, and discouraging simplistic solutions
- encouraging participants to develop their personal authority by listening to their own voices in determining how to live their lives
- encouraging participants to share authority and expertise, and work interdependently with others to solve mutual problems

(Baxter Magolda 2009:251).

Learning partnerships provide good company to learners on their difficult journeys toward self-authorship. Using the metaphor of a tandem bike, I have argued that implementing the LPM means that educators take the back seat from which they can provide guidance while offering learners the opportunity to direct their own developmental and educational journeys from the front captain's seat. This arrangement maximises learners' personal choice and responsibility to manage their own journeys – factors crucial to developing self-authorship.

Learning partnerships are possible in multiple learning spaces in higher education as well as in lifewide experiences outside of education (e.g. parenting, employment). My longitudinal participants experienced learning partnerships with educators, work supervisors, parents, siblings, spouses and therapists (Baxter Magolda 2009). Many of these partnerships were not intentionally designed to promote their development but instead arose from interacting with others who were interested in helping them succeed in various lifewide experiences.

Next I share some examples from the work of colleagues who have implemented intentionally designed learning partnerships in multiple settings. Their work suggests that young adults could reach self-authorship earlier than my longitudinal participants did if the conditions are in place to promote it. I include examples that illustrate learning partnerships in the curriculum, the co-curriculum and those that combine these two curricular environments.

Academic contexts for learning partnerships

Use of learning partnerships in academic contexts suggests that they can promote academic and personal outcomes simultaneously. The two examples that follow highlight explicit efforts to promote academic success by attending to the underlying developmental capacities it requires.

Earth Sustainability: a core curriculum to promote self-authorship
Educators at Virginia Polytechnic Institute and State University (Virginia Tech) organised a twenty-two-credit, four-course sequence on earth sustainability to help students meet core curriculum requirements and develop self-authorship. Virginia Tech is a Research I university with roots in agriculture and engineering that serves approximately twenty-one thousand undergraduates as well as graduate students in over a hundred graduate degree programmes. Designed using the LPM as the pedagogical foundation, the interdisciplinary course series used a spiral curriculum in which learners worked to achieve increasingly complex content learning goals and complex ways of making meaning simultaneously.

Bekken and Marie (2007) describe how learning and development goals were mapped on a four-semester plan to situate learning in learners' current experience and cumulatively challenge them to move toward self-authorship. For example, using assumptions and arguments translated to sorting opinions from arguments supported by evidence in the first semester. In the second semester the goal changed to identifying assumptions, discovering disciplinary biases and recognising complexity. In the third semester learners were asked to evaluate arguments and supporting assumptions and challenge disciplinary bias. In the fourth semester learners were asked to frame arguments from multiple perspectives, justify assumptions and assess evidence. This cumulative progression placed learning in learners' experiences yet simultaneously challenged them to recognise the complexity of earth sustainability. Assignments also placed learning in learners' experiences by asking them to analyse their experience (e.g. analyse their families' food consumption) or engaging in a class experience together (e.g. a service-learning project in a local food-producing community). Multiple instructors presented multiple perspectives, emphasising how their own disciplinary training and beliefs influenced their perspectives. At the same time each class session involved learners sharing their perspectives, which instructors respected and valued. Instructors discouraged simplistic solutions for achieving sustainability, instead opting to explore conflicting perspectives and engage learners in weighing the benefits and drawbacks of various approaches. Assignments were aligned with the learning goals for the semester, always blending analysis of class discussion and readi ngs with learners' own voices.

Of the nineteen students enrolled in the first offering of the series, fifteen were white, three Asian-American and one Hispanic. They were majoring in natural or applied sciences, social sciences and the humanities, and most held jobs. Through analysing written essays about sustainability at the outset of the first course, Bekken and Marie identified the vast majority of the learners as following external formulas. Revisiting their essays at the end of the first term, over half rejected their initial theses as too simplistic. Several noted the value of developing their own visions of sustainability. By the end of the third term learners reported making connections between course material and their personal lives and wrote with an authentic voice that was not evident in earlier terms. A mixed-method assessment of the Earth Sustainability series with these students as well as a matched comparison group included two measures of epistemological development and an interview. These measures, administered at the beginning of the series, the end of the second semester and the end of the fourth semester, revealed that Earth Sustainability students made greater epistemological advances than did the comparison group students. Olson *et al.* (in press) reported that by the fourth semester Earth Sustainability students were abandoning the idea that knowledge is absolute in favour of acknowledging uncertainty and the need for evidence to make knowledge claims. The authors noted that epistemological differences between the Earth Sustainability and comparison students were not significant at the end of the first year, suggesting that a sustained curriculum is key to developmental growth. Overall the success of the Earth Sustainability series supports the notion that content and developmental goals can be achieved simultaneously and that learners in their second year of college can abandon external formulas and begin to author their own perspectives.

Promoting self-authorship through academic advising
Pizzolato and Ozaki (2007) described a retention-focused academic advising programme (STEP: Support to Enhance Performance) modelled on the LPM for students in academic difficulty in one college of a large, public Midwestern research university in the US. The eighteen students who participated in STEP were between twenty and forty-one years old and represented all class years even though 50 per cent were seniors. The group was 79 per cent male, and racially diverse (31.6 per cent African-American or Black, 5.3 per cent Asian, 10.5 per cent Latino/a, 10/5 per cent Other and 42.1 per cent White). These students either had less than a 2.0 GPA for the semester or were on academic probation. The STEP programme involved regular one-on-one sessions with a professional advisor focused simultaneously on academic success skills and how students made sense of their experiences, decisions and themselves as well as how they balanced others' expectations of them.

The STEP advisor was careful not to offer formulas for success, opting instead to engage students in constructing their own success plans. By respecting their thoughts and feelings, she encouraged them to develop their internal voices. For example, she began by listening to their stories about how they came into academic difficulty before engaging them in active problem solving. Her advising sessions focused on who students wanted to be and who they were so that they could craft plans around this information. This focus emphasised their role in making career and other important decisions and situated learning in their experience. The advisor served as a coach, offering her expertise as students made plans and encountered obstacles but inviting students to transfer skills learned from overcoming obstacles and to explore their motivations behind particular behaviours. Sharing authority and expertise in this collaborative partnership helped students learn to value their own voices.

Pizzolato and Ozaki (2007) reported that STEP participants were following external formulas at the outset of the programme. Their academic difficulty provided enough dissonance to set the stage for considering new plans. By the end of the semester, participants were shifting away from external formulas to seeing themselves as important players in deciding what to believe. Pizzolato and Ozaki speculate that this movement is faster than what is typically reported because the intentional use of the LPM helped them connect cognitive capacities to their real-life situations. Routine questioning about why they were evaluating their situations in particular ways may have helped them consider their voices more carefully. Participants ended the programme more convinced that they could have some control over their academic success, more in tune with their own interests and better able to address the pressures stemming from others' expectations. It is likely that these new perspectives would also carry into non-academic decisions.

Other examples of learning partnerships in academic contexts
Educators have successfully used learning partnerships in individual courses as well. Hornak and Ortiz (2004) designed a community college business course using a blend of Ortiz and Rhoads' (2000) Multicultural Education Framework and the LPM. Learners made progress on revisioning their own pasts, learning about other cultures and beginning to understand how culture is created. Hornak and Ortiz concluded that creating learning partnerships in diversity educational contexts would help learners see themselves as intimately involved in the perpetuation and change of culture. Brudzinski and Sikorski (in press) redesigned a large introductory geology course using learning partnerships. They report that once they connected effectively to students' developmental capacities, student confidence on one hundred and twenty-eight learning objectives improved dramatically. They also share their own personal growth in integrating science content with affective dimensions of learning.

Haynes (2004) and her colleagues used the LPM to redesign a four-year writing curriculum in an interdisciplinary undergraduate program at Miami University (Ohio), a public, liberal arts institution enrolling approximately sixteen thousand undergraduates of traditional age. Frustrated that their students were not able to produce sophisticated senior theses, the teachers redesigned the writing curriculum to focus on reading and writing proficiency and critical analysis in the first year. The second year then moved on to learning and writing in the disciplines, followed by interdisciplinary writing. The third year emphasised interdisciplinary methodology and theory. The fourth year capstone then supported students in applying their prior knowledge in writing their senior theses. This gradual sequencing of writing matched students' developmental capacities, guiding them gradually to embrace multiple perspectives and develop their own voices in their writing.

Learning partnerships also guide a Bachelor of Integrative Studies degree offered on Miami's regional campuses, where enrolment includes a non-traditional student population (Hieber and Wahlrab in press). Integrative seminars begin with a focus on understanding the self, including crafting one's own plan of study based on one's own career and life goals. The focus then shifts to one's role in community through service-learning experiences. In the capstone seminar, learners integrate these understandings in creating and developing a culminating project that they will carry forward into their future career and studies. Thus this academic programme attempts to intentionally integrate the various dimensions of students' lives. Student journals in classes assist them in bringing their voice to learning and tracing their own development. Training teachers to use learning partnerships in teaching and advising is also a central part of this programme.

Co-curricular contexts for learning partnerships[1]

College students living on campus face numerous challenges in living away from home, living with peers whose values and experiences differ from theirs and adjusting to living in a community where individual and peer needs must be negotiated. Residential life educators are using learning partnerships to promote learning outcomes in all three dimensions of development. The next two examples highlight a process for community development and a residential curriculum.

Using community standards to promote self-authorship

The University of Nevada, Las Vegas (UNLV) is an urban research institution serving twenty-eight thousand students. Its mission includes a liberal education that prepares graduates for the work force or continued education. Substantial growth of on-campus housing in the early 1990s set the stage for an innovative approach to developing community called the Community Standards Model (CSM). Piper and Buckley (2004) defined community standards as shared agreements among members of a living unit about how they would treat one another. Residential living requires multiple levels of negotiation with others: with roommates on study space, sleep time, visitation and housekeeping; with neighbours on common space use and noise levels; with residents of multiple ethnic, racial and value backgrounds; and with peers whose values vary on alcohol use and sexual behaviour. Many students entering residential living early in their college experience have not yet acquired the developmental capacities to effectively engage in these complex negotiations. The CSM takes into account students entering developmental capacities in engaging them in learning how to participate effectively in relationships.

CSM is a structured process involving three phases:
- Phase I involves staff introducing residents to the concept of community standards and engaging residents in generating an initial set of standards. Encouraging residents of a living unit to establish their own standards (within university and legal parameters) emphasises personal responsibility for behaviour.

- Phase II involves community problem solving when residents feel someone has violated the standards. At students' request, staff convene meetings to discuss how these incidents affected community members. The focus at this stage is on clarifying the effects of behaviour on the community and refining of standards to avoid future violations.
- Phase III involves holding particular residents accountable for alleged violations. When complaints are initiated, staff work with the alleged violator to prepare him/her for the discussion with the community about his/her behaviour. All are encouraged to share their viewpoints, including the alleged violator, with the goal of obtaining an agreement to modify the offending behaviour.

Using both community and individual development theories, designers of the CSM incorporated the LPM into their work. Involving residents in establishing their own standards and holding themselves and others accountable to these standards respects their thoughts and feelings. Learning is situated in their living experience because problem solving takes place in the context of real-life issues of importance to them. Guiding the community to collaborate on solving problems offers practice in sharing authority. Drawing out multiple perspectives and values about daily living and community issues emphasises the complexity of relationships and the importance of bringing one's perspective to the dialogue. Rather than authority figures solving roommate or community problems, residents are actively engaged in learning how to solve problems and in doing so learn about themselves and how to interact more effectively with others.

Piper and Buckley (2004) report that quality-of-life surveys completed by residents at the end of the academic year offer evidence that community standards are effective. Over 70 per cent of the respondents reported that they were more comfortable making their own decisions, more understanding of others, more aware of how they affected others, more open to ideas different than theirs, more responsible, more appreciative of others' uniqueness and more willing to state their opinion. Over 60 per cent agreed that they were more able to stand up for what they wanted and to object to actions they thought were wrong. Because these living units included first- through fourth-year students, staff interviewed students to ascertain their views about community standards from various developmental phases. Those who initially viewed the standards as external formulas to follow began to see them as a process for negotiating needs. Similarly, these students gained confidence in expressing their own needs over time. In addition to helping students abandon external formulas, community standards helped those who were already at the crossroads to move toward self-authorship. Those residents reported gaining increased self-awareness and ability to interact effectively with peers, dynamics that suggested that their internal voices were moving to the foreground. For those who were self-authoring, the experience of interacting regularly with peers around shared standards offered opportunities to refine their beliefs, identities and social relations. This example illustrates that co-curricular experiences can be powerful sites for learning and self-authorship development.

Using a residential co-curriculum to promote self-authorship
Miami University's (Ohio) Office of Residential Life created a developmentally sequenced curriculum for the approximate nine thousand undergraduate students living in the residence halls. This occurred in the context of an overall university initiative to become an Engaged Learning University (Hodge *et al.* 2009). The Engaged Learning University model 'features principles and practices that lead students steadily toward self-authorship in which epistemological, interpersonal, and intrapersonal maturity are integrated' (ibid. 16, 18). Because this philosophy included blending the curriculum and co-curriculum in a vibrant campus community, residential life was an ideal site for engaged learning.

The residential curriculum is guided by an overarching goal of enabling residents to become citizen leaders and engaged scholars within their community. The curriculum contains three tiers that each outline developmentally appropriate learning outcomes in the areas of academic success, community engagement, cultural proficiency and identity development. The three tiers in their model relate to moving in (generally involving first-year students), moving through (sophomores and juniors) and moving out (seniors) of the college experience[2] Using the LPM, the staff crafted moving-in goals for students who are externally defined, moving-through goals for those at the crossroads and moving-out goals for those using self-authorship. Diversity in students' meaning making is acknowledged and accommodated by creating learning partnerships with individual students to match their developmental capacities. Residence life staff receive training in the LPM and self-authorship theory and generate multiple strategies to implement the curriculum accordingly. This example exemplifies constructing the residential environment as a learning space in which students can grow on all three dimensions of development.

Blending academic and co-curricular contexts
Perhaps the most powerful learning partnerships are those that engage all aspects of learners' lives, acknowledging their holistic development. These

partnerships resonate with lifewide learning because they enable and empower learners to integrate various aspects of their lives in the learning process.

Casa de la Solidaridad: cultural immersion to promote self-authorship
Casa de la Solidaridad is a Jesuit study abroad programme focused on justice and solidarity cosponsored by the Association of Jesuit Colleges and Universities, Santa Clara University and the University of Central America. A one-semester-length cultural exchange programme in El Salvador, it challenges students' perceptions about global justice and human liberation and encourages them to self-author their values. The Casa celebrated its tenth anniversary in 2009 and has over two hundred alumni.

Kevin Yonkers-Talz, co-creator and co-director of the programme, designed the Casa to reflect the components of the LPM (Yonkers-Talz 2004). Cultural immersion automatically situates learning in learners' experiences. Their living-learning community, which includes University of Central America students, and field placements bring them into direct contact with diverse others. The complexity of issues associated with poverty permeates the experience. Sustained and guided individual and community reflection in the living-learning community emphasise the importance of bringing one's views to deciding what to believe. The six courses students take while at the Casa integrate the subject matter with their field placements. A praxis course to integrate learning from students' field placements in the community emphasises knowledge as complex and socially constructed. The living-learning community and pedagogy of the Casa model sharing authority and expertise. Mutual relationships within the Casa community and with the Salvadorians define learning as a mutual process. Staff support, community living and the pedagogy of the Casa validate students' capacity to know.

Yonkers-Talz lives with the Casa students and also formally interviews them throughout their experience. He reports that encountering the poverty in El Salvador creates major dissonance for most students despite their preparation for the experience. Participants report that continual reflection on what they encountered in this experience helped them work through questions of what to believe (e.g. about how governments and societies work, define their own views about poverty and justice), refine their sense of their identity and form a vision for their role in the larger world. The interviews suggest that students entered the experience with some notion of expanding their worlds and leave the experience having moved out of the crossroads into self-authoring their beliefs, identities and social relations. The intensity of the experience no doubt accelerates development, yet the learning partnerships provide the crucial support to address significant challenges.

Internships to promote self-authorship
The Urban Leadership Internship Programme (ULIP) at Miami University challenges students to clarify their vocation and identity through a ten-week summer internship involving work, service and urban exploration. The ULIP involves approximately twenty-five sophomores and juniors each year in internships in three urban areas in the state. Once admitted, students work individually with the programme coordinator to design an internship uniquely suited to their goals. The overall design of the programme is intentionally structured to offer learning partnerships with programme staff, internship supervisors and peers.

Egart and Healy (2004) described how they implemented the six LPM components in the structure of the programme. The interns' role and responsibilities in their urban placement and community introduce the complexity of knowledge in these settings. The interns need to negotiate their new environment and identity, establishing their own voice in work and personal life. The interns work mutually with their peers to share authority and expertise. This occurs through a course in the semester prior to the internship, regular meetings in each urban centre of interns placed there during the internship and follow-up conversations with the entire group the semester following the internship. Collaboration among co-workers, roommates, supervisors and the programme coordinators supports students in defining learning as a mutual process. The programme coordinator emphasises that supervisors should give interns substantive responsibility and value their perspectives. Learning is automatically situated in the interns' experience in their jobs and community service in the urban setting. Group work and reflective writing offer validation of their thoughts and feelings as they navigate the internship experience.

Egart and Healy (2004) conducted a formal evaluation of the programme's effect on participants' development. Interns reported that their relationships with supervisors encouraged them to develop their own voices due to sharing authority. The experience of being independent and autonomous in their work roles and their everyday living in an urban environment challenged them to consider their own perspectives in everyday and work decisions. Encountering dissonance in their internships and daily lives in the urban environment called their attention to the complexity of urban issues. Structured opportunities for reflection on their experiences and their role in society led them to view themselves as citizens who could affect change. Participants' shifted from being unsure what role they could play to developing internal beliefs and values that helped them envision active roles they would pursue in the future. This shift suggests a move out of the crossroads into self-authoring one's beliefs, identity and social relations. It also suggests that direct experience, paired with strong and facilitative support, can lead to significant growth in a short period of time.

Learning partnerships in an Honours programme
After successfully developing a four-year writing curriculum using the LPM, Haynes (2004) translated these insights into a total reform of Miami University's Honours programme. Students from all university disciplines participate in the Honours programme throughout their college experience. Taylor and Haynes (2008) explicitly outline a three-tier approach to both the curriculum and co-curriculum that identifies the developmental goals, learning goals, educator expectations and learning experiences that best challenge and support learners at each phase of development. Like the Earth Sustainability course series described earlier, the three-tier approach intentionally structures learning outcomes and educational practice around learners' developmental capacities. The developmental goal of the first tier, where learners tend to follow external formulas, is to help learners see the shortcomings of doing so. The developmental goal of the second tier, where students are at the crossroads, is to help learners listen to their internal voices to decide what to believe and to mutually negotiate with others. In the third tier, where students are becoming self-authored, the developmental goal is to assist them in using their internal belief systems consistently and integrate aspects of their identity.

Taylor and Haynes have recently embarked on a total revision of the Honours programme based on this approach. Educators collaborate with students to identify experiences that will help them achieve learning goals, the students report how they achieved goals in each tier in an electronic portfolio and the staff assesses the portfolio based on rubrics crafted around the developmental and learning goals. First-year students submitted their reflective narratives this year to begin meeting the sequenced learning outcomes. Students' reflective narratives allowed teachers to complete a thematic analysis for key Honours courses to identify developmentally effective assignments and activities. For example, through the thematic analysis for CHM 144.H: College Chemistry Lab, teachers learned that the sol-gel experiment in particular had a large impact on students because the instructor trusted students to create, implement and analyse the results of a long-term experiment and expected students to share their new knowledge in a public forum. Teachers are using the results of such thematic analyses to guide faculty development efforts (K. B. Taylor, personal communication, 3 March 2011).

Self-authorship through learning partnerships during orientation
Although sustained partnerships over time enable educators to provide ongoing good company to learners, an example of building an orientation (induction) programme around the LPM reveals that the process can begin in a two-day orientation experience. Based on her participation in a community of educators working on designing engaged learning, the director of orientation (Stoll in press) initiated changes in Miami University's new student orientation programme. This programme orients students and their parents to the college experience prior to the start of their first college year. The programme focuses on four goals for incoming students: confidence, comfortable, connected and curious. Confidence entails self-efficacy and a sense of one's ability to succeed, comfortable relates to developing a campus support network, connected refers to a sense of belonging and curious relates to openness to new ideas. Recognising that these goals demanded certain developmental capacities, Stoll infused the orientation programme with the LPM.

Three key components of the programme – individual advising, written reflection and orientation leader training – were intentionally designed to support and slightly challenge students' entering tendency to follow external formulas. Student orientation leaders engaged small groups of students in crafting academic and co-curricular goals, which individual advisors then asked the students to share the next day. This approach conveyed respect for students' thoughts and linked their experience to organising their class schedules. Written reflection incorporated into large and small group sessions asked students and their parents to reflect on the information provided and its relationship to their own experiences. Reflections related to how ideas presented related to their prior expectations, their strengths and interests related to choosing a major and their academic and co-curricular goals. Some reflection questions focused on action steps that families could discuss after orientation. Staff and students facilitating these discussions were trained to craft learning partnerships with students and parents. Stoll (in press) collected student and parent feedback that revealed these outcomes: understanding the difference between memorisation and discovery-based learning, students gaining a sense of their role in the learning and advising process, and parents gaining insight into their role as partners to help their students become the directors of their educational journeys. These are remarkable outcomes for a two-day experience. They suggest that the way we frame the college experience with incoming students may predispose them to approach it as a lifewide learning project.

Authoring your life: a lifelong and lifewide project

My longitudinal participants' stories support the notion that learning is a lifelong and lifewide project. Their journeys toward self-authorship took place in classrooms, co-curricular settings, community involvement, employment and in their personal and professional relationships. Growth that occurred in these spaces influenced growth in other spaces. The journeys also illustrate that growth in the epistemological, intrapersonal and interpersonal dimensions is intertwined. This holistic view of learning and development in all of an individual's life spaces resonates with the lifewide concept.

The examples of learning partnerships support the concept that learning and development can occur in almost any context of an individual's lifewide experiences but that experiences that are intense and immersive appear to accelerate development. Having good company in both curricular and co-curricular settings and empathetic and skilled support also facilitates development. Because the LPM emphasises situating learning in learners' experience and respecting their voices, it naturally incorporates various dimensions of their lives into the learning relationship. The challenge of bringing one's own voice to the learning process further reinforces the centrality of the learners' whole lives in their learning and development.

Both learning partnerships and lifewide education aim to promote integration among various aspects of learners' lives. They also both aim to promote self-authorship, recognising it as the developmental foundation for the most valuable complex learning outcomes. Self-authorship enables taking advantage of learning opportunities as well as creating one's own learning infrastructure in various contexts. Research on success in adult life supports the role of self-authorship in managing complexity. Kegan and Lahey (2009) offer numerous examples of how organisational leaders in private corporations and public agencies function more adaptively when they have achieved self-authored meaning making. Kegan and Lahey advance the notion that moving beyond self-authorship to self-transformation – a way of making meaning that enables reflection on one's internal belief system – is actually necessary for the increased complexity these leaders face. Similarly, Drago-Severson (2010) suggests that educators in secondary school systems need self-authoring and self-transforming meaning making to adapt to the complex challenges they face. My longitudinal stories demonstrate how self-authorship helps the participants navigate the challenges of adult work and personal life (Baxter Magolda 2009). Developing an internal voice to guide one's life enables one to recognise and engage in opportunities for growth as well as to identify and develop the kinds of partnerships that support it. Thus substantial evidence exists that higher education must broaden its view to emphasise and gain the benefits from lifewide education. Learning partnerships embrace learners' lifewide experience and promote their capacity to shape their journeys toward self-authorship. The learning parnerships described in later chapters (Chapters 11 to 13 this volume) provide examples of how one UK university has tried to achieve this goal.

Endnotes
1 The term co-curricular is used here to describe campus-based contexts for learning that do not gain academic credit.
2 http://www.units.muohio.edu/saf/reslife/reslife/whatwedo/rescurric.php

Chapter 6

An imaginative lifewide curriculum

Norman Jackson

> The idea of curriculum goes to the heart of what we take higher education to be, of what might be and should be in the twenty first century.
> Barnett and Coate (2005:16)

Synopsis
The vision for an imaginative lifewide curriculum is a vision of a curriculum that engages learners in a deep and enduring way because learners themselves use their imagination and agency to design, create and inhabit their own spaces and places in order to develop. This vision has the potential to embrace all the spaces and places in learners' lives while they are involved in higher education. Such diversity of experiences is necessary to provide the contexts and situations to enable learners to develop the self-awareness, capabilities, qualities and dispositions necessary to survive, prosper and be fulfilled in a complex, uncertain and changing world. A set of principles, based on the ideas discussed in the first five chapters of this book, define the purposes and goals for an imaginative lifewide curriculum.

An imaginative curriculum
In 2001 I facilitated the development of a network of people who cared about students' creative development while they were studying in higher education. We called it the *imaginative curriculum network*.[1] We never defined what we meant by an imaginative curriculum, but in the foreword to the book *Developing Creativity in Higher Education: An Imaginative Curriculum,* Mihaly Czikszentmihalyi wrote:

So if one wishes to inject creativity in the educational system, the first step might be to help students find out what they truly love and help them to immerse themselves in the domain. ... When students are eager to immerse themselves in learning because it is a rewarding, enjoyable task, the basic prerequisites for creativity are met.

(Czikszentmihalyi 2006:ix–xx)

Viewed from this perspective, the essence of an imaginative curriculum is one that by design, encourages and enables learners to immerse themselves in the domains which they find rewarding and enjoyable. The vision of a lifewide curriculum (Jackson 2008a, b; Jackson and Campbell 2008; Jackson 2010) is a vision of a curriculum that engages learners in a deep and enduring way because learners themselves use their imagination and agency to design, create and inhabit their own spaces and places which enable them to develop into the people they want to become. This vision has the potential to embrace all the spaces and places in learners' lives while they are involved in higher education. This would enable learners to gain recognition for the ways in which they are making their own education more complete through all the things they are doing to develop themselves.

An imaginative curriculum is an engaging curriculum. When we engage deeply or immerse ourselves in an experience we are involved intellectually, practically and emotionally – head, body and heart (see Chapters 3 and 10 this volume). Engaging someone is an intentional act. Within the educational context it is motivated by the desire to promote learning and personal development. In higher education intentions are usually framed and made relevant within the context of a subject and the educational goals of a module or programme. Relevance might also be framed using a theme like employability, vocational training or personal development planning. In the context of a lifewide curriculum our intentions are framed by the intention to promote learning and personal development that is relevant to all aspects of a learner's life - in other words their holistic development as a person.

From a learner's perspective, being engaged, or giving focused attention to something, is an intentional act. It requires a conscious decision to be made: in that space between stimulus and response there is a space and in the space I am choosing to 'engage' with the situation at a level that requires cognitive, physical and emotional effort. Engaging learners occurs when:

students make a psychological investment in [their] learning. ... They take pride not simply in learning the formal indicators of success (grades), but in understanding the material and incorporating or internalising it in their lives. Students are engaged when they are involved in their work, persist despite challenges and obstacles, and take visible delight in accomplishing their work. Student engagement also refers to a "student's willingness, need, desire and compulsion to participate in, and be successful in, the learning process promoting higher level thinking for enduring understanding." Student engagement is also a usefully ambiguous term that can used to recognize the complexity of 'engagement' beyond the fragmented domains of cognition, behaviour, emotion or affect, and in doing so encompass the historically situated individual within their contextual variables (such as personal and familial circumstances) that at every moment influence how engaged an individual (or group) is in their learning.
(Wikipedia n.d.)

Hodge *et al.* (2009), describing the philosophy of an *engaged learning university* (based on the educational approach used at the University of Miami, Ohio), explain:

An engaged learning university features principles and practices that lead students steadily toward self-authorship in which epistemological, interpersonal, and intrapersonal maturity are integrated. ... To discover new ideas, learners must possess an internal set of beliefs that guide decision making about knowledge claims, an internal identity that enables them to express themselves in socially constructing knowledge with others, and the capacity to engage in mutually interdependent relationships to assess others' expertise. These capacities cannot be cultivated solely by engaging actively with the raw materials and tools of the academy or by participating in a student-centred classroom, although these are essential. Instead, they emerge gradually when educators foster students' holistic growth through continuous self-reflection, seamless and authentic curricular and co-curricular experiences that steadily increase in challenge, and appropriate levels of support.

... the key tenets of our intentional, engaged learning philosophy:
- Guide students to develop an internally defined and integrated belief system and identity, which prepare them personally and intellectually for lifelong learning.

- Actively engage students in discovering new knowledge in a sequenced, developmentally appropriate way to enable them to evaluate evidence critically, make informed judgments, and act ethically.
- Create a vibrant campus learning community that blends curricular and co-curricular learning opportunities and capitalizes on the roles of all constituents (faculty, staff, and students) in promoting student learning.

Hodge *et al.* (2009: 1–2),

These views are entirely consistent with the idea of a lifewide curriculum, but adopting such a concept would require an engaged learning university to embrace the extra-curricular as well as the co-curricular experiences of students.

Concepts of curriculum

Fraser and Bosanquet (2006) argue that there is no single definition that accounts for the way academic staff understand the term curriculum. they identified four ways in which academics thought about curriculum: 1) curriculum is contained within a unit or module of study 2) curriculum is contained in the content and process of a programme of study comprising a variably prescribed set of study units or modules 3) curriculum is visualised as the students' experience of learning and is negotiated between learners and teachers and includes 'intended and unintended.....transactions' between a learner and a teacher' 4) curriculum is a collaborative partnership between learners and teachers that result in changes for both learners and teachers (Fraser and Bosanquet 2006:274). All these conceptions are based on an assumption that learners learn a curriculum, whether it is designed for them or negotiated by them.

In their study of creativity and curricula in UK higher education, Edwards et al (2006), derived a similar set of perspectives on what academics thought curriculum meant:

> Use varied widely, ranging from 'syllabus' and programme plans, to notions of the hidden curriculum, in which the social, cultural and political context (what some participants described as the 'fuzzier bits') was counted as part of what was taught. ... However, one conception of the curriculum emerged for understanding the broader possibilities for understanding creativity. This was the idea of the lived curriculum as experienced in the classroom. ... The lived curriculum arose dynamically out of interactions with students.
>
> (Edwards *et al.* 2006:60)

Kelly (2004:8) provides a conceptually more valuable definition 'the curriculum is all of the learning experiences that the student has as a result of the educational context.' The strength of this definition is the way it is grounded not in content or structure, but in an individual's experience that takes account of the context for that experience.

The vision for an imaginative lifewide curriculum (based on a lifewide educational context) is for a lived curriculum that is experienced and contemplated by the learner through all the life spaces she inhabits.

In their book *Engaging the Curriculum in Higher Education* Barnett and Coate (2005) drew attention to a significant issue in UK higher education policy debate, namely the near total absence of any discussion or concern for 'curriculum' in the two major reviews of higher education.[2] They attributed this not to carelessness but with the desire by those orchestrating the debate to avoid the challenges posed by serious engagement with the idea of curriculum: 'the absence of the term "curriculum" from these reports is not happenstance. It represents a systematic disinclination to engage seriously with matters concerning higher education as an educational project' (Barnett and Coate 2005:14). 'The absence of the term curriculum is not just a matter of vocabulary; not just a matter of a missing term. Its absence is indicative of systematic interests at work for which the term curriculum would pose difficulties' (ibid. 16).

These authors concluded that the policy debate, as it was framed by these national reviews, 'is tipping [curriculum] into the skills, standards and outcomes model of curriculum rather than a reflexive, collective, developmental and process oriented model' (Barnett and Coate 2005:18). '[This] emerging concept of curriculum neglects more intractable dimensions of human development such as human qualities and dispositions' (ibid. 24).

This critique identified a significant issue and challenge, and provided one of the stimuli for the lifewide curriculum to try to create a more inclusive, developmental and process-oriented curriculum that encouraged and enabled learners to develop as whole people.

Barnett and Coate (2005:51) acknowledge that there were pioneers who were calling on 'concepts and theories of complexity to assist our understanding of curricula' (Tosey 2002; Jackson 2004) and endorsed these ways of thinking 'provided that complexity is understood as characterising the framing and acting out of curricula as well as the forms of human capability that curricula are intended to develop'. The approach described in this book attempts to engage with this challenge.

Framing the lifewide curriculum

A lifewide curriculum is formed around the idea that an individual's curriculum (rather than a programme for a group of students) should enable him to be the person he wants to be and enable him to develop into the person he would like to become. The framing concept of knowing–acting–being developed by Barnett *et al.* (2001), Parker (2003) and Barnett and Coate (2005) helps us understand an individual's relationship with a curriculum.

Chapter 1 argued that a higher education should help prepare people not just for their first job, but for the rest of their lives – lives that require us to continuously develop and adapt and perhaps also to reinvent ourselves. Barnett and Coate (2005:48) highlight some of the challenges of a rapidly changing world for curriculum design maintaining that such concerns have never been accepted as a generally valid way of approaching curriculum design.

> a changing world calls for certain kinds of human capacity and dispositions and for self-awareness and self-confidence. The self is implicated in a changing world. No longer can the wider norms and practices be endorsed: individuals have to work things out for themselves in their own situations. Individuals have to become selves, strong, careful, open, resilient and critical selves. Students' being, willy-nilly, comes into play.
>
> Knowing, acting and being, these then are the three challenges of a changing world that curricula in higher education have to address. ...... there is ... a responsibility on all those at the sharp end in higher education to ensure that curricula with which they are associated are supplying responses of some kind to these three challenges. ... These challenges open up possibilities for universities to do even more justice to their hopes of educating. For example, if 'higher learning' is that form of learning that is appropriate to higher education, it has now to be interpreted as referring to a composite of especially challenging forms of learning that are appropriate to a changing world.
>
> (Barnett and Coate 2005:48-49)

The knowing–acting–being curriculum paradigm developed by Barnett *et al.* (2001) and Barnett and Coate (2005) represents the higher education curriculum as the structure, process and experience for student development across the domains of knowledge, action and self (Figure 6.1).

Analysis of curriculum documents and discussions with course designers revealed that the relative significance, connection and integration of these different domains varies across different discipline areas and types of programme. In science and technology disciplines 'knowledge' is emphasised, with action taking a lesser role, and self residing in the background. In humanities and arts disciplines knowledge is emphasised with self playing a lesser role and action residing in the background. In contrast, in curricula, where there is a professional orientation, action is fore-grounded, with self and 'knowledge' taking a lesser but still important role. Curricula which aim to prepare people for the professions tend also to have a better balance and integration of the three domains. This set of relationships is summarised in Table 6.1.

Figure 6.1 Representation of the knowing–acting–being curriculum paradigm. Source: Barnett *et al.* (2001) and Barnett and Coate (2005:73-7). Circles represent relative emphasis and degree of integration of the three domains in the curriculum of different disciplinary fields: a) science and technology, b) humanities and arts and c) professional disciplines.

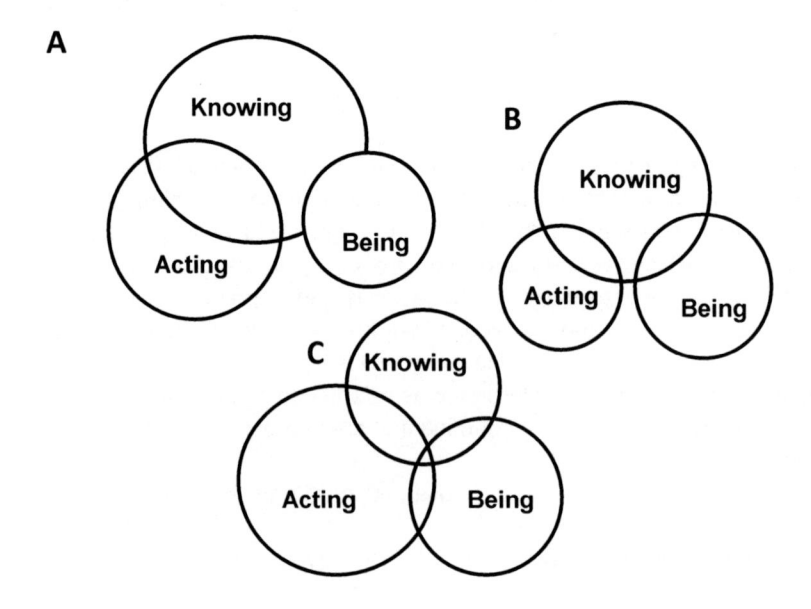

Barnett et al. (2001) and Barnett and Coate (2005) criticised higher education for paying too little attention to the 'self' dimension of curriculum. This is now being addressed systemically across higher education through the introduction of PDP with its emphasis on self-awareness, reflection and planning for self-development.

Table 6.1 Summary of the relationships between knowledge, action and self in different disciplinary areas. Source: Trevitt and Perera (2009), based on Barnett et al. (2001) and Barnett and Coate (2005). In this schema '>' denotes 'has a greater weighting than' and '=' denotes 'has an equal weighting with'.

Broad disciplinary area	*Emphasis across the key domains*
Science and technology	Knowledge > action > self
Arts and humanities	Knowledge > self > action
Professions	Action > self = knowledge

Parker (2003) used this way of framing a higher education curriculum to argue that curriculum designers should move beyond 'the prevalent commodified discourse in Higher Education' and, instead, embrace the idea of a 'transformational curriculum' – one where potentially the student is actively involved in negotiating his own customised approach across the three domains posited by Barnett et al. (2001).

Trevitt and Perera (2009) also utilised this conceptual framework to evaluate the orientations of an autonomous self-regulating professional taking responsibility for his own continuous professional learning and development through his work contexts and practices (Figure 6.2). In this context:

> the very notion of curriculum [as an educator-designed experience for learning] now becomes a more contested one with ... learning in context (or participation in the workplace) taking precedence over classroom-based activities. ... [W]e are now dealing with 'multiple knowledges' rather than a previously implied singular 'knowledge'
> (Trevitt 2010:5)

The continuing professional learning perspective offered by Trevitt and Perera (2009) and Trevitt (2010) 'foregrounds our concern with the on-going process of negotiation of professional identity(ies)' (Trevitt 2010:5).

Figure 6.2, builds on ideas developed by Trevitt (2010). It shows the three curriculum perspectives (knowledge-action-self) developed by Barnett *et al.* (2001) and Barnett and Coate (2005), together with a fourth perspective - continuing professional learning (CPL) added by Trevitt and Perera (2009). The latter proposed the need for a personal 'space for learning'; namely professional lifelong learning where self > action > knowledge, and where embodied knowledge is more important than codified knowledge. This additional perspective also approximates the curriculum space for holistic personal development through lifewide learning where self > action > knowledge and where embodied knowledge is more important than codified knowledge.

Figure 6.2 Curriculum orientations within the knowing-acting-being paradigm. Adapted from Trevitt and Perera (2009) and Trevitt (2010), drawing on the original concept of Barnett *et al.* (2001) and Barnett and Coate (2005). The upper triangle shows the orientations of curricula in formal education. The lower triangle shows the orientations of personal and professional development through everyday work and wider life experiences.

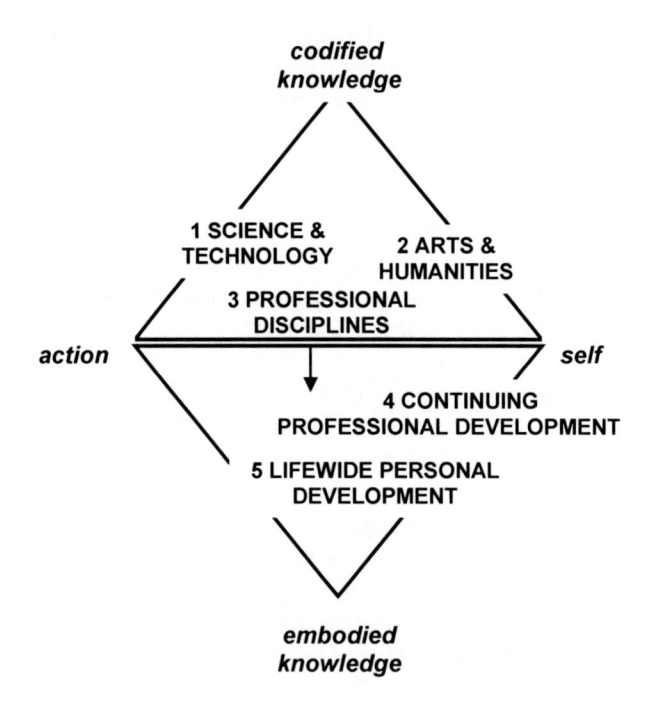

When this conceptual tool is applied to the lifewide curriculum idea we can see that while students' formal education might be engaged through a curriculum that is discipline-based, with one of the three orientations postulated in Figure 6.1, by viewing the curriculum as a lifewide proposition we can see the potential for students to engage in the development of their own identity (or self-authorship: Baxter Magolda 2004 and Chapter 5) more completely through their involvement in the places and spaces they choose to inhabit outside formal education. Through this conceptual lens we can see how they would develop embodied personal knowledges, agency, self-fulfillment and confidence derived from their actions in the situations that they encounter or create for themselves. They are in fact gaining the sorts of experiences, knowledges, capabilities and dispositions that will stand them in good stead when they embark on their professional careers because many of these ways of being and acting, and developing multiple forms of knowledge, are a necessary part of participating and engaging in work.

A curriculum for integration

The ability to integrate our knowledge, imagination and capability in order to act effectively in a given situation and achieve something is core to our functioning. The challenge to higher education is how can we improve students' ability to integrate and apply their learning and development in different contexts.

> Developing students' ability to integrate and apply learning [in different contexts] is an important piece of what makes higher education relevant to today's world. On any given day newspaper headlines point to the need for graduates who are sophisticated in their thinking, able to discern complexity in situations, and motivated to continuously seek better, more responsible, solutions to problems encountered in work, in life and in society ... The current context also requires graduates who are creative; who can anticipate the not-yet-known, and negotiate rapid technological, cultural, and global shifts.
>
> (AACU 2009a:1)

Integrated education is based on designs, facilitation and support mechanisms that seek to enable and empower learners to integrate their experiences and learning from, and in, different contexts and to transfer, apply and adapt their learning to new situations and contexts. The promise of a lifewide curriculum is that it holds more potential for encouraging learners to see themselves as the integrators of their life experiences and their own learning, than an academic curriculum alone.

Integrative learning is an understanding and a disposition that a student builds across the curriculum and co-curriculum, from making simple connections among ideas and experiences to synthesizing and transferring learning to new, complex situations within and beyond the campus.
(AACU 2009b:1)

Integrative education is based on designs, facilitation and support mechanisms that seek to enable and empower learners to integrate their experiences and learning from, and in, different contexts. The *Integrative Learning Value Rubric* developed by AACU (ibid.) identifies four areas of integration: 'connecting skills and knowledge from multiple sources and experiences; applying theory to practice in various settings [and perhaps growing new theories from experience?]; utilizing diverse and even contradictory points of view; and understanding issues and positions contextually' (AACU 2009b:1). All these areas are highly relevant to our discussion on lifewide learning and development.

In the USA the integrative learning movement has grown mainly in colleges and universities that provide a liberal arts education. The movement appears to have grown from a number of reasons:

1. The desire to create greater coherence for the learner of curricular experiences that appear to be highly fragmentary – combinations of major/minor/service components. In the UK, because of the strong emphasis on single honours degrees, there is less interest in learning outside the academic curriculum so this reason is far less pronounced.

2. A concern to make academic learning more relevant and connected to the real world.

    Fostering students' abilities to integrate learning – across courses, over time, and between campus and community life – is one of the most important goals and challenges for higher education. Initially, students connect previous learning to new classroom learning. Later, significant knowledge within individual disciplines serves as the foundation, but integrative learning goes beyond academic boundaries. Indeed, integrative experiences often occur as learners address real-world problems, unscripted and sufficiently broad, to require multiple areas of knowledge and multiple modes of inquiry, offering multiple solutions

> and benefiting from multiple perspectives. Integrative learning also involves internal changes in the learner.
> (AACU 2009b:1)

This reasoning is valid for any higher education system.

3. An appreciation of the challenges of the modern world and the need to develop students' capabilities for, and commitment to, lifelong learning and to the process of continual renewal, adaptation and reinvention that their working lives will necessitate.

> These internal changes, which indicate growth as a confident, lifelong learner, include the ability to adapt one's intellectual skills, to contribute in a wide variety of situations, and to understand and develop individual purpose, values and ethics. Developing students' capacities for integrative learning is central to personal success, social responsibility, and civic engagement in today's global society. Students face a rapidly changing and increasingly connected world where integrative learning becomes not just a benefit ... but a necessity.
> (AACU 2009b:1)

This would also be a valid reason for developing more integrative approaches in any higher education system.

4. An appreciation of the pedagogies and learning capabilities required of a trans-disciplinary world that must transcend discipline-only contexts. But also a recognition that there needs to be a connection between disciplinary and real world study.

> Because integrative learning is about making connections, this learning may not be as evident in traditional academic artefacts such as research papers and academic projects unless the student, for example, is prompted to draw implications for practice. These connections often surface, however, in reflective work, self assessment, or creative endeavours of all kinds. Integrative assignments foster learning between courses or by connecting courses to experientially-based work. Work samples or collections of work that include such artefacts give evidence of integrative learning. Faculty are encouraged to look for evidence that the student connects the learning gained in classroom study to learning gained in real life situations that are related

to other learning experiences, extra-curricular activities, or work. Through integrative learning, students pull together their entire experience inside and outside of the formal classroom; thus, artificial barriers between formal study and informal or tacit learning become permeable. Integrative learning, whatever the context or source, builds upon connecting both theory and practice toward a deepened understanding.

(AACU 2009b:1)

This would also be a valid reason for developing more integrative approaches in any higher education system.

5. An attempt to address the issue of emergence in complex adaptive social systems i.e. the societies in which we live. Emergence is 'the process by which patterns or global-level structures arise from interactive local-level processes. This "structure" or "pattern" cannot be understood or predicted from the behavior or properties of the component units alone' (Mihata 1997:31). It is phenomenon that we can all recognise in everyday life in the real world, but to which higher education traditionally gives little consideration.

6. The need to make better use of the resources we have available within a university environment for educating learners as whole people.

'Learning Reconsidered' is an argument for the integrated use of all of higher education's resources in the education and preparation of the whole student. It is also an introduction to new ways of understanding and supporting learning and development as intertwined, inseparable elements of the student experience. It advocates for transformative education – a holistic process of learning that places the student at the centre of the learning experience.

(NASPA & ACPA 2004:1)

This argument makes considerable sense, especially in a world where resources for higher education learning are ever more costly and scarce. The arguments and thinking elaborated in this proposal are totally consistent with the lifewide learning and education concept.

7. To this list we might add the need to make better use of resources for learning in environments outside the university to which a learner has access.

The vision of a lifewide curriculum is for an educational and developmental design that would improve a university's ability to meet all these concerns. A lifewide curriculum would empower those learners who choose to see themselves as the authors and implementers of their own designs for personal development. It would encourage learners to see the whole of their life experiences as opportunities for their own development and enable them to integrate learning and development from any aspect of their lives into their higher education experience and vice versa. Finally, the adoption of a lifewide concept of learning would provide a university with a rationale for connecting all of its staff and services that support students, their learning, wellbeing and personal development in a common educational enterprise.

A lifewide curriculum

The lifewide curriculum is a response to the challenge of how to design a curriculum that enables learners to integrate their life experiences into their learning and developmental process to prepare themselves for the complexity and uncertainty of their future lives. Such a curriculum shifts the focus from a 'skills, standards and outcomes model of curriculum [to] a reflexive, collective, developmental and process oriented model' (Barnett and Coate 2005:18). It focuses attention on the importance of developing capability, dispositions, knowledge, qualities and confidence for acting in the continuous stream of situations that make up learners lives (see Chapters 3 and 4 this volume) and it shows them that higher education values the choices they are making about how they are choosing to live their lives. In framing the curriculum in this way we are championing the idea that capability is 'essentially one of freedom – the range of options a person has in deciding what kind of life to lead' (Dreze and Sen 1995:11). In revealing his lifewide curriculum a learner is choosing to reveal the life he has chosen to lead: he is revealing how he is authoring his life (Chapter 5).

Propositions for a curriculum that prepares learners for life

The following list outlines emerging propositions for an imaginative lifewide curriculum that would help learners develop the multiple forms of knowing, skills, capability, qualities and dispositions necessary for being successful, effective and fulfilled in a complex, uncertain, changing and sometimes disruptive world. These propositions are derived from the perspectives offered in the earlier chapters of this book and they are intended to support the development of the complex integrated capabilities of highly effective people described by Greene (2004 and Chapter 4 this volume).

An imaginative lifewide curriculum:
1. gives learners the freedom and empowers them to make choices so that they can find deeply satisfying and personally challenging situations that inspire, engage and enable them to develop themselves
2. enables learners to appreciate the significance of being able to deal with situations and see situations as the focus for their personal and social development
3. prepares learners for and gives them experiences of adventuring in uncertain and unfamiliar situations where the contexts and challenges are not known, accepting the risks involved
4. supports learners when they participate in situations that require them to be resilient and enables them to appreciate their own transformation.
5. enables learners to experience, feel and appreciate themselves as knower, maker, player, narrator, enquirer, creator and integrator of all that they know and can do, and enables them to think and act in complex situations
6. encourages learners to be creative, enterprising and resourceful in order to accomplish the things that they and others value
7. enables learners to develop and practise the repertoire of communication and literacy skills they need to be effective in a modern, culturally diverse and pluralistic world
8. enables learners to develop relationships that facilitate collaboration, learning and personal development
9. encourages learners to behave ethically and with social responsibility
10. encourages and enables learners to be wilful, self-directed, self-regulating, self-aware and reflexive so that they develop a keen sense of themselves as designers/authors and developers of their own lives appreciating their learning and developmental needs as they emerge.

This concept of a lifewide curriculum is intended to complement and inform, not replace more traditional forms of academic curriculum – i.e. a 'lifewide' curriculum embraces *all* of a student's experiences while he is engaged in a higher education. The propositions take account of the need for learners to work things out for themselves as they engage intentionally or accidentally in the experiences that they encounter in the real world outside the classroom.

Visualising a lifewide curriculum
When designing educational experiences curriculum designers usually begin with *their* purposes and the outcomes *they* want to promote, and then *they* think about the content, and process, create and organise resources to support learning. *They* decide what counts as learning, and finally *they* evaluate the standards and quality of learning, as demonstrated through one or more assessment methods and tools that *they* have designed guided by criteria *they* create to assist them in making judgements. This is the way teachers generally do things in higher education.

Some designs, particularly where curricula have a strong vocational orientation, require participation in real world environments and problem working (for example through a work or clinical placement) and include assessments of performance that relate to doing a job and performing a role in a work context. In these situations, people other than teachers (e.g. work place supervisors) may be involved in making judgements on performance and achievement. These sorts of learning experiences involve the highest degrees of integration of knowing, acting and being and consequently are more able to prepare learners for the complexity of the professional world.

This is a curriculum for the world of professional practice but relatively few students have this type of learning experience, so the challenge to curriculum designers is how to create opportunity for more students to participate in experiences that will enable them to gain a richer and deeper experience of knowing–acting–being in authentic contexts where they can apply their learning. Our response to this challenge was to turn the problem on its head and ask the question, what if we were to begin with the learner and his life, and see the learner as the designer of an integrated, meaningful life experience? An experience that incorporates formal education as one component of a much richer set of experiences that embrace all the forms of learning and achievement that are necessary to sustain a meaningful life.

This way of thinking resulted in the idea of a lifewide curriculum (Jackson 2008a, b, 2010b) to embrace the idea of an educational design that seeks to empower and enable a learner to integrate his learning from any aspect of his life into his higher education experience. Such a curriculum was also considered by Jackson (2008a) to afford the best opportunity for students' creative development, since the intrinsic motivations that drive creativity are more likely to be present in the spaces that individuals choose to inhabit and to which they devote time and attention.

Figure 6.3 conveys the most inclusive concept of an undergraduate curriculum and the forms of validation and recognition for learning and personal development. It embraces: the academic curriculum, the integrated theory-practice curriculum such as are found in many health and social care programmes, programmes with placement opportunities, community-based service learning opportunities, co-curricular experiences on or off the campus, students' self-determined extra-curricular experiences on or off the campus.

Figure 6.3 Lifewide curriculum map. Source: Jackson (2008a, b and 2010)

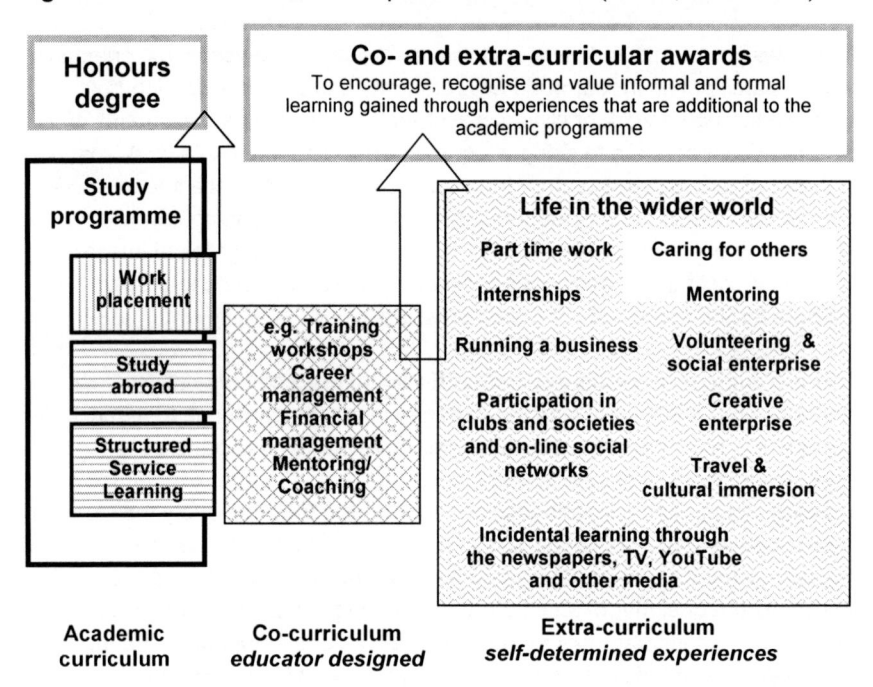

```
                            Co- and extra-curricular awards
   Honours              To encourage, recognise and value informal and formal
   degree              learning gained through experiences that are additional to the
                                       academic programme

   Study
 programme                              Life in the wider world

    Work                       Part time work        Caring for others
  placement
                               Internships          Mentoring
                 e.g. Training
                  workshops    Running a business   Volunteering &
    Study          Career                            social enterprise
    abroad       management
                  Financial    Participation in      Creative
                  management   clubs and societies   enterprise
  Structured     Mentoring/    and on-line social
   Service       Coaching      networks             Travel &
   Learning                                          cultural immersion

                               Incidental learning through
                               the newspapers, TV, YouTube
                                    and other media

    Academic         Co-curriculum          Extra-curriculum
   curriculum      educator designed      self-determined experiences
```

The concrete expression of this idea translates into curriculum map (Figure 6.3) containing three different curricular domains, all of which have the potential to be integrated into a learner's personalised higher education experience and be recognised and valued by the institution:

1. academic curriculum, which may by design integrate real-world work or community-based experiences

2. co-curriculum: educator-designed experiences that may or may not be credit-bearing and for which learners may or may not receive formal recognition
3. extra-curricular experiences that are determined by the learners themselves and constitute all the spaces that lie outside of 1 and 2, above.

The precise form of this curriculum map will reflect the curriculum arrangements of an institution. For example, at the University of Surrey, where these ideas have been developed, the undergraduate academic curriculum contains the following types of programme : three- or four-year programmes integrating theory and academic practice; three-year programmes which integrate theory and work-based practice throughout the period of study; four- or five-year programmes in which the third year is spent in work-based practice and three- or four-year programmes that offer opportunities for study in other countries. The co-curriculum offer (additional experiences that have been designed to support student development) will also vary from one university to another.

The University of Surrey has a long tradition of single honours programmes with a strongly regulated core content (core modules) with relatively little opportunity for optional modules that would permit students to incorporate broader experiences into their credit-bearing programme. But it would also be possible, with an accommodating curriculum framework, to design a lifewide curriculum that was integrated into the credit-bearing structure.

Creating personal meaning

A lifewide curriculum is a personal curriculum. It constitutes the spaces and places in and through which an individual has determined the life he wants to lead. It reflects the choices he has made to create new opportunities for himself in the future. The principle of 'freedom of choice' that underpins the idea of lifewide learning means that the learner must choose to reveal his lifewide curriculum.

A life space map (Figure 6.4) can be used to reveal the spaces and places we inhabit, the things we do in those spaces and places, the significant relationships we have and value, and the ways in which we maintain our physical, emotional and spiritual well-being.

Figure 6.4 My life spaces map (January 2011)

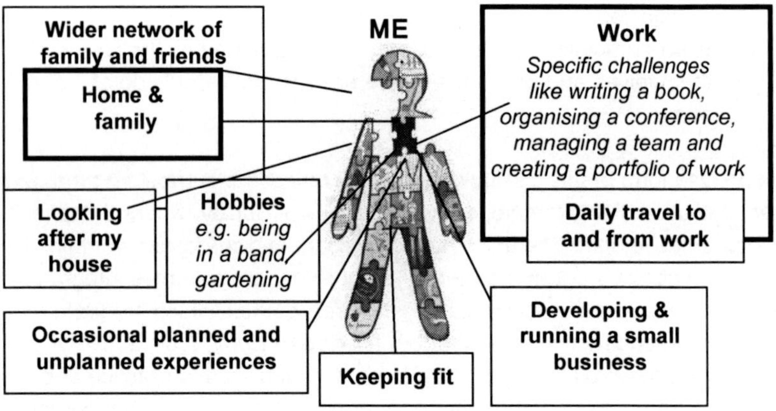

- Wider network of family and friends
- Home & family
- Looking after my house
- Hobbies e.g. being in a band, gardening
- Occasional planned and unplanned experiences
- ME
- Keeping fit
- Work — Specific challenges like writing a book, organising a conference, managing a team and creating a portfolio of work
- Daily travel to and from work
- Developing & running a small business

In creating a life spaces map the learner is revealing something about who he is and what sort of life he is choosing to lead. The creation of a life spaces map can be used to promote reflection on our opportunities for development through the situations that we encounter and create in our daily lives. Every space we inhabit has its own challenges and opportunities each holds the potential for us to exercise our will, harness what we know and can do, develop new knowledge, be creative and resourceful, behave ethically and use and integrate many of our capabilities. In every life space there are opportunities for learning, relationship building and the development of capability that ultimately can be transferred and utilised in other life spaces.

Figure 6.4 shows my own life spaces map. It summarises the life I am choosing to lead at the time of writing (January 2011). My family and home is my most important life space. Day to day, it involves my wife and two children who are living at home, but I have four other children, one at university and three who are older with partners; not to forget my grandson. Beyond this we have extensive branches of the family in Iran, Australia and other parts of England. All in all we have close to 100 members in our blood-related family – there is complexity even within the family domain. Families are great for involving you in the lives of the people you care most about. Capability in this domain is very much geared to supporting, guiding and helping family members develop and live their lives in such a way that they feel valued, enabled and fulfilled. And there is just as much challenge in this as in any other life space.

My house continually challenges me practically and emotionally. It's a lovely but complicated house and there always seems to be something requiring attention, and working out what needs doing, finding someone who can help at reasonable cost or learning how to fix something myself, is a never-ending story. We have a large garden with woodland which needs constant and sometimes urgent attention and my significant challenge at the moment is a rabbit problem. We are under attack and if I can't work out how to deal with this problem there will be more holes than garden. So there is lots of scope for personal development here!

My work, consumes a majority of my time. As leader of the SCEPTrE team it involves my relationships with colleagues in my team, the institution and the wider world, leading and collaborating, planning and decision making, creating activities that others see value in and achieving specific goals, one of which is completing this book by a specific date. Capability in this domain is concerned with *the ways and means we have* to build relationships for accomplishing the things we set out to do, to generate and implement ideas, to sell ideas, persuade others of their value, to negotiate in order to achieve what we value in the belief that it will be of benefit to our students.

I include in my life space map the daily journeys I make to and from work because this is often the time I plan or reflect on daily events or more generally on my work and the other happenings in my life. Many of my ideas or decisions about what to do seem to emerge from my thinking and jottings in this space so it fulfils an important role in my life.

I also involve myself in experiences that help maintain my sense of well-being, like reading, listening to music, swimming and gardening, and more social activities like being a granddad or playing in a band. The latter has its own challenges as we juggle commitments to meet to practise, members leave and are replaced and we 'negotiate' what to play.

Occasional planned and unanticipated experiences which become our temporary life spaces add to the opportunity and the challenges we face. In the last 12 months I have experienced losing my closest friend to cancer, witnessed two of my children getting married and had a family holiday in Egypt. Such experiences (including such things as family bereavement, loss of job or serious illness) are the situations in everyday life that put us in the domain of unfamiliar contexts and challenges that we have to learn to deal with and that may require us to go through a transition in order to adapt to a very different life.

At the time of writing I am approaching a transition point in my life as the SCEPTrE project comes to an end I will be leaving the university. I know I have to create my own future and I have two strands to my strategy. The first is to keep an open mind and to be receptive to any opportunity I can recognise as it emerges. The second is to try to create opportunities for myself, so I have established a business with a partner to capitalise on what I think I am good at and what I know he is good at. We have already begun trading and we are both having to develop our knowledge and capability to try to create a successful enterprise that we hope will provide services that others value and will bring us a sense of purpose and fulfilment.

Final integrating thoughts
This chapter has set out the proposition that:
- The life spaces and places we occupy and the relationships we have and the things we do in them are the most tangible expression of the way we are choosing to lead our life within our current freedom and capability.
- Collectively, our life spaces and places represent our self-determined lifewide curriculum within which our learning and development are planned and managed, or emerge through our day-to-day doings and beings. We need to be able to respond to both planned and emergent situations for development.
- Our life spaces and the relationships we have and the things we do in them hold the potential for our future life. By adding to these life spaces or changing what we do within them we are choosing to lead a different sort of life.
- By revealing our life spaces and places, the relationships we have and the things we do in them we begin the process of explicitly recognising our lives as our most valuable resource and opportunity for learning and developing ourselves.
- The process of creating and reflecting on our life space map can help us think systematically about the life we are choosing to lead and the opportunities we have for which we have for developing ourselves.

John Dewey (1897) said that 'education is a process of living and not a preparation for future living'. Inspired by his friend, Eduard Lindeman framed his vision for adult education in the words I have chosen to frame this book.

> A fresh hope is astir. From many quarters comes the call to a new kind of education with its initial assumption affirming that *education is life* – not

merely preparation for an unknown kind of future living. ... The whole of life is learning, therefore education can have no endings.
(Lindman 1926:6)

Eduard Lindeman's vision for education was not one constrained by classrooms, timetables and formal curricula. His vision was framed by a concern for the educational possibilities of everyday life; non-vocational ideals; situations not subjects; and people's experience. That pretty much sums up my own view of lifewide education.

Endnotes
1 http://imaginativecurriculumnetwork.pbworks.com/
2 Robbins Report (Committee on Higher Education 1963); Dearing Report (1996).

Chapter 7

Freedom to learn: a radically revised pedagogy to facilitate lifewide learning in the academic curriculum

John Cowan

Synopsis
Higher education has progressed fairly steadily to a common pedagogical approach which centres on the idea of *alignment*. In this arrangement, intended learning outcomes are identified and declared; learning activities which will enable the desired learning and development to be achieved are conceived and undertaken with the support of appropriate and effective teaching; and assessment which calls for these outcomes is (ideally) carefully designed and implemented. All three elements are aligned in advance. The same principles and practices underpinned by notions of alignment have been applied to date in most of the purposeful schemes for personal development planning. In this Chapter I argue that lifewide learning, wherein learning and development often occur incidentally in multiple and varied real-world situations throughout an individual's life course, calls for a different approach, and a different pedagogy. Higher education should visualise lifewide learning as an *emergent* phenomenon wherein the outcomes of learning emerge later on, and are often *un*intended. Consequently, they cannot be defined in advance of the activities through which they are formed. This Chapter offers some practical ideas on how lifewide learning might be embedded in academic programmes.

Introduction
The aim of this Chapter[1] is to answer the questions *why* and *how* should we develop and adopt a new and independent pedagogy for curricula which feature and honour students' lifewide learning? I begin with the bold assertion that trail-blazing efforts in lifewide learning have been hampered, to date, by established

academia, which has treated this innovation, at best, as something to be simply added to current practices. In such cases it has been assumed that we can retain the main features of the established approach and graft on additions (in various forms) to cater for lifewide learning. In this Chapter I distinguish between the treatment of lifewide learning virtually as an extra-curricular activity, and its integration as an independent co-curricular component of higher education, with its own appropriate curriculum, assessment and pedagogy – an approach which Baxter Magolda (2009) describes effectively and persuasively in terms of many recent examples of Learning Partnership Models. For I assert here that lifewide learning should be distinct in its own right, and so merits distinct consideration – especially where matters of pedagogy and curriculum design are concerned. Those who want to see lifewide learning sited firmly in learners' programmes are therefore confronted by the challenge of developing and practising a new lifewide learning pedagogy.

Pedagogy of the status quo

Over perhaps the last twenty-five years, a fairly explicit and directive pedagogy has emerged for programmes of higher education in the United Kingdom. The characteristics of this approach are that:

1. Programmes are conceived by teachers.
2. Programmes or courses are subdivided into self-contained modules.
3. Each module has its own explicit learning outcomes which the course team has decided that learners should achieve.
4. Assessment is arranged by the course team to validly and reliably determine achievement of these intended learning outcomes.
5. Learning and teaching activities should be purposefully planned to support achievement of the intended learning and development.
6. The desirable integration and compatibility of items 3 to 5 is described as alignment or constructive alignment (Biggs 2003), and is featured as a desirable goal or ultimate quality of well-designed curricula.

Consequently, assessment by teachers of the achievement of specified competences by learners (confirming what they can do), according to predetermined criteria and at an appropriate level, is a core feature – except perhaps in those few schemes that embody self or peer assessment.

Personal development planning

The advent of planning for personal development as a central feature of learners' programmes (QAA 2000) has created the impression of enhanced

learner empowerment within the traditional structure. Compared with traditional programmes:
- The intended learning outcomes are certainly predetermined; *but they are now chosen and framed by learners who have not yet undertaken the learning journey, and who have an incomplete appreciation of its demands and potential.*
- The assessment is compatible with the intended learning outcomes; *it is conceived according to the same limitations as are the outcomes.*
- Learning activity is planned towards the achievement of the chosen outcomes; *but it is necessarily planned by learners who lack training or experience in the design of learning activity, and are unlikely to conceive innovative learning activities.*
- Most importantly, the overall programme aims, the programme structure and the criteria and levels for judgements are still predetermined by teachers, and so can strongly influence the learners' exercise of autonomy.

PDP-based development in a traditional programme

I choose to test my suggestion that most PDP is to a considerable extent arranged to fit traditional structures. I do this first by considering a complete programme where I am a tutor. The details are as follows:
- In a parallel set of activities, alongside their degree programme, postgraduate MSc(HRM) students have the opportunity to prepare for Associateship of the Chartered Institute of Personnel and Development (CIPD).
- By the time they have completed their MSc programme, students who so wish should have shown themselves capable of planning, monitoring and evaluating their personal and professional development
- Most students begin this programme with little or no experience of planning for development, or evaluating progress. A short introductory workshop, based on manufactured examples, centres on offering helpful advice to the imaginary authors of mid-standard plans and claims; it then helps them to summarise how to plan and claim on the basis of SMART objectives, in terms of advice to themselves as they prepare drafts.
- The expectation (not requirement) is that students will be giving attention at any one point in time to around six objectives, divided between professional, academic and personal aims – without trespassing directly on the MSc syllabus, but otherwise freely chosen.

- During the introductory workshop, the need to begin to assemble relevant data from the outset, in order to inform judgements and substantiate claims, is stressed and exemplified. Students' forward plans should include consideration of the forms of relevant data which they can readily acquire and assemble to inform monitoring and claims.
- The learning communities in which students are grouped for course purposes should form supportive groups for their CIPD efforts.
- Students' learning communities in turn have the facilitative support of a personal development tutor, whose function is to prompt, but never to direct, the students' activities. This style of tutoring is 'nudging', in the Brunerian sense, prompting progress into Vygotsky's Zone of Proximal Development (ZPD). It takes the form of facilitative comment on claims and plans, assembled for this purpose at six-monthly intervals.
- Final claims are audited by tutors, to confirm that the requirements of the CIPD strand have been met and the procedures followed. But the claimed attainment of competences and standards is not assessed. The course team are confident in the ability and desire of self-managing, self-monitoring and self-assessing postgraduate students to prepare themselves adequately for professional life and ongoing personal and professional development, and to satisfy CIPD that they have done so. Our confidence has not so far proved unfounded.

On the face of it, this activity, which is focused on personal and professional development, appears to share many features with the traditionally designed and delivered MSc programme. It has predetermined and explicit learning outcomes (albeit chosen by individual students). Assessment is objective, systematic and appropriate, according to criteria and an expected level of demand which were decided initially by the course team. Assessment decisions are reported to assessment boards and acted upon in the usual way. The status quo remains secure.

The challenge of lifewide learning

I now submit that lifewide learning is so radically different in its nature that if we are to contemplate featuring it in learners' programmes we should ensure that it is independent of constraints arising from the characteristics and practices of other accompanying components of higher education. In particular, we need to radically rethink our pedagogy, beginning from scratch.

Again I choose to use an example to illustrate the points I make, which I claim are general for lifewide learning. My example this time is a mere component of an undergraduate module entitled *Developing Employment Skills*; but it is one whose features are not constrained to conform with those of its traditional senior partner, so to speak. Enrolment on this module is only open to students who have some kind of part-time employment, not necessarily discipline-related, and whose employers will permit these students to use this experience to contribute to their development towards enhanced employability, including the identification of an issue or problem upon which they might reflect constructively.

One component of this module calls for the identification on eight occasions of a critical incident, involving the students or directly observed by them. This should be an incident from which they may generalise and, by so doing, identify a step forward in their development. If students so wish, they can email their reflective logs to a tutor whose Brunerian comments are intended to facilitate deeper reflection. Another component of the module, often arising from a critical incident, is the identification by the student of a problem in their place of employment, and the generation of a possible solution to that problem.

During this one-semester module, a significant number of students find themselves awarded an increase in their basic pay rate; and some are promoted to a higher level of employment, especially when their project is deemed impressive by their employer. However, it has not been simple to negotiate approval and ongoing validation of this apparently successful module within the traditional environment of a conventional university.

For the important outcomes from the two components I have described are unintended, are often highly personal and only emerge as the students' experience progresses. The programme activities were not framed to facilitate specific developments; and the outcomes are at various levels, in a range of domains, and are often very difficult to substantiate, especially when they are in the affective domain. Although the module is assessed traditionally, the assessment which matters most to students, and features in their self-portrayal to employers, is their own self-judgement, framed in their own way, to their own criteria. The associated pedagogy to structure the effective supporting of the students in their creative, reflective and analytical thinking is as undeveloped as is the methodology for e-moderation which is currently perturbing many academics (Vlachopoulos and Cowan 2010).

Table 7.1 compares and contrasts features of typical schemes to support student-led lifewide learning and traditional teacher-led learning.

Table 7.1: Comparing and contrasting student-led lifewide learning with traditional teacher-led programmes

Traditional teacher-led learning programme	Student-led lifewide learning
Planning concentrates on desired outcomes; Outcomes are intended	Design concentrates on worthwhile experiences; Outcomes emerge
Activity designed to achieve outcomes	Learners have various reason for choice of activity
Most of the spaces and places for learning are chosen by the teacher/institution	Spaces and places for learning are chosen by learner
Outcomes and criteria are general	Outcomes and criteria are particular
Assessment is usually by teachers	Learners identify, represent (often in varied ways) and claim their own development
Competence is external judged	Self-knowledge is central
Learning level predetermined against generic level descriptors	Learning level emerges: this level is problematic and is judged against an individual's notion of their previous level of learning
Teachers are directive: concepts of tutor, manager, scholar, even instructor are relevant	Teachers are supportive and facilitative: concepts of coach, guide, mentor, facilitator are relevant
Outcomes, assessment and learning and teaching activities are aligned from the outset	Learning experience leads to development and, after reflective self-evaluation, to a Record of Development and a judgement on development

Complex learning and achievements

Peter Knight wrote many wise words about pedagogy. Pertinent to the present topic are remarks he made at the First International Conference on Enhancing Teaching and Learning through Assessment in Kowloon in Hong Kong (Knight 2005). There he concentrated on what he called complex learning, which for him was development located towards the higher end of the taxonomies of the cognitive and interpersonal domains. These areas were of interest to him at a conference on assessment, because learners' higher level achievements feature complex and changing constructs which do not have the qualities necessary for them to be measurable. He referred to the lists of preferred graduate qualities emerging from the researches of Harvey et al. (1997), Knight (2005) and Brennan et al. (2001), to which reference can usefully be made for amplification. Their comprehensive catalogue of desirable attributes of employable graduates is similar to many of the achievements that students are claiming from their lifewide learning.

Having stressed that complex achievements resist measurement, Knight (2005) went on to argue that, their indeterminate nature impels us to use assessment approaches that are radically different from those in routine use. Like many nowadays he favoured deliberation on the weight of evidence (ibid:2), a methodology which empathises strongly with what is emerging for many as the favoured approach to assessment of lifewide learning. The consequence of this, of course, is for universities to replace warrants with students' claims about their complex achievements (ibid:6).

He also remarked (ibid:4), that we cannot even find reliable and robust ways of fostering complex achievement. Then, in what he described as a digression, but one which is important in the present context, he made five points about fostering the type of complex achievements which lifewide learning values. These were:
- We need to think systemically or holistically about the student learning experience.
- We must eschew approaches which merely "encourage simple learning of complicated material, and offer little to the developments that employers, amongst others, value".
- Curricula which promote self-theories, beliefs about ourselves, about others and about the extent to which we can generally make a difference are more favourable to the formation of the desired complex achievements.
- That development of complex achievements is helped by metacognitive awareness.
- Tasks to promote complex achievements are those which encourage what he called "real transfer".

Rather than 'dumbing the curriculum down', it was Knight's view that it behoves us to actively foster complex learning – which is precisely what lifewide learning sets out to do. Readers of this volume will note much common ground between the aspects of the education process which Knight advocated and the priorities stressed by Baxter Magolda (2009:251) which were:
- discouraging simplistic solutions
- drawing learners' attention to the complexity of their decisions
- encouraging learners to develop their personal authority by listening to their own voices

- encouraging learners to share authority and expertise
- encouraging learners to work interdependently with others to solve mutual problems.

Propositions for a lifewide learning pedagogy

In Chapters 6 Jackson sets out ten propositions to provide guidance to learners (both teachers and students) on the types of situations and experiences that are being encouraged through a lifewide curriculum. These constitute a very real challenge for any programme designers who traditionally do not support these forms of learner engagement. They are worth considering here (Table 7.2) because teacher/tutor designers would need to give careful consideration to these propositions in designing their programme.

Table 7.2 Ten propositions for an imaginative lifewide curriculum.
Source: Jackson, Chapter 6 this volume.

Proposition 1: **gives learners the freedom and empowers them to make choices so that they can find deeply satisfying and personally challenging situations that inspire, engage and enable them to develop themselves**
Proposition 2: enables learners to appreciate the significance of being able to deal with situations and see situations as the focus for their personal and social development
Proposition 3: prepares learners for and gives them experiences of adventuring in uncertain and unfamiliar situations where the contexts and challenges are not known, accepting the risks involved
Proposition 4: supports learners when they participate in situations that require them to be resilient and enable them to appreciate their own transformation
Proposition 5: enables learners to experience, feel and appreciate themselves as knower, maker, player, narrator, enquirer, creator and integrator of all that they know and can do, and enables them to think and act in complex situations
Proposition 6: encourage learners to be creative, enterprising and resourceful in order to accomplish the things that they and others value
Proposition 7: enables learners to develop and practise the repertoire of communication and literacy skills that they need to be effective in a modern, culturally diverse and pluralistic world
Proposition 8: enables learners to develop relationships that facilitate collaboration, learning and personal development
Proposition 9: encourages learners to behave ethically and with social responsibility
Proposition 10: encourages and enables learners to be wilful, self-directed, self-regulating, self-aware and reflexive so that they develop a keen sense of themselves as designers/authors and developers of their own lives, appreciating their learning and developmental needs as they emerge

At first sight it might seem that this learner-centred arrangement encompasses no role for teachers. But closer inspection reveals that the propositions almost all imply teaching persons as the subjects for the various active verbs within their wordings, whose objects grammatically are the learners. If lifewide learning is to become part of the core educational offer of universities, it will surely be teachers or tutors or teacher-planned frameworks that *enable, encourage, support, prepare and give permission or empower* and ultimately *recognise and validate* the learning. It will be their notions of standards in this learning environment that will ultimately be recognised through an award. What is emphasised in Table 6.2 is the overarching importance of the first proposition which must be at the heart of any pedagogic model. The remaining propositions provide guidance on the focus for learning and development, facilitation and collaboration in tutor–student interaction.

Towards a pedagogy for lifewide learning

I now outline some tentative steps towards a pedagogy that might enable lifewide concepts and practices of learning and education to co-exist with other components of programmes in higher education – and vice-versa. In so doing, I have been immensely attracted to Maret Staron's ideas (see Chapter 8) of an ecologically sound learning and pedagogy, with its ever-shifting relationships, and interdependence.

1. It is paramount that lifewide learners have freedom to choose – their aims, their activities through which they will learn and develop, and the criteria by which they will judge their learning and development in due course. Hence their learning during the lifewide experience should be autonomous. The experience should be one within which they are free to plan, manage, monitor, change and evaluate their learning and development. In that sense their activity might be described as 'ring-fenced' from the interference of tutors (Figure 7.1).

2. Outwith the ring-fence are located the various involvements of what may be described as teaching people or people who support the learner and their learning. It is here that the design for a lifewide learning programme is conceived. It is here that the programme team, in many cases in negotiation with learners, will ensure that:
    - roles are defined for learner, tutors, administrators – and assessors, if necessary
    - the mode and expectations of assessment (the persuasive hidden curriculum) are decided and communicated to learners

- whatever statement about the criteria that will be applied is formulated
- potentially useful inputs, whose use is never mandatory nor even presumed, are created and made accessible
- tutors and teachers are available and may be commissioned to provide specialist instruction, information or even advice, as in some problem-oriented project-based learning (Moesby 2006)
- tools of enquiry, and methods used to support enquiries, are available in digest form, for reference
- tools for recording and meaning making are provided, again recognising that there must be freedom of choice in the way learners record and represent their learning. There is no room for a 'one size fits all' approach here.

Figure 7.1 Integrating lifewide learning into the academic curriculum by giving learners the freedom to choose their activities and experiences through the idea of 'ring-fencing'

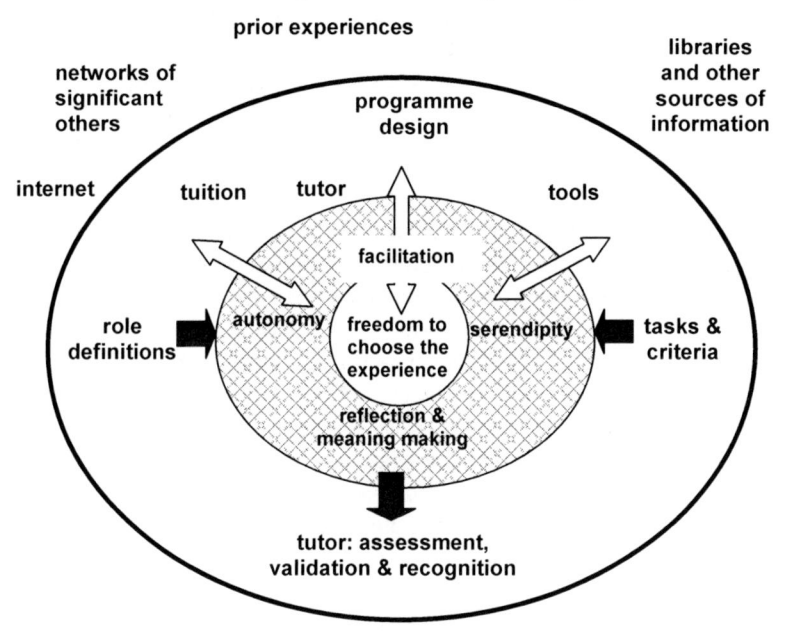

3   Within the ring-fence, the learners should be free to negotiate, decide, plan, prioritise, act, judge and interact as they so wish, as they direct,

monitor and record th eir own representations of self-taught learning. Any tutor's activity within the ring-fence can only be facilitative – to encourage, support, enable, prompt and challenge in a constructive way. The events which occur within the ring-fence, once the lifewide experience has commenced, will often entail serendipitous inputs, unexpected experiences, unplanned affordances and fresh challenges and opportunities – all of which the learners will or should respond to autonomously. During their experiences, the learners will draw on familiar worldwide sources such as the internet, libraries, their own networks of people including peers and of course on their own prior experiences. On conclusion of their focused activity, the learners should reflect within the ring-fenced activity both on their learning and on their development. They should also reflect meta-cognitively on the processes they have followed, and how these, like their development, may benefit from enhancement in their next lifewide learning experiences.

4 Outwith the ring-fence is the tutor whose other function, besides design, facilitation (and perhaps collaboration as knowledge is developed and shared), is the evaluation and validation of the learners' own judgements on their learning and personal development.

Roles of teacher/tutor/educator

These ideas for a pedagogy to support lifewide learning have important implications for the role of the teacher, tutor or significant other who supports learners and their learning. I take guidance here, as my title implies, from the writings and teaching of Carl Rogers (1969, 1983). He spelt out two principles describing the style of a facilitative teacher in contact with learners within such a setting as lifewide learning. The first was that the support of learners in a learner-directed context should feature congruence, unconditional positive regard and empathy, which at times he called genuineness, acceptance and understanding. The second was that the facilitator of such learning should become a fellow learner. Both principles describe with helpful precision an effectively facilitative tutor/student relationship.

Rogers also wrote of the role of teachers in setting up such learner-directed situations. He spoke of *modes of building freedom*. He gave many examples of how to create the conditions for responsible self-directed learning. He discussed how teachers with that intention concentrate on making resources clearly available by thinking through and simplifying the practical steps the student must go through. These are areas of responsibility which should be undertaken and completed, albeit in negotiation with the students, *before* the learning activity begins and hence outwith it.

The three principles of educational practice underlying the Learning Partnerships approach developed by Baxter Magolda (2004) to facilitate learner's journeys towards self-authorship and described by her in Chapter 5 are entirely consistent with Rogers' clear annunciation of the principles of a facilitative pedagogy. However, Rogers, and those who have tried to follow his example, moved rather sooner towards self-authorship and refrained from acting in a guiding role, like the fellow traveller on the rear seat of the tandem in Baxter Magolda's metaphor:

> The first principle, *validating learners' capacity to know* ... invited participants into the knowledge construction process, conveyed that their ideas were welcome, and offered respect that boosted their confidence in themselves. ... The second principle, *situating learning in learner's experience,* was evident in educational and employment settings that used participants' existing knowledge and experience as the basis for continued learning and decision making. ... The third principle, *mutually constructing meaning,* involved educators and employers connecting their knowledge to that of the participants to arrive at more complex understandings and decisions. This welcomed participants as equal partners in knowledge construction, helped them clarify their own perspectives (emphasising autonomy), and helped them learn how to negotiate with others (emphasising connection). The blend of connection and autonomy inherent in constructing meaning supported learners in moving towards the mutuality characteristic of self-authorship.
>
> Baxter Magolda (2004:42–3)

Possible lifewide learning format

1. Teachers design a programme framework which will encourage and permit learners to engage in their choice of lifewide learning

2. The framework provides for learners to freely choose their aims, the activity in which they will engage and in due course the criteria against which they will judge their efforts and development.

3. As a preparatory activity, learners may inform themselves about several lifewide learning experiences and their assessment, discuss their

judgements and the objective making of such judgements with peers, and reflect on what they wish to carry forward from this induction into their own lifewide learning.

4. Learners now firm up on their intentions, presumably moving on from at least a vague intention which led them to express interest.

5. The programme team offers input on the collection and citing of appropriate data to inform judgements in due course by learners of their learning and development during, or as a consequence of, the lifewide learning experience. The team may offer a range of options for the recording and representation of learning and achievements leaving the learner to make the final decision as to which format to employ.

6. The programme framework encourages formative and summative reflections by learners on the process and its outcomes. This can be facilitated by tutors, if the learners so wish.

7. The programme framework makes provision for, but does not require, constructive peer interactions between learners.

8. Learners, preferably beginning this task before the conclusion of their project, collate and analyse the data they have ingathered, drawing out meanings, achievements and results against criteria of their choosing which they provide reasons for.

9. Having formulated their judgments, learners review their experiences and their evaluation of them, formulating a view about the standards of their development and of the processes they followed. They are encouraged to imagine different pathways they might have taken and to reflect on these with the wisdom of hindsight.

10. Learners' claims and reviews are then audited by peers, who seek to check these against programme procedures and the need for objectivity and comprehensiveness. Teachers/peers provide feedback to learners. In doing so they are acknowledging the validity of the personal knowledge and judgements embodied in the claims for complex achievements.

11. Learners are expected, but not required, to carry their reflective self-evaluation forward into an iterative forward plan for further development.

Concluding remarks
Teacher-designed programmes should support the ideals of autonomous lifewide education through careful consideration of propositions that encourage learners' lifewide learning and the pedagogy that supports and facilitates it.

Lifewide learning should feature learning and development for the learners, taking them beyond their level of attainment when the experience commenced. It should not centre upon the display and application of learning and competences which have already been acquired.

The effective use of teachers to promote and support lifewide learning will be in the various activities outwith the ring-fence in Figure 7.1 and (for some) in facilitation and possibly cooperation within the ring-fence. There are two dangers in the facilitator role of which all concerned should be aware:

- It would be readily possible for a gauche facilitator to limit the students' freedom, rather than to empower them as autonomous learners.

- A facilitative tutor who has been involved in an activity outwith the ring-fence when the programme was being formulated may be tempted to wander across the ring-fence to make adjustments while learning is in progress. This would seriously confuse students about their autonomy within the ring-fenced area.
(Vlachopoulos and Cowan, 2010; case study 3).

In some schemes for lifewide learning, there is a risk that catering for and encouraging individual choices may lead to disregard of the socio-constructivist potential of formative peer interaction. However, learners should be encouraged and given recognition for their efforts to create their own networks and relationships for learning and personal development.

This search for a new pedagogy, suitable for lifewide learning, has brought out several immediate findings. The first is the fact that the traditional pedagogy of the status quo is inappropriate. The second is the direct relevance of Rogers' thinking about how to ensure freedom to learn for students, in this case in lifewide learning. The third is the need to carefully consider the roles and activities of tutors once lifewide learning has commenced, lest departures confound the autonomy which the lifewide learners need to enjoy and use.

The lifewide learning process is fundamentally different from most teacher-directed situations in that it begins with the learners choosing an area of activity which may be attractive to the individual for a variety of reasons. Such activities are not purposefully selected and planned in advance to enable the learner to achieve *specific* learning; rather, specific learning emerges only later as a serendipitous by-product of doing.

Insofar as lifewide learning entails planned development, the planning is of arrangements through which the potential of the chosen activity for the learner may best be discovered and realised. Consequently, the assessment of the outcomes must be analytical and reflective; learning and achievement (often complex) should be judged against particular criteria that make sense to the individual in that context – rather than against more general criteria. Lifewide learners thus have to evolve their own frameworks for identifying, analysing and judging their own development in the particular contexts in which it has occurred – rather than being constrained to criteria devised by others. Hence learning outcomes from lifewide learning are *identified through* the assessment or review process – rather than being *confirmed by* it.

The making of objective judgements, about experiences, inputs and competences, is arguably the most demanding of the cognitive abilities, and one for which even graduate lifewide learners can profitably be prepared. Concerns about the assessment of lifewide learning can readily proliferate. Possible areas of development include the demand associated with making personal assessments; the difficulty of informing judgements regarding some of the more sophisticated of the abilities developed in lifewide learning; and the fact that the level of learning and development cannot be known at the outset, and may well be lower than the learner – and society – would have wished. Perhaps the most adequate response to these concerns is to point out that, in subsequent life, in employment, social life and even in interviews, these learners will be judged and rated for what they are, what values they epitomise and what they demonstrate in practice that they can then do – and not by whatever certification they have acquired.

Endnotes
1 This Chapter began life as a background paper to support my presentation at the Student Lifewide Development Conference at Aston University in February 2011.

Chapter 8

Connecting and integrating life based and lifewide learning

Maret Staron

> Life based learning seems initially a utopian/fantasy notion, but we live in a complex world. The notion is an honest attempt to capture the full breadth of our humanity, and apply it to our working life[1]

Synopsis
This chapter provides an overview of a research and development project in Australia that focused on capability development for the knowledge era. A new model, called life based learning, was developed through research and discussion. The basis of life based learning is that learning *for* work is not restricted to learning *at* work and that all our learning and development is interrelated. There are many similarities between the concepts of life based and lifewide learning and it makes sense to connect them. However, in life based learning there is an explicit emphasis on a strength based orientation to capability development and it would be beneficial to further explore this in the context of lifewide education and personal and professional development planning.

Introduction
The concept of life based learning is an outcome of a research project – 'Designing Professional Development for the Knowledge Era' – that examined professional development in the vocational education and training (VET) sector in Australia[2]. The research was motivated by a desire to discover what might lie beyond traditional approaches to professional development. The project team[3] was supported throughout the research phases by an international Working Group, a National Reference Group and wider audiences for feedback and dialogue on research in progress - through forums, journals, website

publications, presentations and workshops. The methodology informing the research drew on phenomenology, hermeneutics and dialogue.

A key question underlying the project was: what needed to change in professional development in the workplace to accommodate emerging technologies, business imperatives and globalisation? Other research pointed to the need to broaden approaches to training and compliance; integrate formal and informal learning; re-examine pedagogy and build capacity; and foster sustainability and resilience. The needs of customers, including students, were rapidly changing, as were the demographics of the workforce. New thinking was required around learning models that supported innovative practice in the field.

The research team's vision was that of rich, diverse, sustainable learning environments, that incorporated continuous inquiry and adaptability in complex and constantly changing settings. The team's value was around choice – that there was no one way to learn; learners knew best how to meet their learning needs; and designing how learning and development fits into and influences their lives - was potentially the best way to go.

The purpose of the research was to develop a business framework that supported this value and vision, and guided workforce planning and development in VET. The assumption was that teachers' learning would directly impact on students' learning. As indicated by Moodie (2004:6), teachers and trainers best develop student learning by reflecting and learning from their own practice as teachers.

What follows is a summary of the research[4], its core concepts, key findings and application of the research in the field. Connections between 'lifewide' and 'life based' learning are drawn out and there is reflection on the research, five years on. Implications for personal and professional development planning within a lifewide concept of learning are considered and suggestions for a strength based approach are provided.

Key concepts

The research commenced with the identification of four key concepts that underpinned a new approach to professional development: broadening the term to capability development and providing a new model called life based learning. The key concepts came from an extensive examination of literature and knowledge gathering in the field. The concepts were:
- knowledge era – the environment

- learning ecologies – the metaphor
- strength based philosophy – the mindset
- business wisdom – the actions.

Knowledge era – the environment
As we move out of the information era into what some are calling the knowledge era of the 21st Century, people are experiencing increasing complexity, diversity, uncertainty, contraction and change. This is reflected in the increasing tension between mechanistic processes vs organic and fluid ways of working and learning; the desire for predictable outcomes vs emergent outcomes; the collection of information vs the generation of knowledge; the desire to have one way of doing things vs multiple solutions. Both the concept of life based learning and lifewide learning acknowledge these contradictory, complex, diverse and changing environments and contexts.

In such environments, how we create knowledge becomes a key issue and *knowledge work* has emerged as a key generic capability. This form of work is non-linear and non-routine, more intuitive, opportunistic and networked and less driven by a pre-planned path or mindset. Knowledge workers reflect this generic capability when they tackle problems in new ways that make sense in new contexts; maintain a balance between productivity and creativity; and collaborate in both face-to-face and virtual environments (Staron, Jasinski and Weatherley 2006:24). The challenge is both individual and organisational: the creation of a happy, productive and effective workforce in environments that are diverse, contradictory and rapidly changing.

Learning ecologies – the metaphor
A new metaphor was needed. Metaphors such as 'bureaucracy' and 'networks' that suited previous eras were no longer adequate for the knowledge era. The research team chose the metaphor of 'ecology' because it embraced the idea of adaptability and 'opposites in co-existence'. They extended the metaphor to that of 'learning ecologies' (Siemens 2003) as a 'best fit' for the changing needs of working and learning. in the knowledge era.

A learning ecology metaphor is: dynamic – with ever-shifting relationships and interdependence informing learning and doing; adaptive – which is a key survival capability within an ecology; and diverse – a core requirement in knowledge work (Staron *et al.* 2006:26). It enables a move away from seeking the 'one way to get it right' to a more open *orientation* to learning – including *multiple* ways of working, learning and living. A learning ecology metaphor also invites us to work with apparently contradictory concepts that often challenge us, such as using an anticipative approach rather than a predetermined approach; using approximations rather than exactness; seeing fuzziness as a strength; and watching self-organisation happen even though there may be no explanation for where the self-organising pattern comes from (Staron et al. 2006:26). The researchers named this more open and adaptive orientation to learning: life based learning.

Strength based philosophy – the mindset

The changing paradigm for organisational change and learning is based on a *strength- or asset-based emphasis* that views organisations as mysteries to be embraced rather than problems to be solved (Cooperrider 2004:99). The focus is on collaboratively identifying what is right and enhancing it. Core strengths and solutions that already exist are identified and the aim is to *amplify* what is working. The spotlight is on the forces that help the organisation to thrive.

However, many organisations still have a culture of deficit based approaches to learning and development. Cooperrider (2004) describes the *deficit based emphasis* as one where organisations focus on what is wrong and 'fixing it' through intervention strategies. Problems are identified, solutions are brainstormed and efforts are made to 'fill the gap' This is an outmoded legacy from the industrial era.

The shift to strength based approaches is more than just wanting to 'think strengths'. It requires a shift in learning systems, processes, practice and mindset. Essentially a paradigm shift. The research identified two underpinning theories that support the shift to strength based approaches – positive psychology (Seligman 2000) and flow theory (Csikszentmihalyi 1990).

Business wisdom – the actions

Organisational wisdom builds on organisational learning and knowledge management (Hayes 2005). Wisdom emerges from the way that knowledge, values, and experience are linked and leveraged to promote learning and growth within an organisation. Baltes (2004) offers as a work in progress, seven properties that are usually part of any definition of wisdom: questioning the conduct and meaning of life; knowing the limits of knowledge and the uncertainties of the world; a 'superior' level of knowledge, judgement and advice; knowledge with extraordinary scope, depth and balance; synergy of mind and character; knowledge used for the good or well-being of oneself and others; and that wisdom is easy to recognise though it may be difficult to achieve and specify.

The concept of wisdom is central to the research project. Wisdom is strength based as it contributes to human well-being and the common good. Wisdom contributes to synthesis, aligning components together into an integrated whole; and wisdom is achievement-oriented as it has a practical orientation and guides thinking and action. (Staron *et al.* 2006:30). A focus on wisdom can help us understand how we work, learn and lead in complex and chaotic environments. It reminds us of the fundamental importance of human development and encourages us to be the best that we can be for the benefit of both ourselves and others.

Key findings
The key concepts and the related practices that the researchers investigated led them to the following three key findings:
- *Capability development* is the new emphasis for working and learning in VET.
- *A strength based orientation* to capability development is most effective for change.
- *Life based learning* is the contemporary framework for capability development.

Emphasising capability development
The research recommended that the term 'capability development' be the preferred term to 'professional development'[5]. The term capability development aligns well with the discourse around the four key concepts and reclaims the importance of people, as well as reinforcing the importance of business imperatives. It focuses on people's *confidence* in applying existing skills in new circumstances (Stephenson and Weil 1992) and integrates a broader range of strength based strategies than does professional development.

The term capability development suits the 'organic', open-system nature of the knowledge era and recognises that both individual and social processes coexist and underpin learning (Staron *et al.* 2006:39). Capability development encourages learners to be self-directed, designing their own situations for learning and sharing their knowledge with others. To support capability development, organisations need to create environments that promote and enable the dissemination of learning for the benefit of all. Both life based and lifewide learning acknowledge the importance of 'capability development' (Chapter 4 this volume).

The research defined capability development as 'supporting people being confident, capable, connected, curious and committed learners who interact with their environment so that they are in dynamic balance between life and work, and who take effective and appropriate action at work' (Staron et al. 2006:40). On reflection, Jackson's reference (Chapter 4 this volume) to capability being the ability to comprehend, evaluate and act in situations of different levels of complexity – as well as Eraut's construct 'everything a person (or group or organisation) can think or do' (Eraut 2009:6), provides a deeper perspective on capability development and it would be beneficial to incorporate such perspectives into a reworking of the researcher's definition.

Figure 8.1 Building new foundations for capabilitydevelopment.
Source: Staron et al. (2006: 41) (© TAFE NSW)

Established professional development practices such as expert centred learning and work based learning (including action learning, mentoring, coaching, communities of practice	Emerging strategies such as conversations, Appreciative Inquiry, talent management, disruptive technology and positive deviance	Openness to future potential - those that are still to emerge

Foundation values and truths such as generosity, sensitivity, authenticity, trust and goodwill

A strength based orientationto capability development
A strength based orientation to capability development does not displace what has gone before. From an ecological perspective, the 'survival of the fittest' can be applied to any strategy that is *being considered for capability development*. *Some* people will prefer known, established approaches while others will require varied and creative opportunities. This mix is best achieved through: incorporating foundation age-old values with known, established practices; providing opportunities for engagement with emerging new strategies; and an openness to future options (Figure 8.1).

Participants in the research forums believed that *values and age-old truths* were fundamental to the success of any strategy. They talked about, for example, being valued, trusted, appreciated and recognised. It became apparent to the researchers that values and truths were an important underpinning to the successful application of strength based capability development strategies.

In a strength based approach, learners are encouraged to take responsibility for their learning and select from as wide a range of strategies as possible and personalise them to meet their needs. Both life based and lifewide learning encourage this. However the lifewide learning concept could benefit from incorporating a more explicit emphasis on a strength based orientation to learning.

Life based learning

Life based learning is the suggested contemporary model for capability development in the knowledge era. Life based learning proposes that learning *for* work is not restricted to learning *at* work. The premise is that all learning is interrelated and therefore it is not easy to separate learning at work from other types of learning adults do (Figure 8.2). Being a multi-dimensional experience, adults engage in a lot of learning other than formal learning. Much of this 'extra curricular' learning influences our thinking and practice at work. This is the same premise that underlies 'lifewide' learning[6].

Figure 8.2 Moving from segmented to integrated learning. Based on Staron *et al.* (2006:44) (© TAFE NSW)

Expert Centred	Work Based	Life based	
Training	Professional Development	Capability Development	Emergent Strengths Holistic
Hierarchy metaphor	Network metaphor	Learning ecology metaphor	Adaptive Diverse Integrated
Learner as passive receiver	Learner as worker	Learner as whole person	Mutual Relationships
Strategies	**Strategies**	**Orientation**	

The aim of life based learning is to allow for more of the 'whole' person to be present at work. It acknowledges that what we learn and experience outside of work can be as important to our work as what we learn and experience at work. Illeris (2003) refers to 'life projects' that link everyday interests with professional learning. Life projects can be, but are not restricted to, family projects, work projects, service projects, leisure-time projects – all of which are integral to the identity of the individual.

Many people have skills, knowledge and attributes that are not acknowledged at work but that could significantly contribute to business results and working relationships. Life based learning recognises the importance of this. It acknowledges *multiple sources of learning* that open up opportunities for developing and using capability (Figure 8.3). The challenge is how to recognise, capture, support and utilise this more open-ended approach for the benefit of both the individual and the organisation.

Both lifewide and life based learning differentiate themselves from *lifelong* learning. Lifelong learning is seen as a continuum of learning throughout life and promotes 'learning for ever', whereas life based learning focuses on the source of learning for the purpose of workforce capability development. Lifelong learning is learning through the whole of a person's journey through life and life based learning is 'learning from the whole of a person's life at any point in time[4].

Figure 8.3 Life based learning – building on and integrating potential. Source: Staron *et al.* (2006) (© TAFE NSW)

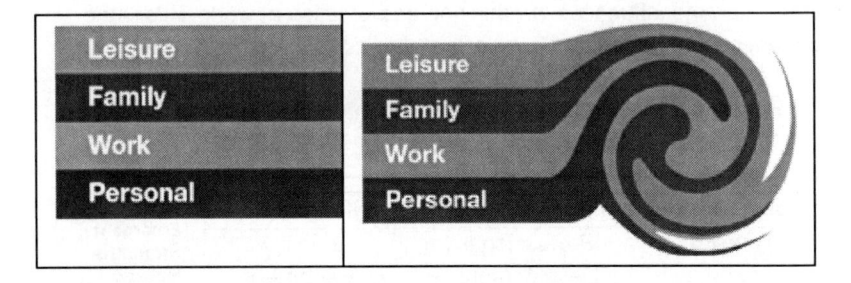

Rather than a list of prescribed strategies, life based learning proposes that it is the *characteristics of life based learning* that best support individuals and groups in the judgements and decisions they need to make about their learning. Characteristics of life based learning (Staron *et al.* 2006:46–7) are that it:

- *Emphasises capability development.* The purpose is to fulfil people's potential.
- *Promotes a strength based orientation to learning.* It is the orientation that makes the difference, not the strategy.
- *Recognises multiple sources of learning.* Supports engagement in varied learning events and acknowledges the associated capability development.

- *Balances integrity and utility.* Mindset matters. Life based learning seeks a balance between integrity of being authentic and utility of the required business results.
- *Shifts responsibility for learning and personal development to the individual.* Learning is a personal and unique event. Individuals need to take responsibility for designing their own learning and choosing options that best meet their personal and professional goals.
- *Shifts the role of organisations to that of enabler.* Organisations need to be places of rich learning, reflection and choice that optimises learning opportunities.
- *Acknowledges that contradictions are strengths.* Contradictions can lead to new understandings, practices and relationships with space for different interpretations of the world.
- *Invests in developing the whole person.* The refocus is on the human factor and 'being' through having a robust sense of self and a sense of relationship with others that enriches knowledge and skills development.
- *Acknowledges human dispositions as critical.* Basic human foundation truths are vital and *what* you know is as important as *how* you know about the world.
- *Appreciates that change is qualitatively different.* Change is both externally and internally oriented. Knowing self is as important as new knowledge and new practicesWhile these characteristics appear in list form, their true strength is in their relationship as an interconnected and integrated whole rather than as separate entities (Figure 8.4).

Figure 8.4 A holistic and interconnected perspective of the key characteristics of life based learning. Source: Staron *et al.* (2006: 47) (© TAFE NSW)

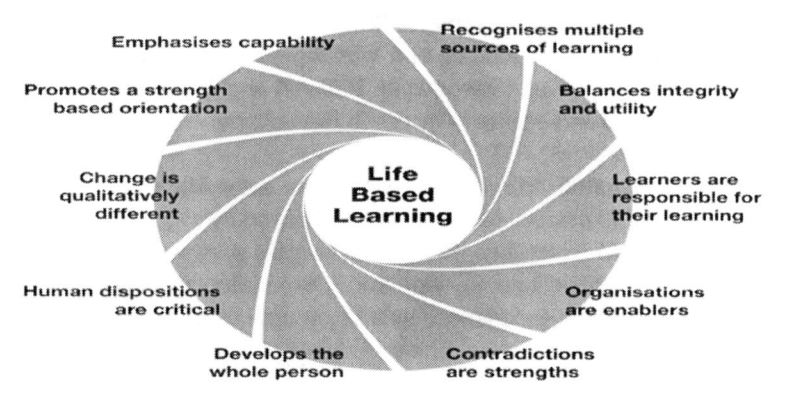

Life based learning model

Life based learning moves us *beyond the familiar models* that have been the predominant models for learning and development in vocational education and training (VET):
- the expert-centred model – focusing on the 'teacher' as the holder of knowledge, skills and experience from which the learner learns.
- the work-based learning model – focusing on learners learning from the 'teacher' as well as from facilitated learning experiences through work projects and action learning processes at work.

Life based learning does not discard the expert centred and work-based learning models. It embeds the models within an *expanded* model of life based learning – it 'grows' the image of learning for work. Being *a model for growth and the realisation of personal potential* (Figure 8.5), life based learning is adaptive, self-facilitated and based on reflexive practice, making use of any strategy appropriate to the task. Strategies can be sourced from any model that works for the individual – whether expert centred, work based or through life experiences. The preference may be for one learning approach over the other or all three may co-exist. Like any model, life based learning will morph and shift over time as people engage with it and reshape it to fit their context.

The four distinguishing features that a life based learning model needs to retain are:
- an emphasis on *strength based orientation* rather than strategy
- explicit recognition of underpinning *foundation truths and values*, which for the participants in the research forums included trust, mindfulness, generosity, consideration and tolerance
- *integration* of the best of traditional formal and informal approaches to learning with learning through life experiences
- acknowledging the *learner as a 'whole' person* who accesses many sources of learning (Staron et al. 2006:49) and who learns in a holistic way (Beard and Jackson Chapter 3 this volume).

In the national research forums, participants were enthusiastic about the life based learning model because it articulated what was familiar and known to them, and proposed a way forward that was tangible and realisable. For them, the benefits of life based learning were that it: expanded perspectives on learning, legitimised life experiences as a key source of learning and acknowledged the whole person. The main types of life based learning experiences that participants identified were: significant life events, developing

Figure 8.5 The life based learning model.
Source Staron *et al.* (2006:50) (© TAFE NSW)

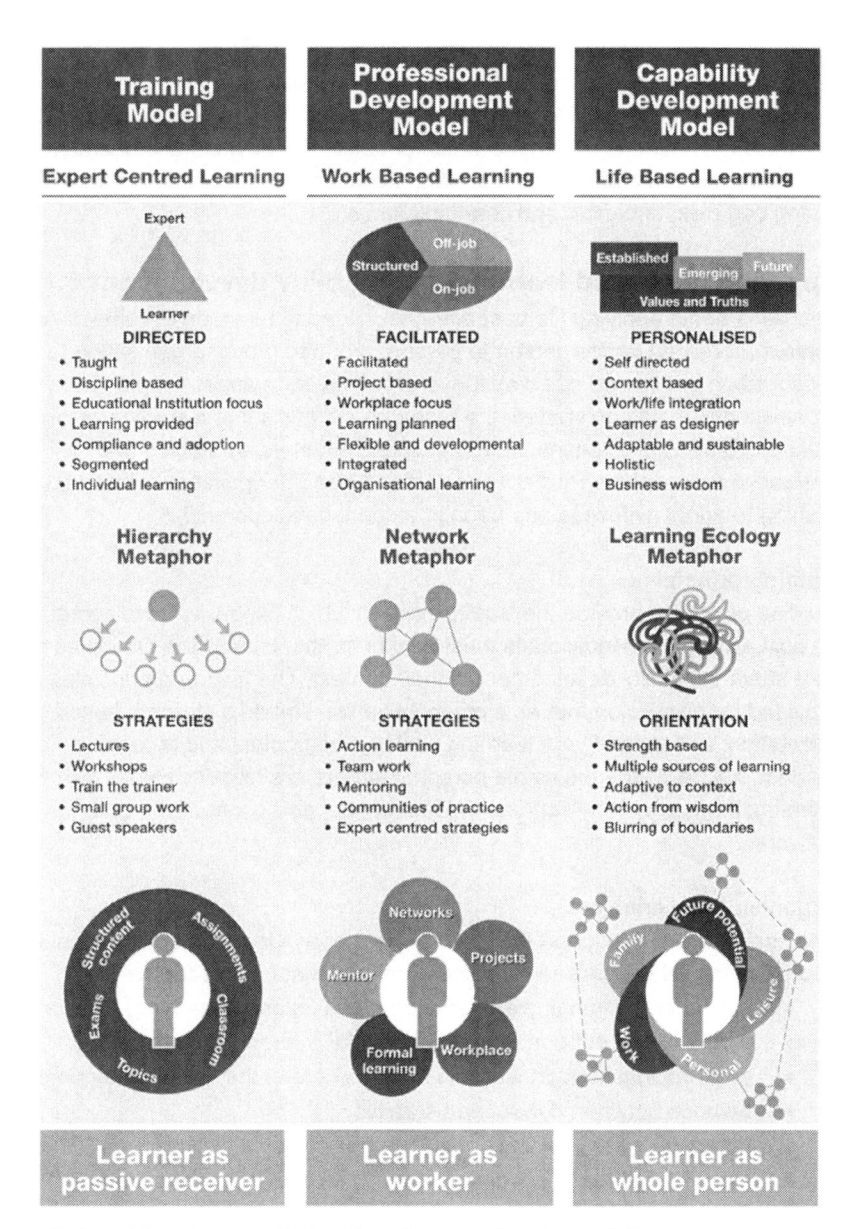

Training Model	Professional Development Model	Capability Development Model
Expert Centred Learning	Work Based Learning	Life Based Learning
DIRECTED	**FACILITATED**	**PERSONALISED**
• Taught	• Facilitated	• Self directed
• Discipline based	• Project based	• Context based
• Educational Institution focus	• Workplace focus	• Work/life integration
• Learning provided	• Learning planned	• Learner as designer
• Compliance and adoption	• Flexible and developmental	• Adaptable and sustainable
• Segmented	• Integrated	• Holistic
• Individual learning	• Organisational learning	• Business wisdom
Hierarchy Metaphor	**Network Metaphor**	**Learning Ecology Metaphor**
STRATEGIES	**STRATEGIES**	**ORIENTATION**
• Lectures	• Action learning	• Strength based
• Workshops	• Team work	• Multiple sources of learning
• Train the trainer	• Mentoring	• Adaptive to context
• Small group work	• Communities of practice	• Action from wisdom
• Guest speakers	• Expert centred strategies	• Blurring of boundaries
Learner as passive receiver	**Learner as worker**	**Learner as whole person**

Life Based Learning: a model for integration, growth and potentiality. © TAFE NSW ICVET a talent and recreational interests. Participants were able to articulate how their life based experiences transferred to the workplace and how it impacted on themselves, their students and their teams.

The research concluded that there is no one way or best approach to successfully implement life based learning – it depends on context. Organisations need to determine which enablers will be most useful and how to effectively support staff in their learning, growth, adaptability and resilience during complex, uncertain and changing times.

Applying life based learning to capability development

Decisions about applying life based learning need to be made in context. As context (or reality) varies person to person, group to group, organisation to organisation there is no one way forward. However, to assist people and organisations in getting started, the research suggests that a starting pointing point could be to re-examine their principles, enablers, strategies and evaluative approaches. Perhaps these ideas also offer pointers to institutions wishing to adopt a lifewide approach to student development?

Guiding principles

Guiding principles provide the 'scaffolding' on which capability development can be built. Groups and individuals must decide for themselves the principles that best serve capability development in their context. The following principles are provided for discussion, not as a prescriptive list: embed a strength based orientation; understand your learning ecology; appreciate and recognise wisdom; acknowledge the whole person; learners are responsible for their own learning; there are many sources of learning; support connections and networks.

Organisational enablers

The enablers aim to support the development of rich learning environments. The following list is provided for discussion and is not a prescriptive list:
- space for exchanging and sharing ideas (informal learning)
- a culture that supports job reshaping for personal growth
- systems that support learners as designers of their own development
- balance between control and creativity
- capitalise on the benefits of an intergenerational workforce
- focus on futures in education rather than futures of education (Slaughter 2005).

Strength based capability strategies

Established capability development strategies (i.e., those strategies that practitioners in the research forums were familiar with) may have a strength based orientation or, if not, can be easily adapted. Practitioners identified established strength based strategies as: action learning, communities of practice, coaching and mentoring. What matters is how these strategies are applied. Unfortunately many practitioners said that strategies such as mentoring have been applied with a negative focus on weaknesses rather than on building strengths.

Many 'new' and *emerging strategies* align well with the concept of learning ecologies and their methodologies have been developed around a strength based focus. Practitioners in VET were not very familiar with these emerging strategies (apart from conversations). They include but are not limited to:

- *Conversations* – which are integral to daily organisational activity and are a source of rich learning. They are central to how we interact and learn as human beings and can be a primary strategy for knowledge generation and relationship building. Candy (2004) suggests that conversations include dialogue with colleagues; asking questions of someone who knows more; and internally, involving introspection and reflection. Many models and tools are available to facilitate conversations. Popular models are World Café[7], Open Space Technology[8] and Strategic Conversations[9].
- *Talent management* - is about identifying, valuing, guiding and nurturing the talents and aspirations of employees (and not just the 'high fliers'). Untapped talent is a wasted business asset. Talent management strategies can cater for varying intergenerational needs; can identify what talent is needed to achieve goals; whether it is available within the organisation or needs to be 'bought in'; and how to recruit, retain and develop that talent.
- *Positive deviance* is about the people who function better and achieve more than others with the same set of constraints and resources as everyone else. These people are known as 'positive deviants' (Crom and Bertels 1999) and they achieve success by defying conventional wisdom. Identifying these people and the principles they apply provides the background to distil the principles of success within that culture.
- *Appreciative Inquiry (AI)* is based on the premise that organisations change in the direction in which they inquire (Cooperrider and Whitney 2002). An organisation which keeps inquiring into problems will keep finding problems and an organisation which inquires into what works

best will keep finding more and more that works well. AI amplifies what works well, thereby building a future where the best becomes more common. AI involves five phases: choosing an affirmative topic; discovering what gives life to an organisation; dreaming of what might be; collaboratively designing what could be; and delivering results through implementation and review.
- *Disruptive technology* - challenges orthodox ways of doing things (Christensen 1997). It can occur through the introduction of a new technology, product, process or service that eventually overturns the existing dominant way of doing things – even though initially it performs worse than the leading technology of the time. Disruptive technologies offer alternatives to established technologies and are perceived by some as being more agile, responsive and empowering.

Evaluation

Traditional methods of evaluation may not suit capability development in rapidly changing and complex environments. They are often deficit based rather than strength based, trainer directed rather than self-directed, past rather than future focused, pre-determined rather than emergent, and event focused rather than personalised. Many traditional evaluative processes are still relevant for certain areas of learning and development, although how effective they will be when evaluating in increasingly diverse, uncertain and complex environments with high levels of innovation and knowledge sharing is questionable.

The research identifies two evaluative approaches that appear to be more aligned to life based learning for capability development in the knowledge era:

- *Appreciative Inquiry (AI)* embeds self-evaluation into the processes used to discover the core strengths and best practices within an organisation. Key evaluative questions have been developed for each of the four phases in the AI process.
- *Most Significant Change* (Davies and Dart 2005) involves regular monitoring and the collection of significant change stories from the field that are shared and discussed across the organisation. The process is relatively easy to use, contributes to the sharing of values, and monitors and evaluates emergent and unexpected shifts and changes.

Life based learning offers a way forward at a time when many industrial era processes are no longer working. It opens the way to re-energising people, honouring what has worked well in the past and realigning current and emerging strategies to a strength based orientation. Life based learning expresses what many people know and feel and provides a dynamic model for capability development in the knowledge era.

Life based learning is holistic in nature, being much more than an 'add-on' or piecemeal approach. It requires astute, context-specific thinking and an openness to intuition and serendipity. It is only a beginning and, as such, will be reinterpreted and applied in various ways.

Throughout the Chapter the reader will be struck by the fact that the thinking developed around the idea of life based learning is totally congruent with that developed for lifewide learning. Both view learning and education for work and future life through the lens of a complex and changing world and both reclaim the importance of the whole person element.

Both see learning and personal development as a whole-of-life venture (or ed*v*enture). Learning cannot always be predicted and it emerges in partly intended and partly unanticipated ways. Both focus on the need for learners to take personal responsibility for designing their own learning and both encourage learners to recognise and take advantage of opportunities as they emerge through everyday interactions and relationships.

Both life based and lifewide learning recognise that individuals integrate and apply what they learn from different parts of their lives to the challenges and problems they encounter in their daily lives. In effect, they transfer their learning to a new context and adapt themselves to perform in, and deal with, the situations in which they are involved.

Although implicit in the lifewide learning idea, life based learning has explored the idea of a strength based approach to capability development much more systematically, and there is advantage in integrating this idea more firmly into the lifewide learning model in higher education.

Applying life based learning (some reflections)

It is five years since the 'Life based Learning' research report was published. During that time people have reacted in different ways to the research. Some have embraced it wholeheartedly and others have ignored it or resisted implementation.

Adoption of life based learning
Initially, the greatest interest was from those involved in e-learning. They viewed the life based learning model for capability development as more A realistic and inclusive than previous learning and development models. Life based learning gave them a holistic learning context through which they could incorporate their extensive global networks, and design when and how they learnt in both virtual and non-virtual learning environments.

Other groups that also responded enthusiastically to life based learning were community and outreach groups involved in on-campus and off-campus learning. The teachers incorporated elements of the life based learning model into their practice, particularly for groups such as refugees and those undertaking community projects. For some, the model aligned well with their community and family-based learning. Teaching section heads have used strength based approaches such as Appreciative Inquiry for planning and supporting staff. In one institute, the life based learning model was adapted to leadership development where potential leaders were provided with multiple self-directed learning options.

During the past two years anecdotal evidence suggests that managers and groups continue to take on board elements of the life based learning model rather than the whole model itself. Most interest is expressed in adoption of strength based strategies such as Appreciative Inquiry and conversation-based learning. The methodologies of these strategies are often modified and adapted to meet local needs. More people are starting to speak the language of learning ecologies, with particular reference to adaptability, diversity and multiple options.

Resistance
Change frequently brings resistance. The 'new' or different way bumps up against the 'old' or common way causing tension. At times, the resistance is strong enough to stall the change. This is not surprising as life based learning entails a paradigm shift. People find it difficult to sustain doing things differently or thinking differently within educational systems that are often bureaucracies that are slow-moving, rules bound, deficit based and teacher-directed. Resistance can come in different forms, such as:
- *Support in disguise*. Senior management can be very supportive until it is expected that they will need to change as well.
- *Change is great as long as it's the change I want to make*. People say 'I love change.' However, I have noticed that they love change provided it

is the change they want and that minimally challenges their world views, habits, attachments or desires.
- *Fear of self-organising systems.* Senior management frequently seem to fear self-organising systems. I assume they equate it with anarchy and loss of control and power.
- *A mismatch between rhetoric and doing.* Often the support for change is in the form of rhetoric and the actions do not match the words. For example, people now speak of facilitation instead of teaching, outcomes instead of outputs, capability development instead of professional development and perhaps in the future life based instead of work-based learning and strength based instead of deficit based strategies - while there is little real change in processes and practice. However, perhaps it is just a matter of time?
- *The need for instant results.* We seem to live in a 'quick fix' society. Change takes time, and when those providing funds cannot see widespread results in short timeframes they frequently withdraw resources and turn their attention to the 'next big thing'.
- *If we can't measure it, we don't value it.* The focus is frequently quantitative against set criteria. A limiting approach that can overlook the change that is actually happening.
- *We don't know our own values.* When people do not know or live by their core values, they may make decisions based on conditioned beliefs or the needs of others and 'sit on the fence', swinging one way and then the other. 'Just tell us what we have to do and we'll do it.' They are unable to follow through consistently with the change because the driver is 'external' rather than 'internal'.
- *Desire for certainty.* Funding bodies often want to know outcomes in advance and there is little (or no) room for emergence of the unanticipated. The surprises are ignored and some of the most important learning is disregarded.

Despite the resistance (which most of us feel from time to time), many do find ways to champion new thinking and doing and to support each other in following their own unique paths of learning and development. Shifts often occur 'underground' and the ecological metaphor suggests that meaningful change will be organic rather than driven through management. We can all make this happen and I hope that people will feel encouraged and supported by their leaders, managers, colleagues, friends and family in sharing their experience and knowledge and assisting others who would like to embrace aspects of life based (or lifewide) learning.

Implications for personal and professional development
During the last few years I have been able to reflect on the research and think about implications for personal and professional development planning. Through my own life experiences and learning I have altered some of my views and gained new insights[10]. Some of the areas I have further examined include: context, learning ecologies, role of attractors, core values, strength based orientation, designing your own learning and enablers.

Context before content
The research advises that application of the life based learning model depends on *context*. However I have observed that most people prefer to launch into *content* and strategies before considering context. Many want a common template for application that everyone can use. In reality this does not work simply because we all have such different realities or contexts.

So what is context? Context can be viewed as the 'container' that the content or learning will sit within. Context therefore varies student to student, lecturer to lecturer, faculty to faculty and location to location.

Learning ecologies – a metaphor for context
Learning ecologies is an exciting metaphor. It is more diverse, expansive and complex than previous metaphors such as 'networks'. It is in its infancy in use in educational settings. I suggest that learning ecologies can be viewed as a *metaphor for context through the lens of learning*.

The purpose of identifying a learning ecology (or context) is to gain a deeper understanding of a persons' (or groups) relationship with their lifewide (or life based) learning environment. This will be unique to each individual or group. For students, it can help them see the 'bigger picture' or have a 'helicopter' view. After examining their learning ecology they can reflect on:
- Assumptions – whether their assumptions about learning help them fulfill their aspirations.
- Strengths – whether their strengths align with their values, goals and purpose.
- Reality – recognise that their reality (or context) is both 'internal' and 'external'.
- What works and what does not work – so that they focus on what works for them and helps achieve their dreams.
- Different perspectives – from which perspective they view their learning ecology, whether mental, emotional, physical and/or spiritual, or

whether a formal, informal or lifewide learning perspective, and what this tells them about their relationship with their learning environment.

Learning ecologies can be expressed in many ways – drawn, written, spoken, thought about in whatever medium is meaningful to the learner A good example of this is SCEPTrE's 'educational vision' (Figure 1.1 Chapter 1 this volume) that symbolically shows the relationship of a learner with their learning environment.

Another way of portraying a learning ecology is through 'five circles' (Figure 8an approach adapted from Armstrong (2003).

Figure 8.6 The five circles of a learning ecology (Armstrong (2003)

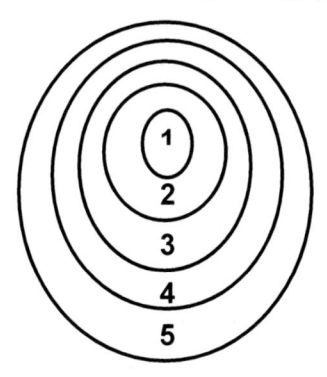

To create your own learning ecology map, draw five circles (as shown in Figure 8.5), reflect on the following and within each circle draw or write your responses:
- In the first circle –those things that are *always, consistently* important and valuable to you in relation to your learning. It may be something about yourself, your friends, teachers, resources, feelings, goals, subjects, educational institutions, time, culture, hobbies, personal learning characteristics, work, skills, etc. It may be one thing or many things, or nothing at all at this point in time. That is fine as there is no right or wrong way to complete the circles.
- In the second circle –those things that work for you most of the time in relation to your learning. You do not have the same certainty about these things as you do for what is in your inner most circle, however they are important to you and influence your learning. You feel happy about these things most of the time.

- In the third circle – place those things that you feel are missing from your learning environment, that you want to acquire because you believe it will help you with your learning. It may be people you want to get to know, things you want to do, knowledge you want to achieve, personal attitude you want to change, etc.
- In the fourth circle –those things that you believe hold you back from maximizing your learning and your potential. It may be aspects of yourself, other people, lack of resources, life experiences, requirements of educational institutions, the work place, etc. Often these are the 'shoulds' in your life or things you resent. Acknowledge it, make peace with it and commit to re-focusing on those things that work for you.
- In the fifth circle –those things that have angered you or hurt you during your learning experiences, whether through family, friendships, life experiences or formal learning settings. Acknowledge it, witness (rather than re-experience) the hurt or anger and do your best to let it go. Turn the energy towards those areas that strengthen your development and creativity.

It may be helpful after completing the five circles to reflect on:
- The opportunities or 'openness' in your context – the areas (people, resources, policies, attitudes, networks, behaviour, technologies, values etc) that allow you some 'stretch' or opportunity to expand and achieve your goals.
- The 'non-negotiables' or barriers in your context – the areas (people, resources, policies, attitudes, networks, behaviour, technologies, values, etc) that inhibit or block your expansion or achievement of goals.
- How to make better use of the opportunities. (It is a bit like playing a game of darts – you want to find the spaces that lead you directly to your goal and to avoid or spend minimum time being blocked or losing ground.)

Sometimes what one person sees as a non-negotiable another sees as an opportunity, or vice versa. This is a reflection of people's differing realities or contexts. At other times there is clear agreement between people about the non-negotiables and opportunities – they share the same reality or context. What kind of a match or mismatch have you experienced between student and teacher learning ecologies? The aim is one of acceptance and making room for all realities.

The role of attractors

An aspect of the knowledge era that has not explicitly been referred to in the research is that of the role of attractors. As we try to make sense of all the information that bombards us, we let some in and filter out the rest. This reflects our *values* because what we value we 'let in'. However, if we are run by our conditioning (rather than our values) the attractor is external to us. We easily get distracted by the competing goals, purpose and tasks that the organisation has set for us. However, when we live our core values we hold the attractor inside ourselves and we attract to us those things that are compatible with our core values. Research suggests that organisations need values-driven people.

Core values

Values are the foundation or bedrock of any approach to personal and professional development. They are not our conditioned beliefs that shift and change over time. Core values (or gifts) are integral to our being. A core value(s) could be, for example, any one of the following: choice or creativity or beauty or happiness or security or transformation or friendship or travel or being in nature or knowledge or prosperity or service or physical strength or courage or faith or as in my case, being authentic – just to give a few examples.

Core values drive what we do – consciously or unconsciously. When strategies, plans or methodologies do not match our core values, then conflict or dissention arises. The core value of one person can 'clash' with the core value of another, such as security versus risk taking. The aim is to have an environment of allowing and space for all. Be clear on what your core value is and whether or not you are prepared to compromise it when you plan or design your learning.

Designing own learning

Designing your own learning is a feature of both life based and lifewide learning. However, designing learning may be quite different to that of planning learning i.e. a shift from rules to that of responsibility.

A design can be defined as the organised arrangement of elements and principles for a purpose (Wikipedia). A learner's own design for learning would therefore consist of:

- *Goals and purpose.* A goal is *what* the learner is aiming for, something that the learner wants to do, for example, develop skills in drumming. The purpose is *why* the learner wants to achieve the goal, i.e. the advantage or benefit, what it will enable, or the direction it will take the

learner in, for example, joining or forming a band who share your musical tastes, having fun, earning some money and recording the band's own songs. Goals are not set in concrete. It may be that when the initial goal (drumming) is achieved, the purpose (joining or forming a band) then becomes the new goal and a new purpose (earning some money or writing and recording a song) is identified. In this way purpose can relate to continual expansion. If goals are in conflict, find a way in which all goals can be achieved. And check whether goals and purpose are congruent with core values.
- *Elements*. In visual design, elements can be, for example, shape, texture, form, value, size, direction and space. They support the uniqueness of each design. They form the 'language' of the design and can be visible and exist separately to each other[11]. What elements in a *learning design* would support the uniqueness of a person's growth and development? I would suggest that it could be the learner's values, context (or learning ecology), vision, strengths, intuition, direction, skills, attributes, passion, life's purpose, etc. What do you think?
- *Principles* – the principles of visual design oversee the relationship between the elements and inform the way a composition is arranged as a whole. They provide a common framework for the design and usually reflect values. Principles for visual design involve balance, unity, contrast, focal points, repetition, harmony, etc. What principles would inform a *learning design* producing a coherent whole? I would suggest: freedom to choose, self-determined action, lifewide (or life based) experiences, strength based orientation to capability development, holistic engagement and holistic learning, openness to what emerges, balanced, contrasting, relationships, social settings, commitment to self-regulation and self-reflection.

Successful designs for personal learning and development incorporate the elements and principles so that they serve the learners own purpose and goals. In such designs teachers adopt the role of facilitator, mentor and coach. One of their important roles is to encourage questioning (see Staron 2011 for examples of questions that might be used to help learners design future learning from a strength-based perspective.

Closing comments
It is important to keep questioning and to accept that there is no one answer or one right way to proceed. However, there will always be ways to proceed that are more effective in one context than in another. In order to gain the full

benefits of a life based approach to learning we must be open to the ever-unfolding nature of learning and development and view them as a process rather than a product. Educating our young people for life begins in the home, embraces the world of family and friends and continues through formal education and work, and all the things people do to add value to and create meaning from their lives. Imagine a world where formal education embraces these ideas and you create a world where life based/lifewide learning for all becomes a reality.

Endnotes
1 This quote is from an anonymous participant in one of the national discussion forums that were organised as part of the research programme
2 The project was jointly funded by the Australian Department of Education, Science and Training (DEST) and NSW Technical and Further Education (TAFE NSW).
3 The project team comprised myself as project manager at the time working in TAFE NSW, Marie Jasinski from Design Planet South Australia and Robby Weatherley from TAFE NSW. I would like to acknowledge the inspiring creativity of Marie Jasinski and Robby Weatherley, their extensive contributions to the research and the fun that we had together. Marie died in 2008 and we miss her.
4 The final research report is titled 'Life based Learning – A Strength based Approach for Capability Development in Vocational and Technical Education' (2006). A separate companion document was also produced titled 'A Business Approach to Capability Development – Considerations and Suggestions for Applying Life based Learning in the Workplace' (2006).
5 Participants in the research forums thought 'professional development was a restrictive term as they associated it with professional groups, training in occupational skills, short courses, workshops or project work. Most preferred the term 'capability development'.
6 Editor's note
7 World Café is a set of methods and tools for fostering an intentional creation of a living network of conversations around questions that matter (Whole Systems Associates 2002).
8 Open Space Technology is a large group process designed to promote conversations for solving real business problems and is a good example of a self-organising and emergent process (Owen 1977).
9 Strategic Conversations aims to create a strategic process and culture through stories captured from strategic conversation workshops (Strategic Conversations website)
10 I would like to acknowledge one my current teachers Catherine Wilkins of Xpand Consulting and her influence on my understanding of what my own truth is.
11 See for example designer Marvin Bartel http://www.bartelart.com/

Chapter 9

Lifewide learning habits of students

Jenny Willis and Norman Jackson

Synopsis
This Chapter examines evidence from students' self-reports of their perceptions of how and where they gain learning and development while they are at university. Two sources of information are used: surveys of students' perceptions of their learning in three domains: the formal curriculum, the co-curriculum and their extra-curricular activities, and essays submitted by students to a series of open competitions which encouraged them to reveal important learning and personal development gained from life experiences.

These data demonstrate the diversity of spaces and places from which students claim development and enable identification of the particular situations from which they believe significant development occurs. While it is clear that the students who responded to these surveys and competitions are engaged in a process of self-determined personal development, there is a tendency to under-value the informal learning and development gained in co- and extra-curricular contexts. The development of greater self-awareness, through a structured and facilitated process would seem to be a worthwhile educational goal.

Introduction
Previous chapters explained the concept and explored the dimensions of lifewide learning in order to justify why the idea has educational value and potential. But what evidence is there that students are engaged in lifewide learning? More importantly, what evidence is there that students are deliberately seeking and finding 'deeply satisfying and personally challenging situations that inspire, engage and develop themselves' (Proposition 1 for an imaginative curriculum that would prepare learners for the complexity of their future lives – see Chapter 6).We might also consider students' self-reported

development to the ideas of self authorship described in Chapter 5 by Baxter Magolda.

Our focus for enquiry into students' lifewide learning habits might be framed around a question like: what evidence is there that students are seeking or creating for themselves experiences that enable them to develop the dispositions, qualities, thinking and decision-making abilities, and practical capabilities they need to be successful and fulfilled in whatever lives they choose to lead?

This chapter draws on two sources of information:
- the results of three online questionnaire surveys conducted between 2009–10 aimed at evaluating the nature of the experiences students utilise to develop themselves and the significance for personal development of these experiences
- four essay competitions offered between 2008–11 inviting students to describe their experiences through which they gain personal development.

Together these sources of information reveal and celebrate the diverse and rich nature of students' experiences and the self-reported significance of these experiences to their personal development.

Lifwide learning orientations
From the data we have accumulated in our research studies we conclude that individuals' lifewide learning can be categorised into one of three orientations.

Career/vocational/employability orientation: where activities focus primarily on personal development for employment, an intended career or vocation. This orientation may also involve an entrepreneurial focus for people who intend to set up their own business.

> the balance of activities I have developed outside of the academic and professional world have not only enhanced my skills to work as a clinical psychologist, they have also provided me with opportunities to learn how to manage myself in new and diverse situations.
> (professional doctorate student)

> When I work as an Associate, I can integrate what I have learnt with clients' businesses and individual requirements and reflect on the knowledge and understanding I have acquired through my professional experiences. I

believe in the development of professional capability alongside academic capability, which is why I have chosen to maximise my exposure to stimuli for learning through different channels.
(MA law student)

Self-actualisation orientation: where experiences are pursued mainly for personal growth, interest, passion and self-fulfilment.

I knew when I started the course that I wanted to do more than was on offer so I chose to study French as well. I found the course very tough but I maintained my commitment to it throughout the ten weeks duration. I was bottom of the class throughout, and out of 10 practice tests only finished above bottom once! However, I am not someone who gives up easily and spent 3 days before the exam studying French from morning until late at night, and in the end it paid off, I got a 2:1 [a good mark] in the exam ... It did teach me that with hard work, commitment, lack of sleep and pure stubbornness you can get what you want.
(Level 1 business student)

The self-actualisation orientation may include a strong explorative disposition in which new experiences are sought simply because of a willingness to try new things.

Ever since starting University almost 4 years ago, I tried to fill my time with extra-curricular activities. I did not have any specific reason to do it, I just liked doing those 'extra' things and learning something new.
(MSc business student)

I have also tried archery, ice skating, trampolining, netball, fencing, ballroom dancing and salsa. I'm a member of the badminton club. On Saturdays I volunteer at the UniSport Kids Sports Club where I help monitor children as they have fun in the gym. I have been elected as the Malaysian Ambassador of the SE England for the London 2012 Games. I occasionally contribute to the university student newspaper (2 articles so far) and I am a member of the newly set up Volunteering Society. I actively participate in Student Union activities such as 'Give it a Go', 'Do More' and I'm a member of the 'International Committee'. I have learned to carve pumpkins, create my own Christmas decorations, visited Shakespeare's houses, Windsor Castle and Bath thanks to the Students' Union.
(Level 1 business student)

Or a combination of these orientations.

Questionnaire surveys

An initial questionnaire was used in 2009 to examine the lifewide learning habits of nurses (Jackson *et al.* 2010). From this pilot study a more substantial questionnaire was developed and administered in late 2009.[1] It comprised a set of questions relating to:
- learning and development within students' programmes
- experiences while at university and the significance of individual experiences to personal development
- perceptions of learning and development gained outside of the study programme.

Respondents rated each dimension on a scale of 1 to 5, with 1 being very little perceived development and 5 very significant perceived development. Qualitative data were also collected to explain ratings.

Survey 1 had 309 respondents representing all four faculties (Faculty of Arts and Human Sciences – FAHS, n = 98; Engineering and Physical Sciences – FEPS, n = 75; Health and Medical Sciences – FHMS, n = 74; and Management and Law – FML, n = 62). They included students at all levels of study (Figure 9.1). A full report of this study can be found online (Willis 2010a).

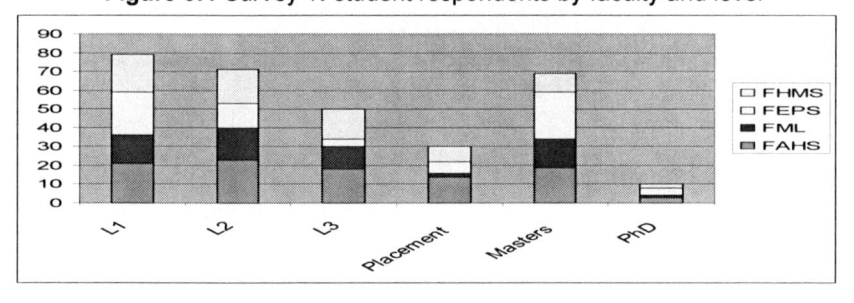

Figure 9.1 Survey 1: student respondents by faculty and level

Survey 2 utilised the same questionnaire but added supplementary questions relating to students' creative development. It was administered to students in creative arts subjects – Dance and Culture, Film, Theatre and Music, and students from Guildford School of Acting (GSA). Sixty-two students completed this survey. A full report of this survey is available online (Willis 2010b).

Figure 9.2 Survey 2: creative arts students by level of study

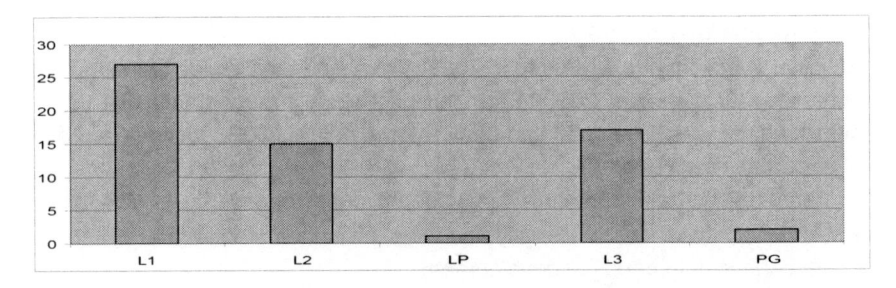

Survey 3 was undertaken at the end of 2010 in order to provide comparative data for non-creative arts students. It used the same questionnaire as previously, with minor adjustments, and was open to Surrey undergraduates in all non-creative arts subjects. There were 206 respondents, distributed across the faculties, as illustrated in Figure 9.3.

Figure 9.3 Survey 3 : student respondents by faculty and level

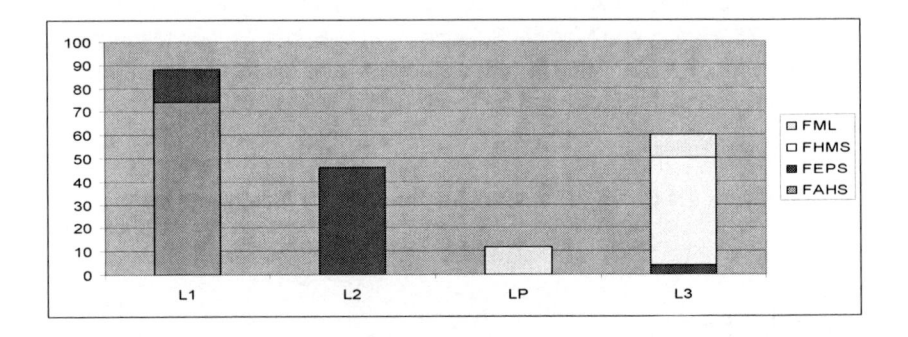

Study and learning habits

Respondents were asked in all three surveys how much time they spent each week on study-related activities. Table 9.1 shows that between 4 per cent and 11 per cent of respondents spend less than 10 hours a week on these, whilst between 19 per cent and 23 per cent spend in excess of 30 hours weekly on activities related to their degree. The norm for the majority in all three surveys is between 11 and 30 hours a week.

Table 9.1 Respondents' weekly study hours (%)

	<10 hrs	11–20 hrs	21–30 hrs	>30 hrs
Survey 1	5	17	56	22
Survey 2	11	35	34	19
Survey 3	4	39	33	23

The first section of the questionnaire focused on activities directly related to the programme of study while the second and third sections of the questionnaire related to co- and extra-curricular activity and personal development. Student responses are summarised in Tables 9.2 and 9.3. These tables show the proportions of students in each survey reporting that an aspect of development was significant or very significant (4 or 5 on the scale used); S1–3 are the three questionnaire surveys.

Table 9.2 also categorises the dimensions of learning and experience across the academic, co- and extra-curricular domains, according to whether they represent career/vocational/employability relevance (speckled cells); personal interest, passion and growth (diagonal stripes); or a mixture of career-specific and more general interests (vertical stripes). The fact that all three forms of shading occur in both domains of activity indicates that students believe that all aspects of learning and development are occurring across their lives.

Learning and development through the academic curriculum

The scores for personal development through the programme of study (Figure 9.4) are mostly high, as would be expected from formal education requiring engagement in learning-oriented activities, with assessment and feedback providing students with 'evidence' of their development. The three groups of students surveyed agree on the most significant (self-management and enquiry skills) and least significant (learning a foreign language) dimensions of their personal development.

Creative arts students (S2) attribute greater importance to creativity, adaptability, team work, listening and verbal skills than do other students. Conversely, subject knowledge appears to be slightly less important to creative arts students.

Table 9.2 Perceived development through curricular and co/extra-curricular activities. Percentages show proportion of students rating this aspect significant or very significant for their personal development.

Curricular Dimensions	S1 309	S2 62	S3 206	Co- and Extra-curricular Dimensions	S1 309	S2 62	S3 206
Subject knowledge	87	79	84	Find/apply for job	61	23	27
Analysis	76	69	82	Interview prep		16	46
Evaluation	69	79	74	Being interviewed	52	18	22
Synthesis	44	53	50	Learning in work context		21	25
Problem solving	65	58	69	Applying classroom learning		23	25
Design solutions	54	58	65	Gaining work experience	55	31	32
Enquiry skills	83	82	85	Understand how business works		18	17
Research skills	78	77	82	Being managed		15	18
Written communication	78	79	77	Professional skills	52	32	53
Verbal communication	67	81	65	Written communication	53	35	30
Active listening	75	87	77	Verbal communication	69	37	34
Use of IT	68	58	65	Graphical/visual communication		19	15
Visual/graphical	40	40	47	Listening skills	71	40	33
Experience real work	64	65	69	Assessing situations	51	31	27
Team work	70	90	71	Find out for action	65	32	28
Adaptability	68	87	71	Make decision with little information		29	25
Leadership	54	63	49	Evaluate/reflect on performance	54	34	26
Being creative	47	87	51	How to improve performance	63	37	28
Being enterprising	39	48	35	How to use IT skills	59	21	25
Ethical awareness	55	50	56	Work with colleagues	68	48	40
Self-management	81	81	84	Interact with others	76	50	45
Reflection, self-evaluation	77	76	81	Interact with clients	50	42	22
Learning language	21	15	21	Socialise with other cultures	69	29	31
				Manage others		16	20
				Manage self	74	37	38
				Manage emotions	61	34	28
				Behave ethically	56	32	33
				Negotiate with others	50	27	24
				Managing challenging responsibilities	20	15	
				Being creative	55	17	51
				Confidence in own abilities	40	35	70

Key		
Career/vocational specific relevance		
Personal interest, passion and growth		
A mixture of career-specific and more general interests		

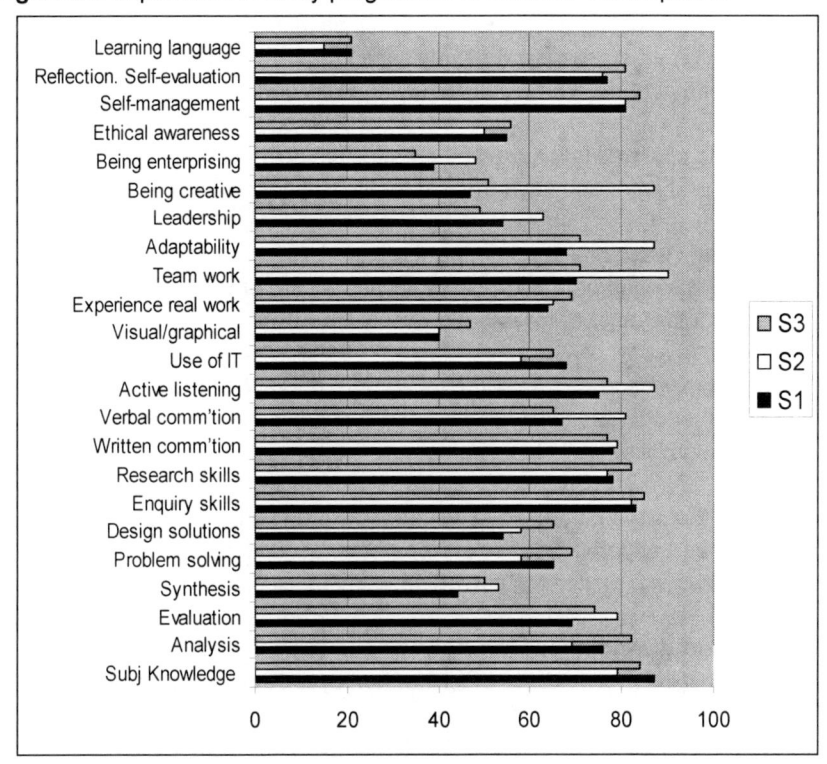

Figure 9.4 Importance of study programme in students' development

Note: Percentages represent the proportion of students rating this aspect as being significant or very significant for their personal development.

Respondents' narrative comments show insight into their development. Many feel they are learning to deal with pressure, often citing study skills and time management as instrumental to their growth.

> Deadlines etc. encourage time organisational skills meaning that as a person I am learning to be prepared and calm (not having to panic about not having things done).

One person describes this process as being helped 'to learn how to learn'. Other key themes relate to management and leadership, as illustrated by this respondent:

> There are lots of opportunities for group work, developing team work skills and communication with peers which will be vital on graduation. Also, the nature of my course means I study case studies to which I have to apply theory, helping me with problem solving skills and analysis.

Creative arts students talk more of their affective development, growth in self-confidence and independence. For instance:

> I feel that I am being taught to be a better all round performer but I am being challenged on a personal basis and so am growing as an adult and gaining knowledge of myself and of how life works.

> My programme encourages me to be more creative than I previously felt free to/thought wise to be. The course is making me more confident in my personal abilities and also as a person.

Learning is therefore perceived as being stimulated by a mixture of practical experience and opportunities to develop personal qualities and capabilities. Variations in group responses can be seen in Figure 9.5.

Learning and development through co- and extra-curriculum
Table 9.3 presents the findings of all four surveys. Dimensions have been shaded according to whether they represent career/vocational relevance (speckled cells); personal interest, passion and growth (diagonal stripes); or a mixture of career-specific and more general interests (vertical stripes). Although there is a mix of all three developmental orientations, a majority of the dimensions represented relate to personal interest and growth. For some students their co- or extra-curricular activities may be unrelated; for example the high significance accorded to new cultural learning is unlikely to be directly related to a programme of study. The table includes the ratings given by student healthcare professionals in the pilot survey (S4). Some dimensions were not included in all the surveys, hence a few cells in the table are left blank.

Some activities can be directly related to their programme of study; for example the high percentage of survey 4 respondents (94 per cent) who have a part-time job that is related to their intended career in the healthcare professions. For instance, a level 1 nurse student commented.

> I have been a member of St John Ambulance for the last 9 years and originally started nursing in 1999. Left for personal reasons and regretted it.

I jumped at the opportunity to go back and do something that I have always loved doing, working with people!

Table 9.3 Perceived development through co-/extra-curricular activities facilitated by the university but not credit-bearing

Co- and Extra-curricular Activities	S1 309	S2 62	S3 206	S4 41
Looking after yourself	80	90	82	88
Being a parent	8	0	3	46
Caring for someone	21	13	18	67
Job related to career		37	29	94
Participating professional training		29	31	
Creating or running a business	7	3	6	8
Volunteering	33	35	31	54
Significant travel experience	40	34	25	
Living in another country	31	21	28	37
Meeting/interacting with other culture	65	55	67	
Coping with personal illness	24	18	36	58
Organising something	52	47	58	60
Fund raising	17	26	17	38
Marathon / challenging experience	14	6	16	20
Duke of Edinburgh Award	4	3	6	7
Learning another language	24	15	26	23
Learning a skill e.g. to drive	24	37	32	42
Experience performing public		69	25	
Learning/playing a sport	31	15	32	28
Learning/playing musical instrument	49	56	17	
Being part of a drama group	21	18	5	38
Other creative enterprises	18	32	21	
Member of a student society		45	41	
Mentoring or coaching others	23	32	32	64
Skills-based activities organised by the Students' Union	33	32	25	4
Participating in careers events	22	11	20	
Participating in SPLASH events (student study skills organisation)	16	8	16	
Other skills-based activities	20	32	24	

We are led to hypothesise that students pursuing certain professions, such as healthcare and creative arts, are more likely to have co- and extra-curricular interests which are closely related to the field of study. Such students are pursuing a career or vocational orientation in their lifewide learning.

Other differences emerge in Table 9.3. The healthcare respondents are more likely to have parenting responsibilities, reflecting the larger proportion of mature learners in this group. They appear to have greater responsibilities as carers, raising the question, was their choice of career influenced by this experience? Similarly, they are more involved in mentoring, an activity which calls for self-confidence and experience, something which may be less highly developed in the other groups. Some of the healthcare respondents' comments confirm these hypotheses:

> I felt quite a strong calling on my life towards maternity care. I've spent some time in South America and seen the difficulties in developing countries. I'd love to spend time abroad caring for people and working with the church.
>
> Wanted to become a nurse upon leaving school – was persuaded against, became computer programmer – square peg in round hole, got redundancy, opportunity to train as a nurse and use life experience as well.

Figure 9.5 shows the percentage of students in each survey who scored a dimension of their co- or extra-curricular experiences as being significant or very significant to their development. It is immediately apparent that the aspect of most developmental significance to all three groups is having to look after themselves. This is consistent with their scores in domain 3 (Table 9.2).

Meeting/interacting with other cultures and organising something are next in importance to all groups. Unsurprisingly, performing in public is highly significant to creative artists, but not to the other groups. The dimensions of least significance (being a parent and running a business) are consistent with the young age of most respondents and do not necessarily represent lifelong values.

When narrative explanations of learning and personal development are examined, we find that co- and extra-curricular activities fall into categories such as:
- *volunteering* – mentoring schoolchildren or other students, charity work, legal support work, tutoring
- *study* – reading, attending lectures, using library and internet, being a course representative, participating in language courses
- *work experience* – part-time and temporary full-time job(s) and internships.

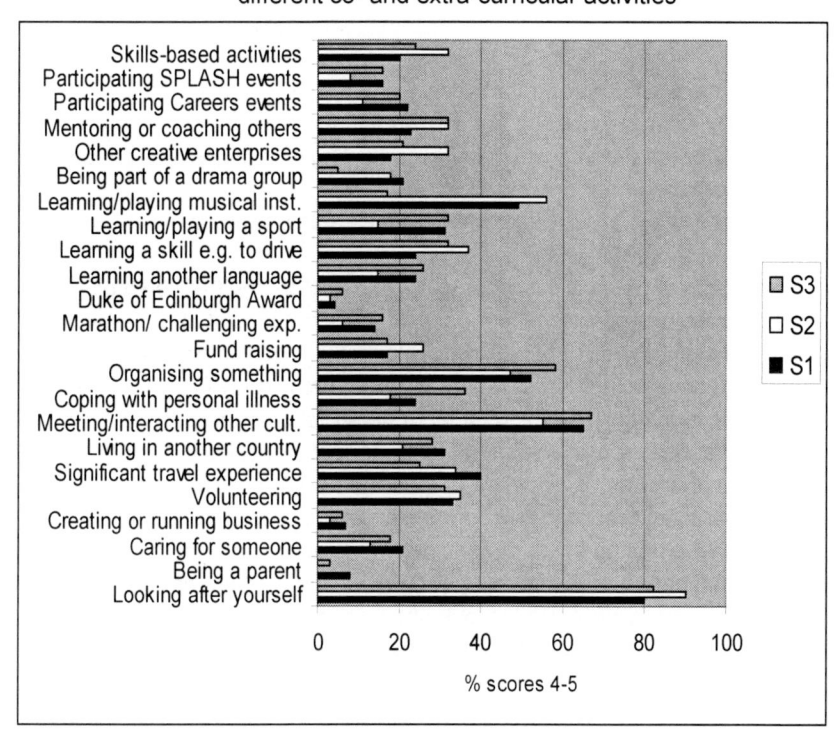

Figure 9.5 Participation in and learning from different co- and extra-curricular activities

Respondents provide insights into what and how they have learnt:

> During my second year I volunteered at a local secondary school as a languages assistant. As well as developing my public speaking skills and gaining self-confidence, I improved my time management skills, I used my initiative, and I learnt to adapt my speech and behaviour to different situations, when communicating with people of different age groups and roles within the school.

> I am currently Court Mentor and am learning a great deal from this role including building relationships in a professional manner, being open minded, and in understanding different people's personalities and views. I also have a part-time job in a retail branch which is increasing my ability to learn about technology and sell products to customers. It is helping me

> learn different ways to increase customer satisfaction, which will be a vital skill once out of study.
>
> (Level 3 engineering student)

> I have done some professional sessional work with bands, and have been constantly writing, recording and performing for years. I have also worked in children's entertainment which involves dealing with many different people and performing under pressure.
>
> (Level 2 music student)

Yet the breadth of co- and extra-curricular experience and the depth of students' qualitative comments contrast starkly with the relatively low scores given to the significance of personal development in this domain, when compared to development through the programme of study (Table 9.2, above). With the sole exception of 'looking after yourself', scores are considerably lower than those for dimensions of learning in the formal curriculum. An objective examination of qualitative evidence (supported by interview data) confirms extensive personal growth in this domain, so why do respondents fail to recognise it when rating these dimensions? One explanation is that this is due to the informal nature of the learning and development in the co- and extra-curricular domains, where desired outcomes are not explicitly specified or predetermined, and formative feedback may be absent. Given the importance of informal learning in the world outside higher education, we would argue that there is a need to raise students' awareness and to provide support to enable them to recognise and value their development in these domains.

But some students do appreciate the extensive personal development they are gaining through what is sometimes an astounding range of experiences: this level 1 engineering student is particularly astute in his appreciation of the importance of his own engagement in activities beyond the academic curriculum.

> Everything I have learned so far has helped me broaden my horizons. From philosophy to music theory and martial arts, it all helps shape us. I am who I am today because of the things I have done. What I will do in the future will depend on the things that I have done and not the things that I haven't done. Therefore it is all relevant. (...) I have practised guitar, karate, I have been part of a team in basketball in my home country and I have studied music theory, philosophy, German, Spanish, ancient Greek, history and sociology.

Student narratives of learning

The second method used to gain insights into the nature of students' lifewide development was through a series of essay competitions which encouraged students to reveal important learning and personal development gained from life experiences. Four competitions were organised between 2008 and 2011, together these competitions yielded 184 narratives.

Orientations in students' lifewide learning enterprise
Taking the 2010 lifewide learning essay competition as an example, the orientation of each narrative was identified. Table 9.4 reveals that in the 30 undergraduate and 18 postgraduate (master's and doctoral) submissions, the orientation in undergraduate essays veered towards self-actualisation (37 per cent of the subset), a combination of orientations (30 per cent) and exploration (23 per cent), whereas the postgraduate essays were predominantly career-oriented (44 per cent) or had a combined orientation (33 per cent). These general patterns probably reflect differences in age and priorities and can be explained in terms of a greater need among postgraduate students to secure entry into the job market.

Table 9.4 Orientation of student narratives in the 2010 lifewide learning essay competition

	Orientation	UG N=30	UG%	PG N=18	PG%
1	Career	3	10	8	44.4
2	Self-actualisation	11	36.7	2	11.1
3	Explorative	7	23.3	2	11.1
4	Combination	9	30	6	33.3

In search of an imaginative curriculum

The first eight chapters of this book highlighted the opportunities for learning and development that a lifewide concept of learning and education affords. Chapter 6 proposed a set of principles for an imaginative curriculum that would help and enable students develop the experience, knowledge, capabilities, personal qualities and dispositions necessary for surviving and prospering in their future world. The evidence we have outlined for students gaining significant development from activities outside the formal curriculum suggests to us that they themselves are embracing the idea of a more complete education by consciously or unconsciously seeking or creating experiences that are in tune with these propositions. In the following section we illustrate, through a small selection of students' narratives (12 in total), some of the ways in which they are utilising their lifewide experiences to develop themselves. While example stories are organised under a single proposition, most can be related to several propositions.

Proposition 1 gives learners the freedom and empowers them to make choices so that they can find deeply satisfying and personally challenging situations that inspire, engage and enable them to develop themselves. *All the stories in this section can be related to this proposition.*

> ***Story A:*** One influential experience lasted mere seconds, but the impact it had upon me then, and will go on to have in the future is endless. The experience that changed everything happened in an average clothes shop in an average town on an average day. It was on that day, in a dim lit, overheated changing room that I realised that the average UK shop no longer made trousers that were big enough to fit my waist.
>
> Up until this point my life had revolved around absent nutritional morals and an unhealthy inactive lifestyle. Everything I was ... was my own doing. This was one of the hardest things about my journey ... to accept my own personal responsibility. ... After this realisation I knew that I had to turn my past lifestyle around in order to create a better future for myself, both in terms of health and opportunity that my weight may have denied me ... a year and a half of sacrifice, development of will and determination saw me drop my weight healthily from seventeen and a half stone to ten, with a reduction in waist size of just under 20 inches.
>
> After I had lost my weight, I set the goal, that by 2009 I would become a Personal Trainer, so that I could give something back to people who were in similar situations to myself. I had grown up overweight. I had little interest in sport and had always underachieved in P.E. sessions throughout secondary school ... It has been over a year now since I qualified as a Level 3 Personal trainer, and I have continued my learning further and further, getting more and more qualified so that I can offer my clients not only advice from my own experience, but also based upon firm academic study ... On top of my university studies I have 10 regular clients who I spend an hour with each and every week, helping them get closer to their goals. The most satisfying thing is that I can have an impact on their journeys, I can get them into good habits and I can accelerate their efforts with my subject knowledge.

I developed so much as a person during my initial weight loss phase, I was able to focus on targets and achieve goals no matter what the barriers. I developed will and determination, and the ability to never give up. All these have helped me during my studies at the University and during my commercial business experiences. As a personal trainer I have learnt so much more though, most of which was completely unexpected. I have learnt what passion is, and how infectious it can be. If you are passionate about your subject, the people you teach too will be passionate about what they are learning, and as a result achieve more. I have built my confidence, so that it is almost unrecognisable compared to a number of years ago.

(Lifewide learning essay competition 2010)

For some students, deep satisfaction comes through engaging in their own spiritual development.

Story B: It is said that when one is going on a spiritual journey, then the progress happens in leaps when he/she comes in contact with someone like RJ. Another thing that I recently did is the 'artofliving' basic course and I liked it because of the things I got to learn. It is an exciting place to be at as there are so many things that are taught in the course with the lightest use of words and in an effortless fashion. They teach some simple but profound value points like:

- Responsibility increases power: so take up more responsibility in life
- Live in the present moment
- Give 100% to whatever you do
- Opposite values are complimentary
- Present moment is inevitable
- Don't see intention behind other people's mistakes
- Expectations reduces joy
- Don't be a football of other people's opinion
- Accept people and situations as they are

I must say that there is no other place where I could have had such knowledge delivered in such a way that it becomes an inherent part of my character. It is because of the teachings in the artofliving family that I have become more confident and capable of taking risk. It has of course helped me in concentrating in my studies and helped me improve my relationships. Also the teacher who I met during the course has taken this personal responsibility of helping me take more and more responsibility in life and to live every moment 100%. She has really given me hope when I had no one else to look for. I know we will remain good friends for life.

(Lifewide Learning Award submission 2011)

Proposition 2 enables learners to appreciate the significance of being able to deal with situations and see situations as the focus for their personal and social development.

Story C: In October, I was selected as one of 21 from all over Europe to attend a Gospel Choir conductor's week-long, all-expenses-paid workshop in Poland. This was an incredible opportunity and for me personally, a life-changing experience. It was inspiring to meet people from so many different cultures and backgrounds, and some with language barriers, but being brought together by the wonderful connection of Gospel music. I was so inspired by this week and longed for others to experience what I had, that when I arrived back at University, I started up a Gospel Choir. Since October last year, this choir has been growing rapidly. We now have a steady 30 attending rehearsals every Monday evening. We've developed so much as a group through performances and recordings, like a local church's carol service and the University's iGala as part of the International Festival. It has been an honour to hold the role of conductor and president of the Gospel Choir and see the passion for it spread ... The church that I attend has loved hearing about the Gospel Choir and how it developed from an idea into a reality, and we are currently in the planning stages of beginning a Youth Gospel Choir in some local schools. So many international students have been attracted to the Gospel Choir. A few have said that they love coming along because it's such a great way of meeting and getting to know others. Others have said that it is the thing they look forward to the most in the week and miss it when on holiday! The Gospel Choir has been nominated by the students as the Best New Society for the Annual Student Awards.

(Lifewide learning essay competition 2010)

A sequel one year later: This year, I have tried not to simply study robotically, (which perhaps was my approach to studies last year) but really delve into my learning and simultaneously broaden my lifewide experiences through and beyond it. It is so important to believe in yourself, especially as a musician and composer. What a privilege it is to be brushing shoulders with such a wealth of gifted musicians! Last year, I thought of myself unworthy to collaborate with these people that I looked up to. I felt a sense that I didn't belong here. However, this year I've realized that I am on a journey of self-discovery.

I met a rapper last year in a strange and uncomfortable environment; we had both agreed to assist an unknown music student in his experiment. I was blown away by this young rapper's talents and fresh, uncorrupted lyrics. For years, I had been praying for a rapper to write with ... and now, I was face-to-face with the answer to my prayers. When he asked me to collaborate with him, how could I have said no? 'First say yes, and work out how to do it later', right? So that's what I did.

This friendship has been so great; we went to London together to meet with one of his producers, and it was such an eye-opener for me to really see what a producer's life was like in the *real* world. They have both come to gospel choir rehearsals to get an idea of the sound for our track and we are now in the process of writing for the choir, him and hopefully an orchestra. Although it is a really ambitious idea, I am thoroughly enjoying the experience and am developing the necessary skills not only through my studies but also through the process of transcribing, arranging and teaching new songs to the choir; something I *never* imagined I'd be capable of doing.

(Lifewide learning essay competition 2011)

Proposition 3 prepares learners for and gives them experiences of adventuring in uncertain and unfamiliar situations where the contexts and challenges are not known, accepting the risks involved.

Story D: Knowing that the union helps fund clubs and societies made me feel like the university was my oyster. I decided to form my own Skydiving club with the hopes that it could be as successful as the other clubs out there. I had never done any skydiving in my life and I thought it would be fun to do. During December I sent an email to my department asking if people were interested in the idea. Within five minutes of having sent the message I had around 30 replies. I took the details of everyone and sent it to the union. I made at least 100 calls to dropzones all over England, France and Spain. The best place to do it ended up being in Salisbury. The dropzone was inside a big army base ... that trained both soldiers and civilians. Being the military, they had the best equipment and a very competent staff. After talking to the manager, he agreed to charge us the cheaper military rates on the grounds that we were a student sports club. To us this meant that jumps could be as cheap as £10 each.

The first trip was very intense for me. Jumping out of a plane is not a natural thing to do and I was afraid from the moment I woke up. On Saturday we did all the training that was required. Six hours of theory and an exam at the end of the day. On Sunday we geared up and got on the plane. I was shaking and felt sick. My first jump was going to be at 3500 feet and I couldn't stop looking at my altimeter. Those were the longest five minutes of my life and every moment I wanted to get off the plane. I looked around and every other person sitting next to me seemed relaxed. At that point I slowed down my breathing and said to myself 'these people are probably just as scared to jump as me, they just hide it better'. Those words didn't make me feel any better.

When they opened the door I felt true terror. The surge of cold air made me shiver even more. The loudness of the engine made me feel frantic and that door was the embodiment of every fear I had ever experienced in my life.
When it was my turn, the jumpmaster shouted:
AT THE DOOR!!
LOOK UP!!!
GO!!!!!!

When I jumped my brain immediately shut down. They call it sensory overload. Your brain is functioning normally but there is so much to take in that it loses the ability to record new information. After jumping the next thing I remember is being debriefed about the jump on the ground. After many more jumps, all that fear has turned into pure adrenaline. I no longer have sensory overload. I'm addicted to the sky and I am happy that the other members of the club are too.

(Lifewide learning essay competition 2010)

Proposition 4 supports learners when they participate in situations that require them to be resilient and that enable them to appreciate their own transformation through the transitions they make. Such situations may be very demanding physically, intellectually and emotionally, and they do not always result in success or achievement.

Story E: L was getting ready for school with one of her other nannies. She became unconscious, something switched out her light, purloined her sparkle, and she was rushed to hospital. It could have been a number of things, her epilepsy, the shunt in her brain, maybe her breakfast went down the wrong way, who knows? Standing in that hospital room, I wanted to run, get out of her life because it hurt too much. I didn't want to face it anymore. But I stayed. Like the water in the ocean; it can't choose its direction, it just gets pulled by the tide in the same direction as the other waves.

We couldn't believe she made it through the weekend ... [she] was a fighter. Seeing her the way she was, not always crying and even managing to crack a smile through those struggled breaths humbled me and gave me strength ... None of us thought twice about the tiresome, endless journeys back and forth to see our precious girl. Nights there weren't easy. The worry through all of the brain surgeries, the endless waiting for her to wake up, the tears on our cheeks, were taking their toll on us all. ... At every opportunity we could steal, every precious moment was spent telling her how much we loved her, and how amazing she was. Always feeling though that the words just weren't enough, no matter how much they were repeated, no matter how many kisses and cuddles accompanied them, it just wasn't enough.

Finally the day came. I heard the dreaded word 'palliative'. There was nothing more we could do. She was going to die ... on 7th October L passed away. ...

L did not ever experience the pleasure of conversation, of walking, running, reading a good book, looking at a beautiful view, choosing her own clothes, making her own food, yet her happiness was overwhelming ... The pure emotion displayed by this amazing young girl has taught me to appreciate everything in life and in the world. I drive along a country lane, appreciate the trees, the music on the radio, the ability to sing along, to be able to climb out of the car myself, everything; the small things which we don't often appreciate being blessed with. When things go wrong, like losing my mobile phone, having no money, putting on a few pounds, struggling with an essay, needing new brakes, tyres and exhaust all in one go ... I take a step back and remember how lucky I am. These small hiccups are only a tiny part of the big world in which we live. Remembering to remember the important things is a skill L has taught me that I hope I will never lose. I realise the importance of appreciating those who you love, telling them so, and making the most of the time and memories you share. I try to pass on this perspective to others, and teach them some of the amazing lessons that L has taught me.

... This is the most intense learning experience I have ever been involved in. Never have I been more immersed in any situation. I believe in any situation, you learn if there is some sort of love involved. If you love the subject you are studying, or the area in which you are writing an essay, or even the environment you are learning in, then you will succeed in learning. Saturated, tangled, absorbed, engrossed; you don't have a choice, the tide takes over you and pulls you in until you are truly immersed.
(Immersive experience story competition 2008)

Proposition 5 enables learners to experience, feel and appreciate themselves as knower, maker, player, narrator, enquirer, creator and integrator of all that they know and can do, and enables them to think and act in complex situations. *All the stories used in this book illustrate one or more dimensions of this proposition.*

Story F: I am in my final year of Law with International Studies and it was always expected that I should go into practice once university finished. Before university, I already had an interest in short story writing and comic script writing but it was only after taking a CSV course in journalism that I decided to pursue writing as a career rather than a hobby, albeit freelance. This freelance ambition has gradually turned into a passion for multimedia journalism which should result in the start of a NCTJ journalism qualification next year.

One of my first opportunities was volunteering as a web based news writer which involved sourcing existing entertainment news stories with a rock, alternative theme from websites and then re writing the story for the relevant audience. Through this given list of websites, I was able to improve my skills involved in spotting a newsworthy story and in meeting the needs of a specific audience. Unfortunately, I was not developing my own writing style as I did not create the initial storyline ... I started applying for the position of voluntary writer with online magazines who were willing to employ new writers. So, I learnt the process of sub–editing and entertainment feature writing ... I was very excited about securing a placement with Life Fm, Brent's local radio station ... As a result, I developed an aptitude for conducting interviews, a vital skill in journalism, Furthermore, I enjoyed interacting with and working with a diverse range of individuals, all passionate about their profession.

My next experience of writing came in the form of my legal affairs internship at the European Healthcare Fraud and Corruption Network, Brussels. One of my tasks was to track EU legal developments and then create a legal/policy based report using these findings. As well as improving my legal knowledge of the EU health care sector, this activity developed my ability to write concisely and I learnt how to implement a policy based opinion based on EHFCN's values and beliefs within sections of the existing news story therefore giving the story a different twist. In hindsight, my law degree also benefited from this placement as I was able to use this information to write my current dissertation on EU health care. The best achievement from this opportunity was that I was able to build a strong portfolio of articles that allowed me to get a paid freelance monthly job writing informative fashion articles with a UK marketing company. EHFCN also made me realise that after I graduate I wanted to pursue journalism as my main career. As a result of my writing opportunities, I have become more interested in current affairs and am able to integrate this skill into my debates in my Politics seminars.

Although I have been successful in my 'online' writing, I still had aspirations to get involved in opportunities that allowed me to create and develop my own story that had particular significance in reality rather than just appealing to an editor's wishes. Thus, I was overjoyed to be chosen as the Amateur Swimming Association's Media Liaison Volunteer where my current task is to conduct interviews with young disabled volunteers interested in participating in the Paralympics and then write articles which are featured on the ASA's website and their magazine The Swimming Times. I have learnt to adapt my interview technique to a situation as I have discovered you need to make young people confident about talking to you as well as liaising with media professionals to document these Olympic inspired moments ... Perhaps, I will make that leap from being a writer to a journalist and learn that magic does not happen only when the pen touches paper.

(Lifewide learning essay competition 2011)

Proposition 6 encourages learners to be creative, enterprising and resourceful in order to accomplish the things that they and others value.

Story G: Perhaps my most prominent hobby during my time at Surrey has been Australian Rules Football – AFL. I took up the sport less than two years ago through an Australian friend, who was coach of a London club side ... After being battered and bruised after my first game or two, I started to learn the rules and train more seriously and managed to make the Premiership play-off finals with my club ... in my second season, confirming us as the second-best team in the country. Playing in a league full of Australians who have played AFL all their lives motivated me to train hard and take the sport seriously (to avoid injury if nothing else!). I was rewarded with a call up to the Great Britain squad ... and was delighted and honoured to be named in the squad for last year's International Cup in Australia. During this period I also organised a charity game for the Great Britain side against an Australian side in my home-town of Sevenoaks, Kent. I organised the event alone, organising a range of generous sponsors; a venue; licensing; food and drink; first aid; printed t-shirts; designing, writing and printing programmes; selling around 250 tickets; and raising several thousand pounds for charity. Needless to say, the effort required for this was huge, as was the learning curve. To have organised such an event on such a scale was very challenging but a real pleasure to behold.
(Lifewide learning essay competition 2009)

Story H: It was in summer of 2009, when a friend from Singapore visited me in London and introduced me to a piece of technology that he thought was 'sale-able'. After carefully researching the industry, I realised that by slightly tweaking the product we could address a big market gap, which could potentially make us thousands of pounds. Once the product was ready, we faced challenges with paying UK manufacturers' high cost, so leveraging upon my personal network I helped establish manufacturing contracts with companies in India. The point to note is that initially it was just a lab experiment and my friend wanted to do something with it! Just by fully utilising my skills, network and resources I connected the dots around the world by bringing in other Angel Investors and established a company jointly operating out of Delhi, Seattle, London, Istanbul and Singapore. Initially this was something I was pursuing out of interest, but once it turned into a success I faced with real challenges pertaining to time as I was already working ten hours a day on my Industrial Placement. But using my effective time management and prioritisation skills, I found enough time on weekends and evenings to run this business ... when my peers were partying and enjoying sunny weekends in summer of 2010, I was hopping flights to establish a global contract between investors. It was unbelievably challenging to be on an industrial placement and at the same time trying to hold conferences on skype with people based in different countries to make imminent decisions. Most importantly, I have gained firsthand experience of the kind of risks my future clients might face while operating in a globally competitive marketplace and all the legalities that are involved with setting up an international business. But personally, it is quite satisfying and I am proud to admit that with the profit ... I could pay off a portion of mortgage on my parents' home in New Delhi.

(Lifewide learning essay competition 2011)

Proposition 7 enables learners to develop and practise the repertoire of communication and literacy skills they need to be effective in a modern, culturally diverse and pluralistic world.

Story I: I went to Quito, Ecuador as part of a volunteer programme organised by the international organisation EIL (Experiment in International Living), in which I lived with an Ecuadorian family, learnt Spanish, and worked as a volunteer on projects. Being away from family, friends, and everything familiar enables you become truly immersed into a different country and a different culture ... I've never had so many consecutive emotional highs and lows as I did in my three months in Quito.

After a month of Spanish lessons, I had 2 months of work. I chose to split my time between teaching English to children in a pre-school in Las Casas, a poor district of Quito, and working in Albergue La Dolorosa, a shelter for children whose families are unable to care for them. Having never done anything like this before, I didn't know exactly what I was expected to do ... My poor Spanish was constantly a barrier between what I was, and what I wanted to be.

My Ecuadorian 'mother' R was a very strong woman. Being a single mother and career woman in a country that is still very chauvinistic and where women can't walk a few yards without the standard catcalls and whistles, she needed to be. She was sharp and I was quite scared of her. In my first weeks, I'd come home from Spanish lessons and she would ask me about my day, my life at home, etc. She was trying to help me, but I'd never spoken another language before and I was struggling with it. She would get frustrated whenever I didn't understand her, and attempt to say it in English in a really loud voice that always felt like she was shouting at me. I would generally let something like that wash over me, but in Ecuador I was very vulnerable and sensitive, and I was often close to tears whilst attempting to speak to her. I dealt with this by basically retreating from her, and trying not to care. I didn't see her as my mother or her apartment as my home. I stayed long hours at work and travelled whenever possible at the weekends with other volunteers, and had some fantastic experiences with them. They would talk about their good relationships with their host families, and I envied them. I questioned my relationship with my actual mother, and decided to make a more conscious effort when I got home. I should have made more of an effort with my Ecuadorian mother too, as the host family is all part of the experience.

This was the lowest point of my time in Quito ... It was absolutely a complete disaster. I've never been in a situation like that before, and I remember thinking at the time that I couldn't believe that this was actually happening. But it had to happen, as it was a revelation of sorts. Once I had let everything out that had been building up in my head, I was able to look on the situation as an observer and see how it really was ...

After nearly three months the city was beginning to feel like home. My Spanish was at its best ... I loved my journey to work in the morning when I could buy fruit on the street, converse with people in Spanish ... One really memorable thing for me was buying curtains for the playroom. As I was dealing with the shop assistant in the drapery store, various customers would come over and try and help us figure out exactly what I wanted. When I had the material bought, the shop assistant took me down the street to a dressmaker, where another conversation of what exactly I was looking for ensued, again with the input of the other customers in the queue, and some pen and paper. It really was such a buzz being able to get by in a country in a way that I had never envisaged when I first arrived.

(Immersive experience competition 2008)

Story J: But it was during a 'R.A.G. Raid' that I can say my life changed. A 'R.A.G. Raid', for those people who don't understand the lingo, is basically, members of R.A.G. taking to the town centre with buckets for any spare change people were willing to donate to the charity we were representing for the day. Towards the end of the day I was approached by two people, a man and a woman, saying they represented a company called 'Home Fundraising'. They both seemed very confident and charismatic and were asking me how I would feel going door-to-door fundraising for charities. Originally sceptical, (it being my third year with important exams pending) I decided to really push myself to see if it was something I would enjoy and it turned out to be the best decision I ever made.

The job entailed a group of us travelling to a destination decided previously (our region was anywhere between Oxford and Brighton) and knocking door-to-door and talking to people from 3pm till 9pm about our charity, trying to get people to sign up to donate as much as they could each month. My few months working at Home Fundraising really made me grow as a person. Fundamentally, [it] taught me the importance of a basic human virtue ... charity. I think a reason for this was my being assigned to the charity Cancer Research UK.

I'll never forget on my first day, knocking on a door and starting from my memorised script about how cancer affects 1 in 3 of us and thinking it was going well, and getting half way through when the woman I was talking to burst into tears and told me she had recently lost her husband to cancer. In a similar vein, at another door, I spoke to a woman holding a baby and as I begin to recite statistics concerning leukaemia and the improving chance of survival, the woman interrupts to tell me her baby has recently been diagnosed ... talking to so many people each day either being personally affected or knowing someone who is affected was such a humbling, eye-opening experience that changed my immediate view on the importance of charity work.

... my time working there literally changed my life. For a law student whose aim in life was to work for a law firm in London and earn a lot of money, talking to people who had lost husbands and children really hit home to me the real importance in life of family and happiness in what you do. After my time spent sharing stories with people on the street I suddenly found it hard to relate to the importance of dividends in Company Law lectures or how to sue people best in Family Law. It completely changed the trajectory of my life and now I am on course to becoming a police officer. This is a goal awakened in me by my time talking to people from all walks of life and feeling as though I really want to communicate and help people every day for the rest of my life. All in all my love affair with charity work and meeting and talking to people has changed my life completely, from one that would have been concerned with profit and money, to one concerned with helping people and talking to communities.

(Lifewide learning essay competition 2011)

Proposition 8 enables learners to develop relationships that facilitate collaboration, learning and personal development.

Story K: I was given the opportunity to be entrepreneurial and work with a team to come up with a business idea and try to put it into action and make a profit from it. Our team chose Battle of the Bands and we set about organising it. The first mistake I made was that I organised the bands, a venue, radio airplay and a date, within 3 days which I now realise was far too fast and didn't give me enough time to really plan anything. The second mistake I made was that I did it all without the team, which meant I forgot one of the main points of the task ... 'The team make a profit'. Inevitably my group failed ... I did learn valuable lessons such as team work really does mean TEAMWORK and contract negotiation is extremely fun, and that I will most likely run my own business when I leave university ...

(Lifewide learning essay competition 2009)

Story L: The choice of volunteering within an infant school came from a desire to help people. My previous work experience had left me behind tills, washing dishes or feeding the elderly. The latter began to show me just how wonderful it is to make a difference in people's lives.

I began as a teaching assistant but soon began to realise how much of a difference can be made in a child's life by the adults who guide them. After just a few weeks I found I lacked the confidence to initially raise ideas within my working team. This I considered to be one of my greatest weaknesses. The need to present my ideas to eight other people in my team terrified me. In one instance after nervously presenting my ideas for a harvest assembly, the teacher I worked with inspired confidence in me just by saying what a good idea he thought it was. My creativity began to exert itself in the research for new stories for the children to enact during their assembly and creating props left me smeared in paint and with a smile on my face. I believe my initial nervousness came from feeling that I was just a student. I had never been in a circumstance where research and ideas I had written down could transform from words on a page to a wonderful show before me that the children could perform for their parents. From that point on I began to consciously contribute during meetings and was no longer held back by the thought that my lack of work experience in education would detract from my ability to make worthwhile contributions to the school.

The ability to form interpersonal relationships with all members of staff came easily to me. I enjoyed working with everyone and found myself being able to differentiate my communicative behaviour between my adult team members and the children within the class. I began to unravel the intricate workings of a child's mind and the fantastic perspectives they can bring to their own learning. This enabled me to teach concepts ever so more effectively, a skill that academic research could not have aided me in. Seeing the children grasp a mathematical concept I had taught them and then perform it independently, was magical. Observations I made of techniques to mediate difficult behaviour, enforcement of school rules, the reward systems available to children and the many ways in which different teachers taught their class left me with an extremely rich perspective. Not only was I learning the crucial skills that many students learn as part of a teaching degree but I was able to evaluate and integrate different teachers' styles to form a style of my very own.

Despite volunteering I treated every job with the utmost importance and attempted to excel myself in what ever I was asked to do. I believe my willingness to do whatever was asked of me and the efficiency and enthusiasm I brought to my work was the reason the school offered me paid work in my fourth month with them. From this I was given my own class for an hour and a half once a week in which I had the opportunity to help them develop their writing ... The difficulties in managing a class independently, preparing much needed resources and planning techniques to engage the children were all experiences working as a classroom assistant would never have placed upon me. The submersion in yet another new environment began to further enrich my knowledge.

My future now seems clearer as I begin preparation for my graduate teaching programme to commence later this year. It's so important that such an overwhelming experience is not feared but approached with determination. As each new experience gradually becomes our familiar, shallow end of the pool, we must push forward towards the deep. For knowledge can never be finite and I believe submersion into new working

experiences is the best way to learn.
(Immersive experience competition 2008)

Proposition 9 encourages learners to behave ethically and with social responsibility.

> *Story M:* I have a brother who is severely visually impaired and categorised as a blind person. As well as being blind his left hand is partly paralysed so that he can not use it. ... I decided to accept the responsibility to take care of my brother in order for him to come to the UK and develop his English skills and follow his dream of pursuing higher education. It was a big responsibility because I had to cook for both of us everyday and clean everything, as he cannot do many of the things that would be done by the average individual. I had to sort out his belongings, take him to places where he needed to be and fill out all his forms. I also had to support him in many other areas of his life. Prior to my brother moving in I thought that caring for him would occupy my time and stop me from my studies and that I would fall behind everyone else on the course. However, I now realise that whilst caring for my brother a whole new horizon opened up in front of me. I discovered that there is much more to this life; this life is not just about me. My personality and character grew so much during this period because of the difficulties I went through and the contacts that I had to make in order to help him. The word 'service' found a very deep new meaning and value in my mind and heart.
> (Lifewide learning essay competition 2009)

Proposition 10 encourages and enables learners to be wilful, self-directed, self-regulating, self-aware and reflexive so that they develop a keen sense of themselves as designers/authors and developers of their own lives, appreciating their learning and developmental needs as they emerge. *All the stories told in this book demonstrate very well how this proposition is given meaning through the lifewide experiences of students.*

Being/becoming authors of their own lives

Baxter Magolda (Chapter 5) draws attention to the importance in personal development of 'the growth of epistemological, intrapersonal and interpersonal complexity' (Baxter Magolda 2004:41). Students enter university at all stages in their epistemological, intrapersonal and interpersonal development. Their programme of study or postgraduate research programme enables them to continue to develop in each of these dimensions but we tend to underestimate the considerable development gained through other experiences outside their formal education.

The first point that can be made is that the propositions for an imaginative curriculum, developed in Chapter 6 and used to organise the student narratives in this chapter, provide indications of the sorts of experiences and engagements that are likely to lead to the situations in which the epistemological, intrapersonal and interpersonal development necessary for self-authorship is more likely to occur. By relating the example narratives to these propositions we are saying that students are engaging with situations that hold the potential for these complex forms of development to emerge.

The questionnaire surveys provide an insight into the range of experiences students are involved in, and an indication of the significance individuals give to different forms of development arising from such experiences. But it is the stories students tell about their experiences and the development arising from such experiences that provide deeper insights into the purposes and meanings individuals attribute to such experiences.

An evaluation of the extent to which an individual demonstrates the dispositions and personal agency of self-authorship is not possible through the data we have gathered. However, Baxter Magolda (2004) identifies three assumptions relating to the perception and use of knowledge necessary for self-authorship which can be used to evaluate students' narratives. These assumptions are: 1) knowledge is complex and socially constructed, 2) self is central to knowledge construction 3) authority and expertise are shared in the mutual co-construction of knowledge among peers.

It is possible to find examples in most of the narratives submitted to the essay competitions of students engaging with knowledge in ways that demonstrate they appreciate it as a complex, highly situated and contextualised, individually and socially constructed, and emergent phenomenon. It is also apparent in the narratives that students view themselves as the developers and users of the knowledge they develop often with others. Here are a few illustrations taken from the extracts above.

- Student (A) developed knowledge to inform his practice as a personal trainer through formal study (for a qualification) and through his work with clients. 'I have learnt so much more though, most of which was completely unexpected.'

- A music student (B) who set up a highly successful Gospel Choir – a collaborative, uncertain knowledge-rich process in itself requiring the considerable development of relational and technical knowledge – formed a new partnership with a rapper through which knowledge and relationships are shared and new musical works are created.

- Student (C) took on the organisation of a new sky-diving society and made over 100 telephone calls to 'dropzones' all over England, France and Spain in order to create a knowledge base to determine the cheapest and best place to jump.

- Student (D) gained some profound insights into her own appreciation of life as a result of the relationship with a disabled child she developed through her role as a care worker.

- A law student (E) engaged in a sustained process of developing the knowledge he needs to be a journalist through volunteering as a web based news writer, as a voluntary writer with online magazines willing to employ new writers, conducting interviews with local radio station and through a legal affairs internship at the European Healthcare Fraud and Corruption Network, Brussels.

- Student (F) developed from scratch, presumably through a combination of observing, reading, discussing and coaching, the knowledge and skill to play Australian Rules Football at a high level. He also organised a significant fund-raising event.

- An engineering student (G) researched the market for a piece of technology before using his network of contacts developed through living in Singapore and though his placement to set up a technology-based business.

- A student on a gap year living and working in Ecuador (H), learning Spanish and working as a volunteer, developed the knowledge, much of it through her host family, that enabled her to adapt to a culture that is very different to her own.

- A law student (I) raising money for a cancer charity, knocking on doors and talking to people and trying to get them to sign up to donate as much as they could each month, found that time spent sharing stories with people on the street completely changed the trajectory of his life.

- Student (J) learnt from the failure of a collaborative enterprise that developing knowledge by yourself to achieve a goal is not going to result in a successful collaborative enterprise.

- Observations made by student (K) of the techniques used by teachers to mediate difficult behaviour, enforce school rules, reward children and the many ways in which different teachers taught their class, gave her 'an extremely rich perspective' with which to inform her own practice as a teacher.

Final thoughts

The data from questionnaire surveys and essay competitions reveal that significant numbers of students (albeit in self-selected samples) involve themselves in experiences beyond and additional to the formal curriculum while they are studying for their degree. Furthermore, the diversity of the forms of development gained through activities outside their programme that students recognise as being significant to their own development, is striking.

The overall inference that can be made from these surveys is that students develop themselves while they are at university through their engagement with their programme of study and through many other experiences outside the formal curriculum. Unfortunately, most of this development is unrecognised and unaccredited. Students themselves recognise this, and when asked whether they would like to receive university recognition for their informal learning and personal development over 60 per cent of students (survey 1) stated they would appreciate the opportunity for some form of recognition.

Learning and personal development are recognised by students as occurring in three curricular domains – the academic, co-curricular and extra-curricular. However, there appears to be a disconnection between subjective ratings of learning in the informal co- and extra-curricular domains and respondents' narrative evidence of the value of such experiences to their development. This results in considerably lower scores for perceived learning in these domains than in the programme of study context. The qualitative evidence might suggest that learning is occurring, but that it is undervalued by respondents. This may be due to academic cultural expectations that learning is packaged around explicit predetermined outcomes, with teachers' feedback or assessment essential to the validation of what counts as learning and achievement. If learners themselves fail to appreciate their learning and development, and are not able articulate this, they will sell themselves short when competing in the employment market, and, more importantly, they fail to recognise their true personal worth.

One way of addressing this issue would be for institutions to explicitly pay more attention to the learning and development gained through co- and extra-curricular experiences and to create the means to validate and honour these forms of learning and development.

> Participating in this award has taught me how the learning I am doing today goes together with the learning I did yesterday, and how new knowledge comes from previous knowledge. I have seen how the things I engage with help me to develop, and I am enjoying growing and learning much more than before now that I can see the value of it. I have learnt to recognise an opportunity and take the chance. These insights make me feel certain that I will continue working on my personal and professional development even after I have completed the award.
> (Lifewide Learning Award submission, March 2011)

Chapters 11 to 13 describe how one university has attempted to create a learning partnership framework (see Baxter Magolda, Chapter 5) to enable learners to think about and represent their informal learning and personal development and to receive recognition for this learning.

Student narratives of their lifewide learning reveal different orientations reflecting different priorities and dispositions. We suggest that individuals' orientations to lifewide learning might take one of three general forms – career/vocation/employability; self-actualisation; or a combination of these orientations, according to their self-determined priorities and wilfulness. There is a suggestion that in some areas, like health and creative arts, students are using the opportunities in their wider lives to gain experience and capability that is more focused on their career intentions/aspirations. A number of stories indicate that personal insights gained through particular experiences become life-changing. As a result perspectives, purposes and orientations change.

Our belief is that students enter university at all stages in their epistemological, intrapersonal and interpersonal development, and that while they are involved in a programme of study or research they are, through their whole life experience, continuing to develop along these developmental trajectories. Students' narratives of their experiences reveal how they as individuals are engaged in 'the growth of epistemological, intrapersonal and interpersonal complexity' (Baxter Magolda 2004:41 and Chapter 5) and further evidence of this involvement in self-authorship will be presented in Chapters 10 to 13.

Endnotes
1 This questionnaire is provided on the additional resources page at http://lifewideeducation.co.uk

Chapter 10

Immersive experience: a rich but challenging environment for transformative learning

Sarah Campbell and Norman Jackson

Synopsis
This Chapter considers the role of immersion in student development. Stories of immersive experiences were analysed to draw out the characteristics of the experiences and the perceptions of learning and development that emerged through such experiences. The most significant theme in stories of immersive experiences is a sense of journey and transition: it underpins the sense of transformational change that is often associated with immersive experience. Our claim is that immersive experiences provide rich environments for developing a range of self-knowledge, understandings, dispositions, qualities and capabilities that are essential for current and future survival and adaptation in a complex, unpredictable and often disruptive world. A lifewide concept of learning and education could embrace the immersive experiences learners encounter in their lives, and facilitate and recognise the learning and personal development they gain through such experiences.

Introduction
Chapter 6 set out a number of principles for the design of a curriculum that would better prepare learners for the uncompromising complexities of the world ahead of them. All are relevant to this chapter but propositions 3 and 4 are particularly relevant and have in part been formed in response to the studies that are reported in this Chapter.

Proposition 3: prepares learners for and gives them experiences of adventuring in uncertain and unfamiliar situations where the contexts and challenges are not known, accepting the risks involved

Proposition 4: supports learners when they participate in situations that require them to be resilient and enables them to appreciate their own transformation

This Chapter considers the idea of immersive experiences. *Immersion* is a metaphorical term derived from the physical and emotional experience of being submerged in water. The expression *being immersed in* is often used to describe a state of being which can have both negative consequences (being overwhelmed, engulfed, submerged or stretched) and positive consequences (being deeply absorbed or engaged in a situation or problem that results in mastery of a complex and demanding situation). Being immersed in an extremely challenging experience might be very uncomfortable but it is particularly favourable for the development of insights, confidence, resilience and capabilities that lead to adaptation or even reinvention of self. The willingness and ability to transform self is increasingly necessary in order to survive the messiness of life. It is in these situations that we need to draw on all our intellectual, practical and creative resourcefulness. Consequently this is where we might usefully explore possible links with Czsentmihayli's concept of 'Flow' (Czsentmihayli 1997) which emerges through from holistic and intense engagement with a significant challenge. and where our dispositions, qualities and capabilities are able to match the challenge.

Because of these intriguing and important learning dimensions to the experience of being immersed we wanted to find out more about how people experience it and how higher education might either create and/or facilitate learning and development from such experiences.

There are considerable ethical issues relating to putting students into physically and emotionally challenging situations, but students intentionally or unintentionally encounter such situations in their lives outside the classroom. Rather than ignore this fact, higher education could support and help learners develop their understanding of how they change through such experiences. In this context the notion of 'enabling' is one of recognising that although such situations are difficult and stressful, they are part of life. They are often the source of profound insight and personal change: change that better prepares people for similar situations and challenges in the future. By considering and validating such learning, higher education can enhance the ability of learners to recognise their own transformative learning and the process of becoming different.

This chapter summarises the results of two studies undertaken at the University of Surrey. The first was an appreciative enquiry undertaken in January 2008 as part of a conference held at the University of Surrey. The conference was deliberately structured to facilitate enquiry through conversation and story-telling about personal immersive experiences. Participants were invited to record a story about one of their experiences which they believed engaged them in an immersive way (an immersive experience). Forty-three stories were donated.[1]

Participants were invited to describe:
- the context/situation/challenge
- the particular characteristics of the situation that engaged them in an immersive way
- the forms of learning / personal development / change that emerged from the situation
- the words/concepts/feelings they would use to describe the experience
- the principles or lessons that they could draw from the story; for example, how this story could inform designs and enrich opportunities for learning through immersive experience in higher education.

The second study involved an analysis of twenty-six stories of immersive experiences submitted by students to an essay competition in January 2008. The invitation contained a series of prompts but these were intended to stimulate not constrain personal narratives. Interpretative Phenomenological Analysis (IPA) (Smith 1996) was used to identify emerging themes. The final stage of analysis used these themes as an analytical tool to re-examine the forty-three accounts of the earlier study.

What is an immersive experience?

The vocabulary used to describe experiences that participants feel are immersive (Figure 10.1 wordle cloud) is rich and reflects the complexity of the experiences and the emotional effects on participants. The following list outlines the situations and the words and phrases that encapsulate these experiences:
- *Situations that require an intense level of engagement, concentration and effort* – words like absorbing, challenge, consuming, determination, discipline, driven, engagement, energetic, immersed, intense and intensive, perseverance, powerful, relentless, self-motivation, self-

reliance, spell-binding, staying power, steep learning curve, time consuming.
- *Situations that require emotional engagement* – words like anxiety, anxious, despair, despondency, distraught, doubt, ecstasy, emotional, embarrassment, enjoyment, every emotion, excitement, fear, humiliation, irritated, joy, exhilaration, fear, frustration, happiness, lonely, loneliness, painful, passion, pride, sadness, satisfaction, scared, stressed, swallowed by gloom, uncomfortable.

Figure 10.1 Words used to describe immersive experiences in stories written by conference participants (top) and students (bottom)

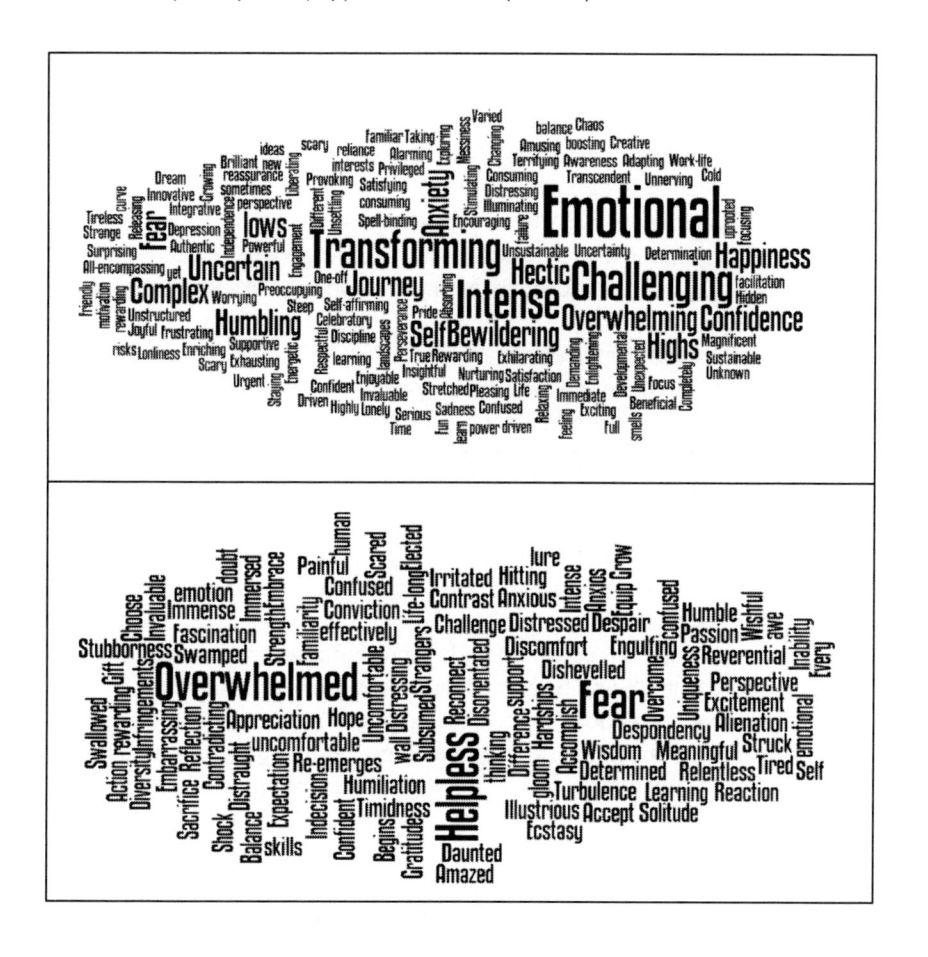

- *Situations that are extremely challenging, sometimes difficult to describe in ways that capture the complexity, in which risk and anxiety are often associated* – words like alarming, all-encompassing, anxiety, challenging (frequently used), competing interests, complex and complexity, demanding, discomfort, engulfing, exciting, exhilarating, fear of failure, hectic, indescribable, messiness, overwhelming, preoccupying, taxing, taking risks, terrifying, time consuming, turbulence, uniqueness, unexpected, unexplored, uncertainty, unnerving.
- *Situations that are uncomfortable or frightening* – words like alarming, anxiety, cold, discomfort, distressing, lonely and loneliness, scary, terrifying, uncertainty, unnerving, worrying, 'I continually felt out of my comfort zone', 'I was forced to exist out of my comfort zone'.
- *Situations where people do not feel in control; involve states of perplexity and uncertainty* – words like bewildering, confused, confused, daunted, engulfed, helpless, hardship, 'I'm only human', indecision, self-doubt, swamped, turbulence.
- *Situations that are not known and require exploration* – words like unexpected, unexplored, uncertainty, exploring, familiar yet new, full of potential, hidden perspective, strange, surprising, 'We explored the concepts'.
- *Situations that stimulate and require reflection and discovery of self* – words like 'It made me reflect on my own skills and attitudes.' 'The impetus to appreciate reflection ... far more constructively than hitherto.' 'To recognise the importance of feedback', 'My questioning and exploration of self', self-doubt.
- *Situations that require creativity* – words like adaptability, creativity, creatively stimulating, invention.
- *A sense of personal change, growth and gain* – words like achievement, awareness [greater sense of], beneficial, 'changing me for the better', developmental, empowering and empowerment, enlightening, enriching, freedom to learn and be myself, grow and growing, insightful, integrative, invaluable, learning, liberating, life changing, meaningful, new understanding, nurturing, overcome, re-emerges, releasing, revelatory, rewarding, self-affirming, self-motivation, self-reliance, transcendent, transforming.
- *A sense of satisfaction, confidence and happiness in coming to terms with or mastering a difficult situation and a creating a new sense of well-being* – words like celebratory, confidence boosting, empowering, happiness, rewarding, satisfaction, satisfying, pride.

Contexts for immersive experiences
Contexts identified in personal stories of immersive experiences include:
- *Challenging cultural situations* – like travel, voluntary service or work in other countries typically compounded by lack of knowledge about the society and language and sometimes compounded by issues like poverty or poor security; for example, finding yourself as a white middle-class teenager in a black African-American urban culture
- *Challenging work situations* – particularly first jobs or new roles, planning and overseeing major events, engaging others and creative work challenge like writing a book
- *Intensive learning processes and environments that others have created*
- *Intensive self-created learning processes particularly relating to postgraduate research*
- *Highly engaged participation in religious/political activity*
- *Intensive engagement in leisure activities*
- *Intensive engagement in artistic enterprise and performance*

The stories of immersive experiences show that the experiences that were selected to embody the idea of immersion were predominantly experiences of choice. Most stories involve people putting themselves into new/unfamiliar and challenging, even risky situations. Many storytellers deliberately and voluntarily put themselves into challenging environments like taking on a job in another country with no knowledge of the language or culture or in a new organisation with little relevant experience, or they chose to engage in particular work, education, self-study or leisure activities that they found challenging.

In some cases storytellers made a familiar place unfamiliar in order to enhance the challenge of the experience – like the story of off-road cycling at night. Here a familiar environment was rendered unfamiliar by the loss of sensory information as a result of riding a bicycle off-road in the dark. The experience involved increased risk of accident but created feelings of excitement and demanded heightened use of senses and off-road cycling skill.

Most of the stories are positive and affirming in the sense that even when the experience was uncomfortable good things generally emerged. However, we also have to recognise that there are circumstances for immersive experience from which good things will not emerge. We must also acknowledge there will be situations where people find themselves immersed in something for reasons beyond their control, i.e. they have not chosen to be in the situation, where life suddenly moves in a direction that was not anticipated and they are precipitated into unfamiliar territory, such as bereavement.

Based on the stories of immersive experiences we can define two sorts of overarching contexts (Figure 10.2). Many experiences are likely to contain a mix of solitary and social activity and also circumstances that involve both individual choice and external circumstances beyond an individual's control.

Figure 10.2 Contexts for immersive experience

Immersion as an essentially solitary experience – contexts for immersion are self-constructed and personal, e.g. reading, riding a mountain bike at night, individual creative and sporting enterprise

Immersion as a co-created social experience –contexts are co-created with others, e.g. work, people in other cultures, playing sport/online games, religious/political communities

- **Immersion as a chosen form of engagement** in a context of individual choice and control, e.g engaging in physical challenge, or starting a business
- **Immersion as a chosen or necessary form of engagement** in a context that has been created by circumstances beyond an individual's control
- **Immersion as a chosen form of engagement** in a context of individual choice, e.g. grappling with a new job, a demanding role, formal learning process, personal research process, team-based artistic performance, living and working in another culture
- **Immersion as a chosen or necessary form of engagement** to cope with a situation that has been created by circumstances beyond an individual's control, e.g. chaos at work, severe illness, bereavement, coping with extreme situations like natural or manmade disasters

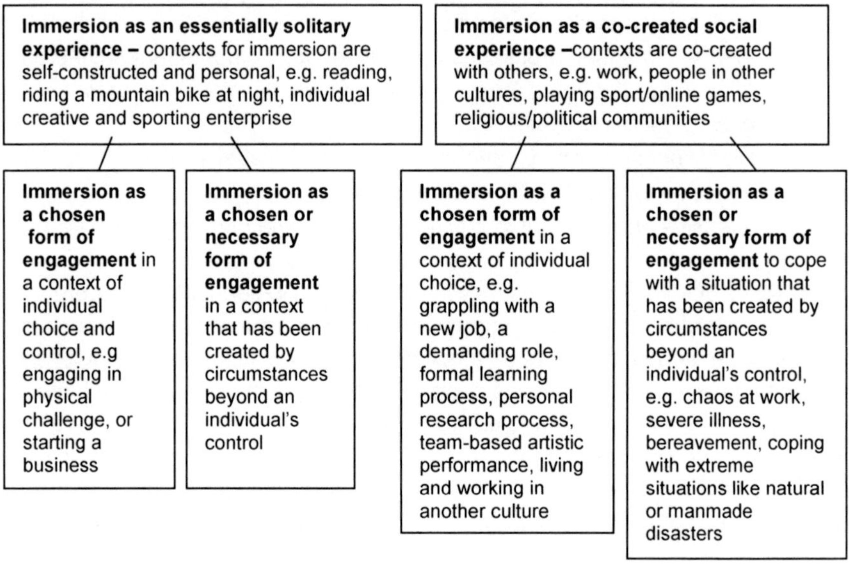

The first category embraces those experiences where immersion is essentially a solitary enterprise (i.e. individuals create the experience through their thinking and actions and do not seek to involve anyone else). The experience of being immersed in a book, the athlete immersed in a training programme, the musician rehearsing for a concert, the scientist undertaking laboratory research that doesn't involve engaging other people, riding off-road at night and playing video games on a computer are all examples of such experiences. We might envisage two situations for immersive solitary enterprise:

- where an individual constructs the environment and conditions for immersive experience – for example, climbing a mountain
- where circumstances require an immersive response from an individual – for example, having to endure and survive a hostile environment if the weather deteriorates badly.

Using the conceptual frame of Stephenson (1998) and Figure 4.1 (Chapter 4), participants have moved from familiar contexts and challenges into unfamiliar settings and challenges. These are often transitional situations; for example, when a student moves from home and school to university, or when someone begins a new job.

The second overarching category is where the immersive experience is much more of a social enterprise – it is co-created through complex social interactions and collaborative enterprise. Again we might envisage two scenarios:
- where individuals place themselves in a challenging social situation and choose to engage in an immersive way – examples might include grappling with a new job or complex work problem, engaging deeply in artistic performance, prolonged travel or exposure in another country/culture with a partner
- where rapid and significant changes in circumstances or the environment require an immersive response in order to get through or survive an event – examples of situations might include severe illness within the family, bereavement and coping with natural or manmade disasters.

Types of immersive experience
Four types of immersive experience can be distinguished in the two studies:
- Experiences that are essentially pleasurable and risk free and do not encounter conditions that are stressful or distressing – like being immersed in a book.
- Experiences that may contain within them pleasurable experiences and outcomes but that also contain physically, intellectually and emotionally challenging, stressful or distressing situations.
- Experiences that are intended to 'block out the light' rather than lead to enlightenment, the murky side of immersive experience. Here immersion has 'links' with homogenisation, 'brain-washing' and the repression of difference.
- Experiences that are painful and distressing, like serious illness or bereavement. They are dominated by emotional low points and outcomes are not generally positive or beneficial. However, positives can be taken from the transformation and surviving that occurs in these experiences, most likely following a period of time and then reflection.

Common features of immersive experiences
According to Baud (2010:8) immersive experience normally involves:

- multiple episodes over time that need to be considered singularly and collectively and typically involve participation in an environment unfamiliar to the learner
- learners allowing themselves to be fully part of the experience : intensive and holistic engagement is a characteristic of immersive experience
- reflection after the event in order to learn from the experience and to be aware that one has learned from it, for meaning to be made and for this to be appropriated into one's wider repertoire of knowledge and skill.

All these things were reflected in the accounts of immersive experiences but the most striking feature is that, despite the huge variety in situations described, there are many similarities in the underlying themes, emotions, changes and experiences of the participants. Appendix 1 presents the themes identified in student accounts, with explanation and supporting quotations. Three overarching themes were identified: the experience, the individual and facilitating factors in transformation.

The experience
This overarching theme encapsulates the immersive experience, as experienced by people writing their stories.
- *Sense of journey* – this is the predominant theme of the stories, demonstrating the type of process of personal development that occurs during an immersive experience. As it is integral to immersive experience, this theme is elaborated in more detail later in the chapter.
- *Emotions* – there is a strong emotional dimension to immersive experiences, and it appears that these emotions are a significant factor in the motivation of an individual to change and a guiding influence throughout the process. This is explained in more detail later in the chapter.
- *Paradox* – external versus internal; small difference versus big challenge; expected versus unexpected; positive versus negative; academic versus real world. This theme captures the contradictions experienced in the stories. It is clear that immersive experience involves juxtaposition in various ways. Dissonance occurs from what is portrayed externally and what is felt internally. Expectations of the experience beforehand are usually not met, and it is the unexpected/unforeseen parts of the experience that bring challenges and change. Experiences swing between extremes of very positive and very negative, and can also be both at the same time. Also, a strong feature in some stories

was the initial shock of the gap between academia and the real world in various ways. This was reconciled by bringing the two together in the end period of mastery.

The individual
This second overarching theme captures what happens to the individuals who engage in immersive experiences and the important changes (transformations) that individuals undergo during the experience.

- *Choice* – choice was important in most stories, where people elected to enter the situation. But the experience was often not what was expected. However, the choice to remain in the difficult situation emerged, as participants chose to learn new strategies and skills to cope with and master a situation. This demonstrates the influence of the freedom to choose or the will to persist.
- *Loss of identity/role change* – there was a clear sense of loss of self, characterised by uncertainty and loss of confidence. What emerged from this was a partial loss of identity and the emergence of a new sense of self, made up from integrating old parts with new parts. This is described in more detail later in the chapter.
- *Perspective change* – this demonstrates how dissonance arises in coping with unfamiliar and uncertain situations, and how negative feelings arise, giving a sense of being overwhelmed. Cognitive reappraisal, or perspective change, reduces dissonance and helps the individual re-evaluate the situation and see it more positively, therefore making it more manageable. Other people are often instrumental in this perspective change.

Facilitating factors in transformation
The third overarching theme identifies some of the factors that influence the process and representation of transformation.

- *Support from others* – the supportive role of others in experiences is important, partly to alleviate loneliness, but also as a way to make sense of experiences, provide other perspectives, help individuals understand their emotions and regain balance. This support was sometimes direct and in other instances was indirect. This is described in more detail later in the chapter.
- *Comparison* – comparisons emerged in the stories, both comparison to others and comparing the unfamiliar to the familiar. Comparison to others was usually self-deprecating, perceiving others as coping when storytellers were not. This sometimes helped to motivate them to

change. Comparing the unfamiliar to familiar emerged perhaps as a way to understand and contextualise the sudden unfamiliarity in which people found themselves.
- *Presentation of situation* – some stories seemingly justified the challenging nature of the situation by presenting the situation as exceptional. This may also have been a way to validate their feelings and difficulties, rather than doubting their abilities; this instead acknowledged their struggle as valid due to the challenging nature of the situation.

Sense of journey

The most common and significant theme in stories of immersive experiences is a sense of journey. This journey underpins the sense of transformational change that is often associated with immersive experience.

An individual's journey often begins with anticipation, which gives way to feelings of being overwhelmed and ends with a sense of mastering or coming to terms with a situation. This pattern is depicted in Figure 10.3.

Figure 10.3 The transformative journey depicted in many stories of immersive experience

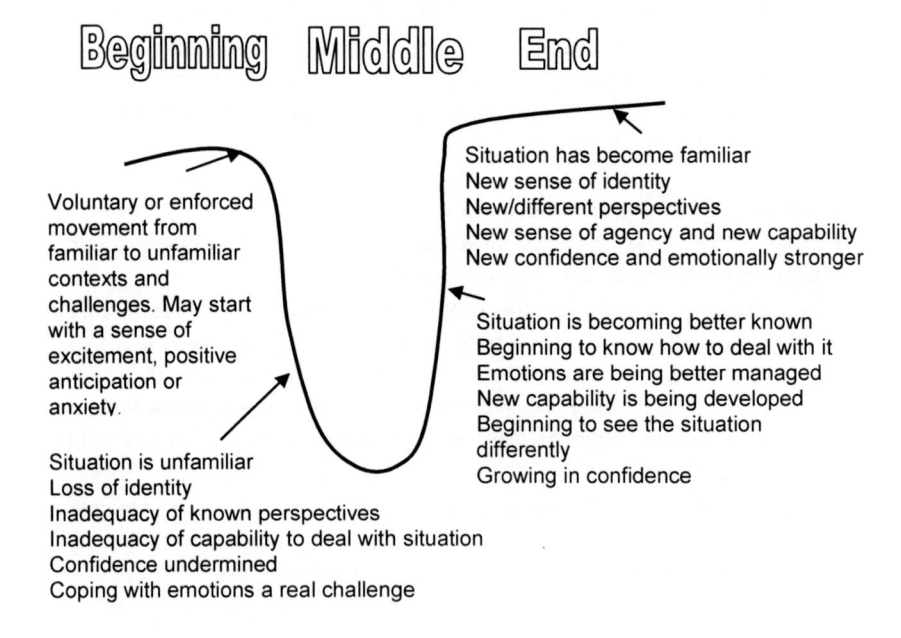

Beginning   Middle   End

Voluntary or enforced movement from familiar to unfamiliar contexts and challenges. May start with a sense of excitement, positive anticipation or anxiety.

Situation is unfamiliar
Loss of identity
Inadequacy of known perspectives
Inadequacy of capability to deal with situation
Confidence undermined
Coping with emotions a real challenge

Situation is becoming better known
Beginning to know how to deal with it
Emotions are being better managed
New capability is being developed
Beginning to see the situation differently
Growing in confidence

Situation has become familiar
New sense of identity
New/different perspectives
New sense of agency and new capability
New confidence and emotionally stronger

In the initial part of the experience most accounts exhibited a sense of excitement and positive expectations or anxiety if the situation was not of their making. During the middle stage of an immersive experience participants felt overwhelmed and questioned the choices they had made and that were available to them, and their involvement in the experience. During the final stage of the experience participants accepted and embraced the experience, having gained control. Individuals recognised that in the case of the experience continuing it would continue to be immersive, but they felt they had control and had learnt strategies to cope with the challenges of the experience.

Another feature of this staged process is the emotional journey participants make. Typically, the journey began with positive feelings (bearing in mind that most participants had voluntarily put themselves into situations which they found immersive). But as the experience unfolds even those who started with positive emotional states progressed into more negative states. The final stage is always characterised by deep positivity – significantly more positive than at any point in the experience as a result of surviving or mastering the situation.

Coping strategies are another feature of the process. Most stories inferred that people felt they had the necessary knowledge, cognitive and affective skills at the beginning of the experience to cope with it. But this stage often gave way to realisations that individuals did not have the necessary skills/knowledge or strategies to handle the situation and lost confidence in their own capability to do so. 'My intellect and understanding is shaken to timidness with all this strangeness.' They had not appreciated how difficult or lonely it would be. This realisation forced people to change, adapt and acquire new strategies and knowledge in order to cope with the challenges in their experience. This change pushed them into the final stage, during which participants developed strategies, awareness and new capabilities. They developed a sense that they had mastered or gained enough experience and changed sufficiently to feel a sense of control. 'So here I was now, suddenly able.'

Many participants experienced a lack of balance in terms of their immersive context and other facets of their lives, which is not conducive to well-being. Most said while they were immersed other areas of their life were ignored, and they did not reach understanding and control until they had reinstated a more balanced lifestyle. It would seem that any immersive situation will entail a period of the situation becoming all-consuming with negative consequences for the rest of a person's life. 'But saturation ... can lead to imbalances in life.' Clearly, from a personal (and perhaps social) well-being perspective it is important for this situation not to be sustained. This is another expression of journey in immersive experiences. The person involved needs to journey from balance to imbalance, but to recognise the learning the person must continue until balance is regained. The motivation to regain balance drives the person to change or learn or to get out of the situation he is in.

The sense of personal change and fulfilment that people gain through an immersive experience is attributed to this pattern of a journey in which a sense of confidence is replaced by a lack of confidence and the necessity to adapt to totally unfamiliar situations (often both contexts and challenges), growing into new and stronger confidence and new capability.

Emotional journey
Many emotions were expressed in personal accounts of immersive experience, including fear, happiness, excitement, guilt, anxiety, fear, shame and unhappiness. What is apparent is that during an immersive experience, very strong, and sometimes overwhelming, emotions are encountered. These strong emotions, in many cases, compelled participants to change or to re-evaluate themselves and their behaviours, either to attain or maintain a positive emotional state.

Emotions play a very important and prominent role in an immersive experience, and it is this experience of coping with and learning to manage emotions that makes the experience so valuable and memorable. Any experience that elicits a strong emotional response makes it very personal and motivates the person to engage with the situation no matter how difficult the challenge. Emotions seem to serve the role of motivating a person to change and to persist in difficult circumstances; although perhaps there must be occasions where they overwhelm the person to the point where they cannot deal with the situation.
In many stories participants have to suppress or control their emotions: 'On the other hand, you have to be calm and collected.' In most cases this was necessary in order to maintain an external representation of oneself, so as not to 'fall apart' during the experience. This awareness of and ability to manage emotions seems important in an immersive experience, and this form of control – that is, suppression – is perhaps the precursor to the participant gaining control over the situation as a whole. This emotional suppression/control is the internal indication to the person that he needs to change in some way to cope with the situation, to 'rebalance' the strong emotions, so the emotions become a signal and then a motivation for change. 'What kept me persevering was my passion.'

Immersive experiences can be lonely experiences, even when there are lots of other people involved. This sense of loneliness may also heighten the emotional experience. In general, participants became more expert in handling their emotions as a result of the experience and developed capabilities for coping with and managing strong emotions in the future. 'I've learnt to cry, to feel pain ... it's essential to talk to people about them.'

Loss of identity/role change
Many accounts of immersive experiences gave rise to a feeling of loss of identity and role change: 'My identity as a student was no longer prominent in defining my contribution. I was an individual working in a firm.' Identity change was also manifest in the desire to become a different sort of person: 'My poor Spanish was constantly a barrier between what I was, and what I wanted to be.'

Loss of identity often led to feelings of being overwhelmed or under-skilled and resulted in strong negative emotions. But through the immersive experience a different identity emerges. This new identity reflects new learning and personal change, and the recognition that this new identity is part of the feeling of transformation. Here is another journey, resulting in integration of the old and new roles and the creation of a more complex person or identity: 'returning to a world where I am surrounded by the paradox of everything yet nothing being the same'.

Support from others
A central sub-theme in most accounts was the role of others in offering support and guidance, and in many cases a feeling that without others the participant would not have survived the experience. In some cases this was indirect support, where participants observed others, and were humbled by, inspired by or admired the resilience of others, which encouraged them to change in order to cope with the experience. 'My Uncle and Aunt were pillars of strength too. The strength, help and support I received from my family, my amazing family, was invaluable.' 'I was blown back by his positive attitude. It gave me strength.'

In other cases the supportive role of others was much more direct and explicit. In many cases participants only gained objectivity and reflective learning, or new strategies, from engaging with other people. The role of other people in facilitating support, reflection and change in an individual immersed in an experience is very important in the individual learning from that experience, as is evidenced from these quotes.

- 'She also told me that when something's wrong, you should put your energy into changing it, rather than letting it get you down.'
- 'His perspective on life left me hungry.'
- '[His] question ... triggered off a change in me ... the mere fact that [he] was willing to teach it to me was enough encouragement ... it showed he believed I was capable.'
- '[She] also taught me the most important things I will ever learn about life. [She] was 9 years old.'
- 'She also told me that when something's wrong, you should put your energy into changing it, rather than letting it get you down.'

Nature of learning
The observations outlined previously begin to reveal the rich nature of learning and development that emerges through an immersive experience. It involves the recognition that:
- *Learning is an active experiential process.* People learn by doing and experiencing things. Personal knowledge grows through the experience and by interacting with others: 'learning from the experiences of others (such as my two French colleagues) was invaluable in helping me to understand this foreign landscape.'
- *Learning involves seeing and making new meanings.* Reflection is an important part of this process: 'learning was initially experiential; later, after the event, predominantly reflective.' 'I was struck by the final wonder ... this triggered a personal exploration of a situation in which I currently find myself. Through it I was able to explore a range of possibilities.'

The learning that participants report raises the issue of what counts as learning: what emerges is a very rich and diverse visualisation and representation of what learning derived through these sorts of experiences means. 'Learning by observing, experiencing, listening, participating, searching for information, asking. [I learnt a] huge amount of a broad/general and subject specific knowledge acquisition happened as a result of this immersive experience.' Situations often demand that we learn quickly and they may force us to make and learn from mistakes. 'I had to learn a lot very quickly, and learn by making mistakes as well.'
- *We learn complex things – like a new language or how a society or culture works.* 'I learnt to speak fluently but at the same time, understood how difficult it is to be completely illiterate.' 'I developed considerable verbal fluency in Russian, moving from an initial lack of

confidence and reluctance to open my mouth for fear of making a mistake, to thinking (and sometimes dreaming) in Russian.' 'I learnt that the British approach to life wasn't the only way, so I learnt how to unlearn. I figured out which parts of my Britishness I wanted to hold on to and which were better discarded. I found out what was really important to me and treasured values like kindness, cheerfulness and courage that go beyond culture.'

- *We learn subtle things.* 'A recognition of the power of the smile and the importance of humour in negotiating and in tense situations.' 'Situations encourage self-reliance and resourcefulness and encourage people to push themselves beyond their comfort zones. The situation, which was highly stressful at times, made me more self-reliant.' 'It made me engage in huge amounts of a priori reasoning, reflection, planning and practice, in the absence of any prescribed, agreed approaches or even content.' 'My own predispositions and interests were encouraged by the circumstances, so that these could be used as resources.' 'I discovered resources in myself of self-reliance, resilience and staying power, even through the difficult times.' '[It has] shown me the importance of risk taking and moving out of one's comfort zone.'

- *We learn physical things and complex skills and competencies.* '… dance movements that then become part of oneself; learning sections of choreography.' 'I learnt to gather and synthesise complex evidence and make judgements about what I had seen and experienced.' 'I also developed skills for embracing differences.' 'I learnt how to build relationships and when to choose not to.'

- *We encounter and recognise ah-ha moments.* 'Not exactly eureka moments, more ah, hah moments as something falls into place, links with something else or I understand more about a situation or experience.'

- *We learn about how other people behave and become more sensitive to seeing the world from other perspectives.* 'I learned how individuals construct their own changing perspectives in learning situations.' 'An understanding that some people just do not see the detail and that it takes hard conscious thought to work with people who have very different thought processes and working patterns when in an immersive situation.' '[I have] a greater respect for others who encounter challenges on a daily basis, particularly people who live in absolute poverty and suffer from terminal illnesses, yet do so in a dignified manner.' 'I learnt to empathise with the front-line teachers and managers that made our education system work.'

- *We learn to think with complexity, with deeper wisdom and new senses of knowing.* 'An acknowledgement that there needs to be vision to create such events, and a realisation that even the smallest of details are important and need to be considered at the visionary stage in order for the big picture to appear complete.'
- *We learn how to reflect more deeply and how to make sense of complex situations through this process.* 'This provided the impetus to appreciate reflection as a practitioner far more constructively than hitherto – and within that to recognise the importance of both peer feedback and an understanding of peer perspectives.'
- *We learn how to create new senses of order.* 'Sense-making is an ongoing project.' 'A feeling of creating order, making sense out of material that was both very familiar to me but which seemed at the outset to be very fragmented.'
- *We learn to see things differently through the forms of learning, personal meaning and the new connections we make in our lives.* 'The learning was about being reminded how teaching and facilitating a learning experience can actually be a trigger for one's own learning – and for the reassertion of one's own learned experiences.'
- *We develop our contextual awareness.* Many of the accounts demonstrate that participants achieve greater understanding of context by comparing what they experienced to the wider context. In some instances this was in relation to the environment or culture. 'Perhaps it's the deep-seated reverence for samurai culture ... or some sense of alienation after the World Wars ... Whatever the social fuel.' For others this was the contextual awareness of their emotions, their learning or their ability to transfer skills. 'I have most certainly adapted it to many different aspects of life.' 'Learning to learn from them was crucial ... I hope will [it] serve me well throughout my career.'

Recognition of personal change

Personal change is often an outcome of an immersive experience and the magnitude and nature of the change is what makes the experience feel transformative. These changes were driven by the necessity to survive the situation and to make the most of the opportunities it held. The amount and quality of change recognised reflects the nature of the immersive experience that is described.

- *Some people moved away from their preferred way of doing things.* 'The insight provided by my mentor threw a lot of light for me on how much of an effort I had made to move away from natural inclinations to adapt to individual coaching situations.'

- *In some situations people are forced to radically change their behaviour.* 'I needed to take a crash course in understanding what it was like to be different. I wore an army coat and converse tennis shoes as an urban uniform. I listened to radio programmes and television that were popular to the African-American community: much of the vernacular and spoken word were [sic] different to me. I [had] to alter the way I behaved: I learned to adopt an unprovocative demeanour and not look up into people's eyes because this was seen as aggressive. I tried to find friends to advise me on protocol; several friends were half African-American and half Indian and were also considered different by their classmates.'

- *People changed their value systems and became humbler.* 'It made me value what I did for a job. It taught me to value difference and helped me become less judgemental.' 'I became (I hope!) less arrogant and more tolerant.'

- *People became more self-aware and gained confidence in their own capabilities.* This was often through the support of others and reflection on what they achieved leading to deeper recognition of their own abilities. This is another dimension of the personal journey embedded in an immersive experience. 'I felt more self-aware and confident to act in a facilitative fashion both with coaches and colleagues ...' '... the eventual growth in confidence to stick with speaking German especially at work. Overall I think that this whole experience made me much more confident and able to tackle new situations.' 'The uncertainty of ever getting through it has been replaced with determination and a trust in my ability.' 'You just trust that you will manage, that you will succeed, that you will achieve ... in confidence.' 'This gave me the confidence.'

- *Immersive experiences develop persistence and self-knowledge about what an individual can achieve.* 'Although there were times when I thought I would go under I didn't. I persisted and with that persistence and my accumulated experiences my confidence grew so that at the end of the process the thought of radical change didn't frighten me any more.' 'Deeper understanding of working with tiredness, endurance: language skills diminish, body can be pushed, working through frustration and difficulty to achieve what perhaps did not feel possible at first.' 'I discovered resources in myself of self-reliance, resilience and staying power, even through the difficult times.' 'I acquired enough resilience to not run away again.'

- *People gain new insights on complex lives and these insights may well connect with or change a person's identity.* 'It made links to what I already knew in a non threatening safe environment. It made me value what I did for a job. It taught me to value difference and helped me become less judgemental. I found that we all had a shared ethos and although we worked in a variety of fields we all wanted the same thing. It made me reflect on my own skills, attitudes and highlighted my strengths. It taught me not to be scared of words. It showed me what child/person centred really means.' 'I became (I hope!) less arrogant and more tolerant.' 'I changed from being a lone, angry rebel to realising that sustaining negativity is a waste of effort and time and that this was better spent finding connections and commonality. I found that shared feelings and experiences were a better basis for establishing lasting common ground than shared opinions. I learnt how to build relationships and when to choose not to.'
- *At the transformative end of the learning continuum immersive experiences fundamentally change people.* 'It's fair to say that this immersive experience was life-changing; I became aware that I could learn anything I set my mind to, taking ownership gradually of a level of confidence that I had never before experienced and that – yes, I can say, permanently – changed my attitude to learning and therefore to myself.' 'I discovered all my limitations as a person, as a Muslim, and as a friend. It was almost like rediscovering me from inside out.' 'I changed from being a novice with no idea what I was supposed to do to someone who could perform the professional role. I reformed my professional identity during that year and became a very different person in terms of my interests.' 'I am not the same person as I would have been had I gone to a suburban all 'white' school.'

The will to be immersed

Understanding what compels people to voluntarily enter an experience that is likely to be immersive, or to turn an experience into one that is immersive by engaging in it in an immersive way, is important if we are to create conditions for immersive experience in higher education. It might be anticipated that committing to a level of engagement that participants recognise as being immersive will require powerful motivational forces, particularly if the experience is sustained over a period of time. The stories participants chose to tell of their immersive experiences were overwhelmingly self-motivated and positive in the sense of fulfilling personal needs, desires and aspirations. In a few stories the reasons for participating in an immersive way were not clear.

Some of the more overt sources of motivation included:
- need/desire for personal development / profound change
- taking on a significant new challenge requiring adaptation/reinvention – motivations to understand/survive/master
- necessity/need to invent (typically connected to taking on a new/significant challenge)
- desire to exploit an opportunity (typically connected to taking on a new challenge)
- desire to learn a language/culture (specific and frequently cited new challenge)
- spiritual desire
- desire to gain professional experience in another culture
- need for stimulation and desire for new experiences
- desire to experience effects
- necessity/need to invent (typically connected to taking on a new/significant challenge)
- need/desire to conduct research (specific context for new challenge)
- passion/excitement/happiness – doing something for self
- doing something for others
- being inspired by others
- modelling immersive behaviour in order to engage others in an immersive way
- coping with situations that were imposed/outside of the control of the individual.

Strong and sustained self-motivational forces are likely to involve a combination of evolving forces. For example, the need or desire for personal development might be connected to taking on a new challenge or exploiting a new opportunity, then having experienced the effects on self and others, the desire continues to build on what has been learnt and applied.

We must also appreciate that an overt motivational force may camouflage other motivations which, although unspoken, might be just as powerful. So need and desire for change/personal development might also be connected deep down to unarticulated desires for a happier, more fulfilling or spiritual life.

Motivations are also likely to change during a complex experience. An immersive experience may begin with an obligation or sense of duty, it might encounter anxiety and fear as a source of negative emotional energy but might progress through senses of satisfaction and enjoyment as difficult situations are mastered and new insights are gained.

Only a few immersive experiences appear to have been 'driven' by circumstances beyond the control of the individual, although the environment and participants' engagement with the environment are key features of most immersive experiences.

Discussion

The immersive experiences described by the participants in these studies clearly engage them in a journey of self-discovery, often brought about by their participation in unfamiliar challenges in unfamiliar contexts (see Chapter 4). Such experiences seem to involve people in a holistic way, physically, cognitively and emotionally. The holistic model of learning and development described in Chapter 3 would appear highly relevant to these sorts of experiences. Through these experiences participants change in ways that they recognise as being substantial and significant. They come to know themselves in deeper more appreciative ways and they are able to transit from one identity to another as they become a different person. We conclude this chapter with a discussion of other research and theories that appear to be relevant to interpreting the learning and personal development gained through an immersive experience.

Making a transition necessitates deep structural change either by changing internally, and or changing the environment. Situations that require us to make a transition create the need for change, but we must choose to break the existing ways of being to create a new way of being (Gerswick 1991). A lot of transition research is focused on life-span milestones, such as school to work, or transition to parenthood (Landmark et al. 2010; Motulsky 2010). What this immersive experience work demonstrates is that there are many transitional situations that can provide the source for revolutionary change. This highlights value of a lifewide concept of education as learners could be encouraged to understand their transitions in a way that would help them prepare for some of the bigger transitions many will have to make later in life.

Transitions involve inter-dependent processes of identity change and repositioning, skills development/learning and the role of strong emotions for meaning making and elaboration (Hale and de Abreu 2010). The ability to understand, make sense of and manage your own and others' emotions is termed emotional intelligence, and it appears transitional processes require these emotional self-management skills (Goleman 1995; Mayer *et al.* 2004, 2008). The motivation and agency of the individual is vital to the change process and for transformation to occur.

In the US large investment was made into developing transition programmes for those with disabilities to improve long-term prospects. The aim was to understand and therefore provide supportive practices that would enable successful transition into new situations such as work and higher education. Landmark *et al.* (2010) review empirical findings to evaluate the practices. These programmes involved fostering self-determination to ensure the individual is the agent of his own life. In particular they helped improve decision-making, problem-solving, goal-setting, risk-taking, self-awareness, evaluation and reflection skills. This is best theorised by self-determination theory (SDT) (Deci and Ryan 2000; Ryan and Deci 2000) where intrinsic motivation leads to individuals being highly motivated to learn, to change and to be active and engaged, eventually resulting in fulfillment and well-being. The key innate components of fostering this intrinsic motivation are competency, autonomy and relatedness (belonging) – all of which can be recognised in participants' stories of immersive experience.

Transitions involve identity change and repositioning (Hale and de Abreu 2010). Changes in identity are influenced by many factors, but past history is important and the new identity that emerges through a transition assimilates new elements with old elements. Manzi *et al.* (2010) suggest that new situational and role demands lead to changes in self-concept as new demands require an assimilation of the old and the new (Li *et al.* 2010; Beard and Wilson 2006). Hale and de Abreu (2010) support a view of process-orientation in adaptation rather than developing to end-states. Individuals cope with the transition ('rupture') by utilising different resources created from their cognitive, emotional and physical capacities. Knowledge of coping with previous transition experiences helps because these knowledge assets can be generalised, internalised and applied to the new transitional situation. Self-determination is important for not giving up and progressing through the transition in order to attain personal goals.

The assimilation of new and old components into a new structure, if integrated and made concrete, perhaps through supportive others, ensures congruence which determines emotional well-being and therefore emotional adjustment following transition (Williams 1999).

Positive or negative adjustment following the transition is proposed to be determined by the change process itself; how it was experienced, managed and encouraged (Williams 1999). Transitions may be negative and harmful as well as positive. Gersick (1991) suggests that evolution (or revolution) is not always improvement. Coping with the change process is important for an individual's emotional well-being and self-esteem. With appropriate support such experiences can be a very enhancing. Other people provide vital emotional support to enable people to progress through the transformation (Hale and Abreu, 2010) and ensure the change is enduring. Relational theory (Motulsky 2010) explains the importance of others in providing the type and quality of the relationship that will facilitate a transition, as was observed in our own study.

A lot of research has explored transitions. Much of it is quite specific in terms of situation such as career change, organisation change, school to work/higher education, university to work, transition to parenthood, transition in special education arenas (Landmark *et al.* 2010) and cultural change (Hale and de Abreu 2010; Ng *et al.* 2009). However, it appears that capability development in coping with and managing transition processes are common across situations (Gersick 1991). Transitional processes enable new capabilities to emerge, that can then be generalised and transferred to other areas of work and life (Ng *et al.* 2009). This conclusion is central to our interest in immersive experiences as a rich environment for learning and personal development. The research suggests that the confidence, insights, dispositions and capabilities that emerge through such experiences can be drawn on in future situations. This is an important conclusion and one that highlights the value of these forms of lifewide learning experience.

The conclusion we draw from our own study is that the overwhelming sources of energy, enthusiasm and commitment to engaging in an immersive way with a complex situation seem to be intrinsic in nature. They seem to be triggered by needs and desires for new experiences and challenges through which people can appreciate and develop themselves. Maslow (1943) developed a framework for analysing the motivational forces behind human behaviour and growth. His model contains five levels of need:

- biological and physiological basic needs – air, food, drink, shelter, warmth, sex, sleep, etc.
- safety needs – protection from elements, security, order, law, limits, stability, etc.
- belongingness and love needs – work group, family, affection, relationships, etc.

- esteem needs – self-esteem, achievement, mastery, independence, status, dominance, prestige, managerial responsibility, etc.
- self-actualisation needs – realising personal potential, self-fulfilment, seeking personal growth and peak experiences.

Table 10.1 Existence-Relatedness-Growth (ERG) theory (Alderfer, 1980)

Growth	An intrinsic desire for personal development. These include Maslow's intrinsic esteem category and the characteristics included under self-actualisation.
Relatedness	The desire we have for maintaining important interpersonal relationships. These social and status desires require interaction with others. They align with Maslow's social need and the external component.
Existence	Provides our basic material existence requirements. They include Maslow's physiological and safety needs.

Maslow's *Hierarchy of Needs* has been extended by other people to include 'levels' ('Cognitive', 'Aesthetic' and 'Transcendence' – helping others achieve self-actualisation). Others have argued that these sources of motivation are all concerned with self-development and self-fulfilment that is rooted in self-actualisation 'personal growth', which is distinctly different to the 1 to 4 level 'deficiency' motivators. Maslow's hierarchical and sequential model has been criticised because in real life people tend to access and utilise different levels of motivation simultaneously rather than sequentially. To address this criticism Alderfer (1980) combined Maslow's five categories into three categories in his Existence-Relatedness-Growth (ERG) theory (Table 10.1).

In contrast to Maslow's hierarchy of needs theory, the ERG theory demonstrates that:
- more than one need may be operative at the same time; that is, needs are not satisfied sequentially
- if the gratification of a higher-level need is stifled, the desire to satisfy a lower-level need increases.

This simpler and more flexible interpretive framework seems to work quite well for characterising the motivational forces that are associated with participants' stories of immersive experiences. The motivations for engaging in immersive experiences seem to be overwhelmingly associated with growth – the personal development, intrinsic self-esteem/self-actualising dimensions of the framework. It would appear that engaging in an experience in an immersive way is a means of satisfying an individual's needs and desires for personal development – for becoming the person he wants to become.

This links strongly to self-determination theory (SDT) (Deci and Ryan 2000; Ryan and Deci 2000). SDT proposes that people have an innate psychological need for autonomy, relatedness and competence, and these influence (through satisfaction of these needs) individuals' intrinsic goal focus and motivation, and determine their sense of well-being. Individual agency, motivation to learn and novel skill mastery are all outcomes of satisfying these needs. Development and self-regulation are important factors. These three needs are proposed as essential to fulfill the human desire for growth and integration. Motivation leads to creativity; therefore, it is important to understand intrinsic motivation as a concept. Intrinsic motivation emerged in participants' narratives in some cases, to deal with an unknown situation, but more generally the motivation to continue in spite of the challenges and difficulties experienced in the immersive experience. Motivation can be authentic, and self-derived, or it can be externally imposed. External imposition is less likely to foster motivation, unless an individual can incorporate the value of this situation into his long-term goal structure. Interest, confidence and excitement arises from authentic, self-derived situations, although our participants still struggled with the unexpected difficulty of experiences they had chosen to enter. However, because they were able to choose this created their sense of autonomy and the motivation that enabled them to continue towards relatedness and mastery. Self-determination is important for persisting through a transition in order to attain personal goals (Hale and Abreu 2010) and our participants demonstrated this in their stories.

Within SDT, cognitive evaluation theory (CET) (Dec and Ryan 2000; Ryan and Dec 2000) suggests that socio-contextual events, such as reward and feedback, enhance feelings of competency, thus the role of other people is vital, as was seen in our narratives. This competency, in turn, increases intrinsic motivation to continue the action, but only if accompanied by a sense of autonomy. Autonomy is increased by choice and self-directed opportunities. Feelings of 'being thrown in at the deep end', while giving rise to strong feelings, allow self-direction and therefore a feeling of autonomy. 'Being thrown in at the deep end', for some participants, created crisis, loneliness and feelings of incompetence. CET suggests that this is a necessary component for autonomy, which in turn influences motivation. It seems that this sense of autonomy may operate at an unconscious level for some participants in immersive experiences.

CET theory suggests that internalisation of processes leads to competence and reflection can be such a useful tool, as this aids internalisation. Structured and facilitated processes, as might be included within practices to support lifewide education, could offer additional support to help learners who are involved in an immersive experience, to gain this sense of competency.

The context is also important, as internalisation and integration occurs where contexts foster support, relatedness and autonomy. This perhaps explains the importance of other people or a supportive network to counter the effects of contexts that do not support these needs. Elaborating on this Kidd (1998) discusses resilience (in relation to careers). This involves emotions and attitudes, particularly flexibility and tolerating uncertainty, and involves self-esteem, autonomy and optimism. These are the personal assets that immersive experiences appear to foster. Immersive experiences have the capacity to continuously develop qualities and capacities for resilience so they can be taken both across life situations and forward into future transitions.

Gersick (1991) argued that all change in natural systems can be explained in terms of a model of punctuated equilibrium drawing on theories from six different domains. The theory assumes long periods of stability (equilibrium) that are punctuated by short periods of revolution, described as 'qualitative, metamorphic change'. Underlying natural systems are deep, enduring structures that determine what persists and what changes during transition periods, which are adaptations to new circumstances. Immersive experiences, based on our research, can be seen as examples of these short periods of revolution in an individual's life process of change.

Levinson's (1978) theory of adult development is used for the domain of 'self'. Levinson explains the strong feelings of loss and instability that arise as deep, enduring structures are threatened during a life-structure transition. The transformational process dismantles the deep structure in order to permit integration of new and old structures. Such transitions involve both loss and the emotions relating to this, and the potential for new possibilities (Hale and de Abreu 2010). This change may take place over several years (Levinson 1978) or shorter timescales (Williams 1999 suggests six months). Based on the accounts in our work, the change process can vary in time but is more in line with Williams, although the learning may accrue over many years and the changes may take a period of time to become enduring.

The profound significance of immersive experience
Through this study we have come to believe that immersive experiences are profoundly important in the development of people. They are particularly important in the significant life-changing transitions that people make throughout and across their lives. What our study has demonstrated is that immersive experiences take many forms and occur outside these widely recognised 'mega transitions'.

Our claim is that immersive experiences provide rich environments for developing a range of self-knowledge, dispositions, qualities and capabilities that are essential for current and future survival and adaptation in a complex, unpredictable and often disruptive world. Students' university experiences in themselves may be immersive but generally students don't recognise them as a discrete immersive experience – perhaps because they are often an extension of the formal educational processes with which they are already familiar and skilful in navigating. We have to look to students' wider life experiences while they are studying at university, to find the sorts of experiences that they recognise as being immersive. Our belief is that such experiences contribute in a significant way to a more complete education. By this we mean the life process that affords an individual the opportunities for developing himself in ways that are necessary to be the author of their own life (Baxter Magolda 2001, 2004, 2009).

> Educators have multiple expectations for the journey that is called a college education. For example, we expect students to acquire knowledge, learn how to analyse it, and learn the process of judging what to believe themselves – what development theorists call complex ways of knowing. We expect students to develop and internal sense of identity – an understanding of how they view themselves and what they value. We expect them to learn how to construct healthy relationships with others, relationships based on mutuality rather than self-sacrifice, and relationships that affirm diversity. We expect them to integrate these ways of knowing, being and interacting with others into the capacity for self-authorship – the capacity to internally define their own beliefs, identity and relationships. This self-authorship, this internal capacity, is the necessary foundation for mutual, collaborative participation with others in adult life.
> (Baxter Magolda 2001:xvi)

A lifewide concept of learning and personal development and the educational practices that support learners' self-development could embrace the immersive experiences learners encounter in the life outside the institutional environment. It is for this reason that we propose that an imaginative lifewide curriculum should prepare learners for and give them experiences of adventuring in uncertain and unfamiliar situations where the contexts and challenges are not known, accepting the risks involved. Our role as educators is to support them when they participate in situations that require them to be resilient and help them recognise and appreciate their own transformation.

Acknowledgements
We would like to thank all the people who contributed stories of their immersive experience to our study. Without their contributions this synthesis would not have been possible.

Endnotes
1 see http://immersiveexperience.pbwiki.com/Stories+of+immersive+experiences

Chapter 11

Surrey Lifewide Learning Award: a learning partnership to support lifewide learning

Norman Jackson, Charlotte Betts and Jenny Willis

Synopsis
In 2009 the University of Surrey embarked on a research and development process to develop an award through which students' lifewide learning enterprises could be encouraged, supported, valued and publicly recognised. This chapter describes the award framework and the learning practices it supports, relating it to the concept of a learning partnership described in Chapter 5. It describes the outcomes of piloting the award and considers the learning and achievements demonstrated by participants in the scheme.

Introduction
The University of Surrey is a medium-sized university (14,000 students) whose mission embraces high-quality research and good-quality undergraduate and postgraduate education. It's educational distinctiveness lies in the undergraduate education it provides, which combines academic theory and practice in discipline-based contexts with real world, practical experience. About 70 per cent of undergraduates are enrolled on either a three-year integrated theory and practice based curriculum, or a four-year programme containing a year-long work placement in environments that are relevant to a discipline and/or a learner's own career orientations. The university believes that this is the most effective form of education to prepare learners for their future lives and this is endorsed by the fact that Surrey graduates are amongst the most employable of any UK university.[1]

Taken at face value it would seem that the university has a very effective educational model, so why should we change it? Closer inspection indicates that, if we exclude programmes that have a statutory requirement for a curriculum that integrates professional practice and academic study (e.g. in health programmes), only 50 per cent of undergraduates participate in our work placement scheme. Furthermore, there are concerns about the ongoing impact of the recession and the dramatic increase in tuition fees in 2012, both of which may impact on four-year programmes. We are in a classic change dilemma – do we sustain a proven model that seems to work well for a significant proportion of students, or do we change what we are doing to adapt to changes in the external environment? A further concern is how might we add value to the experience and development of students who currently do not benefit from this educationally effective model?

The university, through the work of its Centre for Excellence in Professional Training and Education (SCEPTrE), concluded that we need to do three things:
- Create a more engaging academic curriculum: one that is based on independent or productive enquiry.
- Diversify the ways in which the university helps learners develop the capability that is important to being a professional using approaches that do not require a year-long placement (Chapters 12 and 13 describe examples).
- Develop a much broader conception of a curriculum to embrace the idea that learners gain valuable personal and professional development through life experiences outside the current academic and work-based curriculum. We called this a 'lifewide curriculum' to emphasise that the whole of a person's life is brought to bear in their unique learning project that enables them to become who they want to become.

This chapter focuses on the third strategy.

Lifewide learning proposition

The thinking and reasoning outlined in the earlier chapters of this book led us to develop the idea of lifewide learning as one possible means of addressing the second and third of these concerns. The idea of lifewide education was intended to embrace the many parallel and interconnected journeys and experiences that individually and collectively contribute to the personal development of individuals while they are studying for their degrees. We reasoned that by reframing the university's perception of what counts as learning, and developing the means to recognise and value learning that is not formally assessed within an academic programme, learners could be helped to develop a deeper understanding of how and what they were learning in the different parts of their lives. Such enhanced self-awareness is likely to help them become more effective at learning through their own experiences beyond university.

The concept of lifewide learning and a lifewide curriculum was developed through a series of papers (Jackson 2008a, b & c, 2009, 2010a, b & c) and the educational application of the concept developed through the piloting of an award scheme that is described below.

Developing and piloting an award framework

In July 2008, following publication of the University's Student Experience Strategy and Action Plan, SCEPTrE was invited to examine the idea of a lifewide curriculum as a way of developing understanding of the concept of a *more complete education,* which underlies the strategy.

SCEPTrE's response was to propose a *student development award* that embraced and gave meaning to the idea of a more complete education, which we interpreted to mean all the things that students did in addition to their study programmes that made their education more complete. In February 2009, the University's Learning and Teaching Strategy Group invited SCEPTrE to undertake a feasibility study for a 'Surrey Award'. The study was completed and proposals were made to the University Learning and Teaching Committee in January 2010, but the Committee felt that the framework involved too many hours of student effort (300 hours were proposed) and it was too complicated and resource intensive. Revised proposals, which simplified the framework and reduced the time requirement to 150 hours, were accepted by the Committee in March 2010. The framework was piloted between May 2010 and March 2011. The aims of the pilot were to:

- create an award framework and pilot it (including the guidance, infrastructure, operating systems and procedures necessary to promote good learning)
- develop a robust and credible assessment process and develop understanding of standards for learning and achievement
- recruit up to 100 students and support them to enable them to achieve the award or certificates within the framework
- evaluate the process and the outcomes and determine the costs of operating the scheme
- through research and scholarship, develop a knowledge base relating to students' lifewide learning habits

- disseminate the results of the research and development work to the wider community as part of SCEPTrE's national role as a Centre for Excellence in Teaching and Learning.

The framework was developed in two stages: first, building on the work undertaken prior to the pilot, an award was developed and the guidance created; second, a series of certificates was created. The award framework is summarised in Figure 11.1. It comprises an overarching award and a family of certificates formed around themes for personal development. They are unified through the idea of lifewide learning and underpinned by a *Capability and Values Statement* (Appendix 1). The Lifewide Learning Award is made by the university to students who demonstrate, through a portfolio, learning and personal development they have gained through co-curricular and extra-curricular experiences, in line with the requirements for the award. A *minimum* involvement of 150 hours of experience-based and reflective learning is required. Students decide what experiences to include in their portfolio but they have to demonstrate new learning and personal development against the Capability and Values Statement for the award.

Figure 11.1 Lifewide Learning Award framework

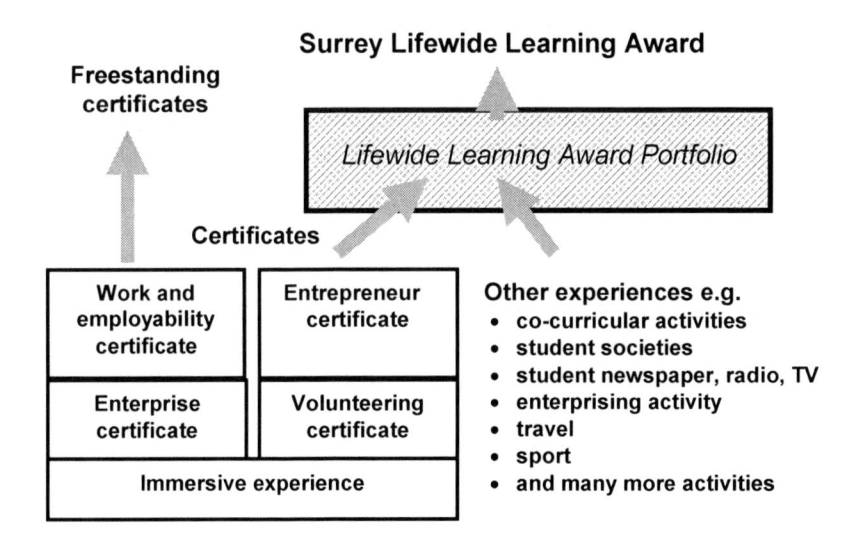

Surrey Lifewide Learning Award

Freestanding certificates

Lifewide Learning Award Portfolio

Certificates

Work and employability certificate	Entrepreneur certificate	Other experiences e.g.
Enterprise certificate	Volunteering certificate	• co-curricular activities • student societies • student newspaper, radio, TV • enterprising activity • travel • sport • and many more activities
Immersive experience		

Certificates provide a distinctive pathway to the Lifewide Learning Award but there is no obligation to include a certificate in a portfolio. They require a minimum of 100 hours of experience-based and reflective learning and they can be taken as freestanding certificates or be incorporated into a learner's portfolio for the Lifewide Learning Award. They provide a means of demonstrating capabilities that are important for employability and for being an effective professional. They complement the traditional means of recognising informal learning gained through the university's professional training scheme. Certificates are underpinned by the same Capability and Values Statement that underpins the Lifewide Learning Award.

The framework is intended to support a lifewide concept of higher education and embrace the idea of a lifewide curriculum which is underpinned by the ten principles for an imaginative curriculum elaborated in Chapter 6.

A learning partnership

Most of our learning involves some sort of partnership. Informally, our partnerships involve parents, other family members, friends, colleagues, peers and virtually anyone whom we believe we can learn from. They also involve formal relationships with teachers and other people who are employed to provide advice and guidance, and the organisations that provide infrastructures and resources to promote and support learning. In lifewide education both informal, self-determined and formal, institutionalised partnerships are necessary and encouraged. Indeed, the added value of lifewide education is in its explicit valuing of all forms of partnership for learning.

The Lifewide Learning Award framework and support mechanisms display the characteristics of a 'learning partnership' (Baxter Magolda 2004b, 2009b and Chapter 5).

The Learning Partnerships Model (LPM) creates an evolutionary bridge by merging three supportive components with three challenges in the learning environment. Support is offered through *three principles*: validating learners' ability to know, situating learning in learners' experience, and defining learning as mutually constructing meaning. Participants reported greater willingness to take responsibility for constructing knowledge and their own beliefs when educators validated their potential to do so. Using their experience offered a foundation for learning provided support in this challenging process. Having learning defined as mutual construction made it acceptable to participate in the process. These supports assist learners in engaging in the *three challenges* of learning environments that promote self-authorship: knowledge is complex and socially constructed, self is central to knowledge construction, and authority and expertise are shared among

Table 11.1 Relationship of Surrey Lifewide Learning Award Framework to Baxter Magolda's (2004a) learning partnership principles LPP

LPP	Infrastructure	Institutional support and engagement
1 Validating students as knowers – *means acknowledging their capacity to hold a point of view, recognising their current understandings and supporting them in explaining their views*	1) Capability and values statement encourages learners to be aware of their knowledge development process 2) Guidance emphasises complexity of knowledge 3) Framework requires learners to make explicit their personal knowledges gained through their lifewide experiences through their portfolio 4) Process for making judgements validates learners' representations of their experiential knowing	1) Through induction process and opportunities for conversation with scheme co-ordinator 2) Through the portfolio checks when feedback is given by scheme co-ordinator 3) Through the assessment process which recognises and values students as developers of knowledge and encourages them to offer their perspectives and views.
2 Situating learning in learners' experiences – *means using students' experiences, lives and current knowledge as a resource for learning and personal development*	The Lifewide Learning Award framework is concerned with learners' experiential learning. Being able to deal with situations is an important focus in the Capability and Values Statement (Appendix 1). The principles on which the lifewide curriculum is based encourage learners to participate in situations that will enable them to develop 'epistemological, intrapersonal and interpersonal complexity' (Baxter Magolda 2004a:41 and chapter 5)	1) Through induction process and informal opportunities for conversation with scheme co-ordinator
3 Mutually constructing meaning – *involves educators, employers and others sharing and connecting their knowledge so that all participants have the opportunity to develop more complex understandings and decisions*	The life place map encourages participants to identify in their everyday situations who they are interacting with and how they are interacting Portfolios and personal accounts encourage participants to reveal who the significant others are in their lives, who help them learn in their different contexts and experiences The creation of a portfolio is itself a constructive, creative, meaning making process	Teachers and employers are only two of many possible 'partners' in an individual's lifewide learning enterprises; others may include parents, other family members, friends, peers, colleagues Significant others involved in supporting the award include the scheme co-ordinator, other SCEPTrE team members (coaching), careers advisors and alumni mentors

knowledgeable peers. Explicit portrayal of knowledge as complex and socially constructed challenged learners to move toward epistemological complexity. Emphasis on the role of the self in knowledge construction challenged them to bring their identity into learning thus moving them toward construction of an internal identity. Sharing of expertise and authority in the learning process engaged learners in mutually constructing knowledge and helped them develop more mature relationships. These six components connect to all phases of the journey because the educator is mutually constructing the educational process with the learner. The partnership adjusts as the learner adopts more complex ways of making meaning.
(Baxter Magolda 2009b:150)

Table 11.1 relates Baxter Magolda's principles for a learning partnership to the infrastructures and support for learning provided through the Lifewide Learning Award framework. Student development is facilitated by a small team (Figure 11.2). The award co-ordinator did most of the day-to-day running of the scheme. An Advisory Committee was created to support the team, with representatives from faculties and industry. The function of the Committee was to act as a think tank to generate new ideas and a sounding board to help the team with decisions. Members of the Committee, particular faculty members, were also expected to be advocates for the scheme. The Committee reviewed ideas, monitored progress, considered plans and discussed results. The Committee also received formal and informal reports from two external auditors.

Figure 11.2 Lifewide Learning Award delivery team and committee structures

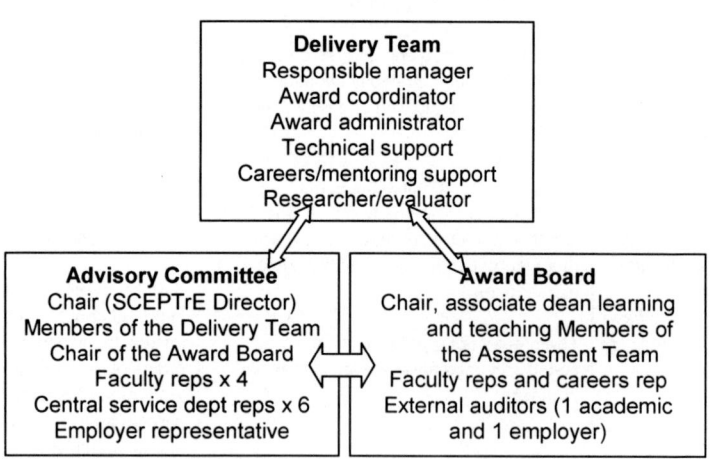

Delivery Team
Responsible manager
Award coordinator
Award administrator
Technical support
Careers/mentoring support
Researcher/evaluator

Advisory Committee
Chair (SCEPTrE Director)
Members of the Delivery Team
Chair of the Award Board
Faculty reps x 4
Central service dept reps x 6
Employer representative

Award Board
Chair, associate dean learning
and teaching Members of
the Assessment Team
Faculty reps and careers rep
External auditors (1 academic
and 1 employer)

The concept of an award for lifewide learning is predicated on students operating independently and self-managing their learning over a period of time (up to nine months during the pilot). To encourage and support this enterprise a website was developed (www.surreylifewideaward.net) to enable students to register and to provide guidance on how to complete the award. The website contained a supplementary 'Student Voice' micro-website that provided many accounts written by students engaged in lifewide learning.

Learners were expected to learn through their experiences independently. This was intentional (to align with the underpinning theory of learning) but it was also pragmatic (to minimise staff costs). Working and learning independently in this way can be a lonely experience so the strategies used to keep in touch with students and keep them connected to the award were vital. Day-to-day support was provided by the award co-ordinator. Support was given in the following ways.

- responses to general enquiries and specific questions by email or telephone
- provision of induction and reflective writing workshops
- informal drop-in conversations
- feedback on portfolios
- reflective learning and writing workshops
- bi-weekly email newsletters celebrating successes of students on the scheme
- ongoing news items for the website
- social events like Christmas party
- help with reflective accounts e.g. if written english was poor
- annual lifewide learning essay prize.

Focus for learning

Situations are the focus for learning and claims for personal development. Eduard Lindeman, writing in 1926 under the influence of his friend John Dewey, provides us with the rationale for focusing attention on situations as the basic building block of living, learning and developing, and this rationale was utilised in the Lifewide Learning Award.

> the approach to adult education will be via the route of *situations*, not subjects. Our academic system has grown in reverse order; subjects and teachers constitute the starting-point, students are secondary. In conventional education the student is required to adjust himself to an established curriculum; in adult education the curriculum is built around the student's needs and interests. Every adult person finds himself in specific situations

with respect to his work, his recreation, his family-life, his community-life et cetera – situations which call for adjustments. Adult education begins at this point. Subject matter is brought into the situation, is put to work, when needed. Texts and teachers play a new and secondary role in this type of education; they must give way to the primary importance of the learner ... The situation-approach to education means that the learning process is at the outset given a setting of reality. Intelligence performs its functions in relation to actualities, not abstractions.

(Smith 2004: quoting Eduard Lindeman 1927)

Figure 11.3 Dealing with situations

```
                    1 Think about
                    /evaluate situation
                    Design/plan actions

3 Reflect on results/    SITUATION              2 Act
learn from experience    challenge, problem,    Be aware of effects and
Enhanced knowledge of    opportunity            adjust actions if
self and how to deal with                       necessary
this type of situation
```

To perform and make things happen we have to be able to deal with and create situations. Our life is full of situations that we have to deal with and deal with in an appropriate and effective manner. When we encounter a situation, no matter what the context, we assess it, decide what to do, do it and, if appropriate, reflect on what happened (Figure 11.3) so that we understand it more. This process is reminiscent of Kolb's (1984) learning cycle, beginning with a concrete experience (the situation we encounter or create).

The award encourages participants to learn and recognise their development through:
- heightened self-awareness of the significance of situations and experiences through which they are learning and developing across their lives
- use of the Capability and Values Statement to draw attention to forms of learning and development that are particularly relevant to understanding and performing effectively in situations
- planning (more like a rough design) for future situation-based learning

- observing and recognising this emergent learning and development and recording of experiences and insights gained through a diary, sketchbook, blog, portfolio, video or other representation
- reflecting on experiences and situations and making more sense of and creating deeper meanings from these experiences
- revealing their meaning making through an integrative account of experiences, learning and development.

For the learner the process begins with enhancing their self-awareness of the many spaces and places they inhabit in which they have their everyday experiences and encounter or create situations. By creating a simple map of their life[2] they reveal how they are choosing to live their lives. Typically, students recognise between four to seven distinct areas in their life, although the boundaries between different areas may be blurred.

In their life map they reveal the building blocks of their life. They show what they do in different spaces and places, and the significant people with whom they interact and learn from. The enhanced self-awareness developed through the creation of a life map is intended to help learners think about the opportunities they have for developing themselves and opportunities for further development. This thinking informs the preparation of a personal development plan. Using the award Capability and Values Statement learners identify where they have had opportunities to develop each element of the statement and where they might further develop capabilities and values in future.

The process of mapping, reflecting and imagining is intended to encourage learners to appreciate their whole lives as the means of engaging with what (Baxter Magolda 2004a and Chapter 5) calls the 'epistemological, intrapersonal and interpersonal complexity' that characterises living and working in the unpredictable world outside formal education. Engaging with such complexity facilitates development of 'one's internal belief system [and] crafting an integrated sense of self' (Baxter Magolda 2004a:29). We agree with this author's claims that self-authorship should be a central aim of higher education, and the Lifewide Learning Award framework addresses, through its focus on learning in and through situations, the three assumptions that underlie self-authorship, namely: 1) *knowledge is complex and socially constructed*; 2) *self is central to knowledge construction* and it is important to define yourself and bring this to your way of learning and being; and 3) *authority and expertise are shared in the mutual co-construction of knowledge among peers*.

Assessing personal enhancements

Lifewide learning poses considerable challenges in an institutionalised environment that seems to value only learning that can be predicted and measured. As we have seen in earlier chapters we are dealing with complex achievements that are difficult or impossible to explain or represent. They include: multiple conceptions of knowledge; capabilities that are integrative in their nature; performance that at best will only ever be partially understood, revealed and explained; and outcomes that are meaningful to an individual because she has been through a unique experience and appreciated their value to herself. Such forms of learning and development are deeply personal and highly situated. Peter Knight (2005:2) offers realistic advice in such situations.

> I am arguing that different sorts of learning and different achievements have to be judged in different ways ... it is a mistake to apply a form of judgement – such as measurement – to achievements that are not, epistemologically speaking, measurable. It is no wonder that so many people have so much trouble trying to measure 'key' or 'generic achievements' or 'skills'. Once we move away from the simplest of the achievements, we are dealing with complex and changing constructs which do not have the qualities necessary for them to be measurable
>
> there are highly subjective areas of human experience ... in which connoisseurship (Eisner, 1985) is an appropriate form of judgement. Connoisseurs are experts with rich knowledge of a field. They offer opinions and argue their points of view but, even so, there are different points of view because the material in question evokes such different subjective responses.

Making judgements about lifewide learning requires an ongoing conversation among a group of peers who are both empathetic and prepared to make judgements based on the evidence of learning that is presented. In reaching judgements as to whether a learner warrants the Lifewide Learning Award assessors were forced to declare what they were valuing and recognising, namely:
- learners' commitments to their own personal development through self-directed and unplanned activities over a period of time
- learners' self-awareness – their ability to recognise that they are learning and developing in different ways through their lifewide experiences

- learners' ability to reveal, explain and communicate their self-awareness of learning, development and personal change using the tools and frameworks provided and artefacts that they created
- evidence of learners honouring the self-directed learning process.

We are not dealing with notions of academic level. We anticipated that the abilities of students to reflect upon their experiences and represent and evidence their self-awareness and development would not vary according to the stage of their education (i.e. a postgraduate student would be better than an undergraduate student); rather, it would reflect individuals' preparedness and capability for recognising and representing their informal learning. Bound up with this preparedness and capability are likely to be cultural issues such as the general reluctance of students in sciences and engineering to reveal personal feelings. The award is intended to enhance this dimension of capability. So the evaluation of the experience by the learner and anyone assessing a learner's claims is an evaluation of the learner's representation of her own enhancement[3] – the journey that she has taken.

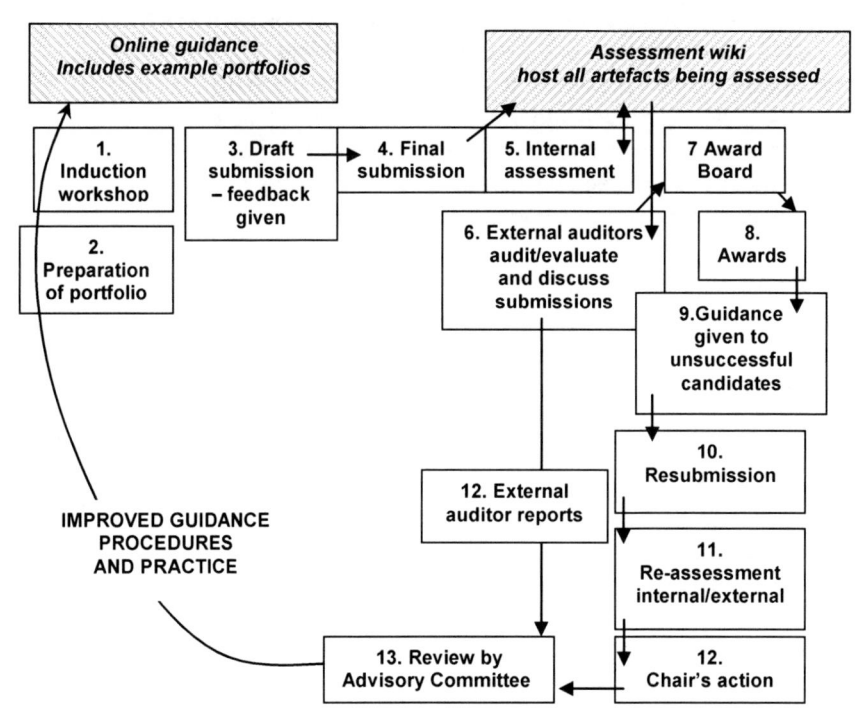

Figure 11.4 Assessment procedures developed through the pilot

Lifewide learning for an individual at a certain stage in her development is revealed and self-judged in accordance with the extent to which it enhances and especially widens her ability to create meaning from her life, and her self-knowledge and capabilities in evaluating and representing her own development beyond her initial stage of development. These perspectives on learning and achievement are consistent with the earlier statements relating to an individual's journey towards self-authorship.

Assessment procedures
Assessment procedures are summarised in Figure 11.4. For the institutional assessor, assessment of a learner's claims for personal enhancement involves reaching an informed judgement about a learner's claims for personal enhancement through the journey they have described in their mediating artefacts (life space map, personal development plan, portfolio, integrative account and perhaps photos, videos, audio records and other items that provide evidence of their experiences and the learning they have gained). Peer review of assessor judgements is through two independent external auditors who had access to learners' portfolios through an assessment wiki. Their role is to audit assessors' judgements on the sufficiency and quality of evidence of learning and personal development and offering an opinion that either endorsed or invited reconsideration of the assessor's judgement. The results of this process are formally presented to an Award Board which makes the final pass/fail decision for each candidate. On completion of the process the External Auditors provide a written report to the University on the assessment process with suggestions and recommendations for improvement. This report is formally considered by the Lifewide Learning Advisory Board.

Patterns of lifewide learning and development
Here we examine the nature and patterns of learning and development (personal enhancements) through the narratives and artefacts students present in their portfolios.

Portfolios
The portfolio is the physical or virtual medium for students to record and represent their learning and development. Its role is intended to encourage learners to develop the habit of thinking about and recording their experiences, drawing out deeper meanings and understandings in the process.

Although the requirements for the award specify that a portfolio be produced containing various documentary artefacts (life space map, personal development plan, evidence of ongoing reflection, final written reflective account and updated CV), the presentation of this portfolio is entirely the choice of the individual. This *freedom to choose* reinforces the self-managed ethos that underpins the award and allows for creative self-expression.

Porter and Cleland (1995) discuss the need for students to have agency over their portfolios and the importance of allowing them to determine what to include, as it allows them to learn from their own 'personal interpretations and insights'. It also fosters a sense of ownership which can lead to greater empowerment for learners, enabling them to become the author of their own stories; expressing this in their own unique voices, in a medium that they feel comfortable with – whether using a video diary, blog or scrapbook.

Adopting this reasoning, participants in the Lifewide Learning Award are able to choose the format and style of portfolio but they are required to demonstrate an ongoing interaction and engagement with it, ensuring that they revisit it at least once a week throughout the process. The emphasis here is on commitment to a process of critical reflection rather than purely listing or describing activities. The portfolios submitted for the award have been rich and diverse (Table 11.2).

Table 11.2 Categorisation of portfolios in the pilot study n=28

'Shoebox'; literally a physical container into which representations of learning are deposited and explained	0
Handwritten diary essentially text based – could be a Word document	9
Scrapbook containing text, photos, drawings and diagrams, and other artefacts like tickets/mementos of events	8
PowerPoint	1
Digital story	1
Blog or wiki	6
E-portfolio	1
Personal website	1
Mixed media – part physical part virtual	1

Some students used blogs and e-portfolios, enabling them to blend or connect technologies and resources such as digital images, audio and video. One student enjoyed the immediacy of being able to record spoken reflection on a mobile telephone when suddenly inspired and was then able to send this directly to her blog. Seeing how people mix and adapt these technologies shows how using a virtual portfolio has the advantage of immediacy and accessibility; being able to add to it from almost anywhere, at any time – for example one blog site that allowed you to update your blog via email or texting from a smart phone.

Such accessibility appeared to be helpful in maintaining engagement and developing the narratives of the experiences through which learning and understanding emerges.

In contrast to the electronic/virtual environments some students opted with enthusiasm to produce a physical portfolio in the form of a scrapbook rich in images and mementos of the events that they had experienced as well as the textual descriptions and reflective evaluations.

Narrative themes
A number of recurrent themes can be recognised in the experiences that students describe in their lifewide learning portfolios and integrating accounts, namely:
- employability and career related experiences
- personal, emotional or spiritual wellbeing / overcoming or coping with challenging situations
- travel and being immersed in new cultures or countries
- involvement in societies or clubs either as an organiser or participant
- personal interests and hobbies
- volunteering, caring for others and mentoring
- being creative and enterprising.

When portfolios and integrating accounts are audited for their content, generalised patterns of responses can be identified (Tables 11.3 and 11.4). These patterns are also manifest in interviews with participants and they seem to represent a fundamental orientation in their pattern of lifewide learning. They were also seen in essays submitted for two competitions on the theme of lifewide learning (see chapter 9). In this set of narratives, five focus on career, employability and development for being an effective professional; thirteen are oriented towards personal growth and self-actualisation; and nine appear to combine these orientations.

Participants are expected to show, in their personal accounts, how their learning and development relates to the Capability and Values Statement. This is normally achieved by relating aspects of their account to specific items in the statement. Table 11.4 shows how statements are referenced in fifteen accounts and also uses the three categories outline above to show the different orientations.

Table 11.3 Orientations in portfolios, integrating accounts and interviews of 27 students who submitted for the Award

1) Career, employability and professional development orientation – *mostly aligned to the goal of developing myself for employment or a vocation/career in a particular field*	G – wants to work in HR, so volunteering and working variously with other people P – hobbies and character traits are strictly aligned with his area of study/career (astronomy and machines) T – event management, but some personal activities e.g. cooking – cultures DP – work experience, music and creative experiences JH – mostly surrounding her learning for the dance management world, though includes some volunteering experiences
2) Self-actualisation – *mostly aligned to personal interests, passions and growth as an individual*	B – choir, leadership, autistic boy, band K – responsibilities at work, mentoring, course rep, leadership in group U – dev. in six months in new culture, personality, language, career goals, casual work C – Brownies, Guides, HCA O – deliberately focuses on these; exemplary, volunteering, setting up own business, hobbies F – painting room, cooking, growing own food, sewing, police officer, learning Spanish M – drama, cooking, dining, gardening, achievements in placement, photography, friends, travel E – coaching and leading canoeing teams, increased self-confidence and transferability of skills I – overcoming her anxiety through facing travel; mentor L – HR research, ALS, course rep all related to her philosophy that personal skills more important than academic Z – SCEPTrE experiences, Mukono work, USA voluntary work AI – vast range of experiences including CoLab, social enterprise, radio, social expeditions FO – St John's ambulance, netball, mentoring, Uganda volunteering, university society
3) Combined self-actualisation and career	H – culminates in her seeking counselling and drawing all together (translation, marriage) N – largely work-related, but then includes SIFE and hospice admin work D – wide range, police, own business, student ambassador, aimed at being person he wants to be R – most career oriented but also conscious effort to broaden her activities e.g. gym, team, language S – career as economist but conscious dev of inter-personal and other skills, travel to India, teaching, cooking, friendships, mentoring A – begins with career focus then moves into his lack of social skills; developed lot as PG, but from an 'abnormal' starting point (autistic?) J – mature student of law, PT in Australia, photographer's, theatre writing, cinema usher, serendipity CF – travel, sport, placement, volunteering, health, skills, creative activities MR – SIFE, volunteering in primary schools, academic rep, academies, language learning

Table 11.4 Analysis of 15 of the 21 integrating accounts (A–O) submitted for the Lifewide Learning Award in March 2011

Capability and Values Statement	A	B	C	D	E	F	G	H	I	J	K	L	M	N	O
1 Managing and evaluating my own development	1	4	4	3	5	1	5	17	8	19	5	4	17	5	4
2 Being able to deal with situations, solve problems, work with challenge and take advantage of opportunity	1	4	6	3	6	1	8	13	4	12	5	5	10	7	10
3 Being able to find out what you need to know to do what you need to do		3	1	4	1	2	4	10	6	13	2		14	2	5
4 Being creative and enterprising	1	2	2	2	2	1	4	9	5	15	1		9	2	6
5 Being a good communicator	1	5	4	4	5	2	5	5	5	15	3	1	10	8	2
6 Being able to work with and lead others	1	5	5	5	6		6	3	4	12	3	4	11	7	3
7 Behaving ethically and with social responsibility	1	2	2	2			2	3	3	11	3	3	5	3	3
8 Other areas for personal dev that are important to me			6					10	2	14	4	1	9	2	
9 My will to be and become who I want to be		6	4	2		1	3	12	5	11	2	6	16	2	5
10 My values and the value I add to my enterprises		3		3			2	10	3	8	3	15	17	1	2
11 My growing confidence in my own ability		3	4	4			5	14	4	11	5	2	1	3	6

Explanation: Numbers indicate the number of times a student claimed this form of development in his/her account. The 21 accounts can be classified into one of three orientations: grey = career orientation (n=3); white = self-actualisation (n=11); speckled = combination (n=7).

As might be expected, every individual's experience creates a unique pattern. As a general rule, those with the greater number of references reveal a richer mix of learning and these learners appear to be more aware of their learning. For example, account J demonstrates, through examining a serendipitous series of apparently unrelated events, how she has come to surmount lifelong anxieties to become a different person. Evidence of the journey towards self-authorship is present in all accounts, even the weaker ones

Career, employability and professional development orientation
Portfolios, integrating accounts and interviews for students with this lifewide learning orientation are focused on experiences and personal enhancement that can be related to their *will* to gain employment in a certain field or to become a certain type of professional. As a generalisation, this tendency is most evident in undergraduate students in their third or fourth year of study who might combine voluntary work, internships or placements or fill their spare time with involvement in communities, groups and informal activities complementary to their disciplinary field which they could relate to their intended career goal. Overseas students often display this career orientation, as illustrated at interview by this postgraduate:

> I think as an international student, when I go back I have to take all the opportunities that are thrown at me. ... I am here for learning and training ... simple as that. Even PhD, as a training period is three years training. It's nothing much. So when I go back I have to be good in knowledge and experience.

A final year dance student filled her portfolio with the dance, arts and cultural experiences she was involved in beyond her studies, including a placement year, several summer internships, travelling to different countries in which she located and attended networking meetings with other artists, and working for an online dance magazine.

> My experiences between June 2009 and June 2010 were remarkably rich ... from planned activities such as internship and voluntary work which contributed to my professional development, to more general life experiences such as travelling to foreign countries and living in a multicultural environment. All of these have contributed so much to the expectations for my future – a career in arts management and a life-long and live-wide process in character building

These types of portfolio often demonstrate a real sense of determination and drive to succeed. In some cases there was evidence of a strategically planned course of action. The following excerpt from a final year music student epitomises this attitude. To strive toward achieving his goals he undertook two internships, was a member of a band, took part in charity gigs and when travelling created sound recordings which he published to his CV-style portfolio website:

> Essentially once I realised I wanted to pursue a career within the music industry in some form, I thought about the processes involved in making something like this become a reality, working out the necessary steps in order to make it happen.

For some there were moments of realisation that connected to their desire to become a professional and represented a transition in their comprehension of what professionalism meant. In some cases this was directly related to a work-based situation while others' comprehension was through becoming aware of the learning occurring in one context of their lives being transferred to another. The statement below captures one student's altered perspective on interviewing following her involvement in a recruitment process while on a work placement.

> Having seen how short listing is done I can now sympathise with those who have to do it and can see how it is very easy to have yourself written off immediately by not addressing the points I have learnt here! For future applications I will definitely think how what I am writing comes across to the person that will be reading it. I will make sure I keep it succinct, to the point and relevant. I will only address the points being asked for. I will ensure I [am] clear about what I am trying to get across.

Vocational focus does not imply only technical knowledge and experience. Students are increasingly aware of the importance to employers of workers' dispositions and transferable skills as expressed by this interviewee:

> Now, when the employer wants to see people with different skills, not just technical skills, that technical skill is developed through education and academics. So I think you develop your social skills ... Social skills are very important ... or soft skills. And you develop by doing different kinds of activities, events, meeting with people, communicating with people, networking, socialising and the best way to do that, especially in the university is involvement in events.

Level 1 and 2 students may still have a strong career orientation but their purpose might be related to building their CV in preparation for applying for a work placement in their third year. A good example of an enhanced CV is offered by student E who both adds and explains the significance of new experiences like coaching.

But the CV loses its importance for some participants. A young dietician admitted at interview that her original objective in undertaking the award was to learn how to condense her frenetic range of extra-curricular activities into a coherent CV, and to be able to add another qualification to it. By the time of completing the award process, she mocked her naivety, confessing, 'My whole focus and aim has completely changed.' Demonstrating the real value she now perceives, she went on: 'Until you start it, until you start doing the reflective process and realise that it does affect you, you don't know what you will get from it.'

Entrepreneurial orientation
A subset of this category is an orientation towards creating or running a business. Students who have this orientation commit considerable amounts of time and energy to activities that are directly or indirectly linked to their business interests. Student D is typical. His list of activities includes being a student ambassador for the university (meeting and greeting visitors, then escorting them around campus); training, working and qualifying as a Special Constable for the police; and undertaking a full-time work placement year setting up his own business – he is now managing director of a not-for-profit technology company. His reflective narrative is packed with evidence of his development, but to quote just one brief extract, he concludes:

> There have been many problems in the business ranging from employee issues to tax issues to banking issues. Through problem solving, persistence and dedication I have been able to overcome many difficult situations, with minor effect on customer relations. There have also been many opportunities, which I have seized and have often resulted in further work and publicity, such as applying and being shortlisted for the Toast of Surrey 2011 Business Awards.

Personal growth and self-actualisation orientation
Portfolios, integrating accounts and interviews of students with this lifewide learning orientation are focused on experiences and personal enhancement that can be related to interests, passions and personal growth or adapting to significant new situations. A number of portfolios submitted were underpinned by an element of personal well-being, a sense of journeying through a challenging situation and the development of new confidence and self-awareness.

> Every day I have to remind myself what I've learned from all the therapy sessions I've had. This is the box that links together all the other boxes, because everything I do to improve myself and get better leads to me being a happier person who loves to be alive more and more every day. Most importantly I'm trying to get my will to live back, and discover things that I love to do, that inspire me, fascinate me and captivate me.

Student F had a sense of writing to someone or an audience even though it was obviously a very personal and sensitive subject matter. Beginning with ' A little bit about me' she offers the reader some background to how she has got to where she is now and concludes this page with the purpose of creating the portfolio:

> It is due to this phobia ... that you will notice that experiences I class as development, you may class as small such as going on a train. But it is doing this that contributes highly towards helping me develop into the person I am trying to get back from before.

This student talks about the sense of achievement she felt in coping with a number of challenging situations and demonstrates how her anxieties have impacted upon many parts of her life but how she is managing these by getting a job over the summer:

> This would normally have caused me high amounts of anxiety ... However, I went for my first day, I was nervous but no more than I feel anyone else would be, and had a good first day. ... Having a ... job such as that had made me come back to university with even more determination to do well ... I am now working twice as hard as I would have been had I not got that job. The job also showed me that I can cope in employment situations without getting anxious like I did the previous year. This is evidence to me that I have progressed.

> [And becoming a mentor] Because I lack confidence, I never had the ability to join any societies and therefore had a limited amount of friends that were either people on my course, or people I live with. I now have friends all over the Campus and I really love walking down the road, or looking out my window and seeing someone I know and who says 'hello' back.

As her confidence grew she tried to help herself more: 'as I have been feeling well I have decided that I am fed up waiting for people to help me and have decided to help myself'. By researching and challenging her own boundaries and comfort zones she is gradually taking on new experiences that are challenging one by one – and seeing the value in confronting them.

Similar growth is recounted by a student who organised a group of volunteers to work in a rural village in Uganda. Referencing her development to all eleven elements of the capability and values statement she concludes:

> This was also a huge challenge to me as I am not naturally outgoing, and I had to really pull myself out of my shell in order to achieve the results I needed. Being the organiser and perceived leader of a group was new to me and extremely daunting; this proved to be one of the most marked times of my life, during which I grew immensely as a person, and developed my confidence through a comforting sense of achievement.

Travelling to new places and being immersed in a different culture is another context with the potential for a great deal of learning and personal growth. Research shows that students who have significant travel experiences (Hansel 1998:87) are more adaptable because they have coped with the surprises and the inevitable problems that arise when travelling. Because they have had to be self-reliant, they are more independent in their thinking, decisions and actions. They become more aware of their home country and culture and are better able to communicate with others and see the world from perspectives other than their own cultural perspective. Much of the personal benefit of travel comes not from what the students learn about the places or cultures they visit, but from the need to continuously make decisions and deal with the demands of daily life in new and unfamiliar settings.

The responsibilities, planning, organisation and self-reliance that travelling can require can provide challenging contexts and new learning situations for any individual. A particularly striking account is found in the narrative of a law student (J) who left school at the age of 17 and returned to full-time education as a mature student. Although experienced in many aspects of life, she had had limited opportunity to travel. Through her own initiative and some chance encounters, she secured a work placement in Australia. The impact this has had on her has been truly transformative, as captured in this extract from her account of visiting Vietnam:

> This past 12 months also saw me conquer some fears that I've had for a while. (...)

It was while we were on a boat trip in Ha Long Bay, exploring the caves and the gorgeous surroundings, that I conquered my fear of water. Something inside me knew that this was a once in a lifetime opportunity and so I stepped into the Kayak and did something I'd not done since I was about 9. It was AMAZING. I felt like I was discovering land for the very first time and I was proud of myself that I let myself do it. I also realised that fears are irrational and I have held myself back through lack of confidence for too long. I hope I will face many more events like this, and challenge myself even further as the exhilaration afterwards can keep your motivation going for months afterwards.

Another student recognises that his love of travel has been a motivator to earn a living, and a source of increased practical skills and of greater self-confidence:

Something I mentioned in both my life map and personal development plan was my love for travelling, which first started during my gap year. I worked for six months in order to travel for two months around South-East Asia, and have travelled to somewhere different every year since then (this year was Morocco, next year over Easter I plan to take a ten-day trip from Rome to Paris via Pisa, Florence, Venice, Milan, Basel, Brussels, Berlin and Amsterdam). Sorting out these trips has helped me to be more organised and responsible, as usually I travel with a group of friends and have to ensure everything is accounted for and sorted out. Similarly, I have found that being in a foreign environment forces me to be more outgoing, whether it involves striking up a conversation with fellow travellers or attempting to ask directions from a local resident.

On a more local, but no less personally significant scale, another student (E) admits: '[I] was a little apprehensive to travel in the underground on my own (it's just too complicated), I had no time to waste.'

International students who come to study at Surrey engage in a transformative experience as they make the transition into a culture that is often very different to their own (see Chapter 13). A Chinese student (U) displays similar insatiability for new experiences and challenging herself. Not content with having made the cultural leap to England, she reveals:

I have a dream that seems it cannot be achieved, it is that I want to work at Swedish Bank and live in Sweden. For an international student, especially

> who comes from China, this sounds ridiculous. I am a Chinese student, my foreign language is English, which will make me special in China but this is not applicable in the UK or Europe. I realized deeply that learning the third language is necessary and useful for me to achieve my dream. That is exactly the reason why I choose French and Italian classes. My friends told me that I cannot handle three languages at the same time finally I will drop or give up one. I feel confused and almost convinced at the beginning, however, I keep asking myself, what is my dream? I cannot abandon any one of them when I am starting to draw the picture in my head.

Incredibly, she has been just one semester in England when she writes this. Her reflective account ends with the challenges she has now set herself in order to achieve her dream:

> Half year in the UK is considerably unbelievable and incredible. A wide range of my ability has improved, as well as my personality, which I did not expect before. However, there are still some aspects I was missing. The rest of my time living in the UK, is adequate for me to change as much as possible. I should start to strengthen my volunteering work and find opportunities to enhance my ethical approach. What I am doing during the first six months is a step closer to my dream, everything is meaningful to some extent. Although now I am working at McDonalds, but I firmly believe that it is only temporary, and in some day, I will find another better job which can get me closer to my dream. I will not stop my pace before my dream comes true; I will keep walking until my dream comes true.

Student societies and clubs on or off campus provide another context for personal development. Here personal growth might be reflected in a sense of responsibility, learning and mastery of new skills, and learning to work with or lead others. Values that are based on good relationships often shine through. Student (B) set up and led a Gospel choir.

> Being in a place of leadership is an absolute honour we are given the opportunity to draw out the gifts in people, get rid of those unnecessary insecurities that hold them back, and bring them to do more than they ever thought they could!

> I was to teach [the choir] some new harmonies that me and a few of the others had only just written – so they weren't fixed in my mind. The way I saw it though, was that the choir would have an opportunity to trial and error

with me, and it'd be a good experience for them. Hopefully it would allow them to really feel part of the making and building of a song.

Another student, drawing on his experience of leading a society, gives a vivid account of how he has developed leadership skills and qualities:

> SIFE had provided me with team leadership skills and taught me how to work as part of a team through various workshops and presentations. I now feel confident in my abilities as a leader. I have attended ... leadership training provided by companies such as HSBC and KMPG, where I learned how to communicate effectively, what it means to be a leader, how to connect your team and effectively manage yourself. Through the year I have helped organize and chaired over 60 meetings this year. Whilst leading I have also involved myself as a team member of every one of our six team projects. By going through the same problems and facing the same challenges as each member, and working together all of which have contributed in developing me as a strong team player. I have learned the importance of planning, of delegation of duties, listening and helping colleagues, and the importance of maintaining a close professional relationship with those you work with. I would now say I am pretty competent in all of the above.

A first year student (L) conveys the exuberance found in many accounts, telling her interviewer:

> The first two weeks of university, I went round and did every society thing going. I did badminton, I did scuba diving, I did rugby, I did fencing again (..) trampolining, and I've kept that one on. I tried some other things as well, but I didn't stick to those. And I work and I volunteer ...

Sporting activities are important areas for personal development for many students:

> I feel that the depth of your relationship off the pitch, is really reflected in how you play on the pitch; you understand each other better, you read one-another's games more easily, and the whole team benefits. Sport is not just the playing of a game. There's so much more to it.

In some instances, sport is undertaken not for pleasure but because it offers a challenge. This is well illustrated by this doctoral student, who had overcome illness and adversity and now found herself on holiday in Cuba with a large group of peers. She explains:

> I'm not really a physical person; I don't really do that much physical activity and ... so I did probably four weeks training, I think, and kind of turned up thinking I don't do heat, and it was 35 degrees here. I don't really do people and there was 15 people in the group and they were really keen cyclists. And I kind of had been training on some old bike which didn't have enough gears and was kind of odd, but on this particular holiday there was one day where we were given the option to either do the 26 kilometres in the morning and at lunchtime get the bus in the next town. Or we could carry on and do the full 84 kilometre cycle. And, as I said, embracing the unknown and challenges I decided that I'd join the other five people who were doing the big one. And so off we went, and we got to kind of the end and there was one kilometre left and it was uphill. And I was like, are you serious? But you know, everyone else was doing it and so I pushed myself and that day I pushed myself in a way that I didn't know was possible. And the sense of satisfaction from getting up that hill and seeing the gates into the town was just ... God, it was like overwhelming and I thought, you know what, I can do this.

This student goes on to attribute her sense of achievement and her new-found confidence to her developing sense of identity.

Volunteering, caring and mentoring create a sense of social responsibility as summarised by this participant:

> I cannot fully explain the feeling of wholeness that accompanies helping someone in a significant way. Every new experience adds to my person, and expands or alters my perspectives. I feel that it has helped me to grow in so many ways, especially in terms of confidence and my capabilities for dealing with unfamiliar situations and to create new opportunities for myself and others.

But it also brings to many volunteers an awareness of reciprocal benefits. Despite previous experience as a Brownies and Girl Guide[4] leader, this language student was fearful of teaching in school and her role as an authority figure. After a few weeks, she had come to the realisation that:

> I saw educational volunteering as me coming into a school and help changing children's lives. I never knew how much we could change each

other's. I saw it as me teaching them, however they ended up teaching me as well. And last but not least, I saw my own development through the teaching, but I never imagined we would develop together.

Similarly, she has learnt from her voluntary work with disabled young people, acknowledging what she did and how her transformation has come about: 'I have learnt through doing, and I did find it quite scary sometimes. Looking back I can see how I turned from clueless to very confident in my volunteer position.'

Volunteering often results in assuming responsibility for others. A final year overseas student holding several voluntary positions recalled one experience she dealt with as a mentor:

> A particular case I had to handle was in the first week of university where a girl kept getting anxiety attacks. She refused to go back to her student accommodation and she wanted to go back home. I spent two hours in Senate House, convincing her on how great university life is. I shared with her my personal encounters and experiences. I remained rational, neutral and [tried] to be not overly emotional. I was nervous as well because I have never handled such a case before. But I pulled myself together and had to choose the right words when communicating with her.

Her personal development is well understood and clearly expressed. She is keen to illustrate it further, with hindsight scorning her previous self:

> I would like to highlight my experience in India. It was always a dream and a personal choice to go to India and see for myself what it is like. All my impressions and misconceptions about India were cleared when I actually met the people on the streets and [spent] days staying with children from the slums. And no, Daravi is nothing like what you see in *SlumDog Millionaire*. I learned to work as a team with 99 other people, we shared rooms, attended lectures, went on visits and volunteered together. We had to be creative when we had to teach English songs and games to the children in the slums. There were times when I felt like giving up, when I could not take the hygiene or the weather, but my love for the kids and the poor made me stay. This summer, I am going back to visit them. I also had to learn a bit of Hindi to communicate, I had to learn to try their cuisines and dance their traditional dancers. This trip taught me to try, adapt and adjust. I am now more culturally aware and I do not form perceptions or make judgemental statements quickly.

Being creative/enterprising makes a significant contribution to personal wellbeing. For this student, the rewards were both intrinsic and practical:

> The cake bake sale was a great success. I made over 50 cup cakes, and between 5–6 of us, we produced over 150 cakes and cookies for sale, making a profit of over £100 towards subsidizing future events for economics students. I was invited to sell cakes half way through a lecture, where I did a short speech to the class to invite them to take a look and buy our cakes, which was very successful and significantly contributed towards us selling all cakes made.

Another narrative describes how a placement year student manages to sustain his extra-curricular interest in the theatre.

> The pantomime enabled me to be more creative, and be myself. As a team we all had to come together to ensure it was as successful as it could be, and help each other out at all times. Without supporting each other at every step of the way it would have failed, and communication, friendliness and willingness to learn were key.

One discovery we made in piloting the award was the new opportunity afforded by the building of a portfolio for creative self-expression. For some students being given permission to create a handmade journal, and knowing that their representations of learning and development in this journal would be appreciated, seem to liberate and energise them. They felt a sense of pride in doing something creative that they could keep or show to people and they spoke of how they looked forward to returning to it. Several said that they would continue with the creative process beyond the award as it helped them see their life in a more meaningful and purposeful way. One person named her portfolio 'Taste the Future'. She told her interviewer that it was just a snapshot, but 'I want to continue it forever. This is just the beginning and I want to continue it.'

For the assessors, it was a privilege to witness beautifully presented scrapbooks full of photographic and hand-drawn images, decorations, mementos, supporting artefacts and explanatory and reflective writing.[5] These mediating artefacts alone demonstrated that considerable time, care, attention, effort and resources had been invested in their production. Implicitly and explicitly, they revealed the significant meaning making process that the student had engaged in. Interviewees described this variously as giving 'permission to dwell on things (…) to think deeper', helping 'me to see what value I get out of life' and making 'you realise what is import to you'. In these cases the portfolio itself was a manifestation of the identity, and the role played by creativity in that identity, of the individual. From the patterns of lifewide learning we can infer that participation in the creation of a scrapbook is characteristic of students who are seeking personal growth and the creation of identity in through their lifewide learning. The way these students inhabit the space in which they create their portfolio seemed to us to embody the notion of 'indwelling' which Polanyi (1967, 1974) describes as the process by which we begin to comprehend and understand something by connecting to it and, literally, living and dwelling in it.

Explorative orientation
Another type of lifewide learning that can be discerned in learners' portfolios is a pattern where the motivation is to explore new experiences which may be only loosely connected and where the *post hoc* meaning making may not be particularly coherent or strong. This explorative disposition (Law 2008) is still motivated by a commitment to self-development, but there is less strategic decision making in the choice of experiences for particular forms of development. What is apparent is that students are open to new possibilities and willing to take risks to try things out for themselves and to learn through the experience. There is a suggestion in the evidence discussed in Chapter 9 that this pattern is more prevalent during the early stages of a student's university career.

One student reeled off an extensive list of co- and extra-curricular activities she engaged in during her undergraduate time. She concluded:

> Each and every one of them taught me something different and I believe they taught me. They also helped me become more rounded and develop my views and see things differently and meet new people and learn how to be more tolerant.

She recognises that although her diverse experiences and interests may appear overwhelming, in reflecting on them she is able to appreciate their collective value:

> And I would do it all over again. I am not saying that everyone should do all of the things I did, but I truly believe that some of these experiences are of paramount importance for a complete education. It's not just about lectures or a perfect academic record; it is about you, about how you develop as a student, as an individual and also as a professional. These things helped me

develop my confidence, use my creativity, develop my English and communication skills and gave me lots of opportunities to work with other students. For me, it all worked perfectly, as to every single one of my three interviews with [company name] it gave me something else to talk about and it got me rid of the tense situation starting with ... 'Wow, so you had 81 for your first year, what else did you do???' And after all these, I know who I am now ... and what's more important, I know who I want to become!

As a postscript, this student went on to secure a work placement with a prestigious company attributing her success to the very fact that she could discuss, with confidence and awareness, the learning and development she had gained from participating in the award.

Facilitating self-authorship

Our educational design for the lifewide learning award was predicated on the desire to recognise and value forms of learning and development that we believe are necessary for being effective and self-fulfilled in a complex, ever changing world. In Chapter 5 Baxter Magolda drew attention to the importance in personal development of 'the growth of epistemological, intrapersonal and interpersonal complexity' (Baxter Magolda 2004a:41). We believe that students embedded in their own ecology of lifewide learning while studying at university are naturally and intuitively developing along trajectories of 'epistemological, intrapersonal and interpersonal complexity'. We sought evidence of this in students' portfolios using the three assumptions relating to the nature, development and use of knowledge (see below). Interviews conducted with students who completed the award reveal how individual students' perceptions of themselves in the world relate to the assumptions that underlie the growth of self-authoring capability and dispositions. A few extracts of interview transcripts or personal accounts are given below to illustrate participants' journeys towards self-authorship.

Assumption 1: lifewide learning exposes learners to epistemological, intrapersonal and interpersonal complexity

It is self-evident from the accounts of participants that they are involved in experiences and situations that expose them to complexity in all these aspects of being. But without help they may find it difficult it to create new and enduring understanding.

> Student K hadn't appreciated the complexity she was involved in because she had not recorded her experiences or reflected upon them.I did do a

> whole bit of extracurricular activities in terms of volunteering, and I think throughout the four years, I look back and it's not that I can't see where I've developed or what I've learnt, it's just really difficult to sort of find concrete things to discuss, because I never documented it. I think ... I wanted something that recognised all the effort that I did put into my extracurricular activities.

Once a facilitative structure for recording and reflecting was available student K began to make more sense of the complexity she was engaged in and the development that has resulted.

> I think more of a positive impact, because I think it just encourages me to keep my extracurricular activities going, etc. You know, it helps me see the learning and those skills then transferred over to my academic practice, which I think I'll find quite useful. You know, the networking, speaking to different people [for example].

And her mother also noticed that she had changed.

> [My mother] She's just so thrilled that, I think ... she's seen the change, like I mentioned, in the last few months, you know, since coming to Surrey, and just the fact that I haven't just been sitting back and doing nothing, or you know, everything that I should have been doing, because she's always moaned about my extracurricular activities.

An example of an epistemological change is illustrated by a Swedish student (O) who revealed how her self-awareness has grown from her interaction with members of the Christian Union. Her parents are atheists, but she has developed a deep religious faith. She sees fellow students who are extreme in their religion, for instance rejecting alcohol or sexual contact. On the one hand she admits, 'They really inspire me because their faith is so strong'; on the other, she feels inadequate for not sharing its depth. Eventually, she has come to compare the extremes typified by them and her parents, and understands that 'I don't have to be one of them'.

Assumption 2: self is central to knowledge construction. Learners define themselves and bring this to their way of learning, work and relationships
Greater self-awareness and a clearer sense of identity (as illustrated by the examples above) leads to greater confidence, which feeds into further activity and self-definition.

A PhD student from Pakistan (HJ) felt he must experience as much as he could during his time in the UK. 'I have to take all the opportunities that are thrown at me.' He demonstrates a keen sense of self, partly borne of his cultural background and perhaps related to his greater maturity:

> I think when I came here and my father told me at the very beginning that knowledge is everything ... And when you're coming in a different culture and I'm the only one from my family coming here, I actually took that, not just academic knowledge, knowledge of the whole thing. So being a researcher, I actually go deep down as well while doing things and I think this is ... this will compliment, basically this will compliment you professional life and your social life even.

Nevertheless, he attributes his growing self-confidence to communication with others, such as through his Student Union activities, as a result of which 'the confidence then came up'. This in turn allows him to take risks and seize opportunities when they come along:

> It's, as I said, you never know about the future ... Like when you do something you have to move on and you have to give another person the place to experience what you have experienced and you move on. And then I think so it's a luck or it's by chance you come across something unique that you don't know about and you want to do it. Maybe because of your previous experiences and ... Like I never imagined in my life, before coming here that I would be taking courses now at Oxford, on a scholarship. I'm doing that right now. So as I said, I am very positive.

This student is fully conscious of the sources of his personal development, explaining that it depends on:

> whether he or she is a risk taker or they actually accept challenges or not. Some people don't accept challenges. They don't take risks. They are very much factual and I think so, I do both. I am factual, but I also take risks and when I find that I think I can do this.

Another interviewee (B) acknowledges that some people find her 'different', and on the surface she appears self-confident in the face of this:
> I'm quite a thinker and I am all about developing as a whole person and I recognise things like that and try and express them to people and they're like,

> oh, that's a bit stupid. Like little things, like I'm lodging with an older couple this year and people find that strange ...

But as she talks on, she begins to reveal her frustration that her self-fulfilment is being impeded:

> I can pass exams, I can do stuff like that, almost without learning anything and it's something I get frustrated about that I'll go to a teacher or, like when I was younger and even now, and say I'm really struggling with this and they look at my grades and they say, no you're not, and they don't help me. Because I want to learn, I don't just want to pass exams.

For her, the award has given her permission to engage in her passions and see that self-realisation transcends domains, bringing success to her personally and academically:

> I can't really express to him how much all of that stuff is allowing me to enjoy my studies more. A bit like last year, I think I was getting a 2:1 [good degree] quite happily and I was working hard, but I think in my head I was like, I don't really want a first, because to get a first you can't really have a social life and you can't really get involved in other things. So it was in my head, I thought, okay, I'll settle for a 2:1 so that I can do Frisbee, I can do gospel choir, I can compose and I can write for bands and do all these things. But from doing those things and from doing the award, it's actually, it's upped my academic, so this year I'm just getting firsts and I'm doing more than I was doing last year with all my extra things. But it's because I'm finally realising that all of those things allow me, give me a purpose and a reason and a passion for doing my work that they all fit perfectly together. So now I'm working at a first, you know.

This sense of permission is a recurrent theme in interviews and narratives alike.

Assumption 3: authority and expertise are shared in the mutual construction of knowledge among peers

A second year engineering student from Spain has learnt the importance of mutually constructing knowledge through his experience with the United World Colleges. Under a scheme which began in the 1960s, scholarships bring together students from around the globe: 'basically they're looking for that sort of person who gets involved, who cares about what's going on around and is sort of like willing to put in effort to sort of like help make things better.' Of his experience there, he recalls:

> And so I got involved in different stuff, for instance, I ran a society ... well, the equivalent would be a society here, like it's called newsflash, where we sort of like collected news from around the world and organised little sort of kind of meetings every week where we would invite all the people to come around. And we would try to get some money from the place where the news was happening to sort of like explain to everyone else, because we got some quite heated debates sometimes.

Continuing his thirst for knowledge, he used the university's reading week to explore the country and meet old friends, only to find that he was inspired beyond his expectations:

> we had a reading week and I spent half of that going to visit a few friends in the North, sort of first I went to Edinburgh and then I went down to York. And there were people I hadn't seen in a couple of years. And it was really inspiring; they were old sort of ex colleagues of mine from college. And so, for instance, I had this brilliant conversation really like I meant with one of the people I stayed with in York, and my friend is studying politics and philosophy which is – I find it a fascinating subject. Like if I hadn't done engineering that's probably what I would've done.

Unfortunately, this student's exuberance for learning makes such demands on his time that he had to withdraw from the award. He expressed real regret and not a little sense of failure, as demonstrated in these two extracts from his interview:

> For someone like me who's really into sort of like the humanistic approach to everything, it was a great opportunity to sort of like take that back, because academically I can't really do that at the moment, it's all sort of like very kind of like technical and theoretical. [...]

> I myself, I am somebody who hates committing to something and not sticking to it, and that's why I failed. I feel really sorry about not being able to complete ...

A very different experience of peer learning is offered by student Q, not at interview but in his narrative:

The mandate of the project was ... primarily to use an open source platform no one in the team had ever built a site of this calibre and complexity. Where to begin? We decided to break off into sub teams to understand what type platform would be suitable. This process was essentially hours of googling and then presenting back to the whole team. It became apparent from the team research that one team member had more of an understanding of the various platforms we could use, and he then inadvertently had become an instructor to us. He would talk us through in depth (and for some time!) how the platform, Drupal works and teach us how build modules on it. Once we had knowledge, we got cracking and completed the first phase of the site on time and no problem that we couldn't solve with the aid of google!

Through a series of chance encounters student L secured a work placement in Melbourne, where she was one of a group of twenty overseas students. In addition to the learning she gained through interacting with them, she describes how she shared her experiences through photographs. By publishing them on Facebook, she was able to involve others in the enjoyment she has derived from the event she recorded, e.g. the exhilaration of climbing Sydney Harbour Bridge, while in return learning from their responses. Reflecting upon her experiences and finding in them an uncanny coincidence of significant encounters, she says:

> I will never ever dismiss anyone who works in a shop or who has retail experience or bar work or anything, because you just don't know what contacts you can make from it. And I do think those sorts of jobs are important, and that's why I've enjoyed them for so long, because of the contacts and the people I've met through them.

Student N gives a vivid account of how she wanted to be 'more proactive' after coming to Surrey to study for a Master's degree. She secured a position as a support worker providing academic and practical support (e.g. as an amanuensis) for students with a disability. Her first student required note-taking, and N's first session with him was an early morning lecture. Because of the early start, she offered him coffee and chatted with him during the break. She describes his reaction as one of shock: he was taken aback that she treated him as a person. He subsequently asked for her to be his supporter, rewarding her with the pleasure of having done her job well. She feels she has learnt much about herself and how alike we all are, whatever our cultural and other differences.

Student N recounts a second vivid experience of learning from her work with disabled students: she was surprised to receive emails during the Christmas break from her tutees, telling her of the grades they had received in their exams. She was touched that they wanted to involve her in their success and recognises in this learning that: 'It's not going to be on your CV or your mark but it says I contributed, I did something, I achieved something.'

Our sense of integration

In the first eight chapters of this book we set out the building blocks for a new lifewide concept of higher education. In Chapter 6 the principles for a lifewide curriculum were elaborated: a curriculum that would embrace in an inclusive way the experiences and situations learners need to encounter and deal with if they are to prepare themselves for their future world: a world that they will help create.

The lifewide learning award framework described in this chapter is our solution to the challenge of supporting these forms of learning and development. In Chapter 3 it was argued that lifewide learning must embrace a comprehensive and holistic notion of learning and personal development and in Chapter 4, drawing on the seminal thinking of John Dewey and Eduard Lindeman, we embraced the idea that situations and the capability to deal effectively and creatively with situations should provide the focus for an individual's learning and holistic development. In Chapter 5 Baxter Magolda elaborated the concept of self-authorship and her beliefs that personal development in higher education must provide opportunity for the growth of epistemological, intrapersonal and interpersonal complexity. We believe that our lifewide concept of education honours, in a pragmatic and practical way, the idea that self-authorship can be a central goal of a higher education that embraces the holistic development of people. The award framework and educational support system we created to promote learning and personal development has the characteristics of a learning partnership (Baxter Magolda 2004a). In judging the outcomes of learning and self-development we believe that students who honoured and engaged deeply with the process gained significant self-knowledge and affirmed who they are and who they would like to become. In the words of one participant:

> Probably one of the greatest benefits of the award was the fact that I had to regularly reflect on whatever I did and how it improved my capabilities, both professional and personal. It is through this reflection that I learnt most about myself, I discovered intricacies of my learning (both explicit and implicit) and how I have developed as a 'whole person'. I can understand now that many

skills gained in one field are transferable and [can be] applied to other spheres of life. I also think that taking part in the award proved to be a very personal journey and in a way helped me to discover who I am, what are my strengths and weaknesses.

Endnotes
1 Between 1996 and 2007, Surrey had an average employment rate six months after graduation of 97.8 per cent, compared with the national average of 93.8 per cent: the highest of any English university. In 2009 Surrey had the highest graduate employment performance indicator (96.9) of any UK university.
2 An example of a completed portfolio containing a life map, personal development plan and personal account can be found in the resources for this book at http://lifewideeducation.co.uk.
3 We are indebted to Professor John Cowan who, in his role as a collegial critical friend, acted as an External Auditor for the Award, and helped the assessors appreciate more deeply the judgements they were making.
4 The Girl Guides Association was set up 1910, and the junior section, called the Brownies, in 1914 to give girls a voice. See www.girlguiding.org.uk.
5 Some examples of students talking about their portfolios can be found at http://lifewideeducation.co.uk.

Appendix 1 Lifewide Learning Award Capability and Values Statement

The Award values and encourages the personal development that you undertake in order to become a more rounded and developed person. We want to encourage you to manage your own development.

1. Managing your own development: the attitudes, skills and behaviours that motivate and enable you to take responsibility for, plan and engage in experiences that enable you to develop yourself. In successfully completing the award you will have demonstrated that you have:
    - taken responsibility for, thought about, planned for and engaged in your own personal and professional development, taking advantage of the opportunities available to you on and off campus
    - reflected on and evaluated the learning, personal and professional development you have gained through the experiences that you have chosen to incorporate into your claim for lifewide learning
    - documented your experiences and what you have learnt from them, and gathered and organised evidence of your learning and development in your Life Skills Portfolio
    - summarised and communicated what you have learnt and how you have developed through a reflective account and an enhanced CV.

The Award emphasises the importance of developing capability to deal with situations (particularly new and challenging situations).

2. Being able to deal with situations, solve problems, work with challenge and take advantage of opportunity: your reflections will show how you have worked with challenge and uncertainty, and engaged with problems in a range of *real world* situations. These stories will reveal how you have understood and analysed a situation, decided what to do, found things out in order to decide what needs to be done, done things and learnt through the experience. In short, how you have made things happen. Your stories will not necessarily reflect success; in some cases stories may reveal how you have had to overcome significant setbacks and demonstrate your resilience in the face of failure.

The Award encourages you to think about these important generic dimensions of capability to deal with situations and make things happen.

3. Being able to develop the knowledge you need to deal with the situation: to be able to find out what you need to know in order to do what you need to do.
4. Being creative and enterprising: you need to be creative, enterprising and resourceful to invent new solutions, adapt to changing circumstances in novel ways and create new opportunities for yourself.
5. Being an effective communicator: to make things happen you need to be an effective communicator, to be able to communicate in ways that are appropriate

to the situation, to be able to communicate to different audiences using different media.
6. Being able to work with and lead others: your reflections will reveal how you have worked and developed relationships with other people and taken the initiative in helping others make good decisions and actions.
7. Behaving ethically and with social responsibility: your reflections will provide a vehicle for showing how you have dealt with ethical issues – how you have decided what is right or wrong, considered the values of others which are relevant in your activities, and tried to do the right thing.
8. Any other capability that is necessary to deal with a particular set of situations.

Through your engagement with the Award you will also have the opportunity to demonstrate these qualities and dispositions:

- Your will to be and become who you want to be: the award is intended to nurture your spirit to become the person you want to be. We are interested in understanding why you choose to do the things you include in your portfolio.
- Your values: your reflections will reveal the values you invest in the enterprises you contribute to and the value you add to the enterprise.
- Your confidence: your reflections will reveal how your confidence has developed as a result of encountering and dealing effectively with situations, accomplishing new things and coping with significant challenges.

Chapter 12

Learning through work

Norman Jackson, Jenny Willis, Michael Eraut and Sarah Campbell

Synopsis
One of the educational goals of a modern higher education system is to prepare learners for the demanding world of work in which they will subsequently spend most of their lives: a world that will be full of challenge, change and disruption. One of the ways in which learners prepare themselves for the world of work is to participate in paid or unpaid work while they are studying for a degree. Learning through work is part of the lifewide learning profile of many, perhaps most students. This chapter draws on three sets of studies and interventions undertaken at the University of Surrey to consider the nature of learning and development in the work environment. It describes a learning partnership model that was developed to support learning through work experiences that are not directly linked to students' programmes. It concludes that much valuable learning and development can be gained and recognised through a lifewide educational model that encourages systematic recording and reflection on the experiences and processes of working.

Introduction
This chapter draws together some of the things we have learnt about student development in the particular contexts of work environments and describes the piloting of a Learning through Work Certificate as part of the Lifewide Learning Award Framework. It seeks to present, connect and integrate three different research and development strategies that were focused on what students were learning and how they were developing in workplace situations.

The **first set of studies** relate to the question *what do we know about how professionals learn and develop in the workplace, and how can we make practical use of this knowledge to improve student development in the work place?* Our starting point was to connect to the extensive body of research into

how professionals learn and develop themselves through work (e.g. Eraut, 1994, 2000, 2004, 2007a & b, 2009, 2010, 2011). Eraut characterised continuous professional practice and ongoing development in terms of what he called 'learning trajectories' (Eraut, 2007a&b, 2009, 2010b). These were used by Willis (2009a) to examine the ways in which students at the University of Surrey were developing themselves through work placements. Eraut's research was used to:
a) evaluate whether students on placement were developing in the same ways as professionals in the early stages of their careers
b) create guidance for students involved in workplace learning on how people learn in the work environment
c) create a self-evaluation tool to help students and tutors analyse the quality of workplace situations and pedagogic support
d) inform development of a framework - the Learning through Work Certificate - that would enable students to recognise and gain recognition for their development through part-time work.

The **second set of studies** addressed the question *how do students engaged in work understand they are developing themselves as professionals?* Students' perceptions of personal professionalism in the work placement environment were examined through two essay competitions. The consequent analysis (Campbell, 2011a) of what being professional means to students undertaking a work placement demonstrated the complex and integrated nature of their development and led to the production of a Guide (Campbell 2011b) to help students preparing for a placement to appreciate the dimensions of professionalism. The study on what being professional means also informed the design of the reflective prompts in the Learning through Work Certificate described below.

Both of the above studies informed the **third intervention** which addressed the question *how can we help students recognise the learning and development they are gaining in part-time work environments and make claims for this development?* The 'Learning through Work' Certificate was designed to be part of the Lifewide Learning Award Framework and was piloted between July-October 2010.

First set of studies: Learning and development trajectories
Learning and development trajectories in the workplace are demonstrated by individuals and teams getting better at what they do and creating more effective, more efficient, innovative ways of working that enable the

organisation/business to be more successful. Becoming better at work can involve many different things (Eraut 2009):
- doing things faster
- improving the quality of the process
- improving communications around the task
- learning quickly
- becoming more independent and needing less supervision
- combining tasks more effectively
- quicker recognition of possible problems
- expanding the range of situations in which one can perform competently
- helping others learn to do the task or part of the task
- increases in task difficulty / taking on tasks of greater complexity
- dealing with more difficult or more important cases, clients, customers, suppliers or colleagues
- creating new and better ways of doing things.

Some of these types of progress could be described as *doing things better*, some as *doing things differently* and some as *doing different things*. Sometimes all three may be happening at once. They all manifestations of people developing themselves.

Progression in dealing with work situations often involves doing the same thing, or not quite the same thing, in more difficult conditions or across a wider range of cases. Although these types of progress seem fairly obvious, people are not always conscious that they are learning things and developing themselves through experience, nor do they remember how or when they learnt something. People are generally not very interested in the dynamic of their own learning. Research on workplace learning (Eraut 2007a, 2007b, 2009, 2011) found that newcomers first recognised that they had learned something when they realised that they were doing things that they could not have done a few weeks earlier. Focusing attention on the how, why and when of learning does lead to enhanced self-awareness and it is these processes and how self-awareness can be used to motivate further development that are of particular interest to our lifewide learning project.

One of the benefits for students engaging in work environments is that they develop the capacity to learn through the activity and social processes of work – learning and personal development associated with learning is a by-product of working. As a result of participating in work environments students are exposed to, and learn from and with others, the cultural knowledge of the organisation, which is then incorporated into their personal knowledge (Eraut 2010, 2011):

- *codified knowledge* necessary for the job in the form(s) in which the person uses it
- *know-how* in the form of *skills and practices*
- personal *understandings of people and situations*
- accumulated *memories of cases* and episodic *events*
- other aspects of personal *expertise, practical wisdom* and *tacit knowledge*
- *self-knowledge, attitudes, values* and *emotions.*

This form of knowledge development and use of knowledge is highly relevant to the idea of self-authorship (Baxter Magolda 2004 and Chapter 5) with its knowledge-based assumptions that 1) *knowledge is complex and socially constructed,* 2) *self is central to knowledge construction* and 3) *authority and expertise are shared in the mutual co-construction of knowledge among peers.*

Table 12.1 Typology of modes of learning in the workplace

Work processes with learning as a by-product	Learning activities located within work or learning processes	Learning processes at or near the workplace
Participation in group processes	Asking questions	Being supervised
Working alongside others	Getting information	Being coached
Consultation	Locating resource people	Being mentored
Tackling challenging tasks and roles	Listening and observing	Shadowing
Problem solving	Reflecting	Visiting other sites
Trying things out	Learning from mistakes	Conferences
Consolidating, extending and refining skills	Giving and receiving feedback	Short courses
Working with clients	Use of mediating artefacts	Working for a qualification
		Independent study

Source: Eraut 2007a, 2007b, 2009, 2010, 2011

Eraut's study of the early career learning of professionals (Eraut 2007a&b, 2011) demonstrated that most learning was not a separate activity but a by-product of their ongoing work; and most of these events involved working with other people. This gave rise to a typology of learning modes of early career learners (ibid.). They are the means by which cultural and personal knowledge are developed.

Table 12.2 Summary of learning trajectories organised into eight categories

Learning trajectory	Details
Task performance	Speed and fluency; complexity of tasks and problems; range of skills required; communication with a wide range of people; collaborative work
Awareness and understanding	Other people: colleagues, customers, managers etc; context and situations; one's own organisation; problems and risks; priorities and strategic issues; value issues
Personal development	Self evaluation; self-management; handling emotions; building and sustaining relationships; disposition to attend to other perspectives / to consult and work with others / to learn and improve one's practice; accessing relevant knowledge and expertise; ability to learn from experience
Academic knowledge and skills	Use of evidence and argument; accessing formal knowledge; research-based practice; theoretical thinking; knowing what you might need to know; using knowledge resources (human, paper, electronic); learning how to use relevant theory in a range of practical situations
Role performance	Prioritisation; range of responsibility; supporting other people's learning; leadership; accountability; supervisory role; delegation; handling ethical issues; coping with unexpected problems; crisis management; keeping up-to-date
Teamwork	Collaborative work; facilitating social relations; joint planning and problem solving; ability to engage in and promote mutual learning
Decision making and problem solving	When to seek expert help; dealing with complexity; group decision making; problem analysis; formulating and evaluating opinions; managing the process within an appropriate timescale; decision making under pressure
Judgement	Quality of performance, output and outcomes; priorities; value issues; levels of work

Source: Eraut 2007a, 2007b, 2009, 2010

Eraut's study (2007a) also identified over 50 learning and development trajectories, each involving the individual to access, integrate and utilise their knowledge, capability, qualities and dispositions in order to perform or accomplish something. At any point in time an individual performing a professional role is either developing or regressing within a particular trajectory depending on the experiences he is gaining through his work. Eraut (2010b) argues that in dynamic work environments the concept of competence-based goals as indicators of a person's workplace capability is far too restrictive. Lifelong learning requires the use of lifelong learning trajectories, which can offer more freedom to be holistic, attend to the emotional dimension of work and appreciate the significance of complexity. Lifewide learning contributes to the holistic development of a person and offers the potential for individuals to develop along some of their lifelong learning trajectories through different parts of their lives simultaneously.

We hypothesised that students on work or clinical placements are also developing to varying degrees along these trajectories in ways that are appropriate to their particular work contexts. Willis (2009a) tested this hypothesis by using these trajectories as a tool to analyse 28 student narratives of how they developed themselves as professionals through their work placement. The students identified 32 factors, either explicitly or implicitly, that they believed were relevant to them being and becoming professional in their particular work context. Each student's narrative revealed a different combination of perceived learning and the aspects of learning and development reported could be related to Eraut's eight learning trajectories (see Willis 2009b for a description of the analysis).

Second set of studies: how students become professional

As Eraut's work demonstrated, fulfilling a professional role requires working with epistemological, intrapersonal and interpersonal complexity. This is more than simply a checklist of things that have to be done; it requires assessing situations often with incomplete information, and making decisions about the best courses of action and then following through to ensure that actions are appropriate and effective. We were interested in concepts of professionalism that students had developed through work experiences. Students who had completed a year-long work placement and/or other work-based experiences were invited to reflect, in a structured way, upon the idea of personal professionalism (their view of what being professional means). An analysis of 22 essays (Campbell 2011) demonstrated that students conceptualised professionalism as a way of being, rather than a checklist of skills and behaviours. The quotes in this section are taken from student essays.

> In essence I believe that personal professionalism is more about the way in which you conduct yourself and your outlook on life.

This way of being is made up of facets such as appearance, manner, conduct, communication, interpersonal skills, attitudes, values, approach, skills and openness to grow.

> Factors such as continuous dedication, learning and commitment to success help individuals to become effective professionals. Not only that but also the extra knowledge that involves ethics, positive attitude, enthusiasm to learn, teach, and many other aspects mentioned above such as respect, passion, persistence and professionalism. In summary, everyone has some degree of personal professionalism but each individual has the ability to develop it through self-improvement.

> People are not only merited on what they know and their credentials, but also on their attitudes and behaviour, so the way I carry myself and the things that I do should be a reflection of what I'm capable of.

Interacting with others (people you work with, managers, customers and clients) appropriately and respectfully, and communicating clearly and directly emerged from student accounts as essential to being professional.

> How you interact with people plays a big part in how professional you appear.

Professionalism is a combination of taught aspects, like knowledge and skills, and experiential, such as interpersonal skills. Students feel you can't be told how to be professional; it is something you learn from direct experience of doing things that require you to be professional, and the conception of it changes as you gain more experience. Becoming professional is a never-ending process.

> Being professional is not something you are told how to do, but something you learn from experience.

Professionalism can also be learnt by observing others as they fulfil their role. Students often stated their own conceptions were a result of observing others either embodying professionalism or conversely being unprofessional. Students also commented that experience had broadened their conceptions of professionalism and helped them to realise that previously held stereotypes of a professional did not capture true professionalism.

> Each member of staff has their own methods and ways of being an effective professional and being in contact with a team like this has helped dispel some of the myths and stereotypes I still had regarding the world of work and being a professional.
>
> I witnessed firsthand the variety of ways to be a successful professional. Whilst each individual may have their own methods of performing their job well, I have noted certain themes that I believe are fundamental in professionalism.

Various skills are important to professionalism, but a key aspect is approach to work, delivered through effective interpersonal skills. Achieving and succeeding requirements of the role, but in a certain way, to a certain standard, to deadlines, characterises professionalism for students. Students have a sense that professionalism must become intrinsic and internalised. If professionalism is internalised, it leads to achieving self-efficacy, self-worth, achievement, accomplishment, a sense of satisfaction and most of all embracing confidence, which in turn strengthens and develops a professional identity. This professional identity helps self-determination and motivation, with the will to do well derived from intrinsically motivated desires.

> I conclude that professionalism is more than simply doing right by the context of one's workplace, but also the personal determination to better oneself in practice and conduct.
>
> Personal professionalism seeps into all we do in life, in both career and social scenarios.

What emerged from accounts was a sense that being professional is about bringing yourself and your personality into the role, enhancing not only yourself but also the role and the organisation. Professionalism is about not only doing what is required or behaving in a way because you are told to, but also doing/behaving because of internalised professional values, doing it for self and self-set standards, arising from intrinsic motivation.

> For me the answer is that a professional works to such standards, not because of the penalties that are imposed if they don't, a bad mark, a sacking for example, but rather they do it because to do anything else would be unacceptable to that person themselves.

I work to high standards because I know that if I did otherwise I would be personally disappointed, the results would not be a reflection of my ability and so I would be letting myself down.

An appropriate set of dispositions is essential to fulfilling the professional role in the right way. The *willingness* to be a certain sort of person behaving in a certain sort of way is paramount. Here are some of the dimensions of willingness identified by student accounts.

- willing to try to perform at a high standard
- openness and willingness to learn and develop for the role, necessitating an ability to listen
- willingness to present yourself in a confident but not arrogant manner
- willingness to do that bit extra, which is necessitated by taking the initiative and an aspect of creativity
- willingness to take responsibility for and learn from mistakes
- willingness to be open to constructive criticism, seeing criticism as positive chances for change
- awareness of different perspectives and willingness to see alternative perspectives to your own
- ability and willingness to both learn from others and teach others; ability to lead and to be led
- willingness to take an active role in being a professional, in the work, and a commitment to growth and self-development
- willingness to be positive and encouraging
- willingness to accept and use feedback from colleagues in order to improve.

These aspects of willingness all amount to a sense of resilience in attempting to be professional. Passion, commitment and seeing the positives in both people and situations all contribute to a climate of encouragement which helps to bring out the best in other people. This fosters another important dynamic in work: the importance of working effectively in a team or collaboratively with others. Students recognised the importance of being able to work effectively with others as well as the ability to work autonomously by taking the initiative. A professional is expected to manage himself and regulate his own behaviour. Knowing your limits of competency, taking responsibility for your own decisions and actions and knowing when to seek help are all important aspects of self-management. Another key aspect of self-management is the ability to manage and regulate emotions. This awareness also enables awareness of the emotions of others and helps to take other perspectives. This ability to manage emotions is an important part of effective interpersonal skills and is captured by Emotional Intelligence theory, which has become a prominent feature in business and organisational research. These are key skills in being an effective leader and employee.

Communication emerged as a vital element of being professional and to the effective use of interpersonal skills. Students' recognised communication occurs through various mediums (telephone, face to face conversation, email, written reports, presentations etc.) and in different contexts with different people. Being able to conduct professional conversations, knowing what / what not to say and how to say it, is part of professionalism. Having the appropriate language is essential as is:

- speaking/writing well, concisely and clearly – being comprehensible
- being polite and respectful – addressing people with their titles is important
- being able to express opinions appropriately
- being approachable
- not being patronising
- willing to share your ideas, knowledge, opinions; having your own voice, ideas and therefore confidence is important to facilitate the sharing of these ideas
- being able to write appropriately in ways that meet the needs and interests of the audience
- when resolving issues, remaining objective rather than being personal
- managing expectations; being clear, direct and concise
- networking skills and building relationships.

Students recognise and appear to cope with the complexity of professionalism, seeing it as something that is embodied in outward appearance and conduct, but also internally in terms of values, attitudes and approach. Students talked of forming a professional identity which results from integrating many of the aspects mentioned above, as well as others. This identity of professionalism is then presumably integrated into the many other identities people hold at any one time; hence some students touch upon taking professionalism not only into the workplace but also into other aspects of life.

Students also recognised the importance of learning from experience, positing that professionalism can only develop from experiencing professional contexts. Students acknowledged that whilst higher education helps develop many of the 'soft' skills inherent in professionalism, these are not realised fully and further developed without the experience of professional contexts. This will help students to realise how transferable many of the facets of professionalism are across situations, which can then benefit them during their time in higher education. This highlights the importance of encouraging and supporting students to engage in professional contexts during while they are studying in order to begin to develop and internalise a conception of professionalism.

The studies described above allowed us to connect a body of research in professional work environments with the experiences of students on work placement. Our next step was to extend our examination of the learning potential of the work environment to situations that were not linked to any formal educational experience or course structure.

Third set of studies: learning through part-time work

In May 2009, 368 undergraduate and postgraduate students completed an online survey inviting them to comment on the opportunities that part-time work provided for personal/professional development. The primary reason cited (100 per cent) was to earn money, followed by the intrinsic motivation of doing something useful and seeking enjoyment (35 per cent). Students also believed that the experience would be useful for their CV, but relatively few students (less than 15 per cent) said that they got a job to develop their skills. Part-time work is predominantly in retail, sales, bar work, waiting, but there are also a range of roles in volunteering, teaching/tutoring, secretarial/temping, cleaning, healthcare and other areas (Figure 12.4). While only a small percentage of respondents claimed that they sought part-time work to develop their skills, a word cloud (Figure 12.5) of 888 responses to the question 'What was the most important thing you gained from your part-time work?' shows that students recognised they gained significant skills and experience.

Table 12.3 provides more detail on the opportunities for personal development that part-time work provided. Over 60 per cent of respondents to the survey believed that the part-time work environment *often* or *always* provided opportunity for the development of professional skills, communication skills, working with others in a team, learning how to interact with customers or clients, learning how an organisation works and how people are managed, learning how to manage themselves, learning how to negotiate with and persuade others, taking on challenging responsibilities and gaining confidence in self. These are all significant dimensions of development for individuals.

Figure 12.4 Wordle cloud showing frequency of responses (n=683) to a survey of part-time jobs. The size of the letters reflects the frequency of response.

Figure 12.5 Wordle cloud showing frequency of responses (n=888) to the question 'What was the most important thing you gained from your part-time work?'

Table 12.3 Opportunities for personal/professional development provided through part-time work (n=363 figures in per cent)

	Never	Sometimes	Often	Always
Finding and applying for a job	14	41	28	17
Gaining interview experience	17	39	25	20
Learning in a work context	10	27	35	29
Applying classroom learning	38	41	15	6
Gaining useful work experience	7	30	31	31
Valuable professional skills	28	28	34	30
Developing communication skills	2	13	31	53
Develop and use IT skills	30	34	22	12
Learning how to work with colleagues or in a team	4	15	32	48
Learning how to interact with customers or clients	1	14	24	58
Learning about how an organisation works	5	26	36	33
Learning about being managed	6	22	40	32
Learning how to manage others	17	35	29	20
Learning how to manage self e.g. turning up on time	4	17	26	53
Learning about business skills and practices.	12	33	32	23
Learning how to negotiate with/persuade others	11	36	35	22
Clarifying future career goals	21	37	27	16
Being given challenging responsibilities	10	30	38	22
Gaining self-confidence	4	13	41	42

Learning through Work Certificate

Convinced that there was value in encouraging students to reflect on and evaluate the learning and development they were gaining through part-time work, in 2009 SCEPTrE developed and piloted a Learning through Work Certificate. This was subsequently aligned to the capability and values statement for the Lifewide Learning Award and incorporated into the Award Framework as a freestanding certificate and as a pathway in the Award. The revised Learning through Work Certificate was piloted between July and October 2010. Eleven students joined the pilot scheme; four withdrew before completing and seven successfully completed the requirements for the Certificate. Their portfolio accounts provide a useful database from which to draw out the learning and achievements they gained through their part-time work.

Educational design

The Learning through Work Certificate provided university recognition for informal learning and personal development gained when students completed at least 100 hours of part-time or temporary full-time (paid/unpaid) work which was not part of a programme of study. In order to receive university recognition for learning and personal development participants had to document their experiences and evaluate the learning and personal development they had gained. Four techniques are used to help students understand, evaluate and reveal their learning and personal development:

- completion of a skills and experiences self-evaluation questionnaire and personal development plan
- online resources to help participants appreciate the nature of learning through work (in contrast to learning in an educational environment) based on the research of Michael Eraut described earlier
- creation of an ongoing reflective diary or blog to record and make sense of their experiences and the learning and personal development gained from them
- reflective account (2,000–2,500 words) – to connect, synthesise and integrate the learning gained through the experience or work. The account draws upon the reflective diary and any other documents or artefacts (such as digital images or audio or video recordings) used to represent learning and personal and professional development.

The Certificate encourages participants to focus on key aspects of personal development that are generic to all work situations and are important to being an effective professional. These are incorporated into the same capability and values statement that underpins the Lifewide Learning Award (Chapter 11). The Certificate also recognises more specific skills that are necessary to fulfil a particular role. A copy of the guidance can be found at http://lifewideeducation.co.uk.

In common with the Lifewide Learning Award, the Certificate encourages students to be aware of and reflect on the situations they encounter and deal with at work. This is consistent with Eraut's research into learning in the workplace.

> *Situational understanding* is a critical aspect of professional work, and probably the most difficult [for a student on first entering the work environment]......because situational understanding tends to be taken for granted by all but newcomers. While newcomers may be well aware of their

lack of situational understanding, they may not get much helpful feedback on it. This is because most people get so familiar with many situations that they cannot imagine anyone else "not being aware of the obvious". Thus newcomers' ignorance of the local culture may not be understood; and there may not be much information to help them learn about the situations and contexts that are so familiar to those around them. Most students on placement need a lot of advice on how best to understand the groups and contexts they encounter....because the tacit dimension of situational understanding is critical.

(Eraut 2011:4

Learning and personal development
The seven participants in the pilot scheme were a mix of male and female, home and overseas students, studying at level 2, P (professional placement year) or 3. Their disciplines included applied psychology and sociology; sociology, culture and media; mathematics; business management; and economics. Each had different levels of experience of paid work, and the nature of their experience ranged from retail through care work, technology support and events management. Some were junior members of a team, others led a small team.

At the start and end of the process, participants were invited to use an audit tool (Table 12.4) to help them think about a) the sorts of learning and development they anticipated from the work and b) the areas of moderate or significant development they had gained through the work experience. Given the diversity of their roles and experience, each profile is individual. The 23 audit dimensions are listed in the second column of Table 12.4. Participants' evaluations of their personal development is shown in the columns labelled 1 to 7, with dark shading indicating considerable development, light shading indicative of some development and blank cells meaning there was little or no perceived development in this dimension. The final column calculates the total score for each dimension, using the scale 1 = considerable development, 0.5 = some development.

The most striking feature of this table is the extent to which participants identified significant or some learning over a majority of the 23 opportunities for learning and personal development listed. All participants believed that they had gained valuable work experience and 14 of the 23 elements of experience were rated 5 (out of a possible 7) for the significance of the learning.

Many of the themes identified as being significant in the earlier Willis (2009a) study relating to student development in the professional training environment, also featured in the narratives of students engaged in part-time working. For example - responsibility/trust, feeling valued, variety of work, new skills or knowledge, dealing with challenging situations, communicating with different types of people, being part of a team, working independently, being organised and able to manage time.

The dimensions that score most highly (Table 12.4 with 6–7 points) are communication and interpersonal skills, personal dispositions/qualities associated with self-realisation and developing self-confidence through successful execution of a responsible work role. Participants express a sense of self-fulfilment having coped successfully with challenging situations.

> [T]he main challenges were managing and prioritising different customer demands with very urgent demands with very short time scales. One of my greatest challenges of my job was to interpret what the customer wants and on a few rare occasions I was in a difficult position, where the customer didn't know or understand what they were asking for. On one occasion [we were] commissioned by a customer to create a podcast of a series of lectures a guest speaker was doing at the University. The customer made it clear through 2 phone conversations that they would like a podcast. After confirming to the customer what a podcast was, we then agreed to take on the project. We filmed the first event and guaranteed that the podcast would be produced within 72 hours onto a DVD. Once the customer had viewed the product, she wasn't happy. The customer expected more than a podcast but wasn't sure what. This was a difficult conversation and in the end we had to cut our losses. This experience has highlighted to me that customer relationships are a complicated beasts and continually evolving as all was not lost as a few months later the ex-customer re-commissioned xxxx to create her some podcasts and now with the right expectations.

A student who undertook a month-long internship in China.

> I feel that I was finally able become an effective communicator because I had improved the way I read other people's emotions through different forms of communication that I originally never really looked at before. In the past, during my time at work I tend to communicate clearly orally or through written communication as there was a slight language barrier between some of my colleagues and I learnt how to communicate and read off body

language and see how they were feeling. Although it sounds extremely elementary, this use to help me decide whether or not a task should be prioritised because my worker was in a rush and also use to help me see what my supervisors and colleagues thought of my work when viewing it.

Table 12.4 Learning through Work Certificate participants' evaluation of new learning through their experiences of work

	Opportunity for learning and personal development	1	2	3	4	5	6	7	Summary
1	Finding and applying for a job								2.5
2	Experience of being interviewed								2
3	Learning about how an organization/business works								5
4	Dealing with challenging situations at work								6
5	Applying classroom learning								2
6	Gaining valuable work experience								7
7	Developing valuable technical skills								3.5
8	Learning professional behaviours								6
9	Developing communication skills								6.5
10	Develop and use IT skills								3
11	Learning how to work with colleagues or in a team								6
12	Learning how to interact with customers or clients								5
13	Learning about being managed								5.5
14	Learning how to manage others								5
15	Learning how to manage yourself eg punctuality								5
16	Learning about business skills and practices.								5.5
17	Coping with and managing emotions								5.5
18	Learning how to negotiate with and persuade others								4
19	Clarifying future career goals								5
20	Being given challenging responsibilities								5.5
21	Being creative and resourceful to make things happen								3
22	Experience of being enterprising								2.5
23	Self-confidence								6

Notes: (n=7); significant new learning = dark grey; new learning = light grey; sum = total for the number of cells that are defined as significant (1) or some new learning (1/2).

Even when they feel they have not been successful, participants recognise the developmental value of their experience, as put by this student who had a month-long internship in China:

> Another area of skill that didn't seem to go so well included my ability to problem solve tasks. I remember being set a vague task from one of my colleagues to create a collage of event pictures that Auditoire had produced so it could be used on the website. The process of it was quite long but it was embarrassing that it took over 5 attempts for me to get it correct and that I stayed in the office until 9:30pm trying to get it correct. It was partially to do with the language barrier as well but I believed that my inability to work out what I had been set reduced my self esteem for a while. I learnt how to move on from the situation as mistakes are always made.

Moving down the scale of perceived significance, dimensions that score 5.5 and 5 relate to aspects of management or being managed, business structure and function, and once more an opportunity to rise to a challenge through being given responsibility. Least perceived development lies in the process of job application and selection, perhaps reflecting participants' prior experience of this or the informal/casual way in which part-time jobs have been found and secured. It is also evident that the nature of the part-time work these students were engaged in rarely offered them the opportunity to apply learning from their programme of study, reflecting the fact that the primary motivation for part-time work is often to earn income rather than to gain career specific experience. The exceptions to this rule, however, shows that part-time work if linked to a field of study and career aspiration can provide valuable and relevant personal development

> Something that I found to be valuable and relevant to my course is applying theory from books on mental disorders to reality, speaking to patients and hearing how that disorder affects them. There is nothing more valuable than getting the opportunity to discuss real life cases from their point of view that you learnt about in a book. A particular example I think of is a patient who had bipolar disorder mixed with alcoholism which they used to self medicate the lows they experienced from their disorder. They shared with me how they felt and acted when experiencing the highs/mania of bipolar in contrast to what it is like to experience the lows of the disorder. It was an amazing experience as I had read about the theory of this disorder extensively however for someone to open up and share with me what it really like for them to live with this disorder is so enlightening. In a book I can read about

the typical behaviour that may be displayed by someone with the condition but the book cannot tell me what was going through that persons head when they were displaying that behaviour and how it feels to look back on it as they are progressing through the treatment.

By comparing the learning they anticipated with what they actually achieved using the self-audit tool (Table 12.4) students were able to recognise how they had changed. An illustration of this process is given below.

> A further difference [I noticed] is the depth to which I went into for the 'Developing communication skills'. In the chart I completed before starting this position I merely ticked the 'some new learning' option for the entire category, and upon reflection of what I have learned so far in these last 3 months I can identify a difference in learning between verbal/oral skills, listening skills, written, designing and media use. These are secondary skills which have developed along the way, I have had no formal training to develop my communication skills, but they have inadvertently improved in the process, something which I am grateful for! I feel that is applies to a large number of the categories on the above list ...

This process of structured reflection is supported by participants' personal diaries or blogs, which they keep in the medium they choose. An extract from one student's blog shows how she used it not simply to record events, but also to analyse her experiences:

> 14th July – Today has been a mad house, with the new releases of Eclipse and Shrek 4th, the cinema was packed with Orange Wednesdays guests. There was not enough staff to cover the number of guests we received. I started to panic and had to do a lot of refunds, I learnt that I need to slow down and keep calm even if there is a huge queue and guests are waiting. Guests appreciate for you to take your time with them so they don't feel rushed.

> 16th July – Today I was called in to the office about a team member harassing the girls. I personally have encountered a few incidents but failed to report it due to it seemed natural for him to do it as a joke. He was dealt with and if he is complained about again then he will be fired from his job as this is not the 1st time this has happened. Apart from that I am now fully trained and confident with in the box office. I haven't spent my full month here because Odeon has not been that straight forward however I am now

trained fully in 3 of the main areas and am now a confident worker who the supervisors are pleased with.

18th July – I am on another close which I appear to be doing a lot of. Over 60 per cent of my shifts are working until past midnight. Now I am fully trained in retail, everything was done quickly except the supervisors were arguing amongst each other saying none of them were doing their jobs correctly. This is slightly worrying if my bosses aren't getting along and can't work as a team as this reflects.

Participants appreciate the value of this process of reflection, as expressed by one who focused her submission around her work in a private clinic:

I feel the whole point of completing this certificate is that it gives me the opportunity to evaluate and consolidate what I learnt from my summer of work experience. On a day to day basis we often do not take the time within our lives to sit down and reflect on what we have learnt, what hurdles we have jumped over and what we should be proud of or on the other hand what we can take away from our mistakes to develop as a person. A major part of what I feel this certificate has given me the chance to do is exactly that, reflect on my work experience at a deeper level than I would have ever thought to have done ... It helped me on days ... of low morale which we can all get when busy with many tasks in our lives by reminding me why I am doing this, what I have learnt so far and how much more I have to learn if I continue. Having come back from the summer and spoken to class members who have not completed the certificate I have to say I feel a sense of accomplishment, I worked hard over the summer and am putting these experiences into the certificate – the words I will put into this I will always have and can look back on in the future to remind myself what I spent the summer doing.

She concludes with words that demonstrate the life-changing impact of her reflecting on her work experiences:

In this work you have to try and keep your work as value free as possible, otherwise it would not be considered ethical. Any emotions or feelings that may arise due to a patient have to be kept aside; otherwise it may cloud your judgment when trying to effectively treat patients. When working with staff alike it is important to remain professional and value free. Through working at the clinic my personal values may have been shaped but this is something that must remain personal and free from my professional life. I however do feel I gained a new sense of self confidence from my time at the clinic, confidence for talking to members of staff (not being afraid to ask questions) as well as confidence when working with patients. I feel I even gained some more confidence at being interviewed, although this was not my first time being interviewed I feel you gain something new from every interview you have.

Conceptions of professionalism
The Learning through Work Certificate encourages participants to reflect on what being professional means to them in the belief that professionalism is a necessary characteristic for appropriate and effective performance in any work environment. Some examples of students' responses are given below.

Student A My views on what makes one a professional have undoubtedly changed over the past few years, and in some cases even more so over this summer. I feel that the key characteristics that demonstrate you are a professional are:
- A mature attitude; being able to draw a line between having a laugh whilst working and immaturity
- An open personality; being the sort of person who can meet a stranger with an open smile and engage and involve anyone in a conversation or project.
- A sense of humility; being able to admit mistakes and to learn from past mistakes to make more justified and informed decisions in the future.
- A democratic countenance; being able to listen to other colleagues opinions when making a decision.
- A flexible nature; being able to adapt to changing situations.

I feel that my placement over the summer has improved these characteristics within me, as well as improving my understanding of what I need to do to become a more effective professional. One significant improvement I feel I have made has been around my maturity, particularly regarding my ability to behave in a much more professional manner around the workplace, despite distractions.

Student B Something else which I feel is appropriate is maintaining a high level of maturity in the workplace and respect for other colleagues. As the youngest member of the team there could be some things I say or do which would not be suitable or which could offend others. I therefore must adopt a certain attitude and adhere to office etiquette to enable myself to not only fit in, but also be respected and considered as a member of the team. This is something which I feel I have managed to do throughout the past three months as I feel I am generally a very mature and respectful person, and have developed this through my working like so far and other activities where I have worked alongside a variety of different people.

Student C Being an effective professional means includes having the ability to:
- Identify any problems and get them sorted out as quickly as possible before they manifest themselves
- Working as part of a team
- Learning from others and give knowledge to others
- Adapt and be flexible when given situations or problems arise
- Learn from previous experience / encounters with previous customers
- Make the job your own by bringing any past experience you have or new ideas

Student D after my experience in China it is possible to become a professional in different ways. Usually when asked what makes an effective professional I would list technical skills such as having the ability to apply numeracy or applying IT. I feel that in the past I have demonstrated such skill but after my experiences in China I believe that an effective professional must at least have the skills listed below:
- Self Management – through time management, being a self starter at tasks and improving skills through constant reflection.
- Problem Solving – by analysing situations and creating appropriate solutions.
- Communication – the ability to clearly express a subject or emotion orally or verbally.
- Team working – through co-operating and respecting others, negotiating with colleagues and realising the interdependency of a team.

I feel that an endless amount of skills could be added to the list but this is the minimum required to become an effective professional.

These perceptions represent much valuable learning gained through exposure to and participation in everyday work situations. They are insights that can be built upon in future and insights that can be shared when they present themselves to prospective employers.

A learning partnership for self-authorship
The Learning through Work Certificate provides another example of a learning partnership (Baxter Magolda 2004 and Chapter 5) through which students' experiences of being and knowing, and their development of personal knowledge (skills, qualities and dispositions necessary to make effective use of this knowledge), enabled them to successfully fulfil their work roles.

The work of Baxter Magolda draws attention to the importance in personal development of what she calls 'the growth of epistemological, intrapersonal and interpersonal complexity' (Baxter Magolda 2004:41 and Chapter 5). As Eraut shows (Eraut 2007) and our students' reveal (Willis 2010; Campbell 2011) the work environment provides an important setting in which students can encounter the conditions that provide the opportunity for growth in being able to deal with complexity.

Examples of students engaging with and appreciating such complexity in the situations they had to deal with has been provided in some of the extracts above and some further examples are given below. All seven accounts revealed, to varying degrees, students engaging in situations that involved the three assumptions that underlie the concept of self-authorship namely: 1) *knowledge is complex and socially constructed,* 2) *self is central to knowledge construction* and 3) *authority and expertise are shared in the mutual co-construction of knowledge among peers.*

Student A took on a part-time summer job at a major supplier of building materials.

> Naturally, some opportunities passed me by, some causing me to miss out on a high value sale. One particularly expensive sale I [nearly] missed out on was when a customer came in looking for a price list of our various timbers and tonne bags of ballast and shingle and the suchlike. After ascertaining that the customer didn't hold an account with us, I proceeded to give him the prices that would be charged to customers that were described as 'cash customers', and were naturally more expensive than the 'trade customer' rates that were set up. The customer was quite shocked that we were around 40p a metre more expensive than one of our largest competitors and began to leave when my colleague came over and rescued the sale. As it

> turned out, the gentleman was part of a large firm who were beginning a new building project nearby and were looking to purchase a large quantity of supplies from us – something that I had failed to enquire about before offering prices.

Student B undertook a month-long internship for an events management organisation in Beijing. Before she went she tried to prepare herself by reading about what it was like to live in China and took lessons in Mandarin, but this did not really prepare her for the significant cultural differences that she had to learn to deal with.

> During my internship, I kept a diary and I learnt that my attitude towards the Chinese culture had changed over time. I firstly entered the country thinking that Chinese people were not welcoming and were too traditional and to some extent narrow minded to eventually become a world economic power. I then realised during the second week into the internship that I had come with a Eurocentric point of view and been slightly unfair and so did my best to give a try and adapt to it. Once I stopped being Eurocentric I realised that I was much more happy in my time during China and felt much more confident with myself ... I learnt that Chinese companies (or at least the company I worked for) placed a high level of importance on hierarchy and sometimes suggestions were not really regarded as useful if you were low in the company's hierarchy. It would sometimes be regarded as rude or going beyond your designated boundary. I learnt that it was best to give advice or suggestions when asked as oppose to using your own initiative.

Concluding remarks

There is no doubt that organisational work environments provide conditions that expose students to the everyday cultural knowledge that underpins the behaviours and actions of the organisation. This knowledge and other knowledge necessary for learners to be effective in their work role are learnt collaboratively and often informally through performing the role. This experience of developing and using these forms of knowledge is valuable to students future learning in other work environments and complements more formalised classroom learning with its strong reliance on transmissive modes of teaching and codified abstract knowledge. These forms of knowledge development and use are important to the development of self-authorship (Baxter Magolda 2004 and Chapter 5).

The work environment is dynamic and because it is full of social interaction, the detail of what happens is unpredictable. In such environments students gain experience of learning how to deal with situations as they emerge. Much of this learning and the personal change/development that results is both generic and transferable i.e. general insights and skilful practices can be used to inform thinking and support action in other situations. The learning partnership model developed through the Learning through Work Certificate, encouraged students to pay attention to the cultural and social interactions in their workplace and to use these events as resources for learning. Fundamentally, this process helped participants reflect critically upon their experiences. The process of making their understandings explicit enabled participants to appreciate even more what they had learnt and how they had changed. This enhanced self-awareness is the most tangible and useful outcome for participants in the process. The mediating artefacts created by participants to reveal some of their learning and development enabled the assessors to appreciate and validate the personal knowledge and newly acquired practical skills.

Through the process of developing and piloting the Learning through Work Certificate we realised the important role played by work in enabling students to learn and develop in ways that are essential for their future employment. These forms of development could be incorporated into a higher education through a lifewide concept of education.

Chapter 13

Adapting to another culture: an immersive experience

Novie Johan and Norman Jackson

Synopsis
International students who make the transition from another culture into the university environment are required to make a significant transition that requires all sorts of adaptive learning, personal change and development. For many students the process is an immersive experience bearing many of the characteristics described in Chapter 10. This chapter describes a Learning Partnership called Cultural Academy that was developed to enable students to reveal the nature of the learning and development gained through the process of adapting to another culture and to gain recognition for this learning through a Certificate that was part of the Surrey Lifewide Learning Award.

Introduction
In Chapter 10 Cambell and Jackson argued that a lifewide concept of learning and education could embrace the immersive experiences learners encounter in their lives while they are studying at university, and facilitate and recognise the learning and personal development they gain through such experiences. In this chapter we take an example of how new educational practices can be created to support an immersive experience that is common to all students as they make the transition to the higher education experience, but it is particularly significant to those students who have to adapt to another culture as they are making this transition. The challenge is how to help these students make the transition and enable them to be more aware of the transformative change that occurs through this process. The knowledge and confidence that is grown through the experience of making difficult transitions is important self-knowledge for a world that is full of disruptions and upheavals (Chapter 10).

Cultural Academy
Cultural diversity is one of the things that make this world a very complicated place and we cannot claim that we educate people for a lifetime of working and learning without engaging with the issue of how we prepare them, or how they prepare themselves, for the culturally diverse worlds they will inhabit. Cultural awareness is something that we all need in order to be able to operate effectively in multicultural organisations and societies, and multicultural universities provide considerable opportunity for these forms of learning and personal development.

In the UK, cultural diversity is a fact of university life. In the case of the University of Surrey nearly 30 per cent of our students originate from over 130 different countries. Surrey is ranked 45th and 68th worldwide for its proportion of international students and staff respectively in the *THES – QS World University Rankings 2010*, a list of the top 600 universities and colleges selected from an estimated 10,000 institutions worldwide. For students, simply living in the multicultural campus society is an education and the societies, events and other activities organised by students themselves enrich this aspect of a more complete education. But the university can also provide opportunity for learning and development that makes use of the valuable resources of students' cultural knowledge and experiences. Our attention was drawn to the possibility space afforded by the co-curriculum – at the University of Surrey these are opportunities for learning that are organised and designed by members of the university in the space outside the formal academic curriculum and they are not credit bearing. Cultural Academy was created in 2007 and between 2007 and 2010 four Academies were organised, each attracting about 20 students from all cultures, levels (level 1 to doctoral) and disciplines.

Educational design
The main intention was to create a process that would not be too onerous on students in terms of their time commitment but would sustain their interest and involvement and permit relationship development over several months. Underlying the design was the commitment to foster conversations that enabled students to share their cultural knowledge and experiences. We also wanted participants to enjoy their experience and to work together to achieve something that they would value and that they believed would add value to their campus community. Examples of these enterprises include:
- making a film of what it was like to live on a multicultural campus
- organising a conference and workshops to share their cultural knowledge and experiences with other students

- undertaking surveys into what it was like to be part of a multicultural campus community
- creating a radio show on the theme of multicultural campus
- organising a multicultural event which included a fashion show, food of the world, an African drum band and other cultural activities, which they called a 'Big Cultural Bash'.

The design was modified for each Academy. In the first Academy, students participated in three workshops, a planning meeting for a conference and an end of process student-led conference. In 2008–9 students participated in three workshops but this time they organised their event (Big Cultural Bash) after the first workshop. In 2010-11, Cultural Academy took the form of two pairs of workshops, one in each semester. To maintain a sense of continuity from one year to the next a wiki was established and each year resources were added so that students could see that they were part of a tradition and the resources they created would be passed on to other students. Our intention was that the Academies would help students develop friendships and good working relationships and this was certainly the case. Students' feedback was overwhelmingly positive with some claiming it was one of the most significant experiences for them while they were at university.

Three important pedagogic ideas underpin Cultural Academy: *collaborative learning* – learning through sharing knowledge and experiences; *productive inquiry* – learning through finding out in order to achieve something; *learning through the experience* of doing something and through *reflection* on experience.

Pedagogic practices that have been used in different Academies include:
- concept mapping – to facilitate personal enquiry into understandings of culture
- cultural enquiry using simple question-based tools
- use of voting systems to reveal patterns of beliefs in response to propositions about culture
- story telling – descriptions of personal experiences and online blogs, creation of digital stories and use of 'Sensemaker' narrative software
- mentoring to encourage conversation and reflection
- film making – enquiry into our multicultural campus, the recording of the Cultural Academy process and the evaluation of the process
- peer 'teaching' – the facilitation of conversation

- questionnaire surveys – online and paper-based surveys of staff and students to gain their perspectives on our multicultural campus
- reflective personal accounts and conversations to consolidate learning using a set of prompts.

Immersive Cultural Experience Certificate
From the beginning, students who completed Cultural Academy and demonstrated their learning through a reflective account were awarded a SCEPTrE Experiential Learning Certificate. With the advent of the Lifewide Learning Award Framework in May 2010 the opportunity arose for a Certificate to contribute to the framework that enabled cultural learning and development to be recognised. The idea of an Immersive Cultural Experience Certificate was born and it became the developmental focus for a SCEPTrE Fellowship by Novie Johan.

The intention was for the Immersive Cultural Experience Certificate to provide university recognition for informal learning and personal development gained when students are immersed in a culture other than their own. The Certificate is intended for three sorts of situations:
- when international students make the transition into the university and they have to assimilate our culture and adapt their behaviours and communications
- when home or international students go on exchange programmes to other universities or on work placements in another country and have to assimilate a new culture
- when home or international students engage in significant travel experiences during vacation periods when they are exposed to and have to adapt to the cultures of other countries.

Cultural Academy provided the vehicle for developing and piloting the Certificate in the first of these contexts with a small group of international student volunteers. The Certificate was developed and piloted in two stages:
- The first stage involved developing and trialing a tool kit and pedagogic strategies to enable participants to think and talk about their transition to another culture and to encourage them to record their understandings (make their personal knowledge explicit).
- The second stage involved a smaller number of volunteer participants in creating a synthesis account of their transition experience, drawing on the personal knowledge they had recorded and drawing out deeper

understandings of their learning and development. This process was aided by a one-to-one interview with the facilitator.

Cultural Academy, autumn 2010
This Academy differed from previous Academies in that recruitment was aimed exclusively at international students who had only recently started at the university. The Academy involved two afternoon workshops six weeks apart with encouragement for participants to meet weekly in small groups to carry on the conversations and relationship building between the workshops. The overall design is shown in Figure 13.1.

Figure 13.1 Design of Autumn 2010 Cultural Academy

Workshop 1 – week 1	Everyday living in another culture – weeks 2, 3, 4, 5	Workshop 2 – week 6
Personal introductions	Keep a ten-minute-a-day diary of cultural incidents	Each trio presents what they have learnt about adapting to another culture
Introduction to Cultural Academy and Workbook	Enter stories of cultural experiences into Sensemaker; at least once a week	Whole group considers the results of the Sensemaker project
Initial examination of the idea of culture based on participants' experiences?	Culture study group to meet three times to share your experiences and plan your presentation around a poster on the theme of *Adapting to the Surrey Culture*	Whole group discussions about how we would recognise these things through a Certificate
Adapting to another culture: creation of cultural lifemap and other exercises using workbook.		
Formation of culture study groups of 3-4 with range of cultural background. Focus on culture shock. Discussion and production of poster. Short presentations filmed.		Award of Cultural Academy Certificate
Introduction to Sensemaker narrative software and first stories written		

The process was underpinned by two workbooks containing tools and frameworks for stimulating thinking and conversation about the transitional experience and recording incidents, thoughts and feelings about the experiences http://www.lifewideeducation.co.uk. Table 13.1 summarises the content of the workbook and shows the reflection, conversational and recording activities it supports.

Process

The first workshop enabled participants to get to know each other and the facilitators to introduce the process. Using the exercises in the workbook, individual reflections and small and whole group conversations explored the meaning of culture. In particular, participants' shared their experiences of culture shock and their initial day-to-day experiences of adapting to the new culture. These impressions were visualised in a poster which was presented to the whole group. Presentations were filmed and the films archived on a wiki. By pooling and capturing experience-based knowledge in this way more perspectives and insights could be gained about the adaptive process.

Table 13.1 Cultural Academy Workbook content – aids to making experiences and personal knowledge explicit

Aids to knowledge development	Activity
Cultural biography (500 words)	Describe where you were born and brought up, your family, the origin of your name, the language(s) spoken in your family, the main cultural influences in your life, the countries you have lived in, your cultural identity.
Culture shock! (500 words)	Describe your experiences, impressions and feelings in the first week after arriving in the England.
Concept map	What does culture mean to you?
Cultural life map	Where in your everyday life do you have experiences through which you gain insights into the influence of culture in the situations you encounter?
Journey of cultural adaptation	Annotate the timeline explaining the emotional journey you are making and the reasons that you feel this way.
Stories of adapting to the English/ University culture using Sensemaker narrative software	Every Friday you will be sent an email inviting you to write a short story about something significant that has happened in the week that has caused you to think about the influence of culture in that situation. You will also be invited to draw meaning from the story and your wider experiences by positioning an X in a triangle that asks you to evaluate the significance of the situation from a variety of perspectives.
Daily diary – ten minute daily reflections	Briefly describe an incident or situation you have found yourself in today that caused you to reflect on culture. What was it that made you reflect on the role of culture in such situations?

Participants were encouraged to develop relationships that would lead to a weekly meeting of their group to continue the conversations and the sharing of cultural experiences. Contact details were exchanged during the workshop to encourage this. Many of the participants agreed to keep in touch through Facebook.

Between the first and second workshop, participants were encouraged to meet their Cultural Academy team informally each week. Not all participants took the opportunity to meet, but those who did reported that they benefited greatly from the experience. Here is an example of a student who honoured the process by recording and reflecting on his experiences and made good use of his team to discuss things that disturbed him about the cultural differences he was encountering.

> I met a British elderly man who was looking for his way to Wates House on the campus. Some distance behind him was his elderly wife looking exhausted from walking around campus trying to locate their destination. The man was carrying a big brief case. He walked up to me and asked for the direction to Wates House and I offered to take him there. As we walked together I felt an urge to help with carrying the brief case for him which is culturally acceptable and expected of young ones in my Country as a sign of respect, even for strangers. But not knowing what is acceptable culturally in the UK to this regard I discarded the thought and just took him to his destination. I didn't feel satisfied for not trying and find out along the line what the outcome would be if I offered to help with the luggage; what will be his response ... where the fears that went down my spine as I discarded the choice to help. ... I'm yet to find out if my decision was right or wrong and general tips as to how respect is shown to the elderly in situations like this in the UK. I'll discuss with my group tomorrow to find out what they know.
>
> (Weekly story collected by Sensemaker)

Participants were also encouraged to complete the exercises in the workbook. Three methods were used to encourage systematic reflection on and the recording of experiences.
- The annotation of a timeline (see below) segmented into weekly blocks of time, to reveal how participants felt and why they felt that way.
- The maintenance of a daily diary (ten minutes per day) recording incidents that caused participants to think about cultural dimensions of a situation.
- The contribution of an anonymised short story each week describing a situation that caused the participant to think about the significance of culture.

This story was sent by email to a database for processing using SenseMaker[1] narrative software (the story above is an example of the types of story told). Students' stories were shared through a booklet prepared for the second workshop.

A traditional English 'cream tea' was organised at the midpoint of the process to encourage participants to come together to share their experiences and aspects of their culture.

The second workshop gave an opportunity for each group to present what they had learned about adapting to another culture. The workshop was essentially a facilitated reflective process and a few important parts of the first workshop were revisited in order to investigate further the process that participants had gone through in the six weeks between the workshops using a second workbook as an aid. This workshop ended with the award of SCEPTrE's Cultural Academy Certificate for those participants who had attended both workshops and submitted their workbooks.

Evaluation of the workshop process
The feedback received from participants indicated that the Cultural Academy helped them develop and share their knowledge about adapting to another culture (scores of 8–10 on 10-point scale in agreement with achieving this aim). Participants believed that it benefited them largely by facilitating their thoughts and reflections about the adaptive process and enabling them to share their experiences and gain more perspectives on the transition through the interaction with others. They felt that meeting and speaking about their concerns with others who were involved in a similar transitional experience and were thus able to understand and empathise with their situation was an uplifting experience.

All participants felt that Cultural Academy provided a good opportunity to meet other students to share their experiences about living in another culture (rating of 8–10 on a 10-point scale of achievement). One participant commented that: "it was the vital aspect in the whole Culture[al] Academy workshop. We built a strong friendship with my team mates." From this positive and trusting set of relationships, they could converse freely and be exposed to different languages, traditions and beliefs. They were able to share their own culture, listen to others talk about their culture and discuss each other's cultural experiences, which they deemed to be a valuable experience. Another participant believed that as a result, "if I meet other [people] from their country I can easily talk to them." They appreciated the opportunity to meet other students from various cultural backgrounds, and appreciated the co-operations and understandings of others.

When commenting on the usefulness of the workbooks, participants indicated that the exercises helped them to reflect on and appreciate the learning gained through the process of adapting to another culture (ratings of 7–9 on a 10-point achievement scale). The additional comments provided by participants were all positive, for example:
- The reflecting process was very effective.
- I reflected a lot and Cultural Academy helped me to share my ideas, my experience, my goal regarding my future adaptation to the U.K. system.
- It made me notice things I was not noticing about myself before.

Besides reflection, the participants also found that the workbook was helpful in guiding their understanding through cultural exercises.

One important outcome of students' learning through the Cultural Academy process is that it gives them an opportunity to learn about other cultures that they were not previously aware of. One participant commented, "through the process, I have learnt [the] other people['s] culture and their life. It means that I can have the chance to share a wide variety of culture and their thinking." While learning about other cultures is an important part of their learning, the main areas of learning suggested by the participants is in the area of their personal view about another culture or their cultural experiences, e.g. how to be positive, optimistic and open-minded; to take responsibility; to take initiative; to not fear asking and seeking support; to be open and willing; to motivate oneself; to take initiative, etc. One participant said that she learnt "to be honest with one's self and express your views openly, frankly", while another said, "I've learned more about myself and what I can be."

Throughout the feedback, students indicate positive aspects of their learning experience during Cultural Academy. Participants felt that taking part was useful in improving both their reflection and their ability to adapt to the campus culture. The words of one participant summed up the general feeling: "The experience helped a lot and had an enormous amount of improvement. Things started to be better and better." Similarly, another participant said: "Things get better and better. I have a lot of new friends, easily get a lot of help and support and take part in many activities. That all enrich[es] my life, I enjoy my life here." One participant explained that by sharing ideas through discussion and presentation, an understanding of one's own culture compared to others' could be more deeply understood. As another participant commented, "Now I know what other people feel, do and act in other cultures."

Piloting the Immersive Cultural Experience Certificate

Having gained experience of using the tools and techniques to facilitate individual learning gained through the process of adapting to another culture, the nine participants who completed Cultural Academy were invited to submit a 2,000-word integrating reflective essay describing the learning they had gained while adapting to another culture in order to complete the requirements for the new Immersive Experience Certificate (Table 13.2). As the workbooks included items 1 to 4, the only additional requirement was the one-to-one meeting to discuss their transition process. Four students submitted essays for the Certificate in March 2011 and all were successful. The next section describes the nature of the learning revealed in student essays and interviews.

Table 13.2 Certificate requirements

To join the programme you will be making a commitment through a learning agreement to evaluate and make explicit the learning and personal development you gain through a minimum of three months' immersion in another culture.
In order to receive university recognition for your learning and personal development you will need to document your experiences and your evaluation of the learning and personal development you have gained in a Reflective Diary (handwritten or word document) or online blog.
Five techniques are used to help you understand, evaluate and reveal how you have changed your understanding and how you have changed as a person: 1) creation of a life map showing where in your life you encounter different sorts of cultural experiences 2) construction of an ongoing reflective diary or blog to record and make sense of your experiences and the learning and personal development you are gaining from them 3) creation of a timeline map showing the journey you have made over the period of time you are involved in the certificate 4) creation of a concept map formed around the idea of adapting to another culture 5) production of a 2,000-word reflective account – to connect, synthesise and integrate the learning you have gained from your experience.
You may include other methods of recording your experiences and demonstrating your learning such as digital images or audio or video recordings. The Certificate encourages you to focus on key aspects of personal development that are generic to all informal learning situations. These are incorporated into a capability statement.

Learning gained through adapting to another culture

Adapting to another culture requires people to move from a world of familiar contexts and challenges into a world where the contexts and challenges are unknown, and where the ability to communicate and understand the contexts and challenges might be hampered by language and perceptual barriers. The norms of behaviour learnt and developed in one culture may no longer be valid and people become uncertain about how to behave. Adapting to another culture involves learning new things and also unlearning some things (at least temporarily). The reflective account provided participants with an opportunity to try to make sense of their transitional experience of adapting to another culture over about six months. By using the tools contained in the workbook to help them reflect on their experiences and their diaries which provided a record of their experiences, they had a wealth of material to draw on in their synthesising accounts.

We used the framework of Campbell and Jackson (Chapter 10) to evaluate participants' accounts of their immersive experiences. The overarching theme of any immersive experience is the sense of journey and this was also apparent in participants' accounts. The form of an immersive experience journey is caricatured in Chapter 10 Figure 10.2 and this general pattern, with some elaborations, could be discerned in the transition stories of participants. Some examples of deep and enduring learning and personal development are represented in the quotations from participants' essays below.

Dealing with culture shock
The process of adapting to a new culture often involves the phenomenon of 'culture shock': the transition from a familiar to an unfamiliar environment where old behaviour patterns become ineffective. According to Ryan & Twibell (2000), culture shock is a transitional process involving a journey in which four stages can be recognised which they called (a) honeymoon, (b) disenchantment, (c) beginning resolution and (d) effective functioning. Cultural change is a stressful process as students' cope with their concerns, anxieties and uncertainties associated with where they live, what they will eat, sleep, health, safety, money, weather, academic challenges and communication. Students who study aboard are unique in that they must not only adapt to a new host culture but also function quickly and effectively in a new academic cultural setting.

In recording their transitional stories, Cultural Academy participants revealed their particular concerns and how they coped with the confusion, anxiety and uncertainty of the situations they found themselves in. Culture shock was expected and had to be dealt with and developing coping strategies was part of coping with and mastering the transition, as described by some participants:

In the event that you experience culture shock in it's [sic] fullest with chronic depression and longing for home, my advice is to meet friends for emotional support. I have not experienced this but I have helped people who were foreign get through downs due to culture shock. Hang out with some people from your country and heal yourself with the culture you missed but don't be scared to return back to the foreign culture, embrace it! You are never alone, and there is always someone there like you who is willing to help.

It has been a wide experience that most of the International students face problems like boredom, monotony during their course, homesick, isolation and loneliness, difficulties socializing due to cultural, history and language barriers etc. Therefore, life and study have not been easy and smooth as I thought at the beginning. ... I also felt a little bit worried and scared, because I have been far away from the support of family and longstanding friends. When I came to UK first week, I terribly missed my parents. My two luggages [sic] were missing after getting off plane, I could not describe this issue very clearly to staff and felt anxious. There were other problems for me at the beginning, such as how to open bank account, how to sign mobile [contract]. Overcooked food and changeable weather also made me negative. In addition, I was afraid to make mistakes when I communicated with someone in English, especially [because] I felt so nervous on the phone. After making some Chinese friends in campus, things were getting better. We cooked together, studied together and went to town together. We can learn and know many things quickly through our activities and chats, such as cooking skills and local news. I was not too shy to talk, and shared my views.

Out of all these challenges, the behaviour and attitude of the people around me [was] my greatest hurdle. I constantly found myself in awkward situations due to me not understanding or being understood properly. ... Another thing which was sort of a culture shock and made me quite unhappy ... is that people didn't touch me much... I'm used to getting a hug or at least a handshake from my friends every time I see them, whereas here people mostly said 'hi' and walked past leaving me in some awkward 'hand stretched out but not shaken' situations. I felt like people didn't want to touch me or were just 'inhuman' by my standards, after all, who doesn't like a hug? But one day I spoke with a friend from Argentina who experienced the same thing ... and he felt the same feeling of 'not getting enough love'. But he explained to me that it is just the culture of the people, everywhere is different. One thing that really made me glad and gave me a very positive impression of the English culture was that when I and my friend told our housemates about this, they always hugged us when we met from then on.

Figure 13.2 Timelines showing how students felt about their experiences of adapting to another culture during the first 12 weeks

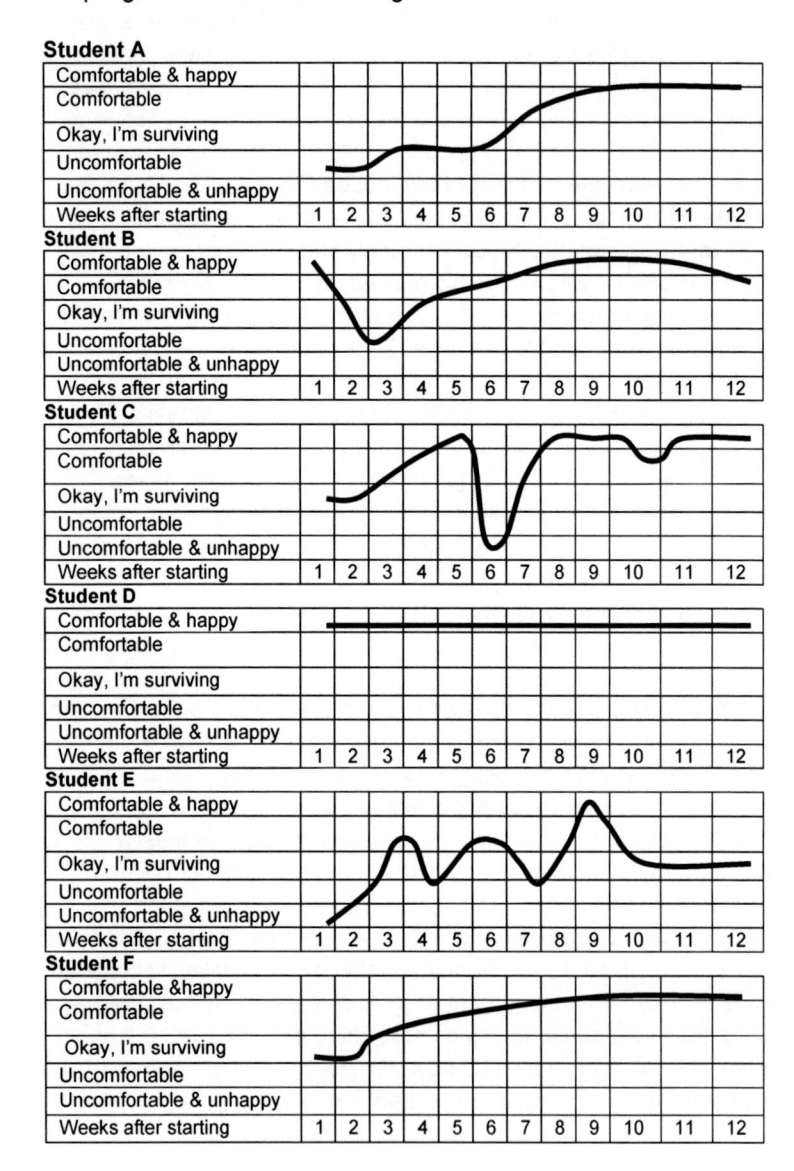

Student A

Comfortable & happy												
Comfortable												
Okay, I'm surviving												
Uncomfortable												
Uncomfortable & unhappy												
Weeks after starting	1	2	3	4	5	6	7	8	9	10	11	12

Student B

Comfortable & happy												
Comfortable												
Okay, I'm surviving												
Uncomfortable												
Uncomfortable & unhappy												
Weeks after starting	1	2	3	4	5	6	7	8	9	10	11	12

Student C

Comfortable & happy												
Comfortable												
Okay, I'm surviving												
Uncomfortable												
Uncomfortable & unhappy												
Weeks after starting	1	2	3	4	5	6	7	8	9	10	11	12

Student D

Comfortable & happy												
Comfortable												
Okay, I'm surviving												
Uncomfortable												
Uncomfortable & unhappy												
Weeks after starting	1	2	3	4	5	6	7	8	9	10	11	12

Student E

Comfortable & happy												
Comfortable												
Okay, I'm surviving												
Uncomfortable												
Uncomfortable & unhappy												
Weeks after starting	1	2	3	4	5	6	7	8	9	10	11	12

Student F

Comfortable &happy												
Comfortable												
Okay, I'm surviving												
Uncomfortable												
Uncomfortable & unhappy												
Weeks after starting	1	2	3	4	5	6	7	8	9	10	11	12

Ward and Kennedy (1993, 1999) drew a distinction between psychological (emotional/affective) adaption and socio-cultural (behavioural) adaption. Psychological adaption can be understood within a stress and coping model and refers to feelings of well-being or satisfaction with transition. Learning to manage emotions is another intangible but essential dimension of the learning that comes from cultural adaptation. The psychological/emotional journeys of several Cultural Academy participants are depicted schematically in Figure 13.2.

Except for student D who felt confident, comfortable and happy throughout the three months of this study, all the students were able to recognise changes in their emotional states, but the journey is different for each participant. Emotional stresses are associated with many aspects of their experience. Homesickness, felt by all participants, is compounded by what many students see as a lack of friendliness of the home culture, but when they experience kindness and generosity this has a significant positive effect on their well-being.

> Another challenge for me was the perceived 'coldness' of the English people. [People from my country] are generally friendly and trusting in the public domain. It is not unusual to strike [up] a conversation with the person behind you in the queue at the bank. In my new country I found that on a bus, everyone stared firmly out the window or into their newspapers, and striking [up] a conversation with a stranger was considered close to bizarre … The English are big on privacy and do not take nosiness lightly. An innocuous question such as whether the expected baby has arrived yet can be found intrusive. In [my country], it is taken for granted that family units will not only stay up to date with each others' affairs, but they have right by default to offer advice, remedies, and in instances step in and take action during any form of crisis. The rule in England seems to be wait until you are told, then you can ask questions. This adjustment has been trying, since I am used to 'intruding', and being intruded upon. I lost a few friends at first because I was accustomed to discussing my problems in painstaking details, then asking for advice.

> The first thing I noticed was the courtesy and friendliness of the people at Heathrow Airport as a security official helped me get to the correct terminal and a shop assistant helped me get a sim card to call a taxi. The taxi driver who transported me to the campus was very friendly and even offered to carry my bags to my room. This left a lasting impression in me.

The HOST scheme links British families with international students. I greatly appreciate Host UK that gives me some opportunities to visit this beautiful and affluent country. It is an excellent way to experience the British culture. The other good thing is the University will pay the cost for you to apply for the visit. I was lucky to be a guest of Mrs....... in this Christmas holiday. I have been to the seaside town of Looe in South West Cornwall. I roamed a long and beautiful coastline of Looe, it is quiet, beautiful and unspoiled, which made me relaxed and happy. I love the boundless sea and blue sky. I also had a big Christmas dinner with [her] daughters and grandchildren in the countryside. They treated me as a member of family, I felt like I was in my home. I am deeply impressed with their hospitality and affability. The weather was cold, but I was warm in my heart. It is really an unforgettable experience for me. In addition, the Friends International Society in Surrey also provides the opportunity to enjoy fun social events, explore life outside of studies and learn more about the Christian faith.

I was shopping at Tesco and I was impressed by the service at the checkouts when I was finished with my shopping. The lady at the checkout was friendly and helpful when she helped me pack my items. Later that day I was also impressed by the customer service at Natwest Bank on campus when the teller was helpful in explaining things to me.

Coping with prejudice and disrespect is another source of emotional stress.

A further challenge I experienced when adapting to English culture [was] the stereotypes that came with my darker skin and my very obvious [foreign] looks. While before I had been one in millions of others like me, now I stood out. There were instances when I was unfairly labelled with the stereotypes given to my countrymen and women. I was referred to as being lazy, a drunk, and good for nothing. I was expected to be loud, callous and uncultured. I was once asked if any member of my family owned a shipping line. These accusations were not necessarily true, but ... I had to bear the brunt for the traits most commonly associated with people from my country or origin.

Developing a positive and optimistic disposition seems to have been one way to overcome feeling homesick, lonely and despondent. Indeed, being able to turn negative emotional states into more positive and optimistic states was considered important in order to cope with the transitional experience.

> There were numerous ... challenges in my path to settling with the culture. All these differences, language, food, weather, behaviour and attitude towards situations, these all affected me and my emotions daily, and not always for the best. I'm a very optimistic and happy-go-lucky person who would require a lot to keep my mood down for long so I usually recovered quickly from negative emotions. I was also always willing to adapt because the English from my experience are very accommodating to people of other cultures and that really boosted my confidence as a person. Because of this mindset I had there weren't any particularly terrible or horrible times I've had as a result of a different culture. However there were times where I felt quite depressed and/or disappointed when I received a different result than what I expected just because of a difference in culture or two. Times where my self esteem hung really low because the people around me weren't reacting as they should. And some times, just plainly being fed up with the way everything seemed different and inhuman.
>
> Adapting to a new culture is a long journey and there are many unforeseen things that could cause a culture shock for people. However, having an optimistic and open minded attitude to anything and anyone of the strange culture is the best thing to do in order to fully adapt and even soak up the new culture. I am optimistic and positive about all experiences and embrace the opportunity to learn as much as I can, thus I believe all of these benefits will enhance my employment prospects and make my life meaningful in the future.

There was recognition that adapting to another culture involved learning new things and also unlearning things that were known through their own culture (at least temporarily).

> Culture ranges from more noticeable behaviours like music to even more subtle and unnoticeable behaviours like how to put your cutlery down after eating (yes it really is complex and different between cultures!). And to the uninformed man, could result in some very awkward and/or embarrassing situations. I am a citizen of [African country], born and raised there with traditional values and grew up learning the way of doing things. With that being said, it is no doubt I had to do a lot of 'unlearning' to do when I came over here to study. I shall talk about the differences in my culture and the English culture and how I started to understand the people here and what I experienced in my journey of adapting to the English culture. To be more specific about the latter of the afore mentioned two, the challenges and

experiences I faced when adapting; coming to an understanding and being understood by the people of this culture; and finally advice for people who want to adapt to a culture peculiar to them.

There was also recognition that changing one's perspectives was an important way of coming to terms with living in another culture.

> My culture is largely family based. The family image and values are the most important thing to a man and everything else like fame, money, pleasure etc comes later. Children learn the importance of family and are usually guided by the parents' wisdom in order to excel in life even when the children are adults. This is quite a contrast to the English culture I've observed which promotes a more 'individual' upbringing for children which promotes children to do more of what they want to do while growing and figure out decisions for themselves with a lot less parental guidance [than our] parents. This came as quite a shock to me at first because I felt that so many children were unruly and lacked respect towards elders and this was clearly because they are given too much room to do what they please while growing. However, there was a situation that altered my view on this. One day out in town, I saw an old lady in the street carrying not too heavy bags and I thought "Oh my God! Where are her children!? They should be carrying that for her", the same scenario in [my country] would be somewhat of an insult to the children that they are not good children to let their parent do such. Imagining the same scenario with my mom, I'd feel like a terrible child for letting her go out at that age. I then went over to her to help her carry the things and she said "I might be old but I'm very capable of taking care of myself" and even more peculiar response! I went home pondering on that response and then asked my teacher who was English why I got that reaction and funny enough she told me that my actions could be seen as insulting in a way, VERY contrary to my original idea of an insult being her children not helping her. And then it hit me, perhaps what I thought was completely wrong ... perhaps they weren't the ones being unruly and ill mannered but 'I' the ill mannered one for insulting her strength and competence. This was a true eye opener for me, it was the first time I ever thought in a different sense and seen the world from a different perspective.

> While at first I was very conscious of myself in the midst of English men, because I was certain everything about me screamed 'foreigner', I came to learn that the reason why I stood out was because I thought so much about it. Gradually, I came to relax and mingle freely, and you would think now that

I was born and bred in Buckingham Palace. Initially I had concerns about blending in; with my accent and my colour, it was made doubly obvious that I did not belong. I have overcome this awkwardness now. For me to blend in, I do not have to be the epitome of the perfect English gentleman, I just have to understand that I carve my own place, that what is of greater importance is that I be comfortable in my own skin.

Life in the UK has been really exciting and challenging as well. However all the way it has made me reflect on my approach to life. It offers a good opportunity to accelerate my growth and also brings a lot of changes to me, which include the self understanding, handling problems, showcase self talent and etc. Generally, I feel it easy and positive to adapt to life in the UK.

When I compare the person I was in February 2010 with the person I have become, I realise that I no longer make generalisations about other people from other countries since I have learnt that each person is unique. I have become appreciative of new people I meet.

And as the unfamiliar situations become more familiar and better understood, confidence grows and there comes with it a sense of achievement, pride and comfort in making a successful transition into a totally different world to what was previously known.

The differences in culture between people is an amazing thing, and to have adapted to one different than mine is something that I will cherish for the rest of my life. Although it may seem unnerving at first, the learning, the growth, the memories and the feeling of triumph are all worth the journey to understanding this magnificent thing we call culture.

Living in England gets easier by the day; I have become to read the nonverbal language that is to be found in any given cultural or societal setting and can only be learned by familiarizing oneself with the culture. While before there were nonverbal cues that puzzled me, or which I missed out on all together, I can now easily pick up on the subtle nuances of nonverbal communications. ... My confidence has greatly gone up. When I was new to England, I second guessed myself at every turn. I had suffered a complex that arose from years of being drilled with the mantra that England and all things English were superior to what I had in my own country. While initially I so badly wanted to fit in that I tried to ape English mannerisms, from speech to dress and a penchant for the races, now I am confident enough of my place that I opt to watch basketball over a game of cricket. I have decided to work with aspects of the English culture that work for me – like the strict observance of time and unerring politeness, while not trying to turn myself into the clone of an Englishman.

Discussion

The case was made in Chapter 10 for the importance of challenging immersive experiences in the transformational (rather than evolutionary) development of individuals. This chapter has focused on a single context for immersive experience: a context that is relevant to all students who leave home to inhabit the unfamiliar environment of a university with its new contexts and challenges. Universities are aware of the challenges of adaptation and they have developed a range of strategies for helping students make the transition from home to independence. Nevertheless, the experience is much more of a challenge for students who are making this transition from a different culture. The Immersive Cultural Experience Certificate focused on this context to demonstrate how personal learning and development gained through the adaptive process could be valued and recognised by students and the university. The first part of the chapter described the process and tools to support and record learning while the second part provided examples of the sorts of learning and personal change that were recognised through the process.

The development of new capability in the English language is perhaps the most obvious developmental challenge for those students with limited language competency. It was a source of psychological and practical challenge for some participants in Cultural Academy.

> My greatest challenge was communication because no matter how keenly I tried to listen, or how carefully I enunciated my words, I neither fully understood native English speakers nor seemed to get through to them. It seemed incredulous that I had been speaking English for the past two decades. This was my greatest frustration since I could not accomplish a task as simple as ordering a plate of fish and chips without bustle. Being unable to communicate hampered with my social interactions. I was at first not confident about trying to make friends because I knew it would take extra effort for us to understand each other. My classes took more effort too, and I was concerned my grades would be affected by my inability to keep up with variations of the nasal Queen's English.

Students recognised that a lack of culturally related knowledge about what was expected of them academically also presented a fundamental challenge to their success (Ham and Wang 2009). This sort of knowledge is essential to academic performance, so mastering it quickly, along with all the other knowledge that has to be mastered, is essential.

> The course is quite intensive, with too much reading and thinking involved. In addition, I never expected to have to speak so much. In China, the teaching is very teacher-centred; the students just listen and take notes. However, there are many pair work and group works in here, actually that is good for us to practice English and communication. Although we have many tasks and assignments, establishing a balance between work and leisure is equally important for us. For the assignments, at the beginning, I felt it was very hard to write down thousand words essay just like a fish out of water, I do not know if I can do that, so I sought some help from staffs [sic] in library. With their friendly help and useful advice, I felt more confident and finished all assignments on time. Therefore if I am not sure about anything, I always try to ask someone.

Beyond these obvious challenges to a student coming to study in a culture that is very different to their own is the need to comprehend the culture, grasp what is expected and develop the capability and confidence to operate and perform in a social, not just academic, sense. This requires students to immerse themselves in the everyday world of those around them in order to learn the ways of being and becoming in the cultural context which they inhabit.

It must be said that many of the generalised features of immersive experiences described in Chapter 10 can be recognised in the narratives and other representations of learning through being in everyday situations created by the students who participated in Cultural Academy. All had begun their experience with a sense of excitement and positive anticipation accompanied by anxiety about the unknown. Most had experienced a significant culture shock when they first arrived that had caused them emotional stress, discomfort and unhappiness and challenged their existing conceptual frameworks for making sense of the world. Some had lost confidence and many had encountered situations that had stretched them emotionally, engendering feelings of negativity, frustration, confusion and anger. Many had felt the loss of their family and friendship networks that encouraged, supported and valued them for the people they are. Through their own agency and effort they gradually overcame their despondency, developed practical coping strategies, changed perspectives and turned their negative feelings into more positive and optimistic thoughts to come to terms and be comfortable with the situation. Making this transition required them to change considerably, and through the tools and frameworks provided by the Immersive Experience Certificate they were able to articulate and represent these changes and the way they felt about them in ways that enabled their learning to be valued and recognised by the university.

In adapting in such a transformative way the students were displaying many of the habits and characteristics of what Baxter Magolda (2001, 2004, 2009 and Chapter 5) terms self-authorship – the capacity to internally define [redefine] their own beliefs, identity and relationships. Self-authorship is the necessary foundation for mutual, collaborative participation with others in adult life (Baxter Magolda 2001:xvi). The development of self-authorship is encouraged and facilitated by 'exposure to epistemological, intrapersonal and interpersonal complexity' (*ibid.*), all of which are present when students put themselves into cultural settings very different to their own. In such situations students realise that they must create the knowledge they need to adapt through active participation and engagement with the world around them. Through sharing their perspectives they come to realise that 'authority and expertise are shared in the mutual construction of knowledge among peers' (*ibid*). We might speculate that the sorts of transformative experiences we have recognised through the Cultural Academy and the Immersive Experience Certificate, accelerate learners along the trajectory to self-authorship as their beliefs, inherited from their cultural backgrounds are questioned, challenged and modified.

> I was invited for dinner by the Chinese students in my flat alongside their friends from other halls of residence. It was great and being part of the culture academy I was proactive during the dinner making the most of the opportunity to learn from their culture. I equally shared with them about my culture. The dinner lasted about three to four hours where in I learnt about their dinning ethics as well as family, government, marriage, history policies to mention but a few. It amazed me why they attached so much importance to eating together as a family even here in the UK away from home. In my country and my home, we hardly eat together on the same table, the most important thing is that you've had your meal be it in the dinning [*sic*] room, your bed room, sitting room or you can go to the toilet if you don't mind (laugh out loud) nobody cares. This Chinese culture made me take a decision to make a difference with my own family and no matter where life takes me (e.g. here in the UK) I can connect to the environment and the

culture around me and 'having a meal together' is a good way of doing that, not just with fellow Nigerians but with the people you find yourself with just as the saying goes 'they that eat together live together'.

Cultural Academy has proved to be a powerful learning partnership for everyone involved (students and educators). The structured and facilitated process encourages development of cross-cultural relationships and engages learners in thinking and talking about the epistemological, interpersonal and intrapersonal complexity associated with the transition they are making. The feedback we have received suggests that for some students it has been one of the most formative experiences they encountered while at university.

Acknowledgements
The following staff and students are gratefully acknowledged for their contributions to the development, evaluation and documentation of Cultural Academy and the Immersive Cultural Experience Certificate: Vasso Vydelingum, Nimmy Hutnik, Sarah Campbell, Duangthida Nuntahpirat, Lori Riley, Hayley York, David Wicksman, Caroline Osinska, Virginia Lam, Mary Lou Tzempelikou, Monty Bal, Ben Mercer and William Patterson, Andra Ilie, Mazio Dadamuga, Nastasia Michail, Can Wang and Khanya Ngonyama.

Endnotes
1 http://www.sensemaker-suite.com/

Chapter 14

Lifewide education: an emergent phenomenon in UK higher education

Charlotte Betts and Norman Jackson

Synopsis
The chapter considers the phenomenon of student development awards that recognise learning and personal development gained through co-curricular and extra-curricular experiences. The scale (over 50 universities) and speed of growth of this phenomenon appears to be unique to the UK higher education system. This chapter describes the characteristics and variations across award schemes and provides a typology of awards. Credibility is an issue within any area of emergent practice and a benchmarking process is described which could provide a system-wide vehicle for quality assurance and enhancement of these new educational practices. The chapter concludes by considering the value of an ecological approach to viewing lifewide education within the lifelong learning paradigm of formal and informal education.

Introduction
This chapter shows that at the end of the first decade of the 21st century UK higher education is witnessing an emergent phenomenon: namely, the growth of student development awards that aim to recognise and value learning and achievements gained through experiences in the co- and extra-curricular dimensions of students' experiences. These are experiences that are additional to the academic curriculum and that generally do not receive academic credit. This assertion is based on a mapping exercise undertaken in 2009–10 (Rickett 2010). Internet-based searches and networking have identified 57 award schemes (Table 14.1) that are either established or are being developed or piloted. An interesting feature of these schemes is that they are distributed across all institutional peer groups but the research-intensive Russell Group and

the 1994 Group of Universities proportionally contain more schemes than other institutional peer groups.

Table 14.1 Universities that have some form of recognition of learning and personal development gained outside the academic curriculum or are developing their scheme (updated from Rickett 2010)

Russell Group	1994 Group	University Alliance	Guild HE	Million +	Other
Birmingham	Bath	Bournemouth	Winchester	Bedfordshire	Aberdeen
Bristol	Durham	Bradford	University of the Creative Arts	Birmingham City	Chichester
Cardiff	Exeter	Lincoln	York St John	Central Lancashire	Dundee
Glasgow	Goldsmiths	Liverpool John Moores		Coventry	Edge Hill
Leeds	Lancaster	Manchester Metropolitan		Derby	Heriot-Watt
Manchester	Leicester	Plymouth		London South Bank	Hull
Newcastle	Loughborough	Salford		Northampton	Keele
Nottingham	Queen Mary	Sheffield Hallam		Roehampton	Kent
Queens Belfast	Reading	West of England			Strathclyde
Sheffield	St Andrews				Swansea
Warwick	Surrey				Worcester
Southampton	Sussex				
	York				
TOTAL 12/20	TOTAL 13/17	TOTAL 9/23	TOTAL 3/6	TOTAL 8/28	TOTAL 11

Award scheme characteristics

Award schemes have developed in a highly situated way so it is not surprisingly that there is great variability in their characteristics. Appendix 14.1 (which can be found at: http://lifewideeducation.co.uk) summarises key features of these schemes. Variations occur in:
- their purpose and focus – personal development, professional development, employability skills, lifewide learning
- what they choose to emphasise – education, employability, leadership, transferable skills
- expectations in the level of student commitment (time and effort involved) in order to achieve an award
- their inclusion criteria – who is included or not included
- scale and level of participation within the student population

- whether students opt in or opt out of the scheme
- types of experiences that qualify for the award – some are more limited than others
- whether the focus is co-curriculum, extra-curriculum or a combination
- whether there are specialist routes or pathways
- how they are assessed, by whom and the criteria used
- how learning is demonstrated – the extent to which critical reflection is encouraged or valued
- the form of recognition – points, credits, certificates
- how they are organised and who organises and coordinates them
- how they are resourced and who is responsible for managing the scheme
- extent of staff involvement – academic staff, personal tutors, central service staff
- level and types of employer involvement – including sponsorships and endorsements
- extent to which the scheme is an explicit part of the university's concept of the student experience
- how schemes are presented and marketed to students
- how awards are made on completion
- whether such awards feature in transcripts
- the degree to which the institution's Students' Union is involved.

Conceptual variations
Our research has tried to identify the key conceptual features that underlie different schemes. While there is much variation and conceptual mixing, our sense is that schemes differentiate at the conceptual level according to whether:
- the approach emphasises whole-person education and personal/career development or attention is focused primarily on transferable and employability skills
- the environments for learning are predominantly controlled/taught or are predominantly experiential
- assessment is primarily through reflective, self-evidencing and reporting or through a tutor-assessed/competency-based assessment
- the experiences that make up the award are predominantly extra-curricular (not designed by the institution and not linked to a programme) or co-curricular (institution-designed, linked to or outside a student's programme)
- leadership skills are seen as either implicit or explicit within the scheme.

Most schemes contain a mix of these conceptual continua but some schemes tend to one or other sides of the conceptual diagram.

Figure 14.1 shows idealised representations of the different foci and approaches that awards are based around – a holistic, whole-person, self-determined focus; a predominantly designed and taught process; an employability approach; and one centred on specific skills or leadership development. Many schemes combine these dimensions. Some examples of awards that can be categorised in this way are listed along with others that might be viewed as hybrid approaches.

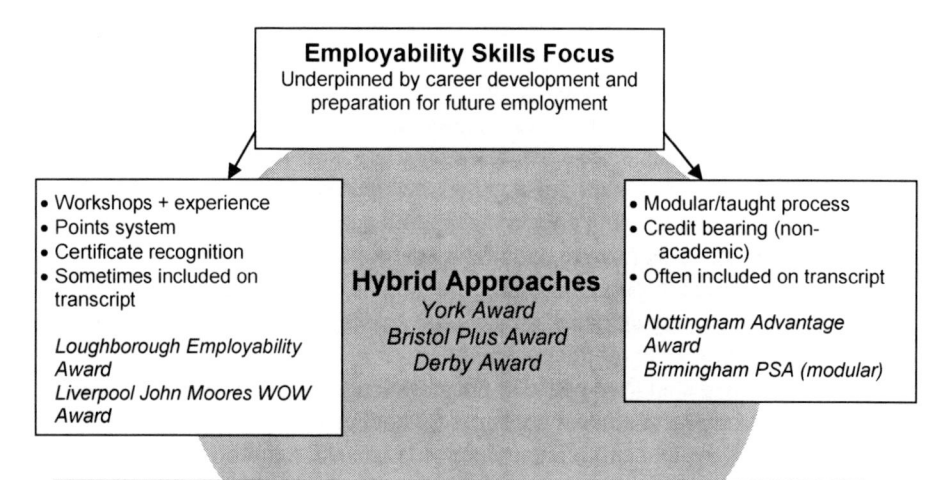

Employability Skills Focus
Underpinned by career development and preparation for future employment

- Workshops + experience
- Points system
- Certificate recognition
- Sometimes included on transcript

Loughborough Employability Award
Liverpool John Moores WOW Award

Hybrid Approaches
York Award
Bristol Plus Award
Derby Award

- Modular/taught process
- Credit bearing (non-academic)
- Often included on transcript

Nottingham Advantage Award
Birmingham PSA (modular)

Holistic Focus

Underpinned by conceptions of learning and capability for life

- Experience + reflection
- Portfolio approach
- Certificate recognition

Plymouth Award
Sussex Plus Award
Surrey Lifewide Learning Award

Specific Skills Focus (e.g. Leadership)

Underpinned by specific skills development and encouragement of [e.g. leadership] qualities
- Workshops + experience
- Academic credit (MLP) or Certified

Manchester Leadership Programme (MLP)
Exeter Leadership Award

An emergent phenomenon

The rapid growth of student development awards between about 2007–11 suggests that we are witnessing a system-wide adaptation that is fundamentally about adding value to the student experience by making higher education more relevant to the lives of learners and recognising that there is more to learning and education than studying a subject. Concerns for employability are a significant driver. With such a rapid growth in these award schemes there is likely to be a multiplicity of reasons. Some of the possible reasons are given below.

- The nature of the traditional single honours course in UK higher education leaves little scope for broader educational considerations especially in research-intensive universities. Student development awards offer a way of embracing forms of development that are not catered for through the academic curriculum.
- The drive for efficiency has progressively reduced contact time: in some courses students spend significantly more time doing things other than studying and student development awards provide the means of recognising learning gained outside the academic programme.
- Many students have to undertake paid work in order to support themselves through university and there is a ready-made context for demonstrating students' employability skills by recognising that work is a valid context for learning.
- The rapid shift from public to privately financed tuition fees corresponds to parental and student concerns for best value for the tuition fee. Institutions that can offer such awards can claim more value for the fee income.
- It is now a universal driver that employability has to be an important outcome of a university education, so demonstrating a commitment to helping students' demonstrate their employability skills is an important institutional consideration.
- The significant support being given by employers and graduate recruiters, as evidenced through sponsorship and direct involvement in institutional schemes, further reinforces the institutional, student and parental beliefs that these schemes are a worthwhile investment.
- There is fear that an institution might be competitively disadvantaged if their competitors offer such awards and they do not.
- There is a genuine desire to broaden and deepen the concept of what a higher education means and to embrace much richer representations of learning that truly embraces the real world beyond the classroom and makes higher education more relevant to students.

The social challenge

As the twenty-first century unfolds, two insights will change the way we think about people, society and politics. First, a better future relies not just on security, economic growth and good government, but also on the development of more capable and responsible citizens. Second, human beings are complex social animals, influenced more by our nature and context and less by calculating, conscious decisions, than we intuitively believe. Personal fulfillment and social progress are more likely if we understand better what drives us to think and behave as we do.
(Taylor 2011)

Such enhanced capability and wisdom can only be gained through deeper engagement with the world and reflective contemplation on our place and presence within it. Our formal educational structures have a pivotal role to play in contributing to both of these personal and social changes but these too also need to change if we are to create a more creative, self-aware and socially engaged society. Formal education has to become more engaged in the holistic development of people as they develop themselves through the whole of their life experiences. As a society we have to adopt not only a lifelong commitment to our own development as people but also to embrace the opportunities for continuous and transformative development that a lifewide approach to education affords. It might be argued that the growth of student development awards that aim to encourage and recognise these more holistic forms of personal development are one of the ways in which we are adapting as a society to meeting the challenge of our own future.

The challenge for emergent practice

Establishing any new field of educational practice is challenging. Establishing standards for learning and development in co- and extra-curricular awards is especially difficult as there is no shared understanding of what 'standards of learning and achievement' means. Each institution is in effect inventing its own standards and operating without the support of an established peer network (like the External Examiner system for subject-based learning) to help validate the process and outcomes. External peers can be incorporated into the assessment process to provide an independent view on standards (see Chapter 11) but it is also important to develop an appreciation of how your own approaches to evaluating learning and the outcomes from your scheme compare with the approaches and outcomes from schemes in other institutions. One collegial way of dealing with this issue is to establish benchmarking groups in which practitioners involved in these schemes participate in a process to share their practices, experiences and understandings so that all might learn through the process. Early in 2011, SCEPTrE approached four other universities with a similar portfolio-based student development award scheme to engage in a benchmarking process aimed at comparing and evaluating the student development schemes operated by the members of the group.

Benchmarking for better understanding

Benchmarking is, first and foremost, a learning process structured so as to enable those engaging in the process to compare their practices and outcomes in order to identify their comparative strengths and weaknesses as a basis for self-improvement and/or self-regulation. Benchmarking offers a way of identifying better and smarter ways of doing things and understanding why they are better or smarter. These insights can then be used to implement changes that will improve practice or performance (Jackson and Lund 2000). It is a 'process to facilitate the systematic comparison and evaluation of practice, process and performance to aid improvement and regulation' (ibid. X). This definition draws attention to the continuum of benchmarking practices from processes that are primarily for developmental purposes to those which are motivated by regulatory concerns. In reality, processes serve both of these purposes although they are likely to be more oriented towards one of them.

Benchmarking methodology

A proposal paper outlining the purpose, objectives, scope and approach was used to explain the process and four institutions agreed to participate. In joining the process participants were hoping to reassure themselves that the approaches they were using were sound, and the outcomes demonstrated by students were appropriate for the achievement of an award, when they were compared with what ot hers were doing. In doing this they believed that the new understandings that emerged could be used to create a typology of practice that could be shared with others. A questionnaire was developed through a collaborative process and once agreed the five participants completed it and posted it on a password-protected website so that each member of the group could see it.

The next stage involved the production of a series of tables to show the variations in practice across participating institutions. Participants then met for a 24-hour meeting and discussed aspects of their awards, drawing on the information provided in the tables. The formal and informal conversations enabled participants to gain deeper understandings and to share perspectives on the challenges. Additional materials were provided, for example student portfolios, so that participants could see how students were representing their learning through the different schemes.

After the meeting participants reviewed and where appropriate amended their responses to the questionnaire in the light of the discussions and sought permission for making the information publically available.

All participants agreed that the opportunity to compare their own approach with what other institutions were doing was valuable. All were interested in learning about new practices that they might also adopt or adapt. They wanted to share the issues and challenges they were dealing with and learn how others were coping or addressing these. All participants shared the sense of isolation or 'loan voice' that they experienced in their own institution, and simply by networking with others they reduced their sense of isolation. All felt vulnerable in an academic world that has little respect for learning that is not within the scope of the academy and all were looking for ways to strengthen the arguments they could use in their own institution for justifying their practice and the resources required to support practice. All were deeply committed to enhancing the student experience and helping students prepare themselves better for the world outside higher education, and all believed that their award scheme was contributing to this process. All were interested in the use of technological aids to support the administrative and learning processes.

Everyone shared the issue of institutional engagement and all were interested in the experiences of others in bringing about change in their institutions. All were interested in understanding the directions of travel and how these award schemes could be connected to systemic policies like personal development planning, e-portfolios and the higher education Achievement Report.
Issues that emerged through the process, although perhaps aired by one institutional representative, resonated with all participants, suggesting that regardless of context and institutional factors there is a set of generic issues that are associated with these forms of educational practice at this point in the evolution of practice. Examples include:

- *Creating an educationally and cost-effective framework.* One that is educationally sound, requires a reasonable but not excessive demand and is cost effective and manageable with a small team.
- *Buy – in from top level management* is essential. Where there is not a senior manager acting as champion the award is not likely to prosper. There are issues when such champions are replaced.

- The fact that these schemes are *often viewed as a 'project' peripheral to mainstream activity*. They are not taken seriously by the institution as they are not seen as 'academic' or crucial to success.
- *The difficulty of convincing academic staff of the value of lifewide learning* and engaging them in promoting/advocating the Award scheme. Most academic staff have little interest in student development beyond their disciplinary interests. This issue is also linked to establishing the credibility of an award and then maintaining it.
- *Reaching students* to make them aware of the scheme and its potential value to them; this is a particular issue in the early stages of establishing an award
- *Reaching out to all students*, not just those who always get involved
- *Retaining student interest and commitment* – typically three or four times as many students register for an award as complete it
- *Providing technological solutions that all students are comfortable with* and find engaging; helping technologically averse students to use an e-portfolio.
- *Helping participants develop the habit of reflection*
- *Creating a sense of community amongst participating students* for what is essentially a solitary act of portfolio building
- *Developing assessment procedures that are efficient and effective* and are scalable and affordable; issues relating to the *assessment* of unique portfolios.
- *Demonstrating the positive impacts on student learning and development*; the need to establish longitudinal research to demonstrate the longer term effects
- *Resourcing – schemes are often run on a shoestring* with typically one main member of staff with help – 'There is often a sense that you're doing this alone and making decisions "on the hoof" without any real back up from the structures which support formal academic learning'
- *The impact of national policies* like the higher education Achievement Report
- *The impact on schemes of the significant increase in tuition fees* scheduled for 2012.

Participants' believed that a benchmarking forum would provide the relationships between practitioners and opportunities for discussion that would help individuals and their institutions to be better informed.

An ecological perspective

We could treat the growth of these student development schemes as an isolated phenomenon. But it would be more valuable to connect and integrate this spontaneous and essentially bottom-up development in one part of our education system to an evolving systems view of lifelong learning, which appears to be the overarching whole-system concept for policy makers in the UK and Europe.

The previous section argued for the use of benchmarking as an organic, self-determined (self-organised) response to the need for developing deeper understanding of practice and for growing a community of practice. This, it might be argued, is an ecological response to the need to learn and develop within a higher education system that is underpinned, at least at the level of practitioners, by collegial values. Hodgson and Spours (2009), drawing on the theoretical work of Bronfenbrenner (1979), argued for an ecological approach to understanding the organisation and governance of lifelong learning in the UK:

> The humanistic language of ecologies, which recognises the dynamics, diversity and complexity, helps practitioner, policy and research communities to move away from mechanistic engineering metaphors.
> (Hodgson and Spours 2009:5)

> The terms 'ecologies' or 'ecosystems' have traditionally been used to refer to dynamic interactions between plants, animals and micro-organisms and their environment, working together as a functional unit. Ecologies are seen as living systems containing a diversity of factors that interact with each other organically; that are literally self-organising, adaptive and fragile.
> (Hodgson and Spours 2009:9)

In the following section we try to embed the idea of lifewide learning and education within this ecological way of thinking about the lifelong learning system of organisation and governance.

While the overall concept of lifelong learning is powerful and undeniable, one of the problems with it is that higher education is seen as one point in a learner's formal education. This book has explored the potential for personal development contained within the informal as well as the formal learning experiences. It is in the detail that makes up the situations of an individual's life that the lifelong journey is enacted and given real meaning. Furthermore, because of its organic, relational and emergent nature, it is the lifewide dimension of human experience that gives lifelong learning ecological significance.

Bronfenbrenner (1979, cited by Hodgson and Spours 2009:10) used the term ecology to propose that human development is influenced by factors operating at different levels of a system within a broad ecological structure, in which each level interacts with and influences the others:

- The *microsystem* contains the factors within a learner's immediate environment (e.g. his curriculum, the day-to-day situations he encounters and his relationships and interactions with the people he meets). This is the level of our lifewide learning experiences, the levels at which our individual situations and our responses to these situations matter. This is the level at which greater self-awareness and reflective engagement with our experiences allows us to appreciate more deeply the how, why, when and where of our own development; and the level at which our will and our agency determines our future.

- The *mesosystem* encompasses the interrelations of two or more settings in which the developing person actively participates; for example, between home or looking after yourself and between formal and informal learning. The mesosystem involves people who have an interest in promoting and supporting learning. In our approach to lifewide learning this is the level at which learners interact with the organisers and facilitators of the student development award framework. It is the level at which guidance is offered and tools, like the lifewide learning map and personal development plan, are provided to help learners make more and deeper sense of their lives, of their being in the world and of how the different parts of their lives interact and interfere. In other words, organised activity in the mesosystem enables people to learn more and better in their own microsystem, and then to use this enhanced self-awareness and capability in future situations.

- The *exosystem* consists of settings that do not involve the developing person as an active participant, but in which events occur that affect, or are affected by, what is happening in the settings which the learner inhabits. This includes, for example, organisations that are responsible for supporting education (schools, colleges and universities) and the public, community and business organisations they interact with. This is the ecological level at which an institution adopts and embeds in its policies and practices a lifewide concept of education and provides the necessary resources and rhetorical support to publicly proclaim that these forms of learning and development are valued. At this ecological level an institution's policy connects to and dovetails with other policies like its learning and teaching, student experience, employability and widening participation strategies. This is also the level where different parts of the organisation – faculties, academic departments, student services and the Students' Union – work together for the benefit of students engaged in lifewide learning. It is also the level at which the university's partnerships with local and regional community, including employers, are utilised for the benefit of learners engaged in lifewide learning. Inter-institutional collegial activity that enables institutions to learn and develop, such as the benchmarking scenario described earlier, is also a feature of this level in the ecosystem.

- The *macrosystem* is the wider society in which all other settings are nested including the socio-economic, cultural and political contexts. It includes government policies and strategies for promoting and supporting lifelong learning. This is the ecological level of the higher education system and the vision is that one day the system as a whole will embrace the idea of lifewide education.

Ecological perspectives not only help us think about the governance of individual institutions, but also about partnership working at different levels of the system. A learning partnership, viewing itself as a 'collaborative local ecology', would be linked to ecologies above and below.

(Hodgson and Spours 2009:14)

The fundamental learning partnership in this lifewide learning ecosystem is between an educational provider and the learner. Using our work at Surrey as an example, this is the framework and the set of relationships that were developed to promote lifewide learning (Chapter 11). This set of relationships and interactions connects in a meaningful way individual learners and their microsystem for learning, with the support for learning and the recognition and validation of learning by the university through the adoption of a lifewide concept of education.

But the university itself is involved in many other forms of learning partnership – for example, learners are enrolled on study programmes leading to a degree.

John Cowan (Chapter 7) shows how the microecology of an individual's lifewide learning could extend and be integrated into mainstream higher education. The university also has links with its local and regional community through a variety of partnerships and associations, and these too could be utilised in an ecological sense for the purposes of lifewide education. For example, it is easy to imagine universities entering new partnerships with their local schools to utilise an adapted lifewide learning award framework to encourage 16–19 students to appreciate their informal learning and personal development, and to utilise such a framework to develop a relationship to encourage progression to the university (far more informative than a UCAS[1] personal statement). This would certainly help demonstrate to young people that learning and development is much more than sitting in a classroom. Similarly we could imagine a university in partnership with a local Lifelong Learning Partnership[2] might use an adapted lifewide learning award framework to encourage adult learners taking their first tentative steps back into the world of formal education. In this way adapted lifewide learning award frameworks could help extend partnerships for learning and provide bridging and transition structures and aids to relationship development in the community surrounding an institution.

Concluding thoughts

The emergent phenomenon of co- and extra-curricular student development awards shows that we are witnessing a system-wide adaptation that is fundamentally about making higher education *more relevant* to the lives of learners and to recognise that there is more to learning and education than studying a subject. In witnessing this shift from more traditional models of education to lifewide education we are in the early stages of a transforming system: one that pays more attention to individuals' learning ecologies. The more firmly embedded these award schemes can be within the student experience, the greater the chance students have of preparing themselves for the real world beyond the classroom.

> In an era of top-down accountability and markets we believe that an ecological perspective on lifelong learning offers ... the potential for a more organic and human-centred approach to the organisation and governance of education, stressing concepts such as inter-dependence, complexity, fragility, resilience and sustainability. It also reflects the learning process itself, emphasising a more connective, participative and exploratory approach that critiques the stress of behaviourist and acquisitive learning.
> (Hodgson and Spours 2009:21)

The added value of the lifewide concept and practice of education is that it gives more and deeper meaning to the fundamental ecology of the everyday learning and development enterprise of an individual. Furthermore, it honours and celebrates individuals' commitment to their own development, rather than simply seeing it as a stage of life to progress through on an individual's lifelong journey. It is also likely that changing perceptions of what counts as learning and personal development will help people appreciate more the lifelong-lifewide nature of learning and personal development that is necessary to live a healthy, productive and fulfilled life.

This book is inspired by a vision for adult education that permeates our thinking about a more complete higher education experience. We can think of no better way of gaining closure in our initial story of lifewide learning than by returning to Eduard Lindeman's inspiring vision.

> A fresh hope is astir. From many quarters comes the call to a new kind of education with its initial assumption affirming that education is life – not merely preparation for an unknown kind of future living. ... The whole of life is learning, therefore education can have no endings
> (Lindman 1926:6)

Endnotes
1 These are the personal statements prepared by people applying to University through the Universities and Colleges Admission System (UCAS).
2 A network of 104 (originally 101) Learning Partnerships were set up across the country in early 1999 to promote a new culture of provider collaboration across sectors (schools, FE, work-based learning and adult and community learning) and to rationalise the plethora of existing local partnership arrangements covering post-16 learning. They are non-statutory, voluntary groupings of local learning providers (ranging from voluntary sector to FE/HEIs) and others such as local government, Connexions/Careers Service, trade unions, employers and faith groups. http://www.lifelonglearning.co.uk/llp/
Example Surrey Lifelong Learning Partnership - http://www.surreyllp.org.uk/

References

Abes, E. S. and Jones, S. R. (2004) Meaning-making Capacity and the Dynamics of Lesbian College Students' Multiple Dimensions of Identity, *Journal of College Student Development*, 45(6): 612–32.

Abram, D. (1997) *The Spell of the Sensuous*. New York: Vintage Books.

Alderfer, C. P. (1980) The Methodology of Organizational Diagnosis, *Professional Psychology*, 11: 459-68.

Alheit, P. and Dausien, B. (2003) The 'Double Face' of Lifelong Learning: Two Analytical Perspectives on a 'Silent Revolution', *Studies in the Education of Adults*, 34(1): 3–22

Alkire, S. (2008) The Capability Approach to the Quality of Life. Online at www.stiglitz-sen-fitoussi.fr/documents/capability_approach.pdf (accessed 11/11/10).

American Council on Education (1949) *The Student Personnel Point of View*. Washington, DC: Author

Association of American Colleges and Universities (AACU) (2009a) Integrative Learning: Addressing the Complexities, Network for Academic Renewal Conference Programme. Online at: www.aacu.org/meetings/integrative_learning/2009/documents/ ILProgram.pdf (accessed 14/02/11).

Association of American Colleges and Universities (AACU (2009b) Integrated Learning Value Statement. Online at www.aacu.org/value/rubrics/pdf/integrativelearning.pdf (accessed 14/02/11).

Australian National Training Authority (ANTA) (2004) Working and Learning in Vocational Education and Training in the Knowledge Era. Online at http://pre2005.flexiblelearning.net.au/projects/resources/PDFutureReport.pdf (accessed 30/12/10

Baltes, P. B. (2004) Wisdom as Orchestration of Mind and Virtue. Berlin: Max Planck Institute for Human Development. Book in preparation. Online at http://library.mpib-berlin.mpg.de/ft/pb/PB_Wisdom_2004.pdf (accessed 30/12/10).

Bandura, A. (2001) Social Cognitive Theory: An Agentic Perspective. *Annu. Rev. Psychol.* 52:1-26.

Barnett, R. (2000) Supercomplexity and the Curriculum. In M .Tight (ed.) *Curriculum in Higher Education*. Buckingham: Open University Press.

Barnett, R. (2005) *A Will to Learn: Being a Student in an Age of Uncertainty*. Buckingham: Open University Press, McGraw Hill Education.

Barnett, R., and Coate, K. (2005) *Engaging the Curriculum in Higher Education.* Buckingham, UK: The Society for Research into Higher Education and Open University Press.

Barnett, R., Parry, G. and Coate, K. (2001) Conceptualising Curriculum Change. *Teaching Higher Education*, 6(4): 435–49.

Barton, W. H. (2005) Methodological Challenges in the Study of Resiliency. In M. Ungar (ed.) *The Handbook for Working with Children and Youth: Pathways to Resilience Across Cultures and Contexts,* Thousand Oaks CA: Sage Publications.

Baud, D. (2010) Locating Immersive Experience in Experiential Learning. In N. J. Jackson (ed) *Learning to be Professional through a Higher Education*, e-book. Online at http://learningtobeprofessional.pbworks.com/David-Baud (accessed 14/02/11).

Bauman, Z. (2006) *Liquid Life.* Cambridge: Polity.

Baxter Magolda, M. B. (1992) *Knowing and Reasoning in College: Gender-related Patterns in Students' Intellectual Development.* San Francisco, CA: Jossey-Bass.

Baxter Magolda, M. B. (1999) *Creating Contexts for Learning and Self-authorship: Constructive Developmental Pedagogy.* Nashville: Vanderbilt University Press.

Baxter Magolda, M. B. (2001) *Making Their Own Way: Narratives for Transforming Higher Education to Promote Self-development.* Sterling, VA: Stylus.

Baxter Magolda, M. B. (2004a) Learning Partnerships Model: A Framework for Promoting Self-authorship. In M. B. Baxter Magolda and P. M. King (eds) *Learning Partnerships: Theory and Models of Practice to Educate for Self-authorship*, Sterling, VA: Stylus, pp. 37–62).

Baxter Magolda, M. B. (2004b) Preface. In M. B. Baxter Magolda and P. M. King (eds) *Learning Partnerships: Theory and Models of Practice to Educate for Self-authorship,* Sterling, VA: Stylus, pp. xvii–xxvi.

Baxter Magolda, M. B. (2004c) Self-authorship as the Common Goal of 21st Century Education. In M. B. Baxter Magolda and P. M. King (eds) *Learning Partnerships: Theory and Models of Practice to Educate for Self-authorship*, Sterling, VA: Stylus, pp. 1–35.

Baxter Magolda, M. B. (2007) Self-Authorship: The Foundation for Twenty-first Century Education. In P. S. Meszaros (ed.) *Self-Authorship: Advancing Students' Intellectual Growth, New Directions for Teaching and Learning*, San Francisco, CA: Jossey-Bass, Vol. 109, pp. 69–83.

Baxter Magolda, M. B. (2009a) *Authoring Your Life: Developing an Internal Voice to Navigate Life's Challenges.* Sterling, VA: Stylus.

Baxter Magolda, M. B. (2009b) Educating for Self-Authorship: Learning Partnerships to Achieve Complex Outcomes, In C. Kreber, (ed) *The University and its Disciplines: Teaching and Learning beyond Discipline Boundaries* Routledge 143-156

Baxter Magolda, M. B. (2010) The Interweaving of Epistemological, Intrapersonal, and Interpersonal Development in the Evolution of Self-authorship. In M. B. Baxter Magolda, E. G. Creamer and P. S. Meszaros (eds), *Development and Assessment of Self-authorship: Exploring the Concept Across Cultures*, Sterling, VA: Stylus, pp. 25–43.

Baxter Magolda, M. B., King, P. M., Taylor, K. B. and Wakefield, K. (in press) Decreasing Authority-dependence During the First Year of College, *Journal of College Student Development*.

Bayne, S. (2008) Uncanny Spaces for Higher Education: Teaching and Learning in Virtual worlds, *ALT-J Research in Learning Technology*, 16(3): 197–205.

Beard, C. (2010) *The Experiential Learning Toolkit: Blending Practice with Concepts*. London, Kogan Page.

Beard, C., Clegg, S. and Smith, K. (2007) Acknowledging the Affective in Higher Education, *British Educational Research Journal*, 33: no. 2, 235-252.

Beard, C. and Wilson, J. P. (2006) *Experiential Learning*. London: Kogan Page.

Bekken, B. M. and Marie, J. (2007) Making Self-authorship a Goal of Core Curricula: The Earth Sustainability Pilot Project. In P. S. Meszaros (ed) *Self-Authorship: Advancing Students' Intellectual Growth, New Directions for Teaching and*

Belenky, M., Clinchy, B. M., Goldberger, N. and Tarule, J. (1986) *Women's Ways of Knowing: The Development of Self, Voice, and Mind*. New York, NY: Basic Books.

Biggs, J. (2003) *Teaching for Quality Learning at University*. Society for Research into Higher Education. Buckingham: OU Press.

Billett, S. (2008) Learning Throughout Working Life: A Relational Interdependence between Social and Individual Agency, *British Journal of Education Studies*, 55(1): 39–58.

Billett, S. (2009a) Conceptualizing Learning Experiences: Contributions and Mediations of the Social, Personal and Brute, *Mind, Culture and Activity*, 16(1): 32–47.

Billett, S. (2009b) Learning to Be an Agentic Professional: Conceptions, Curriculum, Pedagogy and Personal Epistemologies. Abstract and podcast: Learning to Be Professional through a Lifewide Curriculum. Online at http://learningtobeprofessional.pbwiki.com/Stephen-Billett (accessed 20/12/10).

Boisot, M. H. (1998) *Knowledge Assets: Securing Competitive Advantage in the Information Economy.* Oxford: Oxford University Press.

Brennan, J., Johnstone, B., Little, B., Shah, T and Woodley, A. (2001) *The Employment of UK Graduates: Comparisons with Europe and Japan.* Bristol: The Higher Education Funding Council for England.

Bronfenbrenner, U. (1979) *The Ecology of Human Development: Experiments by Nature and Design.* Cambridge, M.A.: Harvard University Press.

Brudzinski, M. R. and Sikorski, J. J. (in press) Impact of the COPEL (Community of Practice on Engaged Learning) on Active-learning Revisions to an Introductory Geology Course: Focus on Student Development, *Learning Communities Journal.*

Cairns, L. and Stephenson, J. (2009) *Capable Workplace Learning: in the 21st Century.* Rotterdam: Sense Publishers.

Candy, P. (2004) Linking Thinking: Self-directed Learning in the Digital Age. DEST Research Fellowship Scheme, Department of Education, Science and Training. Online at http://www.dest.gov.au/ sectors/ training_skills/publications_resources/other_publications/ linking_thinking.htm (accessed 30/12/10).

Callaghan, S. (2009) Cynefin Anecdote. YouTube video. Online at www.anecdote.com.au/archives/2009/04/a_simple_explan.html (accessed 16/02/11).

Cannatella, H. (2007) Place and Being *Educational Philosophy and Theory* 39, Issue 6, pages 622–632.

Campbell, S. (2011a) Personal Professionalism: The Students' Perspective. In N. J. Jackson (ed) *Learning to be Professional through a Higher Education.* Available at http://learningtobeprofessional.pbworks.com/w/page/ 38212255/Personal-Professionalism-the-students'-perspective (accessed 28/05/11).

Campbell, S. (2011b) Student Guide to Personal Professionalism Online at: http://beingprofessional.pbworks.com/w/page/37825348/FrontPage (accessed 4/05/11).

Christensen, C. (1997) The Innovator's Dilemma: When New Technologies Cause Great Firms to Fail. Boston: Harvard Business School Press.

Cell, E. (1984) *Learning to Learn from Experience.* Albany: State University of New York Press.

Clark, T. (2005) Lifelong, Lifewide or Life Sentence, *Australian Journal of Adult Learning,* 45 (1): 47–62.

Committee on Higher Education (1963) *Higher Education: Report of the Committee Appointed by the Prime Minister under the Chairmanship of Lord Robbins 1961–63,* Cmnd. 2154, London: HMSO.

Conklin, J. (2006) Wicked Problems and Social Complexity in Dialogue Mapping: Building Shared Understanding of Wicked Problems. Online at www.cognexus.org/id26.htm#age_of_design (accessed 12/11/10).

Cook, S. D. N. and Brown, J. S. (1999) Bridging Epistemologies: The Generative Dance between Organisational Knowledge and Organizational Knowing. *Organizational science*, 10(4): 381–400.

Cooperrider, D. L. (2004) Keynote speech. Virtual Organisational Development Conference. Online at http://icohere.com/vod/Index.htm (accessed 30/12/10).

Cooperrider, D. L. and Whitney, D. (2002) *Appreciative Inquiry: The Handbook*. Euclid Ohio: Lakeshore Publishers. Online at http://appreciativeinquiry.case.edu/uploads/ Resources_for_AI.pdf (accessed 30/12/10).

Counselling. Research and draft prepared by Deirdre O' Connell (AWCCA Program, George Brown College) for the Metropolitan Action Committee on Violence Against Women and Children. Online at http://www.metrac.org/resources/downloads/strength.based.learning.lit.review.pdf (accessed 02/01/11).

Covey, S. R. (1989) *The 7 Habits of Highly Effective People*. London and New York Free Press.

Covey, S. (2004) *The 8th Habit: From Effectiveness to Greatness*. London and New York: Simon and Schulster.

Critchley, R.K. (2006) The Ageing Workforce – to rewire or rust. Paper prepared for the TAFE NSW International Centre for VET Teaching and Learning.

Crom, S. and Bertels, T. (1999) Change Leadership: The Virtues of Deviance. *Leadership and Organization Development Journal*, 20(3): 162–8.

Csikszentmihalyi, M. (1990) *Flow: The Psychology of Optimal Experience*. New York: Harper and Row.

Czikszentmihalyi, M. (2006) Foreword – Developing Creativity. In N. J. Jackson *et al.* (eds) *Developing Creativity in Higher Education: An Imaginative Curriculum*, Abingdon: Routledge, pp. xvii–xx.

Dearing, R. (1996) Report of the National Committee of Inquiry into Higher Education. London: DfEE. Online at www.leeds.ac.uk/educol/ncihe/ (accessed 25/02/11).

Deci, E. L. and Ryan, R. M. (2000) The 'What' and 'Why' of Goal Pursuits: Human Needs and the Self-determination of Behavior, *Psychological Inquiry*, 11: 227–68.

Dellas, M. and Gaier, E. L. (1970) Identification of Creativity in the Individual, *Psychological Bulletin*, 73: 55–73.

Deleuze, G. and Guattari, F. (2007/1980) *A Thousand Plateaus*. London: Continuum.

Department for Education and Skills (DfES) (2004) *Putting the World into World-class Education: An International Strategy for Education, Skills and Children's Services*. Online at http://www.planning.ed.ac.ul/Pub/documents/DfESIntStrat.pdf (accessed 09/03/11).

Desjardins, R. (2004) *Learning for Well Being. Studies in Comparative and International Education*. Stockholm: Institute of International Education. Online at http://books.google.co.uk/books?hl=en&lr=&id=OXu3h86EsNcC&oi=fnd&pg=PP8&dq=Determinants+of+Economic+and+Social+Outcomes+from+a+Life-Wide+Learning+Perspective+in+Canada+ Author:+Richard+Desjardins&ots=z9pP_wEh_W&sig=_vwiOHqJIZ821H0c09aAOWwqFEM#v=onepage&q&f=tru (accessed 26/1/11)

Dewey, J. (1897) My Pedagogic Creed. Online at http://en.wikisource.org/wiki/My_Pedagogic_Creed (accessed 31/01/11).

Drago-Severson, E. (2010) *Leading Adult Learning*. Thousand Oaks, CA: Corwin.

Dreze, J. and Sen, A. (1995) *India: Economic Development and Social Opportunity*. Oxford: Oxford University Press.

Dweck, C. (1999) *Self-theories: Their Role in Motivation, Personality and Development. Essays in Social Psychology*. Philadelphia USA: Psychology Press, Taylor & Francis Group.

Edwards, M., McGoldrick, C. and Oliver, M. (2006) Creativity and Curricula in Higher Education: Academics' Perspectives. In N. J. Jackson *et al.* (eds) *Developing Creativity in Higher Education: An Imaginative Curriculum*, Abingdon: Routledge, pp. 59–73.

Egeland, B., Carlson, E. and Stroufe, L. A. (1993) Resilience as a Process. *Development and Psychopathology*, 5: 517–528.

Egart, K. and Healy, M. (2004) An Urban Leadership Internship Program: Implementing Learning Partnerships 'Unplugged' from Campus Structures. In M. B. Baxter Magolda and P. M. King (eds) *Learning Partnerships: Theory and Models of practice to Educate for Self-authorship*, Sterling, VA: Stylus, pp. 125–49.

Eisner, E. W. (1985) *The Art of Educational Evaluation: a Personal View*. London: Falmer Press.

Eraut, M. (1994) *Developing Professional Knowledge and Competence*. London: Falmer Press.

Eraut, M. (2000) Non-Formal Learning and Tacit Knowledge in Professional Work, *British Journal of Educational Psychology*, 70: 113–36.

Eraut, M. (2004) Transfer of Knowledge between Education and Workplace Settings. In H. Rainbird, A. Fuller and A. Munro (eds) *Workplace Learning In Context*. London : Routledge, pp. 201–21.

Eraut, M. (2007a) Early Career Learning at Work and its Implications for Universities. In N. Entwistle and P. Tomlinson (eds) *Student Learning and University Teaching. British Journal of Educational Psychology*, Monograph Series.

Eraut, M. (2007b) Feedback and Formative Assessment in the Workplace. In *Assessment of Significant Learning Outcomes*, TLRP seminar series.

Eraut, M. (2007c) Learning from Other People in the Workplace, *Oxford Review of Education*, 33(4): 403–22.

Eraut, M. (2008) Using Research into How Professionals Learn at Work for Enhancing Placement Learning. Proceedings of the WACE Symposium Sydney.

Eraut, M. (2009) How Professionals Learn through Work. In N. Jackson (ed.) *Learning to be Professional through a Higher Education.* Online at http://learningtobeprofessional.pbworks.com/How-professionals-learn-through-work (accessed 03/01/11).

Eraut, M. (2010a) Understanding Complex Performance through Learning Trajectories and Mediating Artefacts. In N. Jackson (ed.) *Learning to be Professional through a Higher Education.* Online at: http://learningtobeprofessional.pbworks.com/w/page/33724569/ Understanding-Complex-Performance-through-Learning-Trajectories-and-Mediating-Artefacts (accessed 03/01/11).

Eraut, M. (2010b) The Balance between Communities and Personal Agency: Transferring and Integrating Knowledge and Know-how between Different Communities and Contexts. In N. J. Jackson (ed) Learning to be Professional through a Higher Education. Online at http://learningtobeprofessional.pbworks.com/w/page/25260594/The-Balance-between-Communities-and-Personal-Agency (accessed 28/04/11).

Eraut, M. (2011) Improving the Quality of Work Placements. In N. J. Jackson (ed) Learning to be Professional through a Higher Education On-line at: http://learningtobeprofessional.pbworks.com/w/page/39548725/Improving-the-quality-of-work-placements (accessed 28/04/11)

Ewell, P. T. (2005) Across the Grain: Learning from Reform Initiatives in Undergraduate Education. Discussion paper 3: Understanding How We Accomplish Complex Change in Higher Education Institutions. Higher Education Academy. Online at www.heacademy.ac.uk/resources /detail/resource_database/id548_complex_change_in_heis_paper3 (accessed 20/12/10).

Fraser, S. and Bosanquet, A. (2006) The curriculum? That's just an outline, isn't it? Studies in Higher Education 31 (3) 269-284.

Gardner, H. (1983) *Frames of Mind: The Theory of Multiple Intelligences.* New York: Basic Books Inc.

Gergen, K. (1999) *An Invitation to Social Construction.* London: Sage.

Gersick, C. J. G. (1991) Revolutionary Change Theories: a Multilevel Exploration of the Punctuated Equilibrium Paradigm. *The Academy of Management Review,* 16: 10–36.

Greene, T, R. (2004) *32 Capabilities of Highly Effective People in Any Field.* Online at www.scribd.com/doc/2162334/32-Capabilities-of-Highly-Effective-Persons (accessed 16/02/11).

Hale, H. C. and de Abreu, G. (2010) Drawing on the Notion of Symbolic Resources in Exploring the Development of Cultural Identities in Immigrant Transitions, *Culture Psychology,* 16: 395–415.

Hall, R. (2006) Workplace Changes: change and continuity in the workplaces of the future. Paper prepared for the 'Designing Professional Development for the Knowledge Era' Research Project. TAFE NSW International Centre for VET Teaching and Learning.

Hall, R. (2010) How Can Technology Help Us Realize the Learning Potential of a Life-wide Curriculum? In N. J. Jackson and R. K. Law (eds) *Enabling a More Complete Education: Encouraging, Recognizing and Valuing Life-wide Learning in Higher Education.* Online at http://lifewidelearningconference.pbworks.com/E-proceedings (accessed 03/01/11).

Ham, G. and Wang, W. C. (2009) Mind the Gap? A Case-study of the Differing Perceptions of International Students and Their Lecturers on Postgraduate Business Programmes, *International Journal of Management Education,* Oxford Brookes University.

Hamer, R. and van Rossum, E. J. (2010) Linking Learning Conceptions to Self-authorship and Beyond. In M. B. Baxter Magolda, E. G. Creamer and P. S. Meszaros (eds) *Development and Assessment of Self-authorship: Exploring the Concept Across Cultures,* Sterling, VA: Stylus, pp. 45–65.

Hansel, B. (1998) Developing an International Perspective in Youth Through Exchange Programs. *Education and Urban Society,* 20: 177–95.

Harvey, L., Moon, S. and Geall, V. with Bower, R., (1997) *Graduates' Work: Organisation Change and Students' Attributes.* Birmingham: Centre for Research into Quality (CRQ) and Association of Graduate Recruiters (AGR).

Haynes, C. (2004) Promoting Self-authorship through an Interdisciplinary Writing Curriculum. In M. B. Baxter Magolda and P. M. King (eds.), *Learning Partnerships: Theory and Models of Practice to Educate for Self-authorship,* Sterling, VA: Stylus, pp. 63–90.

Hieber, M. and Wahlrab, E. (in press) Moving Toward Self-authorship: Building a Degree Program for Engaged Learning, *Learning Communities Journal*.

Heron, J. (2001) *Helping the Client: a Creative Practical Guide*. London: Sage.

Hodge, D. C., Baxter Magolda, M. B. and Haynes, C. A. (2010) Engaged Learning: Enabling Self-Authorship and Effective Practice, *Liberal Education*, 95 (4). 16–23. Online at http://www.aacu.org/liberaleducation/le-fa09/le-fa09_EngagedLearn.cfm (accessed 18/01/11).

Hodgson, A. and Spours, K. (2009) Collaborative Local Learning Ecologies: Reflections on the Governance of Lifelong Learning in England. Inquiry into the Future of Lifelong Learning. National Institute for Adult and Continuing Education, Paper 6. Online at www.niace.org.uk/lifelonglearninginquiry/docs/IFLL-Sector-Paper6.pdf (accessed 12/04/11).

Hornak, A. and Ortiz, A. M. (2004) Creating a Context to Promote Diversity Education and Self-authorship Among Community College Students. In M. B. Baxter Magolda and P. M. King (eds), *Learning Partnerships: Theory and Models of Practice to Educate for Self-authorship*, Sterling, VA: Stylus, pp. 91–12.

Illeris, K. (2002) *The Three Dimensions of Learning, Contemporary Learning Theory in the Tension Field between the Cognitive, the Emotional and the Social.* Florida: Krieger Publishing.

Illeris, K. (2009) Lifelong Learning as a Psychological Process. In Jarvis, P. (ed) *The Routledge International Handbook of Lifelong Learning*, London: Routledge, pp. 401–410.

Jackson, N. J. (2004) Using Complexity Theory to Make Sense of the Curriculum. LTSN Working Paper. Online at www.palatine.ac.uk/files/1040.pdf (accessed 14/02/11).

Jackson, N. J. (2008a) The Lifewide Curriculum Concept: a Means of Developing a More Complete Educational Experience? SCEPTrE paper. Online at http://lifewidecurriculum.pbwiki.com/A-more-complete-education (accessed 25/05/10).

Jackson, N. J. (2008b) A Life-wide Curriculum: Enriching a Traditional WIL Scheme through New Approaches to Experience-based Learning. Proceedings of the WACE Symposium Sydney 2008.

Jackson, N. J. (2008c) Tackling the Wicked Problem of Creativity in Higher Education. Background paper for keynote presentation, ARC Centre for Creative Industries and Innovation, Brisbane, June. Online at http://imaginativecurriculumnetwork.pbworks.com/w/page/19802613/FrontPage (accessed 20/12/10).

Jackson, N. J. (2009) Surrey Award: A Design for Integrative Learning Association of American Colleges and Universities Conference, Integrative

Learning: Managing the Complexities. Online at http://lifewidelearning.pbworks.com/Integrative-Learning (accessed 25/05/10).

Jackson, N. J. (2010a) Learning to be a Self-Regulating Professional: The Role of Personal Development Planning. In N. J. Jackson (ed.) *Learning to be Professional through a Higher Education.* Online at http://learningtobeprofessional.pbworks.com/w/page/32872854/Learning%20to%20be%20a%20self-regulating%20professional (accessed 27/01/11).

Jackson, N. J. (2010b) From a Curriculum That Integrates Work to a Curriculum That integrates Life: Changing a University's Conceptions of Curriculum. *Higher Education Research & Development,* Work Integrated Learning Special Issue 29 (5): 491–505.

Jackson, N. J. (2010c) Enabling a More Complete Education. In N. J. Jackson and R.K. Law (eds) Enabling a More Complete Education: Encouraging, Recognizing and Valuing Life-wide Learning in Higher Education. Online at http://lifewidelearningconference.pbworks.com/E-proceedings (accessed 25/05/10).

Jackson, N. J. (2010d) Developing Creativity through Lifewide Education. Online at http://imaginativecurriculumnetwork.pbworks.com/ (accessed 01/05/11).

Jackson, N. J. and Campbell, S. (2008) Learning for a Complex World: A Lifewide Curriculum. Proceedings of the WACE Symposium, Sydney, October 2008, pp. 246–53. Online at http://workintegratedlearning.pbworks.com/w/page/14753698/FrontPage (accessed 20/12/10).

Jackson, N. J., Fellows, C. and Leng, J. (2010) Adding Value to the Education of Nurses, Midwives and Operating Department Practitioners through a 'Life-wide' Curriculum, *Nurse Education Today,* 30 (2010): 271–5.

Jackson, N. J. and Lund, H. (2000) Introduction to Benchmarking. In N. J. Jackson and H. Lund (eds) *Benchmarking for higher education.* Buckingham: SRHE and Open University Press.

Jarvis, P. (2007) *Globalization, Lifelong Learning and the Learning Society.* Abingdon: Routledge.

Jarvis, P. (2009) Learning to be a Person in Society: Learning to be Me. In Illeris, K. *Contemporary Theories of Learning,* Routledge: London, pp. 21–34.

Jenkins, H. with Clinton, K., Purushotma R., Robison J. and Weigel, M. (2006) Confronting the Challenges of Participatory Culture: Media Education for the 21st Century. The MacArthur Foundation. Online at http://digitallearning.macfound.org/atf/cf/%7B7E45C7E0-A3E0-4B89-AC9C-E807E1B0AE4E%7D/JENKINS_WHITE_PAPER.PDF (accessed 07/12/09).

Keeling, R. P. (ed) (2004) *Learning Reconsidered: A Campus-wide Focus on the Student Experience*. Washington DC: National Association of Student Personnel Administrators and American College Personnel Association.

Kegan, R. (1982) *The Evolving Self: Problem and Process in Human Development*. Cambridge, MA: Harvard University Press.

Kegan, R. (1994) *In Over Our Heads: The Mental Demands of Modern Life*. Cambridge, Massachusetts: Harvard University Press.

Kegan, R. and Lahey, L. L. (2009) *Immunity to Change: How to Overcome It and Unlock Potential in Yourself and Your Organization*. Boston, MA: Harvard Business Press.

Kidd, J. M. (1998) Emotion: An Absent Presence in Career Theory, *Journal of Vocational Behavior*, 52: 275–88.

King, P. M. (2010) The Role of the Cognitive Dimension of Self-authorship: An Equal Partner or the Strong Partner? In M. B. Baxter Magolda, E. G. Creamer and P. S. Meszaros (eds) *Development and Assessment of Self-authorship: Exploring the Concept across Cultures*, Sterling, VA: Stylus, pp. 167–85.

King, P. M. and Baxter Magolda, M. B. (2011) Student Learning. In J. H. Schuh, S. R. Jones and S. R. Harper (eds), *Student Services: A Handbook for the Profession*, San Francisco, CA: Jossey-Bass, pp. 207–25.

Knight, P. T. (2005) *Assessment and Complex Learning*. Proceedings of the First International Conference on Enhancing Teaching and Learning through Assessment. Kowloon, Hong Kong.

Knight, P. T.(2006) A Note on 'Ways of knowing'. Unpublished notes.

Kolb, D. (1984) *Experiential Learning: Experience as the Source of Learning and Development*. Englewood Cliffs, NJ: Prentice-Hall.

Kuh, G., Schuh, J. H., Whitt, E. J., Andreas, R. E., Lyons, J. W., Strange, C. C. et al. (1990) *Involving Colleges: Encouraging Student Learning and Personal Development through Out-of-class Experiences*. San Francisco, CA: Jossey-Bass.

Kuh, G. D., Kinzie, J., Schuh, J. H., Whitt, E. J. and associates (2005) *Student Success in College: Creating Conditions That Matter*. San Francisco, CA: Jossey-Bass.

Lakoff, G and Johnson, M. (1999) *Philosophy in the Flesh*. New York: Basic Books.

Landmark, L. J., Ju, S. and Zhang, D. (2010) Substantiated Best Practices in Transition: Fifteen Plus Years Later, *Career Development for Exceptional Individuals*, 33: 165–76.

Law, R. (2008) *Get a Life – an Introduction to Explorativity*. Published by Lulu.com.
Levinson, D. J. (1978). *The Seasons of a Man's Life*. New York: Knopf.
Lindman, E. C. (1926) *The Meaning of Adult Education* New York: New Republic. Republished in a new edition in 1989 by The Oklahoma Research Centre for Continuing Professional and Higher Education.
Luke, T. W. (2002) Digital Discourses, On-line Classes, Electronic Documents: Developing New University Technocultures. In K. Robins and F. Webster (Eds) *The Virtual University? Knowledge, Markets and Management*. Oxford: Oxford University Press.
Mihata, K. (1997) The Persistence of 'Emergence, in R., A. Eve, S. Horsfall, & Mary, E. L. (eds) *Chaos, Complexity & Sociology:* Myths, Models & Theories, Thousand Oaks, Ca: Sage. 30-38.
Manzi, C., Vignoles, V. L. and Regalia, C. (2010) Accommodating a New Identity: Possible Selves, Identity Change and Well-being across Two Life-transitions, *European Journal of Social Psychology*, 40: 970–84.
Maslow, A. H. (1943) Theory of Human Motivation, *Psychological Review*, 50: 370–96.
Mayer, J. D., Salovey, P. and Caruso, D. R. (2004) Emotional Intelligence: Theory, Findings, and Implications, *Psychological Inquiry*, 60: 197–215.
Mayer, J. D., Salovey, P. and Caruso, D. R. (2008) Emotional Intelligence. New Ability or Eclectic Traits? *American Psychologist*, 63: 503–17.
Mezirow, J. (Ed.) (1990) *Fostering Critical Reflection in Adulthood: A Guide to Transformative and Emancipatory Learning*. San Francisco, CA: Jossey-Bass.
Mezirow, J. (Ed.) (2000) *Learning as Transformation: Critical Perspectives on a Theory in Progress*. San Francisco, CA: Jossey-Bass.
Mezirow, J. (2000) Learning to Think Like an Adult: Core Concepts of Transformation Theory. In *Learning as Transformation: Critical Perspectives on a Theory in Progress,* eds. J. Mezirow and Associates, San Francisco: Jossey-Bass. 3-33.
Moesby, E. (2006) Implementing Project Oriented and Problem-based Learning – POPBL – in Institutions or Sub-institutions, *World Transactions on Engineering and Technology Education*, 5(1): 45–52.
Moodie, G. (2004) Making Students and Teachers the Heart of VET Policy. Griffith University. Online at http://www.avetra.org.au/Conference_Archives/2004/documents/PA018Moodie.pdf#search='making%20students%20and%20teachers%20the%20heart%20of%20VET%20policy (accessed 30/12/10).
Mortiboys, A. (2002) *The Emotionally Intelligent Lecturer*. Birmingham: SEDA Publications.

Motulsky, S. L. (2010) Relational Processes in Career Transition: Extending Theory, Research, and Practice, *The Counseling Psychologist*, 38: 1078–1114.

NAES (National Agency for Education Sweden) (2000) Lifelong Learning and Lifewide Learning Stockholm. Online at *www.skolverket.se/ sb/d/193/url/.../pdf638.pdf%3Fk%3D638 (accessed 11/11/10).*

NASPA (National Association of Student Personnel Administrators) and ACPA (American College Personnel Association) (2004) Learning Reconsidered: A Campus-wide Focus on the Student Experience. Online at www.myacpa.org/pub/documents/LearningReconsidered.pdf (accessed 12/12/10).

Nowotny, H., Scott, P. and Gibbons, M. (2001) *Re-thinking Science: Knowledge and the Public in an Age of Uncertainty.* Cambridge: Polity.

Oakeshott, M. (1989) *The Voice of Liberal Learning* (Edited by Timothy Fuller). New Haven: London.

O' Connell, D. (2006) Brief Literature Review on Strength-based Teaching and

OECD (Organisation for Economic Co-operation and Development) (2001) The Well-being of Nations: The role of Human and Social Capital. Paris: OECD. Online at www.oecd.org/dataoecd/36/40/33703702.pdf (accessed 19/12/10).

OECD (2007) Understanding the Social Outcomes of Learning. Paris: OECD. Online at http://ul.fcpe.rueil.free.fr/IMG/pdf/9607061E.pdf (accessed 19/12/10).

Olson, D., Bekken, B. M., Drezek, K. M. and Walter, C. T. (in press) Teaching for Change: Learning Partnerships and Epistemological Growth, *Journal of General Education.*

Ortiz, A. M. and Rhoads, R. A. (2000) Deconstructing Whiteness as Part of a Multicultural Educational Framework: From Theory to Practice. *Journal of College Student Development*, 41(1): 81–93.

Owen, H. (1977) *Expanding Our Now: The Story of Open Space Technology.* San Francisco: Berrett-Koehler Publishers, Inc.

Palmer, P. O'K. and Owens, M. (2009) Betwixt spaces: student accounts of turning point experiences in the first-year transition , *Studies in Higher Education*, 34 (1): 37–54.

Parker, J. (2003) Reconceptualising the Curriculum: from Commodification to Transformation. *Teaching in Higher Education*, 8(4): 529–43.

Pascarella, E. T. and Terenzini, P. T. (2005) *How College Affects Students: A Third Decade of Research.* San Francisco, CA: Jossey-Bass.

Perry, W. G. (1970) *Forms of Intellectual and Ethical Development in the College Years: A Scheme.* Troy, MO: Holt, Rinehart and Winston.

Piaget, J. (1950) *The Psychology of Intelligence* (M. P. a. D. Berlyne, Trans.). London: Routledge and Kegan Paul.

Piper, T. D. and Buckley, J. A. (2004) Community Standards Model: Developing Learning Partnerships in Campus Housing. In M. B. Baxter Magolda and P. M. King (eds), *Learning Partnerships: Theory and Models of Practice to Educate for Self-authorship*, Sterling, VA: Stylus, pp. 185–212.

Pizzolato, J. E. (2003) Developing Self-authorship: Exploring the Experiences of High-risk College Students, *Journal of College Student Development*, 44(6): 797–812.

Pizzolato, J. E. (2004) Coping with Conflict: Self-authorship, Coping, and Adaptation to College in First-year, High-risk Students, *Journal of College Student Development*, 45(4): 425–42.

Pizzolato, J. E. (2010) What Is Self-authorship? A Theoretical Exploration of the Construct. In M. B. Baxter Magolda, E. G. Creamer and P. S. Meszaros (eds), *Development and Assessment of Self-authorship: Exploring the Concept across Cultures*, Sterling, VA: Stylus, pp. 187–206.

Pizzolato, J. E. and Ozaki, C. C. (2007) Moving Toward Self-authorship: Investigating Outcomes of Learning Partnerships, *Journal of College Student Development*, 48(2): 196–214.

Pollard, A. (2003) Learning Through Life – Higher Education and the Lifecourse of Individuals. In M. Slowey and D. Watson (Eds) *Higher Education and the Lifecourse*. Maidenhead: McGraw-Hill / Open University Press.

Porter, C. and Cleland, J. (1995) *The Portfolio as a Learning Strategy*. Portsmouth: Boynton/Cook Publishers, Inc.

Quality Assurance Agency for Higher Education (QAA) (2000) Personal Development Planning. Online at http://www.qaa.ac.uk/academicinfrastructure/progressfiles/guidelines/pdp/ (accessed 15/02/11).

Quality Assurance Agency for Higher Education (QAA) (2009) *Personal Development Planning: Guidance for Institutional Policy and Practice in Higher Education*. Online at http://www.qaa.ac.uk/academicinfra structure /progressFiles/guidelines/PDP/PDPguide.pdf (accessed 3/10/11).

Rickett, C. (2010) Mapping the Terrain: Survey of Co-curricular and Extra-curricular Awards. In N. J. Jackson and R. K. Law (eds) Enabling a More Complete Education, Conference Proceedings, University of Surrey, April 2010, pp. 94–101. Online at http://lifewidelearningconference.pbworks.com/w/page/25747103/e-proceedings (accessed 12/04/11).

Rittel, H. and Webber, M. (1973) Dilemmas in a General Theory of Planning, *Policy Sciences*, 4. Amsterdam: Elsevier Scientific Publishing. pp. 155–9.

Ryan, R. M. and Deci, E. L. (2000). Self-determination Theory and the Facilitation of Intrinsic Motivation, Social Development, and Well-being, *American Psychologist*, 55: 68–78.

Rogers, C. R. (1961) On Becoming a Person: A therapists view of psychotherapy London: Constable.

Rogers, C. R. (1969) *Freedom to Learn: A View of What Education Might Become.* Columbus, Ohio: Merrill.

Rogers, C. R. (1983) *Freedom to Learn for the 80s.* Columbus, Ohio: Merrill

Rychen, D. S. and Salganik, L. H. (2003) *Key Competencies: For a Successful Life and a Well-functioning Society.* Cambridge, MA: Hogefe and Huber.

Saleeby, D. (1997) *The Strengths Perspective in Social Work Practice.* New York: Longman Publishers, Inc.

Savin-Baden, M. (2008) *Learning Spaces: Creating Opportunities for Knowledge Creation in Academic Life.* Maidenhead: McGraw-Hill / Open University Press.

SCEPTrE (2010) Immersive Cultural Experience Certificate Guide. Online at http://culturalacademy.pbworks.com/w/page/ 9905020/FrontPage (accessed 12/04/11)

Schuller, T. and Watson, D. (2009) *Learning through Life: Inquiry into the Future for Lifelong Learning (IFLL).* NIACE.

Schunk, D. H. and Zimmerman, B. J. (1998) *Self-regulated Learning: From Teaching to Self-reflective Practice.* New York: Guilford Press.

Seligman, M. (n.d.) Authentic Happiness website. Online at www.authentichappiness.com (accessed 30/12/10).

Sen, A. (1985) Well-being, Agency and Freedom: The Dewey Lectures 1984, *The Journal of Philosphy*, 82: 169–221.

Sen, A. (1992) *Inequality Re-examined.* New York, Cambridge, MA: Russell Sage Foundation, Harvard University Press.

Sheets-Johnstone, M. (2009) *The Corporeal Turn, an Interdisciplinary Reader.* Exeter: Imprint Academic.

Siemens, G. (2003) Learning Ecology, Communities and Networks: Extending the Classroom. Online at http://www.elearnspace.org/Articles/learning_communities.htm (accessed 30/12/10).

Skolverket (2000) *Lifelong Learning and Lifewide Learning.* Report for Swedish National Agency for Education. Stockholm: Liber Distribution.

Slaughter, R. (2005) Emerging Paradigms in the Knowledge Era: New Ideas and Practice. Paper prepared for the 'Designing Professional Development for the Knowledge Era' Research Project. TAFE NSW International Centre for Teaching and Learning (an in-house paper; no longer available online).

Slowey, M. and Watson, D. (Eds) (2003) *Higher Education and the Lifecourse*. Maidenhead: McGraw-Hill / Open University Press.

Smith, J.A. (1996). Beyond the Divide between Cognition and Discourse: Using Interpretative Phenomenological Analysis in Health Psychology, *Psychology and Health*, 11: 261–71.

Smith, M. K. (2004) Eduard Lindeman and the Meaning of Adult Education. *The Encyclopaedia of Informal Education*. Online at www.infed.org/thinkers/et-lind.htm (accessed 05/05/11).

Snowden, D. (2000) Cynefin, A Sense of Time and Place: An Ecological Approach to Sense Making and Learning in Formal and Informal Communities. Conference proceedings of KMAC at the University of Aston, July 2000 and Snowden, D. (2000) Cynefin: A Sense of Time and Space, the Social Ecology of Knowledge Management. In C. Despres and D. Chauvel (eds) *Knowledge Horizons: The Present and the Promise of Knowledge Management,* Bost on: Butterworth Heinemann.

Snowden, D. J. and Boone, M. (2007) A Leader's Framework for Decision Making. *Harvard Business Review*, November: 69–76.

Staron, M. (2011a) Life-based learning model – a model for strength -based approaches to capability development and implications for personal development planning. Keynote presentation 'Student Lifewide Development Symposium', March 1st 2011, Aston University, Birmingham Available on-line at: http://lifewidedevelopment symposium. pbworks.com/f/Maret+Staron+FINAL+PAPER.pdf (accessed 10/05/11)

Staron, M., Jasinski, M. and Weatherley, R. (2006) Life-based Learning: A Strength-based Approach for Capability Development in Vocational and Technical Education. Australian Government Department for Education Science and Training and TAFE NSW. Online at http://learningtobeprofessional.pbworks.com/w/page/32893040/Life-based-learning (accessed 30/12/10).

Stephenson, J. (1992) Capability and Quality in Higher Education. In J. Stephenson and S. Weil (eds) *Quality in Learning*, London: Kogan Page.

Stephenson, J. (1998) The Concept of Capability and Its Importance in Higher Education. In J. Stephenson and M. Yorke (eds) *Capability and Quality in Higher Education*, London: Kogan Page.

Stephenson, J. and Weil, S. (eds) (1992*) Quality in Learning: A Capability Approach in Higher Education*, Ch. 1. London: Kogan Page.

Stoll, E. (in press) Engaged Learning through Orientation, *Learning Communities Journal*.

Taylor, K. B. and Haynes, C. (2008) A Framework for Intentionally Fostering Student Learning, *About Campus: Enriching the Student Learning Experience*, 13(5): 2–11.

Taylor, M. (2011) RSA keynote speech 'Enlightened Enterprise' June 2011 http://www.businessgreen.com/bg/opinion/2077883/-enlightened-enterprise

Thomas, D. and Seely Brown, J. (2009) Learning for a World of Constant Change: Homo Sapiens, Homo Farber and Homo Ludens Revisited. Paper presented at the 7th Glion Colloquium by Seely Brown, June. Online at www.johnseelybrown.com/Learning%20for%20a%20World%20of%20Constant%20Change.pdf (accessed 20/12/10).

Thomas, D. and Seely Brown, J. (2011) *A New Culture of Learning: Cultivating the Imagination for a World of Constant Change.* Available through Amazon

Torres, V. (2009) The Developmental Dimensions of Recognizing Racist Thoughts, *Journal of College Student Development*, 50(5): 504–20.

Torres, V. (2010) Investigating Latino Ethnic Identity Within the Self-authorship Framework. In M. B. Baxter Magolda, E. G. Creamer and P. S. Meszaros (eds), *Development and Assessment of Self-authorship: Exploring the Concept across Cultures*, Sterling, VA: Stylus, pp. 67–84.

Torres, V. and Hernandez, E. (2007) The Influence of Ethnic Identity Development on Self-authorship: A Longitudinal Study of Latino/a College Students, *Journal of College Student Development*, 48(5): 558-73.

Tosey, P. (2002) Teaching on the Edge of Chaos. Complexity Theory and Teaching Systems. LTSN Imaginative Curriculum Working Paper. June. Available on-line http://www.palatine.ac.uk/files/1045.pdf (accessed 09/05/11).

Tremblay N A, (2000) Autodidactism: an exemplary model of self-directed learning. In G A Straka (ed) Conceptions of self-directed learning, theoretical and conceptual considerations. New York, Waxman p207-220.

Trevitt, C. (2010) The Teaching Portfolio in Higher Education, and the Nature of Knowledge, Curriculum and Assessment in Continuing Professional Learning (or Development). In N. J. Jackson (ed) *Learning to be Professional through a Higher Education* (e-book). Online at http://learningtobeprofessional.pbworks.com/w/page/31685076/The-teaching-portfolio-in-higher-education (accessed 14/02/11).

Trevitt, A. C. F., and Perera, C. (2008) Learning about Professional Learning: A Curriculum Where 'Self' Takes Precedence Over 'Action' and 'Knowledge' (in Medicine)? Online at http://learningtobeprofessional.pbworks.com/f/P_ChrisTrevitt.pdf (accessed 25/02/11).

Trevitt, A. C. F., and Perera, C. (2009) Self and Continuing Professional Learning (Development): Issues of Curriculum and Identity in Developing Academic Practice. *Teaching in Higher Education,* 14(4): 347–59.

Vlachopoulos, P. and Cowan, J. (2010) Choices of Approaches in E-moderation: Conclusions from a Grounded Theory Study, *Active Learning and Teaching in Higher Education*, 11(3): 213-224.

Vygotsky, L. S. (1978) *Mind in Society*. Cambridge MA: Harvard University Press.

Walker, M. (2006) *Higher Education Pedagogies*. Milton Keynes: SRHE and Open University Press.

Ward, C. and Kennedy, A. (1993) Psychological and Sociocultural Adjustment During Cross-cultural Transitions: a Comparison of Secondary Students Overseas and at Home, *International Journal of Psychology*, 28: 129–47.

Ward, C. and Kennedy, A. (1999) The Measurement of Sociocultural Adaptation, *International Journal of Intercultural Relations*, 23 (4): 659–77.

Whole System Associates (2002) Café to Go! A Quick Reference Guide for Putting Conversations to Work. Online at http://theworldcafe.com/cafetogo.pdf (accessed 30/12/10).

Williams, D. (1999) Human Responses to Change, *Futures*, 31(6): 609–16. Online at http://www.eoslifework.co.uk/futures.htm (accessed 23/02/11).

Willis, J. (2009a) In Search of Professionalism. In N. Jackson (ed.) *Learning to be Professional through a Higher Education*. Online at http://learningtobeprofessional.pbworks.com/w/page/15914954/In-Search-of-Professionalism (accessed 02/01/11).

Willis, J. (2009b). Professional Training, Critical Reflection and Peer Support: Making the Placement Year Work for Others. Online at http://sceptrefellows.pbworks.com/w/page/6835971/Jenny-Willis (accessed 05/05/11).

Willis, J. (2010a) Becoming a Creative Professional. Online at http://creativeinterventions.pbworks.com/w/page/27822835/Becoming-a-Creative-Professional (accessed 19/04/11).

Willis, J. (2010b) Lifewide Learning Report. August. Online at http://lifewidelearningdocumentsforsceptreportal.pbworks.com/f/Lifewide%20Learning%20Report%20August%202010.pdf (accessed 19/04/11).

Willis, J. (2010c) Developing Professional Capability through Professional Training at the University of Surrey. In N. J. Jackson (ed) *Learning to be Professional through a Higher Education*. E-book. Online at http://learningtobeprofessional.pbworks.com/w/page/23781822/Developing-Professional-Capability-through-Professional-Training-at-the-University-of-Surrey (accessed 28/04/11).

Wikipedia (n.d.) Student Engagement. Online at http://en.wikipedia.org/wiki/Student_engagement#Definitions (accessed 24/02/11).

Wood-Daudelin, M. (1996), Learning from Experience through Reflection, *Organizational Dynamics*, 24(3): 36–46.

Yonkers Talz, K. (2004) A Learning Partnership: U.S. College Students and the Poor in El Salvador. In M. B. Baxter Magolda and P. M. King (eds), *Learning Partnerships: Theory and Models to Educate for Self-authorship*, Sterling, VA: Stylus, pp. 151–84.

Yorke, M. (1999). The Skills of Graduates: a Small Enterprise Perspective. In D. O'Reilly, L. Cunningham and S. Lester (eds) *Developing the Capable Practitioner*, London: Kogan Page, pp. 174–83.

Zimmerman, B. J. (2000) Self-regulatory Cycles of Learning. In G. A. Straka (ed.) *Conceptions of Self-directed Learning, Theoretical and Conceptual Considerations*. New York: Waxman,

Index

AACU, 109, 110, 111, 112, 322
Abes and Jones, 78, 79, 84
about the book, 18
Abram, 43, 322
achievements, 2, 29, 30, 31, 35, 74, 127, 128, 134, 222, 232, 237, 273, 308
   complex learning, 128
adaptive learning, 286
agentic, 13
Alderfer, 217, 322
Alheit and Dausien, 32, 37
ANTA, 322
Appreciative Inquiry, 149, 150, 152, 326
assessing personal enhancements, 232
assessment of lifewide learning, 128
autodidactic, 56, 57, 58
autodidactic model of learning
   Tremblay model, 57

Baltes, 140, 322
Bandura, 13, 322
Barnett, 12, 13, 15, 18, 22, 41, 75, 77, 100, 104, 105, 106, 107, 108, 113, 322, 323
Barnett and Coate, 104, 105, 106, 107, 108
Barton, 63, 323
Baud, 201, 323
Bauman, 37, 49, 323
Baxter Magolda, 2, 4, 5, 19, 47, 59, 60, 70, 76, 77, 78, 79, 80, 81, 82, 83, 84, 86, 99, 109, 123, 128, 133, 161, 188, 189, 192, 193, 220, 226, 227, 228, 231, 251, 257, 264, 283, 284, 306, 323, 324, 327, 329, 330, 332, 335, 338, 340
Bayne, 23, 324
Beard, 5, 13, 18, 39, 41, 44, 45, 51, 53, 55, 57, 146, 215, 324
Beard's holistic model of learning
   being and becoming, 51
   belonging, 43
   doing, 44
   feeling, 45
   knowledge and knowing, 46
   sensing, 42
becoming a person, 51
   Carl Rogers, 52

becoming professional, 266
being a person, 53
Bekken and Marie, 87, 88
Belenky et al, 78
belonging, 13, 42, 43, 97, 215
benchmarking
   student development awardss, 314
   methodology, 314
Biggs, 123, 324
Billett, 13, 324
Brennan et al, 127
Bronfenbrenner, 317, 318, 325
Brudzinski and Sikorski, 90

Cairns and Stephenson, 65, 66
Callaghan, 70, 71, 75, 325
Campbell, 19, 20, 101, 194, 261, 262, 266, 283, 296, 307, 325, 331
Candy, 149, 325
Cannatella, 43, 325
capability, 4, 10, 14, 18, 53-54, 61-75, 105, 113, 120, 138-44, 151, 159, 162, 192, 205, 216, 223, 233, 251, 257, 259-65, 273-74, 304, 305, 318, 322, 337-39
   32 capabilities of highly effective people, 73
   as an integrated set of functionings, 67
   as self-awareness, 67
   concept, 62
   definition, 62
   dependent and independent, 67
   in creating knowledge, 139
   perspectives on, 64
   relationship to context and problems, 68
Capability and Values Statement, 225, 226, 227, 230, 231, 236, 238, 259
capability development, 137, 141, 142, 148
   strength-based approach, 63
   strength-based strategies, 149
   diagram building new foundations diagram, 142
capable people
   characteristics, 66
Cell, 52, 325
change,
   organisational to permit life based learning, 152
Christensen, 150, 325
Clark, 37, 325

co- and extra-curricular
    student development awards, 313
co- and extra-curricular domains, 165, 172, 191
co-curriculum, 287
codified knowledge, 48, 108
cognitive evaluation theory, 218
cognitive maturity, 47, 59
Committee on Higher Education, 121, 325
concept mapping, 288
Conklin, 11, 326
Cook, 13, 326, 335
Cooperrider, 140, 149, 326
Covey, 3, 15, 16, 53, 61, 62, 326
Cowan, 18, 19, 122, 126, 135, 258, 320, 339
Critchley, 326
critical incident, 126
Crom, 149, 326
Csikszentmihalyi, 140, 326
Cultural Academy, 286-307
    design, 290
cultural awareness, 287
cultural enquiry, 288
culture shock, 296
curriculum, 12-19, 74- 77, 87-96, 100-17, 122-23, 128-31, 160, 165, 168, 172, 173, 189, 191, 194, 222-23, 226, 229, 257, 287, 308-12, 318, 329
    absence of natiuonal debate, 104
    concepts, 103
    designing, 105, 123
    for integration, 109
    residential, 91, 93
Cynefin framework, 70

Dearing, 121, 326
Deci and Ryan, 215, 218
deficit based approaches to learning and development, 140
Deleuze and Guattari, 34, 35, 37, 38
Dellas and Gaier, 1
designing learning
    shift from rules and procedures to responsibility, 157
Desjardins, 9, 327
Dewey, 120, 229, 257, 327, 336
disruptive technology, 150
Drago-Severson, 98, 327
Dreze and Sen, 62, 113
Dweck, 13, 327

ecology of lifewide learning, 251
educational needs 21st century, 11
Egart and Healy, 95
Egeland et al, 63
Eisner, 232, 327
embodied knowledge, 108
emergence, 50, 56, 74, 112, 153, 203
emotional experience, 46
emotional intelligence, 214
emotional literacy, 45
emotional stress, 299
engaged learning university, 102
engagement, 101
engaging curriculum, 101
engaging learners, 101
epistemic community, 50
epistemological maturity, 78
epistemological, intrapersonal and interpersonal complexity, 19, 59, 60, 188, 193, 227, 231, 251, 257, 266, 283, 306
epistemology, 13, 47, 72
Eraut, 13, 20, 49, 72, 73, 142, 261, 262, 263, 264, 265, 266, 274, 275, 283, 327, 328
Ewell, 17, 328
Existence-Relatedness-Growth (ERG) theory, 217
experience-based learning, 12
extra-curricula learning, 22, 32, 33, 37

flow, 195
Fraser and Bosanquet, 103
Gardner, 42, 52, 329
Gergen, 42, 329
Gersick, 216, 219, 329
Greene, 73, 74, 75, 114, 329
Hale and de Abreu, 214, 215, 216, 219
Hall, 329, 332
Ham and Wang, 305
Hamer and van Rossum, 78
Hansel, 243, 329
Harvey et al, 127
Haynes, 90, 96, 329, 330, 338
higher education's role
    in preparing students for life, 76
Hodge et al, 2, 5, 93, 102, 103
Hodgson and Spours, 317, 318, 319, 320
holistic model of learning, 39, 53, 55, 57, 72
holistic model of pesonal action, 53

342

Homo Faber, 48
   human as maker, 50
Homo Sapiens, 50, 338
   man as knower, 50
Hong Kong school system
   lifewide learning approach, 10
Hornak and Ortiz, 90

identity
   change, 215
Illeris, 42, 58, 143, 330, 331
Immersive Cultural Experience Certificate, 289
immersive experience
   contexts for, 200
   sense of journey, 204
   situations, 196
   types of, 201
immersive experiences, 19, 45, 58, 85, 194-21, 286, 296, 304, 305
   concept, 195
   for learning and development, 194
indwelling, 51, 250
integrated education, 109-10
integrative learning, 110-11
internal voice, 83, 85
intrinsic motivation, 215, 218, 268, 271

Jackson, 1, 18, 19, 20, 24, 39, 53, 61, 101, 104, 115, 116, 129, 142, 146, 160, 163, 194, 222, 224, 261, 286, 296, 308, 314, 323, 325, 326, 327, 328, 329, 330, 331, 335, 338, 339
Jarvis, 37, 42, 330, 331
Jenkins, 14, 331

Keeling, 77, 332
Kegan, 2, 39, 40, 76, 77, 78, 98, 332, 335
Kidd, 219, 332
King, 77, 84, 323, 324, 327, 329, 330, 332, 335, 340
Knight, 46, 127, 128, 232, 332
knowing–acting–being
   conceptual framework for curriculum, 106
knowledge, 5-16, 27-29, 37, 39, 40, 42, 45- 59, 64-68, 72, 77, 80, 83, 88, 90, 94, 95, 96, 103-13, 127, 132, 133, 137-39, 141, 145, 146, 150, 161, 165-75, 181, 187, 189, 190-94, 199, 202, 205, 208, 211, 215, 220, 224, 226-40, 251-59, 261, 264, 265, 267, 270, 276, 282-93, 305-06

academic contexts, 106
dissemination through story telling, 49
Eraut's model of personal knowledge, 49
knowledge abd knowing
   Boisot's conceptual model, 47
Kolb, 230, 332
Kuh, 77, 332

Lakoff, 43, 332
Landmark, 214, 215, 216, 332
Law, 80, 163, 180, 185, 250, 329, 331, 333, 335
learners
   as designers of own learning experience, 138
learning
   and developing as a person, 39
   as belonging, 43
   as knowledge and knowing, 46
   as sensing, 42
   autodidactic self-directed model, 56
   being and becoming, 51
   self-regulated learner, 53
   six dimensions of, 41
   the emotional dimension, 45
   Thomas and Seeley Brown perspectives, 50
   through the experience of doing, 44
learning and development in the workplace, 262
learning ecologies, 139, 154
learning ecology map, 155
learning ecology metaphor, 139
learning partnerships
   academic contexts, 87
Learning Partnerships, 19, 86, 133, 226, 323-24, 327, 329-30, 334, 335, 340
learning spaces, 23-25, 30, 33-38, 86
learning through work, 261-285
Learning through Work Certificate, 261, 262, 273, 274, 277, 281, 283, 285
learning trajectories
   eight categories, 265
   Michael Eraut, 262
Levinson, 219, 333
life based learning
   adoption, 152
   characteristics, 144
   implications for professional development, 154
   key concepts, 138
   model, 147
life space map, 117, 118, 119, 120, 231, 234

example, 118
lifebased learning 19, 137-158
　application, 148
　concepts 139-41
　evaluation, 150
　guiding principles, 148
　model, 146
　moving from segmented to integrated learning, 143
　organisational enablers, 148
lifelong and lifewide
　the challenge for universities and colleges, 31
lifelong learning, 1, 2, 9, 22, 24, 25, 102, 111, 144, 266, 308, 317, 319, 320
　ecological perspective, 317
lifelong-lifewide learning paradigm, 8
lifewide curriculum, 12, 16, 18, 100-121, 129, 221, 223, 224, 226, 227, 257
　curricula domains, 116
　framing, 105
　map, 116
　personal curriculum, 117
　preparation for life, 113
　propositions, 113
　rationale, 100
　student as designer of their own, 16
　vision, 101, 113
　visualising it, 115
lifewide education, 1, 4, 17, 18, 20, 22, 24, 31, 32, 37, 39, 43-46, 49, 50, 57, 59-67, 70-73, 78, 84, 98, 137, 219, 223, 226, 308, 319, 320
　nurturing imagination, 66
　transformative concept, 22
　value of a holistic model of learning, 57
lifewide learning, 4, 9, 10, 13, 18, 19-37, 43, 53, 61, 98, 110, 112, 117, 122-37, 142-43, 155, 160-63, 169, 173, 192, 216, 222-29, 232, 234, 236, 239, 241, 250-51, 257, 259, 261, 263, 309, 316-21
　academic value, 32
　an ecologically supportive pedagogy, 130
　assessment, 136
　becoming a person, 29
　classification of spaces, 33
　comparing and contrasting teacher and student-led learning, 127
　concept, 24
　ecosystem, 318
　entrepreneurial orientation, 241
　explorative orientation, 250
　forms and places used by students, 26
　forms of learning, 27
　HE student examples, 26
　integrating it into the academic curriculum, 131
　language of qualities and dispositions, 28
　nomadic learners, 34
　orientations, 161
　origin of term, 9
　pedagogy, 123
　personal growth and self-actualisation orientation, 241
　possible design for incorporation into academic programmes, 133
　propositions to guide pedagogy, 129
　questionnaire surveys, 163
　research studies, 161
　roles of teacher, tutor, educator, 132
　social challenge, 313
　the radical nature of, 125
　timeframes and rhythms, 25
Lifewide learning Award
　assessment procedures, 234
lifewide learning.
　the challenge of, 125
lifewideness, 1-5, 18, 77
　concept, 2
Lindman, 20, 121, 321, 333
liquid age, 23
liquid learning, 22, 23, 37
　concept, 23
Luke, 23, 333

managing emotions, 299
Manzi, 215, 333
Maslow, 4, 216, 217, 333
Maslow's Heirarchy of Needs, 217
Mayer, 215, 333
meaning-making, 5, 39, 40, 43, 78
　the basic structure behind, 79
metacognitive, 47, 67, 128
metaphor, 49, 79, 86, 133, 139, 143, 154
Mezirow, 2, 76, 333
Mihata, 112, 333
Moesby, 131, 333
Moodie, 138, 333
more complete education, 2, 19, 61, 173, 220, 224, 287
Mortiboys, 45, 333
motivational forces
　Maslow (1943), 4
Motulsky, 214, 216, 334

NAES, 9, 334
Narrative, 49, 236

344

NASPA, 18, 112, 334
Nowotny, 24, 334

Oakeshott, 25, 334
OECD, 9, 10, 334
Olson, 88, 334
Open Space Technology, 149
organisational change
   strength- and asset-based paradigm, 140
Ortiz, 90, 330, 334
Owen, 159, 334

Palmer, 43, 334
Parker, 105, 107, 334
participatory culture, 14
Pascarella, 77, 334
PDP, 53, 107, 335
Perry, 78, 334
personal development planning, 53, 85, 101, 315, 337
   influence on higher education designs, 123
   involving students in the process, 125
personal enhancements
   patterns of personal development, 234
personal growth and self-actualisation, 241
personal knowledge, 264
   formss of knowledge and knowing, 264
Piaget, 78, 79, 335
Piper, 91, 92, 335
Pizzolato, 78, 79, 84, 89, 335
Pollard, 31, 37, 335
Porter, 235, 335
portfolio
   types of lifewide learning portfolio, 234
   narrative themes, 236
positive deviance, 149
positive psychology, 63, 140
professional development, 31, 108, 125, 137-38, 141, 159, 192, 223, 237, 239, 259, 271-74, 309
professional learning, 107
professional lifelong learning, 108
professionalism
   communication, 270
   concepts of, 266
psychological adaption, 299

reason, 41, 43
reflection, 5, 22, 32, 35-37, 49, 53-56, 67, 73, 94- 98, 102, 107, 126, 142, 145, 149, 158, 166,198, 201-02, 207-11, 215, 219, 235, 257, 261, 267, 269, 279-80, 282, 288, 290, 292, 294, 310, 316333, 339,
   use of life space map to promote, 118
research studies
   immersive experiences, 196
   longitudinal study of young adult learning, 79
Rickett, 308, 309, 335
Rittel, 11, 335
Rogers, 40, 51, 52, 53, 59, 132, 133, 135, 336
Ryan, 215, 218, 296, 326, 336
Rychen and Salganik, 10

Saleeby, 63, 336
Savin-Baden, 23, 34, 38, 336
Schuller, 21, 336
Schunk, 53, 336
sel-authorship
self-actualisation, 4, 8, 19, 162, 173, 192, 217, 236, 237, 238, 241
   lifewide learning orientation, 241
self-authorship, 2, 4, 5, 6, 19, 59, 76, 78- 89, 93, 98, 102, 109, 133, 189, 193, 220, 226, 231, 234, 239, 251, 257, 264, 283, 284, 306
   academic advising, 89
   accelerated development, 98
   and internship programmmes, 95
   and lifewide learning, 94
   co-curriculum contexts, 91
   crossroads, 81
   cultural immersion, 94
   following external formulas, 80
   key components, 83
   lifelong - lifewide project, 98
   orientation programmes, 97
   promotion through learning partnerships, 86
   residential co-curriculum, 93
self-awareness, 3, 40, 42, 52, 65, 67, 93, 105, 107, 160, 215, 224, 230, 231-33, 241, 252, 263, 285, 318
self-determination theory, 215, 218
self-efficacy, 54, 55, 56, 64, 66, 97, 268
self-regulated learning
   model, 54
self-regulation, 53-56, 61, 72, 158, 218, 314
   concept, 53
   reflection and meaning making, 55
Seligman, 140, 336
Sen, 61, 62, 65, 327, 336

Sensemaker, 288
sensing, 13, 42, 67, 72
sensory intelligence, 42
Sheets-Johnstone, 43, 336
Siemens, 139, 336
situations
   concept of dealing with, 230
   focus for learning, 229
   levels of complexity, 70
   Stephenson's conceptual framework, 68
   use of Cynefin framework to analyse, 70
Skolverket, 37, 336
Slaughter, 148, 336
Slowey and Watson, 37
Smith, 196, 230, 324, 337
smooth and striated spaces
   Deleuze and Guattari, 34
smooth spaces, 34-35
Snowden, 70-71, 337
Staron, 19, 64, 130, 137, 139, 141-147, 158, 337
Stephenson, 64, 65, 67, 68, 69, 70, 75, 141, 201, 325, 337
Stoll, 97, 337
storytelling, 49
strength based orientation, 137, 141, 142, 143, 144, 149, 154
strength-based approach, 63
   characteristics, 63
striated spaces, 34
student development award
   benchmarking, 314
student development awards 308
   characteristics, 309
   generic issues, 315
   reasons for, 312
studentland, 44
students
   as customers, 24
   as learning nomads, 24
students' creative development, 100
supercomplex world, 12
Surrey Lifewide Learning Award, 222-60
   award framework, 225
   pilot, 224

Talent Management, 149
Thomas and Seely Brown, 12

Torres, 78, 79, 84, 338
Tosey, 104, 338
transformation, 5, 41, 43, 63, 98, 114, 129, 178, 195, 201-03, 207, 215-16, 221, 248
   factors involved, 203
transformational learning, 77
transformative experiences, 59, 306
transition, 20, 34, 36, 37, 43, 58, 78, 119, 194, 214-19, 240, 244, 286, 289, 293-96, 299, 303-07, 320, 334
   making a, 214
   research, 214
Tremblay, 56, 57, 338
Trevitt, 107, 108, 338
turning point experiences, 44
typology of modes of learning in the workplace, 264

Vlachopoulos, 126, 135, 339
voice, 3, 4, 33, 76, 80, 81, 82, 83, 88, 91, 95, 98, 99, 184, 258, 270, 315
Vygotsky, 125, 339

Walker, 62, 339
Ward and Kennedy, 299
wicked problem
   preparing students for a complex world, 11
Wikipedia, 8, 102, 157, 339
will
   importance in learning and development, 15
   to be capable, 75
Williams, 215, 216, 219, 339
Willis, 19, 160, 163, 222, 261, 262, 266, 276, 283, 339
wisdom
   fundamental importance to human development, 141
Wood-Daudelin, 339
World Café, 149

Yonkers Talz, 340
Yorke, 337, 340

Zimmerman, 53, 54, 61, 336, 340

Lifewide Education Community Interest Company
www.lifewideeducation.co.uk

Our passion, hope and purpose
Our aim is to contribute to the development of people by promoting the concept of lifewide learning and education and providing encouragement and practical help to individuals and organisations who want to adopt, adapt and implement the idea.

A more complete education
Our vision for a more complete education is captured in the words of Eduard Lindeman 'the whole of life is learning therefore education can have no ending.' A more complete education unites and integrates formal education with learners' own attempts to develop themselves through their lifewide experiences.

Serving the needs and interests of our community
As a Community Interest Company we are a social *not for profit* enterprise working for and with the communities of practitioners who care about students' development in a holistic, whole of life sense.

1) Our research and scholarship aims to encourage further development of the concept and practice of lifewide learning and education. The products of this enterprise are made available through a book that can be purchased through the website and articles that are distributed free through the website.

2) The services we provide are intended to support individual practitioners and organisations that wish to promote a lifewide approach to learning, personal development and education. We provide an on-demand help & advice service, make contributions to professional development programmes and offer a benchmarking service to enable organisations to compare their practices and outcomes.

3) Our advocacy and public engagement activities aim to influence the thinking and actions of educational practitioners, institutional and political decision makers.

4) Our fundraising activities are intended to attract donors and sponsors to support our not for profit educational work.

5) The awards we make to students in higher education aim to value and recognise their attempts to make their own education more complete through the learning and personal development they gain through their lifewide experiences.

Our services are provided on a cost-recovery basis and any profits are reinvested in the enterprise. By purchasing this book you are supporting our work.

To join our community of interest
Lifewide Education c.i.c. is a community-based organisation that works for and with its members. If you share our vision and you would like to receive regular updates on our work, attend our events or contribute to our enterprise, please visit our website to join our community of interest.